America's Destruction of Iraq

Michael M. O'Brien

Cover Photograph

People walk past destroyed buildings in the Sadriyah outdoor market, located in a predominantly Shi'ite area of Baghdad on Sunday, February 4, 2007. The day before, a suicide bomber driving a truck loaded with a ton of explosives obliterated the market, instantly killing more than 135 people while they shopped. The total injured was nearly 350. It was one of the deadliest suicide bombing attacks since the beginning of the U.S. invasion of Iraq in 2003. The following day I saw this picture on the cover of Star and Stripes, the newspaper for U.S. military personnel. I decided then it would be on the cover of this book. (AP Photo (with permission)/Khalid Mohammed)

Visit my website at:

www.warfare-inc.com

To Mom and Dad

THIS BOOK IS BASED ON actual events. I use my real name. I have omitted the names of certain people and organizations I write about in a negative light for the sole purpose of avoiding a law suit. That by no means diminishes the things they did, or the consequences of their actions. The only names I retain are those of public figures or organizations.

Acknowledgements

I would like to express my sincere thanks to Dr. Anita Gadhia-Smith, Psy.D, who gave me much appreciated advice on the first edition of this book, *America's Failure in Iraq*, and Charles Protzman for his editing assistance. I would also like to thank U.S. Army Colonel (retired) Douglas Macgregor, for his insight into combat operations during Operation Desert Storm. Thanks also to Tyler Drumheller, who met with me and told me about his experience at the Central Intelligence Agency, and about his book. Andrew Bacevich provided me with a broader look at the "military-industrial complex" in the modern world. Lawrence Sellin (U.S. Army Colonel (retired)) has provided on-going insight into the crazy world of political correctness, and just where it is leading the United States.

I want to thank Joyce Battle for her project, *The Iraq War- Part I: The U.S. Prepares for Conflict, 2001*. This extensive compilation of statements made by the key players in Washington who planned our invasion of Iraq is without equal.

I would also like to express my thanks and gratitude to my West Point classmate, Michael Sheehan. Mike was the Ambassador-At-Large for Counterterrorism the last two years of the Clinton administration. He is currently head of the Counterterrorism Center at West Point, which was given to the academy as a "gift" by my class, the Class of 1977. Mike's leadership in diplomacy and counterterrorism rank him at the highest levels of our government. The Counterterrorism Center would not have been possible without the generous support of Vinnie Viola, another West Point classmate and former president of the New York Mercantile Exchange, and owner of the Florida Panthers.

And I want to thank John Stapleton of *A Sense of Place Publishing* for encouraging me to update and re-publish my story, Xavier Comas of *Cover Kitchen* for his inspirational cover design, and Rahul Singh of *Anant Corporation* for his marketing excellence.

Iraq

(Courtesy: Nations Online Project)

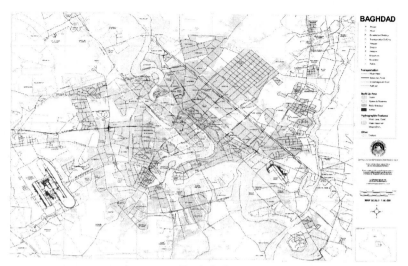

Baghdad

Sadr City is the large rectangular-shaped area to the northeast, across the Tigris River from the International Zone (IZ). Baghdad International Airport (BIAP), the headquarters of NMF-I, is to the west of downtown Baghdad. Route Irish is the highway connecting the IZ and the airport.

(Courtesy: The National Imagery and Mapping Agency)

Baghdad City showing the International Zone, formerly called the
Green Zone, and surrounding area. This photograph shows
the exact same area as the map above.

(Courtesy: Iraq Slogger)

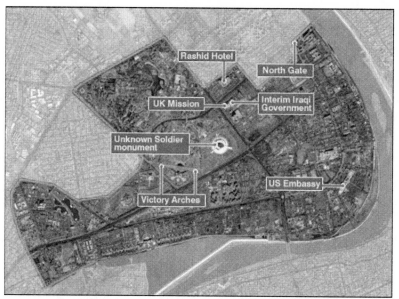

Closer view of the International Zone (Green Zone). The Iraqi Ministry of Defense is the large building just below and to the right of the North Gate (upper right corner of the Green Zone). The Republican Palace is the building labeled "US Embassy" at the bend in the Tigris River (lower right).
(Courtesy: War News Updates)

"The only thing necessary for the triumph of evil is for good men to do nothing."

Edmund Burke (1729-1797)

"Conscription forms armies of citizens, voluntary enlistment forms armies of vagabonds and criminals."

Napoleon Bonaparte

"I had other priorities in the '60s than military service."

Dick Cheney prior to becoming U.S. Secretary of Defense (1989)

Contents

Glossary of Acronyms

BIAP	Baghdad International Airport
CAFTT	Coalition Air Force Transition Team
CENTCOM	Central Command
CFLCC	Coalition Forces Land Component Command
CIA	Central Intelligence Agency
CMATT	Coalition Military Assistance Training Team
CPA	Coalition Provisional Authority
CPATT	Coalition Police Assistance Training Team
DG	Director General
DHS	Department of Homeland Security
DoD	Department of Defense
EFP	Explosively Formed Penetrators
FAR	Federal Acquisition Regulations
FBI	Federal Bureau of Investigation
FBO	Foreign Buildings Operations
GRD	Gulf Region District, U.S. Army Corps of Engineers
HATT	Health Affairs Transition Team
IED	Improvised Explosive Device
IGE	Independent Government Estimate (for construction contracts)
IRMO	Iraq Reconstruction Management Office
IZ	International Zone
JASG	Joint Area Support Group
JCCI	Joint Contracting Command-Iraq
JHQTT	Joint Headquarters Transition Team

JSOC-I	Joint Special Operations Command-Iraq
K-1	Kirkuk
KBR	Kellogg Brown & Root
KMTB	Kirkush Military Training Base
M-4-TT	Ministry of Defense Logistics Transition Team
MNC-I	Multi-National Corps-Iraq
MNF-I	Multi-National Forces-Iraq
MNSTC-I	Multi-National Security Transition Team-Iraq
MOD	Ministry of Defense
MODTT	Ministry of Defense Transition Team
MOF	Ministry of Finance
MOI	Ministry of Interior
MOITT	Ministry of Interior Transition Team
MWR	Morale, Welfare and Recreation
NGA	National Geospatial-Intelligence Agency
NSA	National Security Agency
OBO	Overseas Buildings Operations
OHS	Office of Homeland Security
OIF	Operation Iraqi Freedom
PSD	Personal Security Detail
RFP	Request for Proposals (for construction contracts)
RPG	Rocket-Propelled Grenade
SEIU	Service Employees International Union
SF	Special Forces
SOW	Scope of Work (for construction contracts)
WMD	Weapons of Mass Destruction

Introduction

THE IS A TRUE STORY. It is a story of how one very powerful country destroyed a very weak one, while all along professing to save it. It describes my personal experiences between the First Gulf War and the outbreak of Operation Iraqi Freedom, details my 14 month experience in Iraq from July 2006 to September 2007, and ends with an overview of the current situation in Iraq. *America's Destruction of Iraq* is the story of how the United States of America proceeded to destroy the very country it professed to the world it was trying to save. President George W. Bush told the world that Saddam Hussein was about to use nuclear weapons, gas, or biological agents, "weapons of mass destruction," or WMD. This was not true, as I will describe in detail. Bush invaded Iraq, a sovereign country that presented no threat to the security of the United States, which is a violation of international law. After the United States invaded Iraq, our subsequent efforts completely failed. Yet we stayed in Iraq trying to save it from various fundamentalist Muslim groups, including al Qaeda (now the Islamic State), that began to appear seemingly out of thin air. The United States attempted all this with mismanagement and botched planning on a scale never seen before, by people who were supposed to know what they were doing.

To provide a better understand of the problems in Iraq today I begin with a brief look at the Gulf War of 1991. Because that conflict was not terminated effectively by George H.W. Bush, it started a domino effect in the Middle East. Twelve years later his son, George W. Bush, went back to 'finish' the job, but it didn't work out. On the contrary, it was a complete failure. The domino effect started by the father was blown out of control by his son. (At the time of this writing another son, Jeb Bush, is planning to run for president in 2016!)

In addition to America's failure in Iraq since 1991, I draw analogies to our failure in Afghanistan as well. At the outset, however, the primary difference between Iraq and Afghanistan must be stated up front—the United States had valid reasons for going into Afghanistan after the events of September 11, 2001, but we didn't have any valid reasons for invading Iraq in March of 2003. This difference has plagued our country since, and will haunt us for decades to come.

My journey to Iraq began in July 2006, working for a defense contractor based in Alexandria, Virginia. I spent 14 months there and came back in September 2007 a different person. My eyes were opened by the things I will describe in this book. My eyes were also opened to a bigger problem in America that most people don't have any idea exists. That problem is the subtle, and sometimes not so subtle, abuse of power. This is shared by both the civilian leadership, which implements its power through the military it commands. But this power has to be fed. It is fed by the "military-industrial complex" that President Eisenhower warned us about when he left office in 1961.[1]

Since my return from Iraq nothing has improved there. On the contrary, it's gotten much worse, as I feared it would. It took Barack Hussein Obama more than four years to make good on his campaign pledge to withdraw U.S. forces from Iraq, but thousands of security contractors—mercenaries—remain there. When Obama finally decided to send more troops to Afghanistan, he sent less than half what was originally requested by the ground commander.

That ground commander, General Stanley McChrystal, was later fired for insubordination of his Commander-in-Chief. It was Obama who gave McChrystal his job, and his fourth star. Obama allowed Stan McChrystal to retire at four-star general rank, even though he didn't hold the rank for three years, as required by Army regulations. Stan McChrystal should have been demoted to three-star rank, and then forced out of the Army. Because he wasn't, he now gets paid $60,000 per speech, and teaches "Leadership" at Yale University.

Neither Iraq or Afghanistan are at peace, their insurgencies continue, Coalition soldiers are still getting killed, and innocent civilians in both places are being slaughtered routinely. Both are being "managed" by Barack Hussein Obama in the same way— withdraw all "combat" troops, leave "non-combat" troops there indefinitely, then have the U.S. Department of Defense hand

---

[1] "Eisenhower's Farewell Address to the Nation," January 17, 1961.

over military operations to the U.S. Department of State, who in turn hands these operations over to mercenaries, euphemistically referred to as "security contractors."

Both conflicts are offspring of the way the United States has been fighting wars since World War II. The U.S. never officially declared war in Vietnam. Instead, LBJ muscled the Senate into passing the Gulf of Tonkin Resolution in 1964, because he knew he would never get a formal declaration of war from Congress. Only two U.S. Senators voted against the resolution. One of them, Senator Wayne Morse, voted against it because he said it violated the Constitution, which it did. We don't send uniformed soldiers to fight what we now call "police actions." We send mercenaries instead. Sure, we send soldiers in the initial stages, but then contractors take over, led by Regional Security Officers from the State Department to give the mercenaries their legitimacy and legal cover.

This is where the "military-industrial complex" that Dwight Eisenhower warned the country about has led us. Because our national leadership is weak, and doesn't have the backbone to declare war and tell the American people what is really going on, we send a token force of soldiers and tens of thousands of contractors, tell the American people it's a "police action," and the public isn't any the wiser to what's really going on.

Since the Second World War, when it comes to waging war and using its political and military might in a just manner, and for causes that make sense, the United States has failed. This began during the Korean War, but took on a whole new identity during Vietnam. We had a few minor excursions after that, but things picked up again with the Gulf War of 1991, then again with Operation Iraqi Freedom, the invasion of 2003. We used to fight honorably and use our power to great effect, to win swift and clear objectives, but those days are for the history books.

I was always so proud to be an American, but then I went to Iraq. I'm still proud to be an American, but not proud of our national leadership, not one bit. Growing up we were always the guys in the white hats, the good guys, but after my experience in Iraq that has all changed. The best word to describe my transformation is: *disappointment.* The word "proud" connotes accomplishment, achieving something good. What good have we achieved in Iraq? The only things we have 'achieved' in Iraq are the tremendous growth of the "military-industrial complex," and appalling loss of life. There is nothing about our invasion of Iraq that I have to be proud of. Such was the intensity of my feelings when I returned from Iraq, that I felt compelled to write this book.

I am not a professional writer. I am not a politician. Nor am I a political or policy wonk. I graduated from West Point and served in the Army as an Infantry officer, then entered private industry. I have spent the past 26 years in commercial real estate in Washington, DC. The capstone of my professional experience was serving 14 months in Iraq as the Real Estate Advisor to the Iraqi Ministry of Defense in Baghdad. I was a contractor.

As the wise saying goes, "Those who do not study history are doomed to repeat it." When George W. Bush invaded Iraq in March of 2003, he and his senior staff clearly demonstrated they hadn't learned a thing from the mistakes our country had made before. He then proceeded to make those same mistakes again, only on a larger scale. I can only hope, in the terrible histories of the Iraq Wars of 1991 and 2003, that in some small way this book will help to prevent these mistakes being made again.

This book is my own work, and in my own words. It can be looked upon as a historical account of actual events witnessed by one who was there, on the ground, and by one who lived at the time they occurred. Having spent 14 months in Iraq, I have experience those who never went there, or who spent very short periods of time there (days or weeks) don't have. As a result, my observations of events I witnessed or were part of are based on fact, not conjecture. I also offer my account—in most cases my opinion as well—of events I did not witness but know quite a lot about from those who were there, many of whom I know personally.

I hope this book informs those who want to learn more about America's intervention in Iraq, what happened afterwards, and where Iraq is today.

Mike O'Brien
Arlington, Virginia
February 2015

PART I: OPERATION DESERT STORM

1—Mission Not Accomplished

ON THE EVENING OF FEBRUARY 28, 1991, I dropped by to visit my mother at our family home in Bethesda, Maryland. The TV was on and suddenly the show was interrupted by the network announcing a Special Report about to be broadcast. Within a few seconds President George H.W. Bush came on the air and announced he was ordering the cessation of all hostile action in Iraq, and that he had ordered all American troops to stop any further advances and action against Iraqi forces. He went on to say he had ordered the immediate return of American soldiers home from the battlefield.

I was dumbstruck. I turned to my mother and said this was the worst news I had ever heard. Why on earth were we not going all the way to Baghdad? Why on earth were we letting Saddam Hussein off the hook for his invasion of Kuwait? I couldn't understand why we were stopping our troops half way to Baghdad, when we had Saddam by the short hairs, his troops sprinting back to Baghdad as fast as their 'camels' could take them, with the world watching on CNN as we kicked him from one side of the desert to the other. What had gotten into the President? What had happened? Indeed, what was he smoking?

The nation seemed to go into a drug-induced euphoria over hearing the news. But to me this was the worst thing the President could have done. I remember saying it was probably the worst political-military decision of the century. I never regretted my words—until one night twelve years later.

Within days General Norman Schwarzkopf, the CENTCOM (Central Command) Commander and commander of all allied forces in theater, said the President's decision to end hostilities was a mistake. In no time he was 'taken behind the wood shed' by Bush, and we never heard another thing from Norm about the President ending the war as he did. Later, the story became very clear. The night before the President's announcement General Colin Powell, then the Chairman of the Joint Chiefs of Staff, and General Schwarzkopf, were directly asked by the President for their recommendations. Powell strongly recommended ending hostilities, while Schwarzkopf was ambivalent. He had the chance to say we should continue to press forward, which is what he thought we should do, but he wimped out and went along with Powell. That was why he was making his statements to the press. But it was too late by then. The horse was out of the barn, and wasn't coming back.[2]

Why did Bush do it? There are many reasons thrown about, but the one that has been heard the most is the 'power vacuum' theory. The theory goes if we had captured Saddam Hussein and removed him from power, it would have created a 'power vacuum' in Iraq. The theory follows that this would have led to the countries surrounding Iraq to swarm in, while at the same time civil unrest would have broken out inside Iraq itself.

I don't buy that theory, and never did, because there were half a million allied soldiers right there, in Iraq and Saudi Arabia, at the end of the war. The odds of Iran and Syria invading Iraq, while half a million allied forces were still there, were nil. The odds Sunni and Shi'ite radicals starting a war against each other, with that much allied force there to stop them, was equally small. The power vacuum theory doesn't hold up against the fact there were 500,000 allied troops on the ground, equipped with the new M1A1/2 Abrams tank, to stop anything that would have started in Iraq at that time.

There is another theory, equally weak, that was thrown around at the end of the Gulf War. That theory relates to the limits of the United Nations resolutions authorizing the Coalition to remove Saddam Hussein and his forces from Kuwait. Apologists for George H.W. Bush and Colin Powell claim the resolutions only allowed us to remove Saddam from Kuwait, and nothing more. If so, why did we cross the Iraq border in pursuit of Saddam's forces, and continue until we were half way to Baghdad by the time President Bush ordered everyone to stop? We had already violated the UN resolutions, so the idea that we couldn't go after Saddam doesn't hold water. We were pursuing his forces with the full knowledge of the President, and had every intention of going all the way to Baghdad until the President ordered a stop to offensive operations.

---

[2] John Barry, "The Day We Stopped The War," *Newsweek,* January 20, 1992.

Warrior's Rage: The Great Tank Battle of 73 Easting, was written by retired U.S. Army Colonel Douglas Macgregor. An army major at the time, he was the Operations Officer for "Cougar Squadron," the 2nd Squadron of the 2nd Armored Cavalry Regiment during Operation Desert Storm. Colonel Macgregor was at the "head of the spear," the point of the armored assault against the Iraqi Army as it exited Kuwait. His personal experience during Desert Storm sheds light on the glaring mistakes that were made by the generals in command, who were taking their orders from Washington.

By December 1990, Schwarzkopf had already given Lt. Gen. Frederick M. Franks (not to be confused with Gen. Tommy Franks), the commander of VII Corps, his marching orders.

> "I think it's pretty obvious what your mission is going to be, Fred." Schwarzkopf said, moving his hand along the desert corridor to the west of Kuwait. "Attack through here and destroy the Republican Guard. Once they're gone, be prepared to continue the attack to Baghdad. Because there isn't going to be anything else out there."[3]

Schwarzkopf 's orders to Franks were to destroy Iraq's Republican Guard. From the outset, however, LTG Franks was cautious and never displayed the aggressiveness needed. Schwarzkopf knew this, but instead of directly telling Franks to develop a more offensive attitude, he told Franks to replace anyone in his command who did not ruthlessly attack the enemy. This was Schwarzkopf's roundabout way of putting some spine in Franks' back, but it fell on deaf ears. Franks didn't change at all, and the results showed. Norman Schwarzkopf should have canned LTG Franks. According to Macgregor:

> But this is where the corporate mentality of the club of generals came into play, rather than the pragmatic professionalism required of a true soldier. Franks was one of the "good guys." Schwarzkopf, Franks, and

---

[3] Douglas Macgregor, *Warrior's Rage: The Great Tank Battle of 73 Easting,* (Naval Institute Press, Annapolis, MD, 2009), p. 11.

Gen. Carl Vuono, the chief of staff of the Army, had been friends at West Point.

And so Schwarzkopf did not act. He did not do what he must have known to be his sworn duty. Despite the bluff and bluster and his commanding presence on television, he lacked the character required of a true wartime leader who had the lives of hundreds of thousands of his own men to consider, as well as the responsibility of delivering a decisive strategic result to the nation. It is hard to find a better example of the difference between the character required of a military leader and the mentality of corporate careerism that in fact prevails.[4]

Macgregor goes into detail about the lead-up to the Coalition assault against Iraqi forces in Kuwait, and their escape back to Baghdad. What is very clear in his description is the complete lack of aggressiveness on the part of LTG Franks, and Gen. Schwarzkopf's failure to do anything about it. The key corps commander of U.S. armored forces was a weak leader, which is the same as saying he wasn't one. His boss, the overall commander, did nothing about it from the beginning of the conflict, through to its conclusion.

Saddam Hussein's regime was rescued from destruction not by the heroic efforts of Iraq's Republican Guard but by the uninspired and timid leadership of American generals who if they had some knowledge of war, lacked the temperament for it. Too many were bureaucrats in uniform, men with personalities that always saw danger, never possibilities. None of them were really players in a coherent, coordinated operational plan.[5]

Unfortunately, despite the overwhelming force President Bush provided, the mission of VII Corps—

---

[4] Ibid, p. 12.

[5] Ibid, p. 209.

the destruction of the Republican Guard Corps—was not accomplished. Filled from the outset with apprehension based on predictions of heavy casualties —apprehension that spread down to the battalion level—pointing again and again to the Iraqis' presumed capabilities and the danger of open flanks, General Franks, the VII Corps commander, and his subordinate commanders moved with extreme caution that guaranteed the escape of between fifty and eight[y] thousands of Iraq's Republican Guard troops, seven hundred tanks and other armored fighting vehicles, and a fleet of helicopters.[6]

By the time 500,000 American and coalition soldiers attacked Kuwait on 23 February, only 200,000 Iraqi soldiers were still there from the 400,000 that had been deployed to Kuwait in January. Of these, 87,000 were taken prisoner, and approximately 25,000 were killed. Due to the tactics of VII Corps "creeping up slowly on the Iraqis while pouring fire on them," the rest of the Iraqi troops were able to escape. The American generals thus avoided the battle they didn't want to fight in the first place.

> General Schwarzkopf, the CENTCOM commander in chief, definitely understood the importance to the attainment of this vital strategic interest of destroying Iraq's Republican Guard Corps. Without the Republican Guard to protect him, and impose his tyranny on the people of Iraq, Schwarzkopf knew, Saddam Hussein and his regime would be vulnerable to attack and destruction from his numerous enemies inside Iraq's borders.[7]

> Because the Republican Guard Corps was allowed to escape, Saddam Hussein was able to stay in power. Because he stayed in power and, predictably, refused

---

[6] Ibid, p. 217.

[7] Ibid, p. 211.

to honor his commitments, a combination of Saddam's brutality and his abuse of the Oil for Food program killed thousands of Iraqis every year for a decade and led, inevitably, to Iraq's second major confrontation with the United States and extended the slaughter.[8]

My only disagreement with Doug Macgregor is his contention that another conflict between Saddam Hussein and the United States was inevitable. However, because Saddam wasn't removed from power (i.e., terminated) when we had the chance in 1991, he was still around in 2003. By still being around in 2003, George W. Bush invaded Iraq on the bogus premise Saddam possessed WMD.

As events unfolded, a strange moral and political blindness clouded the vision of America's senior political and military leaders. General Schwarzkopf himself concealed the truth of the VII Corps' failure to fulfill its mission of destroying the Republican Guard. At the postwar press conference on 27 February 1991, he was asked by a British journalist about the escape of the Republican Guard: "You said the gate was closed. Have you any ground forces blocking the roads to Basrah?"

Schwarzkopf answered, "No."

When the journalist pressed the issue, asking, "Is there any way they can get out that way?" Schwarzkopf again answered, "No."[9]

The damage had been done. America's war with Saddam would continue at terrific cost to the people of Iraq, and enormous cost to the reputation of the United States.

Saddam Hussein should have been removed in 1991, but our country's military (Powell and Schwarzkopf) and political (Bush) leadership were weak in the knees. Even a three-star corps

---

[8] Ibid, p 215.

[9] Ibid, p. 217.

commander didn't possess the courage or the fortitude to execute the mission given to him by his commander, a four-star general, who in turn did nothing to change the situation. Why did these men stay in the U.S. Army if everything they had done for 35 years was in preparation for this moment? The answer is obvious based on their actions: the army was a job, and they were very good at doing what was necessary to get promoted in that job. Being effective combat leaders was not important for promotion. Being good yes-men was. As proof that performance means nothing once an officer reaches the highest level—LTG Franks was promoted to four-star general for the job he did during Operation Desert Storm.

It is clear the United States had every opportunity to oust Saddam Hussein at the conclusion of Operation Desert Storm. But Desert Storm was never really "concluded." Because we left Iraq as fast as we could, there was no chance of Saddam Hussein being overthrown. If we had remained for a period of time, his enemies would have had the courage to take him out, or at least try. But our generals were too concerned with parades down Pennsylvania Avenue, memoirs and speaking fees, while our politicians were already thinking of ways to capitalize on Operation Desert Storm by using it to get them elected during the next campaign cycle.

There was nothing preventing the United States from getting another resolution from the United Nations authorizing the pursuit and capture of Saddam Hussein. The justification for this would have been to punish him for what he had done when he invaded Kuwait, and preventing him from doing something else. With Colin Powell as Chairman of the United States Joint Chiefs of Staff, we would have gotten anything we asked for.

The fact is UN resolutions are weak and mean nothing in practical terms. They are merely political props so heads of state can fall back on them to say they have world backing. Why does the United States need the approval of the UN to do what it feels is necessary? Are we afraid of the UN and what it will say against us? You bet! That is exactly why we defer to the UN any time we want to defend ourselves or our allies. When we have a weak leader in the White House he always has to go to the UN for permission to do anything. This is another reason for the decision of President Bush that fateful night. He wanted the world and the UN to like him, to think he was a nice guy, to let them know he really cared what they thought about his actions. The fact is the United Nations is a corrupt and ineffective organization. It's only purpose is to employ connected fat cats from third world counties who live the "life of Reilly" in Manhattan while the their countrymen back home starve. It is an organization made up of people who accomplish little, but get paid a lot, and are given far more importance than they deserve.

In the final analysis President Bush stopped hostilities because he was weak and deferred to Colin Powell to make decisions he should have made himself as Commander-in-Chief. In the end Powell simply told him what to do. Colin Powell is a liberal and a peace lover. Being a peace lover is not necessarily a bad thing, but is disastrous if it is the primary consideration affecting the decisions of a four-star general and the Chairman of the Joint Chiefs of Staff of the United States. Not to say that generals don't love peace, but peace should not be a general's primary objective. A general's primary objective should be the total defeat of the enemy. With that defeat he can assist his political leader achieve *their* primary objective, which is the peace that comes only after the enemy's total defeat. Powell was a professional failure—he did not totally defeat the Iraqi Army, which was his duty and his job.

Colin Powell had an identity crisis. He could never decide who he really wanted to be. He claims he's a Republican but acts like a liberal Democrat. He wore a uniform but acted like a diplomat. He tried to be both when he should he have focused on what he was being paid to do, wage war. Instead, he wanted to achieve peace before achieving military victory. He put the cart before the horse. His priorities were backward, and for that we are paying the price today, and will continue to for years to come. Fortunately, we don't hear much from Colin Powell anymore.

However, Colin Powell deserves credit for one major thing; the use of overwhelming force to defeat the Iraqi army during the Gulf War. When Iraq invaded Kuwait on the morning of August 2, 1990, the world stood in shock primarily due to its disbelief in Saddam's stupidity. He had been rattling his saber for months, but no one thought he would actually invade Kuwait.

When he did invade, the first response of the United States was to get UN approval to defend Kuwait and kick Iraq back across the border. It was Colin Powell who espoused the use of overwhelming force, and for this he will go down in history as a brilliant military leader.

But the concept of overwhelming force is nothing new. U.S. Army doctrine and training has always called for a force ratio of at least 3/1 if attacking an enemy who is in a defensive position. This meant if we were going to attack Iraqi forces in Kuwait and kick them back across the Iraqi border, we would have to go in with at least three times as many troops as they had on the ground. With complete air superiority and 37 days of non-stop bombing, the Iraqi army was devastated and no match for our forces. Powell knew this and still said we needed half a million soldiers there when the bombing ended and the ground attack began. He was completely correct.

His worshipers now call this the "Powell Doctrine." It isn't any such thing. I learned this as a cadet at West Point in the mid-1970s, before anyone knew who Colin Powell was. All he did was take a principle of war that has been around for centuries and put it to effective use. Because Powell used it and it worked, it's been called the "Powell Doctrine" ever since.

Powell got his way and the troops were sent over. But many questions remain to this day. Why didn't we use our troops to their full effect after all the trouble we went through to get them there? Why didn't we use them to capture and topple the Saddam regime when we knew he was killing his own people?

The United States didn't care at all about Saddam Hussein, a former ally. We just wanted Kuwait oil, and Saddam was disrupting its continued flow. Did President Bush send half a million troops over there to kick Saddam out of Kuwait because Saddam had invaded a neutral country and violated international law, or was it so Kuwait could continue to ship oil to us? If so, then our entire reason for going over there was truly disingenuous. It wasn't to rid the world of Saddam Hussein for the righteous reason of his violation of international law—it was to get him out of Kuwait so we could continue receiving their oil. All the talk of atrocities committed by Saddam meant nothing to President Bush and Colin Powell because we could have taken him out then and there. We sent 500,000 troops there. Why did we bother? Instead, we left him alone after he went back to Baghdad with his tail between his legs.

The rational response to the 'power vacuum' theory is this: we had enough troops on the ground to stand up to anything that Iraqi insurgents, Iran, or any other threat could have thrown against us. The reasons Bush gave us for pulling out and leaving Saddam in power don't hold up. We had the forces in place.

What is the use of massing overwhelming force if you don't use it to its fullest extent? The United States and its allies had nearly half a million troops on the ground in Kuwait, Saudi Arabia, and later in Iraq, and stopped. Why? We have never gotten a straight answer from anyone.

The President said he couldn't go any further, but if the sanctions prevented him, as he said then, why did he ask Powell and Schwarzkopf what they thought? If the sanctions were that specific he didn't need their opinion. He asked them because he knew he had the option to continue if he wanted to, but he also asked them because he wanted to hear the answer they gave him, and they all knew it. Wanting to be loved by the media and respected by Colin Powell, the president totally ceased aggressive action without giving any thought to what the consequences would be. Colin Powell started off on the right foot by massing overwhelming force in Saudi Arabia, but then lost his nerve and backed off once we got ourselves into the fight and started killing Iraqi forces by the thousands. Isn't that what war is all about? Isn't that why Powell was a career Army officer? But Powell's media popularity had gone to his head long before this. He became their hero, and their puppet.

If we had used the troops we sent there, captured Saddam Hussein, and waited for the dust to settle, we would not be in the mess we are today in Iraq, and in the entire Middle East. We would have had the forces in place to protect the Iraqi people while they decided for themselves what government they wanted, and we would have been there to help them achieve that goal, with the number of U.S. forces on the ground to protect them while they worked to get there. With half a million soldiers on the ground, who would have tried to stop us from protecting the

Iraqi people while they decided their own destiny? The answer is —no one.

Then there's Norman Schwarzkopf. He had the opportunity to tell the President to continue on toward Baghdad, but failed to do his duty. Then Schwarzkopf had the nerve to blame the President for his decision after he was given the chance to speak his mind but didn't have the courage. Too little, too late. General Schwarzkopf is looked upon as a hero. I hope he enjoyed watching events in Iraq on TV after he went home. He had a major hand in creating these events along with Powell and Bush. Another George Patton? There is no United States general officer who could have failed to achieve the success Schwarzkopf did with all the tools he had at his disposal. The U.S. Air Force handed Norman Schwarzkopf 37 days of non-stop bombing to soften up military targets in Iraq, and at the same time he had half a million soldiers, with their full complement of equipment. The Iraqi armed forces were being blown away by the U.S. Air Force without any air cover of their own. Bozo The Clown could have gotten the same results ol' Norm did. But when it came to being tough and standing up for what he believed when the President asked for his opinion, he chickened out. Schwarzkopf went along with Powell because he lacked the fortitude to disagree with him. Yet they both got paid millions after the war to tell everyone how great they were.

The simple fact is our modern day political and military leaders are not the men of courage or fortitude they used to be. Now, they "talk the talk," but can't "walk the walk." They are collectively afraid of the media and what people will think of them if they choose to make the tough, but necessary, decisions required by men in their positions. They can't cut the grade.

Military officers become increasingly afraid and weak as they advance in rank, for the simple reason of politics. They don't want to upset their careers from further advancement. One has to wonder where the loyalty to their soldiers was. Making full colonel is a very hard thing to do, and making Brigadier General is just about impossible. To rise to the rank of one-star general is a feat few achieve. But making it to four-star general is harder to do than getting struck by lightning. There is only one way to get there and that is to never, ever, say anything that will raise eyebrows, or anything against the 'party line.' In today's world, to state what is *really* going on is professional suicide if one wants to make general officer. It has been heading this way since the Second World War. General officers were not as timid and shy during the Civil War or later. Ulysses S. Grant was a perfect example. President Lincoln gave him command of all the Union Armies, even though he was known to have a drinking problem, because he got results. Lincoln was heard telling his senior military staff that he would buy a case of liquor for any officers who would fight as well as Grant did. Military results, military success—that was what Grant delivered to his political commander-in-chief, because Lincoln stayed out of his way. Lincoln took those results and transformed them into political goals and objectives. One did his job, while the other did his. They worked well together, and stayed in their respective 'swim lanes.'

But things started to change toward the end of World War II and Korea. The strong generals started to get slapped down by the weak ones, or by politicians who had their priorities backward. Look what happened to General George Patton, who was furious when Eisenhower wouldn't let the U.S. Army go into Berlin. "Ike" wouldn't let U.S. forces go to Berlin because he had become a political general. In reality, he had always been. Roosevelt had cut a deal with Stalin allowing the Russian army into Berlin first, giving Eastern Europe to "Uncle Joe" as a bonus. Look where things ended up. Was Patton wrong?

General Douglas MacArthur wanted to go after the Communist Chinese army during the Korean War. He was completely correct wanting to deal with the communist Chinese and North Korea while we were there and in a position to do something about them. Everyone was saying MacArthur wanted to go nuke. But he got sacked by Truman, who had gone nuke a few years before, and yet that was OK. We then got involved in Vietnam to stop the very thing MacArthur was trying to prevent more than a decade earlier—communist Chinese expansion. So who had it wrong, MacArthur or Truman?

Today it's totally different. Today's generals, like weak politicians, want to be liked by a media which will always hate them and be anti-military. Colin Powell is the best example of this. Today's generals testify before Congress and give flowing speeches prepared in advance by their staff officers and tested for response and reaction by their PR people. Decisive military results are not as important as looking and sounding good on TV, especially in front of Congress, and getting good newspaper coverage the following day. These are the important factors to generals now. Powell and Schwarzkopf were not real military leaders. They were four star generals who were in reality high level executives of a large corporation whose staffs did all the work while they spoke in front of cameras. Remember Schwarzkopf on TV day after day during Desert Storm? He was in love with himself. And by all appearances he looked to be at least 150 pounds over the Army's weight limit. Soldiers get drummed out of the service every day for the very same thing. But Schwarzkopf was a four-star general, so he was off-limits. That is not the "leadership by example" we were taught at West Point, Norm's *alma mater*. He must have had his desert fatigues tailored so he could button them up the front. They sure don't sell his size at the military clothing store.

When they had the chance to be real generals, which meant waging war toward the total defeat of the enemy, Powell and Schwarzkopf failed, and failed miserably. If they were really doing their jobs they would have told the President to press on when he asked his bogus question. There would have been no doubt in their minds what their answer would be. If they were real generals, they would have asked the President why he was asking the question in the first place.

Their jobs were to advise the President on how to destroy Saddam Hussein and his military forces, not to advise him of the political ramifications of continuing the attack. But it was the President himself who failed the American people by feeling the need to ask Powell and Schwarzkopf for their opinions. It was his decision to make, not theirs. If Powell and Schwarzkopf were doing their jobs it is very conceivable they would have replied, when asked for their opinions, that they could not imagine why he would want to stop aggressive actions against Saddam's forces? It was up to the President to tell them he had decided to stop, but instead he asked them for their opinions on something he shouldn't have asked them at all. Politics is the President's job. Destroying the enemy is his generals' job.

After breast cancer surgery my aunt was asked by her doctor what follow-on treatment she preferred to have, the more intense and painful, or the less. She opted for the lesser treatment, and died a year later. Why on earth was her doctor asking her? Who's the doctor and who's the patient? In a very similar way Powell and Schwarzkopf share the blame with President Bush for the disastrous way the Gulf War ended in 1991.

But the Gulf War did not simply end that night when the President got on TV and announced the cessation of hostilities. That was the end of Phase I. The next phase would prove far worse for the Iraqi people. It would have been better for them if we had never gone back.

When the Gulf War ended President Bush could report back to his titular superiors at the UN he had ended the war according to their resolutions. He then spearheaded the follow-on sanctions which embargoed the Iraqi economy, effectively destroying it and the lives of average Iraqi citizens. When I went to Iraq in the summer of 2006, I saw the effects of the sanctions with my own eyes. Iraq became a black market economy, with people who would never have taken a bribe or a kick-back before now openly accepting whatever it took to feed their families. Before the Gulf War the Iraqi dinar, the unit of currency, was about three to the dollar. When I was there in 2006-2007, it was about 1350 dinar to the dollar. Iraqis got paid in cash that was handed to them in piles too large to carry in their pockets. They had to put their monthly pay in bags to carry home.

The sanctions didn't hurt Saddam in the slightest. They certainly hurt the Iraq people, however. While U.S. Ambassador to the United Nations during the Clinton Administration, Madeleine Albright responded to a U.N. report that the sanctions had killed more than 500,000 Iraqi children under the age of five: "I think this is a very hard choice, but the price—we think the price is worth it."[10] Most of Saddam's 21 palaces were built by foreign construction companies with money he hauled in under

---

[10] "Child Deaths Rise Sharply in Iraq under U.N. Sanctions, U.N. Says," *60 Minutes* (May 12, 1996), *Deutsche Presse-Agentur*, August 12, 1999; FAIR, November/December 2001.

the watchful eyes of the United Nations during the sanctions— instigated by George H.W. Bush—after the Gulf War. Saddam personally became richer than he was before the Gulf War. The money coming in from the food-for-oil program was scratch. It wouldn't feed a dog. But if he fed his people with the money he was raking in with illegal oil sales, the world would have wondered where it came from. He was happy to keep it all himself. And why not, especially if the UN and the U.S. knew about it anyway? It was all a big act by Saddam to make it look as though the sanctions were really hurting Iraq. They were hurting the Iraqi people, but not him. He was building one palace after the next with the money he was being paid by illegally selling oil through the son of Secretary-General of the UN, Kofi Annan.

In the Middle East where there's oil there's money, and where there's money there's terrorism. An example of the deteriorating situation in Iraq was the Islamic State's capture of the Baiji oil refinery in 2014. The Baiji refinery is one of the largest in the country. The Islamic State has been using money from the Baiji oil fields to fund its terrorist organization (i.e., murder more people).

But the sanctions did far more than just destroy the Iraqi economy and destroy the Iraqi way of life. They also created unrest and desolation, perfect recruiting grounds for future terrorist organizations and insurgents bent on destroying the Iraqi government and anything else they could. When men have jobs and can support their families they aren't going to jump at the chance of becoming terrorists and killing their neighbor. But when young men have no job, nothing to do, see no reason to start families, and the western world has left them instead of saving them from their dictator, they'll take the best offer they can get. This is exactly what happened after the Gulf War.

The "No-Fly Zones" were created after Desert Storm to stop Saddam from sending his aircraft into Kurdish areas in the north and Shi'ite areas in the south. But when he wanted to fly his helicopters into them to 'deal' with things, Norman Schwarzkopf let him do it. What did Schwarzkopf think Saddam was going to do once his aircraft flew in, drop off toys? Saddam sent his aircraft into the No-Fly Zones to bomb and gas his own countrymen while Schwarzkopf, Bush and Powell watched. It was easy for the world to gasp in horror at the atrocities they saw, but how could Bush, Powell and Schwarzkopf sleep at night knowing what they had done by letting Saddam off the hook, and the opportunity they had lost? The generals didn't do their jobs as generals, and the President didn't do his as Commander-in-Chief and the leader of the free world.

Then there's Colin Powell. The My Lai massacre occurred on March 16, 1968. Six months later a soldier wrote a letter to General Creighton Abrams, the new commander of all forces in Vietnam, accusing American soldiers of atrocities against Vietnamese civilians. A 31-year-old U.S. Army major named Colin Powell was assigned the task of investigating the soldier's letter and its allegations, which did not specifically mention My Lai.

> In his report, Powell wrote, "In direct refutation of this portrayal is the fact that relations between American soldiers and the Vietnamese people are excellent." Powell's handling of the assignment was later characterized by some observers as "whitewashing" the atrocities of My Lai.[11]

> In May 2004, Powell, then United States Secretary of State, told CNN's Larry King, "I mean, I was in a unit that was responsible for My Lai. I got there after My Lai happened. So, in war, these sorts of horrible things happen every now and again, but they are still to be deplored."[12]

Major Colin Powell's investigation was not very thorough. The My Lai massacre had occurred just six months earlier, but he came to the determination the Vietnamese people just loved the U.S. soldier. If Powell had plans for making general, writing an investigative report finding fault with anyone, especially senior officers, wouldn't go over very well. Forget the mission he had

---

[11] Robert Parry and Norman Solomon, *Behind Colin Powell's Legend – My Lai*, (Consortium for Independent Journalism, July 22, 1996).

[12] "Interview on CNN's Larry King Live with Secretary Colin L. Powell," May 4, 2004.

been assigned—let other people do the real investigative work. Looking at the way things turned out for Colin Powell later in life, his apparent whitewashing of atrocities being committed by U.S. Army soldiers in Vietnam seems to have paid off.

As the years passed after the Gulf War, Saddam Hussein rose to power again, but this time to even greater power than before the war. He was now a 'player' on the world scene, where he had only been a small actor. He declared himself to be the victor in the Gulf War for one simple reason—he was still alive. In his world and culture, that's all that matters. By letting Saddam live, but far worse stay in power, he could declare himself the victor. His countrymen, and the countries surrounding Iraq, had to admit he had a point. His propaganda apparatus had his people convinced he had 'beaten' the United States. All over Baghdad we saw murals and paintings showing Saddam and his forces kicking our butts during the Gulf War. That's what the Iraqi people believe happened. He was also allowed to gas his own people with our permission, which stoked his ego even more. On top of that, he could keep all of his country's oil money for himself because of the sanctions we and the UN imposed, and his people were now weaker than ever for the same reasons. The true winner of the Gulf War was the very man we defeated—and should have destroyed—Saddam Hussein. Is there any wonder he got bolder as time went on? He truly got away with murder. Saddam was on top of the world.

To quote Doug Macgregor once more:

> How ironic it is that General Colin Powell and President George H.W. Bush allegedly halted combat operations at the hundred-hour mark on humanitarian grounds and from fear that the global media would castigate the United States for annihilating Iraq's remaining forces—namely, the Republican Guard Corps. And yet, the cost in blood and treasure to both the United States and Iraq would have been a fraction of what it has been thus far. Yes, 20/20 hindsight is perfect, but the case can be made that the decision to "take it easy on the defeated Iraqi enemy" was the

most *inhumane* thing President Bush and his generals could have done![13]

For the way he allowed the Gulf War to end, which set the stage for things to come, George H.W. Bush has been getting a 'free pass' from the media, the American people, and from world opinion. Whenever I fly into Houston International Airport and see the snappy statue of him in the terminal, I have to turn away. The current situation is as much his fault as anyone alive, but his son came in to 'finish the job,' and proved to be a bigger disaster than his father.

---

[13] Macgregor, p. 224.

2—September 11, 2001

I was lying on my hotel bed at around 8:30 in the evening trying to get to sleep. I had gotten food poisoning the night before and hadn't been able to go to work that day, so the rest of the team went on without me. The phone rang and I picked it up. It was Michael Jackson on the other end. Not Michael Jackson the King of Pop, but Michael Jackson the Administrative Officer from the U.S. Embassy in Dhaka, Bangladesh, where I was at the time. I'll never forget what he said to me: "Mike, are you watching TV?" I remember thinking it was an odd question, but figured he may have been asking just to see if I was OK and that I had something to do. I said I wasn't, to which he replied, "Well, you need to turn the TV in your room on right now. A plane just slammed into one of the towers at the World Trade Center, and another one just hit the second tower. We're under attack." That's how it started for me.

Mike told me to stay at the hotel until the Embassy notified me, and to keep the team I had brought with me to Bangladesh at the hotel too. No one was allowed to go anywhere without the Embassy's permission. How and why I was in Bangladesh on 9/11/01 is a story in itself.

I was a political appointee in the administration of George W. Bush, having worked on his campaign at its national headquarters in Austin, Texas. I had taken part in the vote recount in Florida, being flown in the middle of the night with a dozen other people to Miami, to begin working the next morning with several hundred other Republican operatives observing the recount at the Miami-Dade County office building in downtown Miami.

The entire recount process and the grounds surrounding it are a topic for another book and another time. Suffice it to say, from one who was there, the Gore campaign wanted human error and the popping chads to overturn the election of Bush. The more the vote cards were handled, the more likelihood the chads, which were pre-punched little squares perforated into the cards, would pop out and call the vote into question. That's exactly what the Gore campaign wanted to happen. They wanted the election to be overturned by man-handling the cards, which was tantamount to tampering with previously fine vote cards. It was all a scam. I personally caught the county employees who were doing the recount making several mistakes, all in favor of Gore. This was because Gore was doing the recount only in predominantly Democrat counties in the state, which increased the likelihood that mistakes and un-counted ballots would go in his favor. Human error played a big role in it all. Every time the cards were held up and the county employee called the results out, they were calling mostly for Gore. They got into the habit of doing this and ended up mistakenly calling Gore's name out, when the vote was not for him. I stopped this when it happened, and the county employees were shocked they had made the mistake. They didn't even know they had done it. Such were the tactics of Gore's camp. To this day, every time I see the liberal bumper sticker, "Hail to the Thief," it makes my skin crawl. Gore tried to steal the election, not the other way around. He just went about it the wrong way, and didn't pull it off. When Gore failed to call for a recount in the entire state of Florida, but only in the four (later three) most heavily Democrat counties, he showed his real intentions and the recount for the scam it was.

We never even got to see all the ballot cards in Miami-Dade County. The Democrat-controlled County Election Commission had already gone through and done their own recount (there were at least three recounts, for a total of at least four times that the vote cards were handled. It's no wonder chads were popping out all over the place). If the Commission looked at a vote card and could not determine who the vote was for, then it went ahead and made its own decision who the voter 'intended' to vote for. In other words, the Democrat-controlled Miami-Dade County Election Commission had been given the gift of clairvoyance and was casting the vote on behalf of the voter whose intention the Commission couldn't determine in the first place! Of course, if a vote card had half a dozen chads popped out, then the Gore camp could say it was impossible to determine who the person intended to vote for. It was all nonsense. Because the vote cards had been handled so many times after the original vote had been cast, now there was no way to determine who the vote was meant for the night of the election. But the Gore camp twisted and turned this scenario on

Michael M. O'Brien

its head, with the help of the liberal media. The real story, which is being told here, never came out. Now we're just left with "Hail to the Thief" bumper stickers by liberals who haven't got a clue what really happened, and don't care. They just wanted Gore to win and Bush to lose, whatever the cost to the dignity of the election process which they don't care about either.

The Commission decided who got these mystery votes, weeks after the voter had made their own decision in the privacy of the voting booth, and then placed all these special vote cards in sealed envelopes by precinct. No one was allowed to open these envelopes, and if we did we would be thrown out of the room where the recount was taking place. No one ever saw these cards, but what we did see was the tally of these votes written on the outside of the envelope. Someone from the Election Commission had written in a magic marker what the vote tally was of the cards sealed inside the envelopes, and that was that. The predominant majority of these votes were for Gore, but we'll never really know who the votes were for. It was not open to the public to see what these cards even looked like. We never got to make our own determination of who the vote was for. It was a completely closed process.

At one point they spread us out and bused about half of us north to West Palm Beach to observe the Palm Beach County Election Commission's hearings. Sitting right in front of me one day was New York Congressman Jerry Nadler. Actually, Congressman Nadler was sound asleep. He just sat in the pew slumped over, snoring himself away. For those who don't know who Jerry Nadler is, it's not hard to pick him out of a crowd. He's about 5' tall, and 4' wide, and one of the most obnoxious members of the U.S. House of Representatives.

After the "Republican mob" brought the vote counts in Florida to a halt, we all flew back to Austin to wait. The Florida Supreme Court, all but one of whose members were liberals, did what no one thought possible, and ordered the recount to start again—this time for every county in the state! We were all blown away. Within a day I was on another flight heading to Inverness, Florida, in beautiful Citrus County on the Gulf Coast.

Al Gore should be ashamed of what he put this country through for 35 days. He didn't care about the American people.

22

He only cared about himself and getting into the White House. And he certainly didn't care one bit, and neither did his 'lawyers,' about tampering with the voting process and with the vote cards. His lawyers just cared about the incredible money they were hauling in. The entire Gore-inspired recount was a mockery of the sanctity of the American voting system and the honor of the individual's right to vote for who they want. The Gore campaign, with the able assistance of the Florida Supreme Court, openly and willingly tampered with valid vote cards and ballots for the purpose of overturning the original vote in only three counties in the state. If Gore really thought the state of Florida was messed up, why then didn't he contest the count in the entire state? He didn't think the votes were messed up in the state of Florida, he just wanted a recount in four counties to surpass the 1,000 vote margin Bush had over him. That's all the recount was to Gore. It was never about the integrity of the voting system in Florida, or possible abuses of it. It was just about how much abuse he could get away with, with the permission of the Florida Supreme Court, in order to steal the election from Bush who always had the majority of votes from the night of the election. With Gore in 2000, and Al Franken later in Minnesota, it's the same. If you are a Democrat and within 1,000 votes—steal it. Or at least give it one hell of a try.

After the election was finally decided I was given a job on the Presidential Inaugural Committee back in Washington, DC. Because of what Gore had put everyone through, the Bush Inaugural Committee had less than half the time to prepare for the numerous inaugural balls held throughout Washington. There were nine balls that night, with the ball for everyone from Texas held at the old DC Convention Center, which has since been demolished. This was not the "Texas Ball" people hear so much about. That's the one where the "Who's Who" go to look cool in their tuxedos and their brand new boots they just bought the day before. All the hot single women in DC want to get a ticket to it to grab some stud with money from the Lone Star State who flies in for the event on daddy's jet.

When George W. Bush was sworn in everyone was scrambling for a job in the new administration. I was no exception. I landed a job at the Department of Agriculture where for three months I did absolutely nothing for eight hours a day, and then split as fast as I could before my head exploded. But one day I got a call from Presidential Personnel, the office that places political hacks in jobs in the new administration. (By the way, all new administrations do the same thing, Republican and Democrat.) The person at the other end of the line asked me if I would be interested in going over to the State Department, to the office called Foreign Buildings Operations, or FBO. This is the branch of State responsible for the design and construction of U.S. embassies and consulates around the world. It's a huge operation, almost like a global real estate development firm. Having been in commercial real estate for more than 15 years at the time, I jumped at the opportunity. But what really amazed me was that someone at Presidential Personnel had actually looked at my resume.

I interviewed with a retired U.S. Army two-star general named Charles Williams, who was a Colin Powell worshipper. When Powell was tapped to be the Secretary of State, he called Chuck Williams in to do an assessment of FBO, ostensibly to determine the condition of its installations around the world, but really to pull him into the job of running it. To his credit, Powell saw the need for an overhaul of FBO, which would entail an overhaul of the infrastructure of all United States diplomatic facilities around the world. Because real estate, and commercial facilities in general, isn't given much thought by diplomats, this was commendable on Powell's part. I think he was given a heads up as to the terrible condition of our facilities around the world prior to taking on the job at State. Maybe he actually listened to diplomatic staff on his many travels around the world, and took notes and promised to fix things. More likely, General Williams sold Powell on the need for this, in the process creating a job for himself. Either way, I give Powell a lot of credit for seeing this need, and General Williams for responding as he did.

General Williams had been busy between the time he retired from the U.S. Army and when he took over the job at State for his good friend Colin. After leaving the Army, General Williams went to New York City to become head of the City's School Construction Authority. He left following an audit finding that he had given misleading information on the progress of his projects.[14] After that he came to Washington, DC, to head up the renovation of all the facilities owned by the DC School System. He had been hired by Julius Becton, also a retired U.S. Army general and head of the DC Public Schools, which is another story of complete disaster. He left that job after another audit said he authorized poor contracting procedures and left the school system open to waste and fraud.[15] What is interesting is that General Williams does not mention the DC Schools job on his bio, most likely because the effort was a failure. He doesn't allow his name to be associated with failure. He just leaves it off his resume. After the DC Schools fiasco he took over the construction of the Dulles Toll Road, called the Greenway, in suburban Loudoun County, Virginia. This is the recently completed road that extends past Dulles International Airport west of Washington, DC, and goes to Leesburg, Virginia, where it ends. The road is beautiful and is expensive as hell. It is a great way to avoid taking the narrower, traffic-filled back roads of modern day Loudoun County, which are awful. General Williams completed the project and has its success well documented in his resume.

General Williams' bio states he "has had an exemplary engineering and construction management career, first in service to his country in the military and now as a civilian. His outstanding leadership, innovative abilities and vision have contributed dramatically to the engineering and construction management profession." It also states he is a graduate of the Senior Manager in Government Program at Harvard University. According to the bio he received a "BS" Degree from Tuskegee Institute. There is no indication what his major was. I was informed while at FBO that General Williams doesn't have an engineering degree. He had been a two-star general in the U.S. Army Corps of Engineers.[16]

It was after the Dulles Toll Road project that Powell asked Chuck Williams to do an assessment of the State Department's

---

[14] Glenn Kessler, "Construction Woes Plague U.S. Embassies," *Washington Post*, August 17, 2007.

[15] Ibid.

[16] "General Charles E. Williams," *Alabama Engineering Hall of Fame*, 1996.

overseas facilities, and then asked him to take the job permanently. General Williams described the offer from Powell as one he simply couldn't refuse, but he was also looking for a job at the same time. General Williams, after what he called "careful deliberation" with his wife, decided to accept the job as Director of FBO for his good friend Colin. General Williams was in awe of Colin Powell. I believe Williams was the one who planted the bug in Powell's ear about the need for an overhaul of FBO and our country's diplomatic infrastructure around the world, and then begged Powell for the position. What a great job for Chuck Williams as he went into retirement.

When he took over FBO, he did so with vigor. But then again he was used to being in charge. He was the type of 'leader' who would make changes for change's sake in order to leave his mark on the organization. The need for the change wasn't important, but leaving his mark was. FBO would be no exception. General Williams began to run FBO like a military unit. Anyone who's been in the military, especially officers, knows there are many different ways to manage and lead people. There is leadership by example, and there's leadership by the strength of the person's personality. But then there's leadership by authority (i.e., rank), whereby the person in charge dictates and the rest must, and will, follow. This is the worst kind of leadership, but it was the style used by General Williams. For example, he refused to ride the elevator with the staff. They were beneath him. The guards in the lobby would hold an elevator just for him when he walked in the front door of the building. General Williams didn't ask, he ordered. He didn't request, he demanded. That style is tough in an army unit, but in a civilian organization it stinks.

I love to tell the story of when the senior staff was invited by General Williams to his home for a Christmas party. We were greeted at the door by the general and his wife, then he directed (i.e., ordered) us downstairs to the basement where there was an open bar. No hanging out by the front door—just straight downstairs. Upon reaching the bottom of the stairs we were hit in the face by a pictorial history of General Williams' career, of his entire professional life. Nearly every picture on the wall, and there were a lot of them, was of him. Every promotion throughout his long career was photographed, with the picture mounted on the wall along with a brief description of the rank he was achieving, the date and other key information about the photograph. Only someone planning a wall like this would have made sure these pictures were taken, and then saved all of them over a period of 30 and more years. There was an artist's sketch of the general with his staff at one of his last commands. It was a humorous caricature of him on an Alaskan dog sled, holding a whip, and his staff were the sled dogs! Of course, General Williams has a big grin on his face. He loved that sketch. Such was his 'leadership' style. It wasn't until the end of the tour of his basement wall that we saw photographs of his wife and his children. One picture of each, if I recall. How touching.

Wanting to leave his mark on the organization, what better way to do this than change its name? Instead of FBO, for Foreign Buildings Operations, General Williams changed it to OBO, for Overseas Buildings Operations. Now everyone calls it "OBO."

Morale at OBO went down the tubes because bureaucrats do not like change in any way, shape or form. People wanted to quit, but the ship didn't sink because in the end government employees will go through hell rather than give up their job security and their retirement. They'll bitch and moan and count the days until they retire, in some cases counting days into the thousands. This was the situation when I started to work for General Williams. He was able to talk the Sectary of State into promoting his position, which forever had been a Deputy Assistant Secretary. The general's position was elevated to Assistant Secretary, befitting of his ego. He was allowed by Powell to attend the Secretary's morning briefings, which no Director of FBO had ever been able to do. When he spoke to the staff he would say we were on the "Powell-Williams Team." I'm sure he has a picture of his promotion to Assistant Secretary somewhere on his basement wall by now.

I was asked by General Williams to be the Director of a new division he had created under his new reorganization. FBO never had a branch strictly devoted to planning. In the past FBO only reacted to needs that came up; i.e., waiting for a roof to fall in before installing a new one on the building. But General Williams created a new organization just for planning, devoted strictly to determining where facilities were in their 'life cycle,' and making a list of all facilities throughout the world based on this research. OBO developed a new 5-year plan, with posts (the State Department refers to all its locations as "posts") listed in descending order based on need of renovation, repair or complete replacement. To his credit, this was a very good thing for General Williams to have initiated. Based on this list my staff would go to the post, perform an assessment of the condition of the Embassy or consulate facilities, which included ancillary buildings such as residential housing and warehouses, and produce a report for the architects and engineers back at OBO to decide the next course of action. This was why I was in Dhaka on September 11, 2001.

I left Dhaka three days after the attacks, after meeting with the U.S. Ambassador, Mary Ann Peters, to say goodbye. She and I had a very interesting conversation about the events of the past few days, the main point being her contention that the world would never be the same again. One of the members of the team and I flew to Bangkok and then to London, arriving to a mob scene at Heathrow Airport. I've never seen an airport in the condition I saw Heathrow the day we arrived there, which was September 14th. We got in at 8:00 in the morning, and had a connecting flight to Dulles around 11:00 a.m. Of course, all flights had been cancelled for the preceding three days, but we were told they might start flying again later that day.

My co-worker and I were waiting in one particular line, when one of the American Airlines employees told us to wait in another line across the way. She walked us over to it, and we proceeded to wait again, but this line wasn't too long, so there was hope. When we got to the counter the young lady asked us for our tickets and passports, and when she saw "DIPLOMATIC" across the top she took them, asked us to wait, and then disappeared. We waited there for about 20 minutes. When she came back to the ticket counter she handed us our boarding passes and wished us good luck. I asked her how we had gotten on the flight. She pointed to the word across the top of our passports, and said two people had been bumped to get us on the next flight out, which was scheduled for about 5:00 that evening.

The staff at Heathrow Airport were wonderful. This was the first of many instances where I would see goodness in people, total strangers. Everyone felt sorry for Americans then, and for what we had suffered. It brought out the good in just about everyone, with one exception, which I will mention shortly. The hotel staff in Dhaka, all Muslims, were wonderful too. They kept offering their sympathy to us and saying how sorry they were for what our country was going through. It was a beautiful thing.

Sure enough, we got to the gate and the word got out that flights were going to start again. One flight left for Chicago before ours, but then ours left for Dulles—the first to land there from Heathrow since the events of the days before. I sat next to a Middle Eastern man who never said one word the entire flight. He must have been scared to death. He never left his seat to go to the bathroom. I can't blame him. When the wheels touched the ground the entire plane started clapping and cheering. It felt great to be home, but greater still to be an American. The guy next to me disappeared.

I would return to the States to hear stories of what people had experienced that fateful day. FBO (now OBO) was located in Rosslyn, Virginia, the part of Arlington County just across the Potomac River from Georgetown, the trendy area of Washington, DC. When the plane hit the Pentagon people in my building who worked on the upper floors saw it hit. One of my friends was on the phone talking to a friend in New York City, who was describing the planes slamming into the World Trade Center towers. Just then she looked out the window and saw the plane hit the Pentagon. She went into shock and walked out of the building, taking 12 flights of stairs to the ground floor, and pulling a fire alarm on the way out to clear the building. She walked all the way home, and didn't come back to work for a week. She was still in shock when she told me her story two weeks later.

After the April 18, 1983 U.S. Embassy bombing in Beirut, Lebanon, followed by the Marine barracks bombing on October 23, 1983 in that same city, the State Department asked retired Navy Admiral Bobby Inman to chair a commission on improving security at U.S. foreign installations around the world. Our country has a habit of freaking out every time a disaster happens, then in no time everyone forgets all about it. As a result, the "Inman Report," as it became known, ended up being used as a paperweight at the State Department. However, by 1:00 in the afternoon on September 11, 2001, every copy of it was being pulled off the shelves at FBO and dusted off. All of the sudden, the Inman Report *was* influential in setting security standards for U.S. Embassies around the world. But because the events of 9/11/01 were so incredible, the report was only the beginning.

After the attacks of September 11, 2001, the State Department had a new mandate—the physical security of its facilities around the world. Now the State Department had a whole new set of problems as far as its buildings were concerned, and they weren't just leaky roofs and bad plumbing. For example, what would happen to buildings located in cities like Paris, where they sat right along the sidewalk and anyone could reach out and touch the walls with their hands, where any terrorist could pull a car loaded with explosives up against the wall of the building and set it off, killing everyone inside and outside of the facility within hundreds of feet? What would the U.S. do with these buildings, located around the world, worth billions of dollars not only for their historical value, but also for their incredible locations in the most important cities in the world? We couldn't just look at buildings for their repair or replacement any more. We now had to consider their complete relocation outside the city centers where they had been for decades. The costs would be enormous. OBO had an annual budget of $1 billion dollars. The cost of relocating embassies would be astronomical, take years to accomplish, and would call for a whole new way of doing business for the State Department. This was the situation during the time I spent there.

Although he had a rough start when he took over FBO, after the events of 9/11 there couldn't have been a better person in charge than General Williams. The Department of State needed a military leader to run that operation. We were at war. We didn't have time for debate or discussion. We had to get things done. Who better to lead us than a retired two-star general from the U.S. Army Corps of Engineers? Before 9/11, General Williams' style didn't work at OBO. After 9/11, that's exactly what was needed.

After 9/11 happened I saw for the first time the cost we would pay for the many failures of the new administration of George W. Bush. When Bush was elected he kept George Tenet in his job as Director of Central Intelligence. Why he did this was beyond my comprehension. I remember wondering at the time, well before 9/11, why Bush would keep Tenet, a Clinton hack, in this immensely important job. The conventional wisdom around Washington was that his father, Bush the First, recommended Tenet stay in his job at CIA because Bush the Elder liked him. If that is indeed true, it is another example of the flakiness of Bush the First, and his desire to be liked by liberals. George Tenet was a liberal with no practical experience to run the CIA before Clinton gave him the job. He had been head of the Congressional committee staff responsible for the oversight of the CIA—that was it. He had never been a 'spook,' and had never been directly involved in the collection of intelligence. All he had ever done was run the committee staff that reported to the members of Congress who provided oversight of the CIA, the committee that gave the CIA the money it needed to run. He was a glorified administrator.

But the real stinker was the effect this decision of George W. Bush's had on the people who had worked so hard to get him elected—people like me who had fought in the trenches in Florida on the recount. After all, why does someone vote for a presidential candidate? Well, one of the reasons is because of the people they hope he will place in his administration. A good example is a pick for a Supreme Court Justice. This single selection is one of the main reasons we vote for a presidential candidate, because it will have lasting implications for years to come. The Director of Central Intelligence may not be a Supreme Court Justice, but the position is certainly one of the most critical in the Cabinet. Allowing George Tenet to remain the Director of the CIA was a slap in the face of everyone who had worked to get Bush elected in 2000, contributed to his campaign, voted for him, and fought for him in the states Gore was trying to steal. We did not expect to get stuck with Tenet, a Clinton holdover. I for one didn't fight in the trenches in Florida during the recounts, to get stuck with a Clinton hack like Tenet.

Another issue that must be discussed, which wasn't noticed until after 9/11, was Bush's complete and utter failure to hold people accountable for their incompetence. I worked on his campaign in 2000. I was at his national headquarters in Austin. One of his major points during the campaign was the issue of "personal responsibility." Bush stressed over and over the need for people to be responsible for their actions, and to be accountable for them. He was placing personal responsibility back on the shoulders of the average American, and we liked what we heard. It was 'Reaganesque.' Personal responsibility is one of the touchstones of the conservative movement, and was so at the time of the founding of this country. Stand up for yourself, and take responsibility for yourself. These are the hallmarks of what made this country great. They embellish capitalism and a free market economy and society. Work hard and reap the rewards of your labors. They are also the battle cry of those who are against big government and the liberal-socialist movement. But when 9/11 happened what did Bush do in this critical area? Absolutely nothing.

I am not aware of a single person losing their job, or a single federal employee in a position of responsibility for the security of our country getting fired or forced to retire. That wasn't 'Reaganesque,' it was the same thing that would have happened in Moscow if a high level member of the Communist Party screwed up. Nothing would happen to him either. Needless to say, those same people still have their secure federal jobs, or have since retired with no loss of their precious pensions. This is despicable. We suffered because senior FBI agents and managers in Phoenix failed to heed the warnings of their own agents, because there was no coordination between domestic and non-domestic intelligence agencies, and because peoples' jobs and careers were more important than raising the red flag and digging into things that were beginning to pop up and raise eyebrows.

For the last two years of Bill Clinton's administration his Ambassador-at-Large for Counterterrorism was my West Point classmate, and one-time roommate, Michael Sheehan. Shortly after the USS Cole was attacked in the port of Aden, Yemen, a meeting was held with Madeleine Albright, the Secretary of State. Also at the meeting were Richard Clarke, Clinton's

Counterterrorism Advisor, Secretary of Defense William Cohen, Director of Central Intelligence George Tenet, Attorney General Janet Reno, Mike Sheehan, and others. Clarke wanted to go after al Qaeda, and had a plan in place to do so that he had been working on for months. A vote was taken of the participants at the meeting and he was the only one in favor of retaliation against Osama bin Laden.

Janet Reno thought retaliation might violate international law so she wouldn't support it. George Tenet wanted more definitive proof that bin Laden was behind the attack, although he thought he was. Madeleine Albright was concerned about the reaction of world opinion to retaliation against Muslims, and impact it would have in the final days of the Clinton Middle East peace process. And Defense Secretary William Cohen didn't consider the Cole attack "sufficient provocation" for a military retaliation. So much for his sailors. Michael Sheehan was particularly surprised that the Pentagon did not want to act. He was quoted saying to Clarke: "What's it going to take to get them to hit al Qaeda in Afghanistan? Does al Qaeda have to attack the Pentagon?

Instead of destroying bin Laden's terrorist infrastructure and capabilities, President Clinton phoned the president of Yemen asking for better cooperation between the FBI and the Yemeni security services. If Clarke's plan had been implemented, there is a good chance al Qaeda's infrastructure would have been destroyed and bin Laden killed or in custody, and September 11, 2001 would have been like any other sunny day.[17]

Based on what happened at this meeting, no one thought the attack on the USS Cole was worth doing anything about, other than Richard Clarke and Mike Sheehan. All of these people were responsible for the defense of our country and the protection of our people, which includes going after anyone who kills our citizens, especially our armed forces overseas. Yet, Muslim opinion was more important to them than the lives of United States sailors, and the sovereignty of one of our ships. According to Janet Reno, we might have been violating international law if

---

[17] Richard Miniter, "Losing Bin Laden: How Bill Clinton's Failures Unleashed Global Terror" (Regnery Publishing, 2003), as reported by Kathryn Jean Lopez, "Clinton's Loss?: How the previous administration fumbled on bin Laden," *National Review Online*, September 11, 2003.

we retaliated! We certainly didn't want to violate international law. I wonder if Al-Qaeda asked that same question before it attacked the USS Cole. Al-Qaeda should have an international law scholar like Janet Reno on its staff to make sure that doesn't happen again. Maybe Reno can contract out to Al-Qaeda as its "Risk Management Officer," to make sure that it's in compliance.

To take it a step further, it's OK if a bunch of Wahhabi Muslim extremists murder 17 of our sailors, but God forbid we go after the bastards who did it and offend the Muslim world. (Wahhabism is the conservative sect of Islam espoused by its extreme radical wing, including Al Qaeda. It is not followed by most of the Muslim world which essentially disavows both its teaching, and its practices.)

The only conclusion that can be reached from this meeting is that Madeleine Albright, William Cohen, George Tenet and Janet Reno felt the sensitivities of Muslims was more important than the lives of our dead sailors, and our nation's honor. What other conclusion can anyone come to? What is beyond comprehension was that Madeleine Albright didn't want to take retaliation because it would hinder the Muslim "peace" talks that Clinton was conducting. But a Muslim terrorist attack while the talks were going on could be overlooked. One might conclude Clinton's "peace" talks weren't going very well. Maybe he should have started them sooner. Whatever Clinton and Albright did in the world of diplomacy was praised, yet they couldn't do anything in response to the attack on the USS Cole!

Then when 9/11 occurred, Madeleine Albright had the audacity to accuse Bush of not doing anything to prevent it. Bush had been in office for 8 months at the time, yet Clinton had been in office for a full eight years before 9/11. During Clinton's time in the White House we had the attack on the USS Cole, the Embassy bombings in Africa, the explosion at the World Trade Center, and other attacks. Clinton was indirectly responsible for 9/11 by not grabbing bin Laden when he had the chance.

The day before the attacks, on September 10, 2001, Clinton gave a speech to Australian business leaders in which he admitted he could have killed bin Laden but decided not to. It took almost 13 years for the story to emerge in the mainstream American media that Clinton could have killed Osama bin Laden long before September 11, 2001, but instead he let him go.

> "I'm just saying, you know, if I were Usama bin Laden — he's a very smart guy, I've spent a lot of time thinking about him — and I nearly got him once." Clinton said on a recording of the Australian business meeting. "I nearly got him. And I could have killed him, but I would have to destroy a little town called Kandahar in Afghanistan and kill 300 innocent women and children, and then I would have been no better than him. And so I didn't do it."[18]

Bill Clinton had the opportunity to kill Osama bin Laden, knowing at the time he had been responsible for the deaths of dozens of United States citizens, not the least of whom included military personnel and diplomatic staff. But by his own admission he chose not to. This didn't stop Madeleine Albright from spouting her bile at George W. Bush for failing to get bin Laden before 9/11.

After the attacks on September 11, 2001, George W. Bush could have shown the American people he wasn't going to allow those responsible for preventing it to get away with their failures. Yet, he did nothing. This was the beginning of an era where no matter what happened, or how bad things were planned and executed, George W. Bush would not do a thing to punish the people responsible, and worse, would back them to the hilt in the face of overwhelming evidence that they were completely incompetent. His loyalty to his staff, a great asset when times are good, would prove his undoing when times were bad.

As mentioned above, one of the problems with the events of 9/11, indeed one of its causes, was the lack of coordination between the intelligence agencies of our government. The Federal Bureau of Investigation, for example, is responsible for domestic intelligence, for tracking and apprehending individuals who are spying on the United States within our borders. During the Second World War the FBI was famous for apprehending

---

[18] "Clinton on Sept. 10, 2001: I could have killed bin Laden but 'I didn't'," *Fox News*, July 31, 2014.

German and Japanese spies found in the United States. On the other hand, the Central Intelligence Agency is the primary asset responsible for ensuring our nation's security beyond our borders, our own 'James Bonds.' Because he was so out to lunch and out of touch with the realities of the murky world of 'human intelligence' collection, Bill Clinton enacted official policy that essentially barred our intelligence-gathering agencies from dealing with people of 'unpleasant character.' Look at what the results of this have been, and add 9/11 to the list.

The Clinton administration went as far as it could to diminish our nation's intelligence collection capabilities, indirectly enabling the 9/11 hijackers. In 1995 a memo was written by Jamie Gorelick of the Clinton Justice Department, who served under Janet Reno of Branch Davidian massacre fame. The Gorelick memo drastically widened the so-called "wall of separation" of intelligence collection and intelligence sharing between the domestic and international intelligence agencies of the United States government. Her memo was the single main reason for our intelligence agencies' inability to coordinate their efforts leading up to 9/11.

Yet, this same Jamie Gorelick was a member of the commission appointed by the President to investigate the circumstances leading up to the events of 9/11. (The National Commission on Terrorist Attacks Upon the United States, also known as the "9/11 Commission" or the "Kean/Hamilton Commission.") During the course of the 9/11 Commission hearings it was discovered that one of the single most important players in the events contributing to the tragedies of that day, was in fact a member of the same Commission investigating the events contributing to the tragedies of that day—Jamie Gorelick!

In an April 14, 2004 opinion piece, *The Washington Times* was scathing in its criticism of Ms. Gorelick, declaring that "she had been among the most partisan and aggressive Democratic panel members in questioning the anti-terror efforts of the Bush administration." *The Times* suggested that instead of cross-examining witnesses, Ms. Gorelick should have been required to testify about her own behavior—in particular her 1995 memo making it more difficult for the FBI to locate two of the September 11 hijackers, who had already entered the country by the summer of 2001. Ms. Gorelick's memo, written to FBI Director Louis Freeh and U.S. Attorney for the Southern District of New York, Mary Jo White, ordered them to "go beyond what is legally required," in order to avoid "any risk of creating an unwarranted appearance" the Justice Department was using Foreign Intelligence Surveillance Act (FISA) warrants to undermine the civil liberties of terrorism suspects.[19]

The Times wrote that her memo had a devastating effect into the investigation of al Qaeda operations in this country in the summer of 2001. In late August 2001, the CIA told the FBI that Khalid Almidhar and Nawaf Alhaznmi had entered the country, but FBI investigators refused to permit criminal investigators with knowledge about the recent al Qaeda attack to join the manhunt. In addition, a search warrant to examine the computer of Zacarias Moussaoui, whose interest in flying aircraft had attracted so much attention, was rejected because FBI officials were afraid of breaching Jamie Gorelick's wall.[20]

What authority did Ms. Gorelick have to order Freeh and White to "go beyond what is legally required" of an existing statute? Clearly, Ms. Gorelick wanted to go beyond existing law to ensure the "civil liberties of terrorism suspects" were not infringed—to her standards:

> ...the practical effect of the wall was that counterintelligence information was generally kept away from law enforcement personnel who were investigating al Qaeda activities. But Ms. Gorelick's memo clearly indicated that the Clinton administration had decided as a matter of policy to go even beyond the law's already stringent requirements in order to further choke off information sharing.[21]

If Ms. Gorelick hadn't written her memo the requirements of FISA could have been followed, and our law enforcement and intelligence agencies could have still shared information. But her

---

[19] "Jamie Gorelick's Wall," *Washington Times*, April 15, 2004.

[20] Ibid.

[21] Ibid.

memo did just what it was meant to do—intimidate our law enforcement agencies and personnel from doing anything they feared might get them into trouble with her, the mighty Janet Reno, and the Clintons (Hillary got Jamie her job at DoJ).

Ms. Gorelick ordered Freeh and White to go beyond an existing statute. She's a lawyer, yet she ordered them to follow her own interpretation of FISA rather than follow the law as written, so that the rights of terrorists wouldn't "appear" to be infringed upon in any way, shape or form. The civil liberties of suspected terrorists was more important to the Clinton administration than legally sharing information that was raising red flags and might save American lives. But that didn't stop Jamie Gorelick from blaming the Bush administration for the tragedies of September 11, 2001, six years after she wrote her memo.

When news of the memo came out Jamie cried in outrage that her integrity was beyond reproach. But wouldn't questioning her about the memo be one of the most important things the 9/11 Commission needed to do? One would think so. Isn't that why the commission was created by the President? Instead, the Chairman of the 9/11 Commission, Governor Thomas Kean, got in front of the microphones and blasted everyone and anyone who dared to ask about the memo or Jamie Gorelick's involvement. She was placed off limits by the Chairman of the very commission assigned to investigate the events of 9/11, thereby keeping from the American people any details of Jamie Gorelick's role leading up to the terrorist attacks on September 11, 2001. If they couldn't discuss Jamie Gorelick's memo, or even ask her about it, why bother to have the 9/11 Commission at all? It should have been called "The President's 9/11 Whitewash Commission."

(More has come out since the 9/11 Commission's report concerning Jamie Gorelick's work at Fannie Mae. On April 7, 2005, *The Washington Post* reported that Fannie Mae "employees" had falsified signatures on financial reporting documents, shifting operating expenses incurred in 1998 to later years. The moves erroneously inflated Fannie Mae's profits for 1998, thereby raising the amount of funds in the bonus pool for its top executives to $21.7 million. Jamie Gorelick, the Vice Chairman of Fannie Mae at the time, got a bonus check for $779,625. I don't recall any Fannie Mae executives being prosecuted or going to jail. I guess Fannie Mae considered forging the financial records of a US-owned corporation 'outstanding performance.' The criminal mismanagement of both Fannie Mae (the Federal National Mortgage Association, or FNMA), and Freddie Mac (the Federal Home Loan Mortgage Corporation, or FHLMC), and the criminal conduct of its managers has directly contributed to our nation's financial disaster. Yet, Jamie got a bonus of nearly $800,000 for doing such a great job. Not only did she contribute to the events of September 11, 2001, she contributed to our country's current financial collapse—and has been cashing in the whole time.)[22]

Throughout all the 9/11 investigations the President did nothing, or if he did anything he spoke in platitudes about how great a person was, how great their service to the nation had been, etc., etc., etc., blah, blah, blah. In the case of Jamie Gorelick, all we got was doubletalk about what a great person she was, and that her integrity was beyond reproach. So much for the American people getting the full story, or even close to the full story, about how 9/11 was able to happen, how we might have been able to prevent it, and certainly what was being done about it. One thing is for sure, no one lost their job or their precious pension as a result of the biggest intelligence and security disaster ever to happen to this country; and yet, they all worked for the man who campaigned on the platform of personal responsibility. Not only did George Tenet keep his job after the election of George W. Bush, he kept it after 9/11 too! We would see over and over again how Bush would fail to enforce that same promise, and fail to hold people in his administration accountable for one screw up after another. By this time we were seeing it happen every day.

But in order to make the leap from the events of September 11, 2001, to our attacks in Afghanistan and later Iraq, another critical failure of George W. Bush must be brought to light. After the attacks on the World Trade Center and the Pentagon, and the plane crash in Pennsylvania, George Bush could have done anything he wanted. He could have gotten anything he asked for,

---

[22] Kathleen Day and Terence O'Hara, "False Signatures Aided Fannie Mae Bonuses, Falcon Says," *The Washington Post*, April 7, 2005.

and the American people would have given it to him. Even left-wing comedian and gay rights activist Rosie O'Donnell, best known for *The Rosie Show*, backed him! If she would, that speaks volumes for the support he had, if he had only used it. But instead of grabbing the bull by the horns and doing what he should have done, what he could have done, George Bush squandered the best opportunity any president since Franklin Delano Roosevelt had after Pearl Harbor to bring the country together in the face of catastrophe. Because Bush was a weak president, like his father, he failed to act. He failed to do the one thing he should have done—he failed to reinstitute the draft to increase the size of our armed forces.

Those who think this idea preposterous are reacting with the same knee jerk we always get when the word "draft" is mentioned. The President went on about the "global war on terror" after 9/11. If indeed we were now involved in a global war on terror, how were we going to fight it with the Army half the size it was only a dozen years before? In the late 1980s Germany was unifying and the Cold War was ending. The U.S. Army overreacted with "Operation Quicksilver" in November 1989, reducing the size of the Army's strength by 23%, from 750,000 to 580,000.[23] It should have been called "Operation Quicksand," because that's where we are now. Before the reduction the Army had about 18 fully operational combat divisions. After the reduction it was down to around 10. At that time a division consisted of about 20,000 soldiers, and was either an Infantry or armor division. (In a division there are three brigades, as well as support units. If at least two of the three brigades are Infantry, then it is an 'Infantry-heavy' division. If at least two of the three are armor, it is an 'armor-heavy' division. If all three brigades are Infantry or armor, then it is an 'Infantry' or 'armor' division. Today we are abandoning the divisional makeup of the U.S. Army and going to Brigade Combat Teams.)

If the President declared to the country that we were in a global war on terror, and of course our own country had been attacked, how could he possibly think this war could be fought with the post-Clinton manning strength that now had the Army

---

[23] John J. Mcgrath, "An Army at War: Change in the Midst of Conflict," (Combat Studies Institute Press, 2005), p. 515.

at around 10 operational divisions? It was Bush's perfect opportunity to make use of the Selective Service System, which males have to register with within 30 days of their 18th birthday. (Women don't have to register. Neither do males who have changed their sex to 'female.' I suppose that's one way of avoiding the draft.) I never served in Vietnam, but I registered for the draft in case the country needed me. But today our country is locked into the 'all volunteer' military, which is nothing more than a social welfare system that throws money at kids who want to buy a new car. We pay our soldiers out the nose to enlist, and then pay them out the nose to stay, and then pay them out the nose to go to college, and then offer huge bonuses to re-enlist. True, most are there because they want to serve, but how many would be there without the financial incentives? The true patriot is one who serves but really doesn't want to. The true patriot is the guy who was drafted during Vietnam and had a million things he would rather have been doing, but went because he had to. The true patriot is the one who went to Vietnam against the war and paid the ultimate sacrifice. Is today's 'volunteer' soldier a true patriot like the Vietnam draftee, when he gets paid out the nose for everything and was probably unemployed? It's easy for today's volunteer to say he joined to serve his country. But would he have joined without the money and the bonuses? Today we have a mercenary force, not a volunteer force. If it was a true volunteer force, our soldiers would serve for their basic pay and nothing more. Every time I see recruiting commercials on TV for college and the like, I have to laugh. A volunteer force—where? To most soldiers today it's not a vocation or a call by their nation to serve, it's just a job.

One possible reason why the draft is unacceptable is because the country doesn't want to see women having to register for it, and actually getting called up. What would the country think if men started to get drafted, but not women because they don't have to register for it? In our politically correct society that doesn't look like a fair deal, and it probably wouldn't look like one to young men of draft age either. Even though feminists want women to be able to do everything men do, drafting women is the last thing they want. As a result we can't take all the steps needed to protect our country from further disaster in the post-9/11 world we live in today. Something has to be done about this, but people in power refuse to look at it. They are afraid and won't act, and the country is weaker and less defended for it. If women serve in the military, they should have to register for the draft when they turn 18 just like men do. We talk about equality, but ignore it in this case because we don't want to face the realities of warfare and the image of women being drafted like the men.

Today's soldiers, most of them good and decent people, are bought and paid for. The majority of those in the service today —other than our true combat forces who really want to serve their country—are there because it's the closest alternative to being unemployed. Yet during Vietnam, which started with the draft, the services were made up of men from all walks of life, all levels of the economy, and all levels of education. The flaw with the Vietnam draft, as during the Civil War, was that there were too many ways to avoid it as Bush, Cheney and Clinton did. Yet, even though there were ways for cowards to get out of Vietnam many, like Tom Ridge, Al Gore and John Kerry did serve. Ridge enlisted as a common Infantry soldier after having graduated from Harvard, and Gore served even though he was the son of a United States Senator and could have gotten out of it with a phone call from his dad. And John Kerry, even though he lied about his heroism and faked his decorations, did serve in combat and was in the thick of things (albeit for only three months) in the Mekong Delta. Gore and Kerry both served their country in Vietnam, while Bush and Clinton avoided it.

What about all the protests against the Vietnam War back in the '60's and '70's? The protesters screamed at the cameras about the immorality of the war, and about the innocent civilians we were killing. Yet, when Nixon and the Pentagon caved and ended the draft, all those protests stopped on a dime. As soon as they knew they weren't going to be drafted, the bleeding hearts against the war suddenly realized they weren't against the war anymore. What happened to the immorality of the war and all those innocent civilians we were killing? Now, those former protesters could relax and smoke all the pot they wanted, in the knowledge they weren't going to get called up. And what about those innocent civilians in Vietnam we were supposedly killing? All of the sudden they weren't the protesters' problem anymore. The anti-war movement wasn't based on the immorality of the war, but the fact that those protesters were cowards afraid of getting shot at. The end of the protests as soon as the draft was called off speaks for itself.

The biggest coward of them all was Dick Cheney, who got five draft deferments during the Vietnam War, the last one when his wife got pregnant. In a 1989 interview by *Washington Post* writer George C. Wilson prior to becoming the Secretary of Defense, Cheney said: "I had other priorities in the '60s than military service."[24] A reasonable person might conclude Dick Cheney was trying to avoid Vietnam. But he was still confirmed as Secretary of Defense, whose job it is to send soldiers to war. Cheney's comment begs the question: what "other priorities" did he have other than military service during the Vietnam War? What was he doing that was more important than serving his country, getting his wife pregnant? How many soldiers got their wives or girlfriends pregnant but went to Vietnam anyway? How many of them never came home and never saw their child? I guess they didn't have better things to do than Dick Cheney.

It never ceases to amaze me how men who avoided military service have no problem sending young men into combat and possibly to their death. How can they look themselves in the mirror every day? But then, they don't really care, so it doesn't bother them. What they really care about is themselves, their egos, and their position in life. They say they care about others, especially our soldiers, but their actions speak otherwise. President Bush went on about "the troops" he cared for so much, admitting he gave up golf so it wouldn't look like he was enjoying himself too much as the body count continued to climb in Iraq. It's nice to know that soldiers' lives are the moral equivalent of a golf game.

When our country is faced with catastrophe the only viable solution is to drastically increase the size of our active duty military forces with a draft, and volunteers. But our country refuses to consider a draft, instead relying solely on volunteers, the reserves, the National Guard, and contractors. Who would

---

[24] "Profile of Dick Cheney," *ABC News*, January 6, 2006.

not agree we were faced with probably the biggest catastrophe in our history after 9/11, which continues today? With a draft the Army and Marines could have grown in strength, and we would have had the forces needed to go into both Afghanistan and Iraq. To think we could pull off both operations without resorting to the draft is insane, yet that is exactly what Bush did. He never declared war, because that is politically incorrect today as well. So, we went into both Afghanistan and Iraq without a declaration of war, i.e., without a clearly defined enemy, purpose, objective and mission, and without the troops to accomplish any of it. On top of this, we went in without an exit strategy.

3—The Office of Homeland Security

After the 9/11 attacks the President asked Tom Ridge, the Governor of Pennsylvania, to come to Washington to head up a new office in the White House, the Office of Homeland Security. Governor Ridge had been a close advisor to George Bush during the campaign the previous year, with talk of him possibly being Bush's Vice Presidential running mate. But Ridge is pro-abortion, so that idea never went far.

Tom Ridge was sworn in as the nation's first "Advisor to the President for Homeland Security," his official title. Unknown to many, he was actually Condoleezza Rice's counterpart: she was the President's Advisor for National Security, and he the Advisor for Homeland Security. Another little known fact outside Washington was the setup of the Office of Homeland Security, which by its structure and location proved to be completely impotent.

The Office of Homeland Security was made a part of the Executive Office of the President, assigned directly to the White House. This was done because the President has the power to do most anything he wants with his own immediate staff. If he had tried to create the Office of Homeland Security outside the Executive Office of the President, Congress would have been able to get involved and it would have taken forever to create the office, if it was ever created at all. Due to limitations of space, most people assigned to the Executive Office of the President don't work in the West Wing itself, but across the drive in the Old Executive Office Building. Some are a block away in the New Executive Office Building on 17th Street. The Old Executive Office Building (the "OEOB") is one of the most beautiful buildings in Washington, having been at various times the Navy Department, the War Department, and the State Department. Today it is an extension of the West Wing, housing staff of the Executive Office of the President. So, when someone says they are on White House staff and work "in the White House," they are on the staff of the Executive Office of the President and very likely don't work in the West Wing, but in the Old Executive Office Building next door.

However, there was more to the structure of the Office of Homeland Security (OHS) than just where it was on an organization chart. Being a part of the Executive Office of the President, and not a stand-alone agency, OHS had extremely limited powers. In effect, it had no real power at all. For example, when OHS was established it could not direct any other component of the United States Government to do anything. It was merely a staff element of the White House. Rather than being in the OEOB next door to the White House, its offices were physically located several miles away from the White House at a U.S. Navy facility called the Nebraska Avenue Complex (the "NAC"), located at Ward Circle across from American University. The NAC had been the headquarters of Naval Intelligence during the Second World War, and was the home of the Navy's international arms sales division at the time of the 9/11 attacks. Homeland Security kicked out the occupants of one of the buildings on the NAC grounds and completely renovated the interior. It was quite an impressive task, and done in minimal time.

Being a political appointee at the State Department's Overseas Buildings Operations bureau, I was a square peg in a round hole. I had civil servants working for me. One of them went out of her way to make my life and that of everyone around her as miserable as possible. She had a reputation in the State Department for being a total malingerer, a complete drain on the system. She didn't work, but instead complained to the Federal Employees Union (yes, there is such a thing) whenever someone tried to make her do her job, which I had the nerve to do. With the Federal Government being what it is she wasn't going anywhere, but I could. I got no support from General Williams with this malcontent, after he had hired me and put me into the job, or from my direct superior, a career Senior Foreign Service Officer who made it very clear he didn't like Republicans, and who I shouldn't have been reporting to in the first place.

Never having been in a high level political job before, General Williams didn't realize he was feeding me to the wolves when he placed me in direct charge of bureaucrats. Being a political appointee I should have been in a policy position, where I would report directly to him. It could have worked out if it hadn't been for the woman on my staff, who did everything possible to undermine my authority and destroy the cohesion of the office. But General Williams didn't have the courage to support me and do something about her, so I was on my own. I saw the writing on the wall.

The one person who showed her true colors after 9/11 was this woman, who was on my team in Dhaka, Bangladesh. The morning of September 12, 2001, she was making a joke about the attacks of the previous day. We were eating breakfast in the hotel restaurant and she started joking about how "afraid" she was to be an American, and how she better hide her passport, ha, ha, ha. She thought it was all very funny. The rest of us just looked at her.

I decided to visit the State Department's "White House Liaison Officer." The liaison officer in a Federal agency is the person responsible for all political appointees placed in that department. I asked one of the staff if I could get another job, either within the State Department or elsewhere. The next thing I knew I was being asked if I would like to work for Tom Ridge in the new Office of Homeland Security (OHS) in the White House. Of course I said yes. Who wouldn't want to do that? I interviewed and was selected to be the Senior Director for Administration in OHS, in charge of Personnel, Security, Information Technology and Facilities for Tom Ridge. I was on loan from the State Department to OHS for one year. In the Government this is called a "detail." Because OHS didn't have budget authority to have its own permanent staff, save for about a dozen people, all its staff were people from other agencies on detail like me. The entire homeland security of the United States was being coordinated by a dozen full-time staffers and about 50 other people, political and full-time employees, all on loan from their other government jobs.

One of my responsibilities was for the building that OHS occupied at the NAC. Inside the building was a large room set up with plasma screens and a wide array of communications equipment. It was set up just like an Operations Center, but because OHS had no direct authority over anyone, or any other government agencies, we couldn't even call it what it was, so instead we called it the "Coordination Center." To call it an

Operations Center would have meant we had the operational authority to tell agencies what to do. All we could do was 'suggest' what they should do and monitor them. If an agency didn't want to do what we 'suggested,' they didn't have to. OHS was a lion without any teeth. All of this was because of where the Office of Homeland Security was placed, which was within the organizational framework the Executive Office of the President. If it had been placed outside that, and had been made a department of the Executive Branch of the Federal Government, things would have been completely different. The results of not doing this were felt everywhere. We had no budget, we had no authority, we had no permanent staff beyond about 12 people, we didn't even have the ability to call our operations center what it really was.

The Office of Homeland Security had essentially two missions. The first was to set up a national homeland security staff and organization to coordinate the efforts of the rest of the government. This involved bringing other federal agencies together to work toward a common goal. It also brought together all federal, state and local "first responders," the ones who are the first to respond to any sort of domestic threat. And it brought in private industry's latest technology to fight the new 'enemy.' Industry would soon prove to play a major role in the effort to protect the homeland. In a classic win-win effort industry stood to gain financially by bringing to the government the latest technology, thereby making huge amounts of money, while at the same time the government would get what it needed to fight terrorism with the most modern technology available.

The second mission of the Office of Homeland Security was to draft the legislation creating the new "Department of Homeland Security" that was only being talked about then, but was well on its way to becoming reality. The staff members of OHS spent most of their time doing both of the tasks mentioned here. Some, however, spent all of their time entirely devoted to drafting the creating legislation, although officially they weren't supposed to be doing anything but the first of these two missions. One of my colleagues at OHS, a 30-something university professor named Dr. Richard Falkenrath, was the primary drafter of the legislation that created the new

Department. The law merged 22 agencies into one Cabinet Department, to include FEMA and the U.S. Secret Service. Why these were brought into the new Department is anyone's guess. It makes no sense to me, but then it wasn't my job to write the legislation, nor to approve what Dr. Falkenrath wrote. Other than these two glaring examples of fluff mixed into the new Department, Dr. Falkenrath did an incredible job at OHS, especially for such a young person. His knowledge of government and the workings of its institutions was remarkable. He later became the Deputy Mayor of New York City for Counterterrorism, the post that had previously held by my West Point classmate, and former Clinton Ambassador-at-Large for Counterterrorism, Michael Sheehan.

As the months went by the new department became the most talked about topic in Washington. How many agencies would be folded into it? How many employees would it have? How much authority would it have? How many regional offices? Where would it be located? The list went on. I was involved in many meetings on the future location of the new department headquarters. Would it be in Washington or located outside the city, or even in another part of the country? Would it be a federally owned building, or leased by the Government for 10 or 20 years? Who would get the deal, who would win this huge procurement, standing to make hundreds of millions in land and development fees? The Congressional delegations from Maryland, DC, and Virginia all got involved, wanting the new agency headquarters to be located in their jurisdiction for employment and business revenue. Federally-owned buildings don't pay real estate taxes. But if the building was leased, the owner would have to pay real estate taxes to the local government, raising millions in revenue for its coffers.

The District of Columbia was at the forefront of these discussions, mainly due to its standing as the jurisdiction most in need. This is primarily because its inept administration, corrupt institutions and socialist government are always in need of Federal cash to operate and make political payoffs. Congress usually gives the District what it wants, only to see U.S. tax dollars poured down the drain because of the bribes, payoffs and bloated bureaucracy of the District Government. The leader of this effort was Representative Eleanor Holmes Norton, the current member of the U.S. House of Representatives for DC. She has the distinction of having been elected to her first term after it was brought out by her opponent a week before the election that she and her husband had not paid their taxes for years. Their combined income was well over $500,000, yet they couldn't pay their taxes. And they were both lawyers, "officers of the court." She blamed her husband for not filing their tax returns and took no responsibility for it at all. If Marion Barry could get elected term after term, when everyone knew he was a crack head, what did it matter that Eleanor Holmes Norton didn't pay her taxes?

Having spent nearly 10 years at the U.S. General Services Administration (GSA) in leasing and construction for the Federal Government, being involved in the management of the new department's huge portfolio of facilities would be right up my alley. This was especially true in light of the fact that the 22 agencies merging into the new Department of Homeland Security all had existing space and real estate totaling hundreds of individual leases and Federally-owned locations. What would happen to these assets when they got combined into one department? Most of the space the Federal Government occupies is leased. These leases aren't just going to expire because the Government wants them to. I had been a Contracting Officer at GSA, with warrants (i.e., licenses) to execute real estate leases and construction contracts. I would have been a valuable asset to the newly forming Department of Homeland Security, especially working with GSA, my old agency.

Once the law creating the department was signed by the President all the heavies started rolling in, including a Republican hack named Janet Hale, who was the designee to be the new Under-Secretary for Management. She was brought over from the Department of Health and Human Services, where she had been the Assistant Secretary for Budget, Technology and Finance for just a year. Janet Hale was obviously on the fast track. Unfortunately for the new Department of Homeland Security and the American people, part of Hale's responsibilities would be all of the new department's real estate and facilities. This would be a huge undertaking, and I knew it. I asked her if I could assist in any way, but she never gave me the time of day. I guess I wasn't one of 'her people.' So much for my big plans of getting a high level job in the new department.

I saw first-hand the effects of Janet Hale's 'executive management' skills after I returned from Iraq and went to work as a consultant at U.S. Immigration & Customs Enforcement (ICE), one of the many components of the Department of Homeland Security. I was employed there by a large firm under contract to the agency. When I arrived at ICE, I was told one of the policies Janet Hale had implemented throughout DHS was the concept of "shared services," whereby one agency does work for one or more others in addition to itself. It's supposed to trim costs and increase efficiencies. It sounds good, which is all that counts, but it makes absolutely no sense in the real world. It's a coordination and management nightmare.

For starters, the agency doing the work is going to concentrate on its own needs before doing anything for another agency it's supporting. Why would it do otherwise? It also created problems because one agency isn't familiar with the space needs of another, causing miscommunication and poor development of space requirements. And it added an unnecessary layer of bureaucracy to a process that was already time consuming and extremely complicated, which anything to do with real estate is. It drastically affected the acquisition and delivery of the facilities needed by ICE, numbering hundreds of individual projects per year.

For example, whenever ICE needed space it had to go to U.S. Customs & Border Protection (CBP) first, which in turn went to GSA, instead of ICE going to GSA on its own. On top of all this ICE had to pay a "mark-up" to CBP for its services, and then pay a "mark-up" to GSA for its services too!

This 'Rube Goldberg' arrangement created by Janet Hale affected ICE's ability to provide the most basic support to its staff. Eventually ICE canned Janet Hale's "shared services" concept entirely, which was slowing down its space acquisitions by months, causing needless confusion and duplication of effort. The policy didn't cut any costs or save any time. It just made everything worse, wasting time and money instead of saving it. But it sure sounded good.

The agency that provides real estate services for all Federal departments is GSA—where I happened to work for nearly a decade. Janet Hale saw this on my resume in 2003, but I was not part of her entourage so my services were never called upon. The real estate and facility needs of the new "Department of Homeland Security" would be huge. Staff would be needed on its first day of operation with the skills to deal with these requirements, not the least of which was working with GSA to manage the space needed for its numerous sub-agencies and bureaus.

But Janet Hale was a budget person (i.e., a 'bean counter') not a real estate person, so how would she know this? I had years of Federal real estate experience, and was offering to help in this critical area. Setting up the new Department of Homeland Security would be one of the most demanding and complicated undertakings of the Federal government since the Second World War. The services and help I was offering to Janet Hale (and to my country and the Bush administration) were totally ignored and pushed out the door.

By 2008, ICE was just starting to form its own facilities branch from scratch, five years after DHS had been created. It is the second largest law enforcement agency in the federal government after the FBI, but because of Ms. Hale's "shared services" management style it was created without its own facilities staff. My company was brought in as the de facto facilities staff at ICE until it could get its own facilities program on its feet, costing millions of dollars in consulting fees, in addition to what was being paid to CBP for its services. Some savings.

If its facilities program wasn't bad enough, ICE's budget management system completely was broken. Different people, offices, budget codes and layers all worked against each other, and on top of each other, with the paperwork bouncing around like a pinball. Even in Janet Hale's field of expertise (budget) DHS was in terrible shape. It was like watching a scene from the Keystone Cops.

Most of the senior managers at the newly created Department of Homeland Security had never done the work they were hired to do. Many of the GS-15s and SESs never managed similar organizations, or did similar work, before they arrived. (GS-15 is the most senior level below SES, the Senior Executive Service.) This was especially true in the area of management and support, the areas that fell under Janet Hale for all of DHS. For example, the person responsible for the real estate program at ICE had no prior real estate experience. She had previously worked for the Inspector General, and had been an Internal Revenue agent before that. But she and the woman in charge of all management at ICE were buddies, so she got the job.

DHS desperately needed Federal executives with years of experience in their respective fields. Instead, ICE was staffed with inexperienced friends of people who were able to get into DHS on the ground floor. In the case of facilities, the person with this responsibility at ICE should have worked in Federal government real estate and facilities for 20 years or more. Actually, this person should have run the Facilities Division at another federal agency before they took over at ICE. Instead, facilities at ICE was being run by a person learning on-the-job who didn't have a clue what she was doing.

The turnover of senior managers at ICE was incredible. Because people were placed in positions who didn't have a clue what they were doing they ended up getting "fired," which in government-speak means they were moved into another job. It is just about impossible to get *fired* from the Federal government. You just get moved instead. In one department at ICE five different women were put in charge over a period of just 18 months!

The best example of the damaging effects of Janet Hale's management style was when Hurricane Katrina hit New Orleans on August 29, 2005. The city was essentially wiped out. Entire sections of it were uninhabitable, as well as the offices and other facilities of most Federal agencies, to include ICE. Because it had no facilities or real estate staff due to Ms. Hale's shared services concept, ICE had none of the personnel needed to set up temporary space for its employees in New Orleans in the aftermath of the disaster. It wasn't until two years later that ICE had work space in New Orleans so its staff could perform its mission. The assignment to acquire and set up space in New Orleans was given to an employee of my firm, a contractor. He was sent there because ICE had no one on its staff to do it. As one might expect, consistent with Janet Hale's shared services concept, CBP was frantically trying to find space for its own staff before it lifted a finger to find space for ICE.

Immigration & Customs Enforcement was left with no facilities after Hurricane Katrina swept through the Gulf Coast, no one to secure the facilities and property that had been devastated, and no one to find new facilities for its staff to function. Janet Hale's "shared services" management style was a joke when things were normal. It was a disaster when things weren't. If the Department of Homeland Security is supposed to be there in any emergency and under all conditions, it needs facilities and staff to do this, especially when disaster strikes. That's its mission. How can it help the American people when an emergency wipes its facilities out along with everyone else's?

While Janet Hale was riding around in a limousine and attending meetings as the Under-Secretary for Management at DHS, its bureaus and sub-agencies were being staffed-up with rank amateurs and friends of friends who didn't have a clue what they were doing. It was all based on the "who-you-know" system of Federal employees looking for a promotion, and political appointees on a power trip.

Ms. Hale left DHS to work for Deloitte, one of the largest consulting firms in the country, no doubt getting highly compensated for her management expertise—and her government contacts. Like General Williams, Janet Hale is a "graduate" of Harvard. She has a Master in Public Administration from the John F. Kennedy School of Government there.

Present at many of these meetings over the new DHS headquarters were senior staff from the General Services Administration. GSA's Chief of Staff was a fellow named David Safavian. He would walk in and start running the show, while the rest of us watched in awe. Safavian was a Washington, DC 'wunderkind,' having come up the ranks of the conservative lobbying world on K Street. At one time he had worked for Jack Abramoff, who would later be indicted and sent to prison for bribery. It so happened that during the Abramoff investigation, none other than David Safavian had sold his position as the GSA

Chief of Staff to help his old buddy Abramoff in his attempt to get some sweetheart deals on Government-owned land in DC. Safavian had e-mails of the deals on his Government computer, and was indicted too. He went to Federal prison for perjury and using his GSA position for financial gain, but his conviction was later overturned.

In the end Tom Ridge decided not to do anything regarding the location of the new department and it is still located at the NAC, but not for long. DHS started to move its headquarters from the NAC to southeast Washington, DC to the area known as Anacostia, by far the most dangerous area in the Nation's Capital. It's a combat zone where most of the murders take place. It was decided that DHS would take over a large part of the federally-owned hospital for the severely mentally ill called St. Elizabeth's. This is where John Hinckley, the man who tried to assassinate President Ronald Reagan, has been confined all these years. And why did DHS decide to go to St. Elizabeth's? Simple, to make use of all the federally owned land there that no one else wants. It makes sense financially, but who in God's name would want to work in Anacostia? They will have a tough time getting Federal employees to take jobs there. Maybe they should offer combat and hazardous duty pay. So far the only building constructed for DHS on the St. Elizabeth's campus is the new headquarters for the U.S. Coast Guard.

> …with the exception of a Coast Guard building that opened last year, the grounds remain entirely undeveloped, with the occasional deer grazing amid the vacant Gothic Revival-style structures. The budget has ballooned [from $3 billion] to $4.5 billion, with completion pushed back to 2026. Even now, as Obama administration officials make the best of their limited funding, they have started design work for a second building that congressional aides and others familiar with the project say may never open.

> …some officials have long been skeptical of the [DHS] headquarters project — over whether it is necessary and whether enough funding will ever be

obtained, according to people familiar with the undertaking.

"It's just not going to happen," said a......... congressional aide. "The money doesn't exist."[25]

I've been to the St. Elizabeth's campus many times, and have toured the new Coast Guard Headquarters building, which is 1.2 million square feet and cost $3.4 billion—for one building! The exterior is all glass, and the grounds contain storm water ponds that are supposed to add to the environment. Instead, they are huge pools of muddy water. The building has won numerous architectural awards, which is all GSA cares about. But what about the blast effects from shattered glass?

The Coast Guard Building has won the following awards:

- The Design Build Institute of America: 2013 Design-Build Honor Award
- Associated Builders and Contractors, Inc.: 2013 Excellence in Construction Nominee-Mega Project
- NAIOP-Commercial Real Estate Development Association (Maryland/DC Chapter): 2013 Excellence Awards-Best Institutional Facility
- Washington Building Congress-Craftsmanship Awards: 2013 & 2014-Exterior Stone, Landscaping, Green Roof, Curtain Walls, Architectural Millwork

While on a tour of the Coast Guard building we were shown the "cafeteria." There was nothing to it. The entire room was about 2,000 square feet, for a staff of 3,700 people! GSA has requirements that dictate the size of a concession facility for federal buildings based on its size and the number of people who work there. This doesn't come close. We didn't even have to ask why the cafeteria was so small, before the fellow giving us the tour volunteered. It turns out none other than Eleanor Holmes-

---

[25] Jerry Markon, "Planned Homeland Security headquarters, long delayed and over budget, now in doubt," *The Washington Post*, May 20, 2014.

Norton demanded the cafeteria be small in order to force the occupants of the building—the Coast Guard employees—to walk or drive off the campus in order to find a place to eat. This was Ms. Norton's way of increasing business for the eating establishments in the neighborhood. The "neighborhood" (or should we call it "the hood") is in southeast DC, the area with the highest crime rate in the city, and one of the highest in the country. Ms. Norton doesn't appear to care about following federal construction guidelines, or paying her taxes. She only cares about bringing business to her constituents so she'll get re-elected. That's fine, but not when it's being done with federally-funded construction.

In 2003, while the new department was being planned inside the walls of OHS, Congress was busy debating over it and using its creation for its own political gains. Having an ego of my own, I already had plans of where my corner office would be in the new department's classy new building. But Congress, being what it is, blew everything out of that corner window. One day it was discovered the draft legislation creating the new department had a little clause in it concerning the status of its Federal employees. The legislation stipulated they would not be afforded the same 'protections' as the rest of the Federal government, whereby they could be terminated based on the most ridiculous of reasons— their performance.

Some of the agencies being merged into the new department were under collective bargaining, meaning management couldn't do a thing without the various Federal employee unions agreeing. If the unions didn't like it, then it couldn't be done. The new cabinet department being created to defend our homeland wanted to eliminate this so management would have the flexibility to reassign staff, terminate employees for poor performance, and so on. When this was discovered the AFL-CIO, and every other major labor union went nuts, but the one that really blew its stack was the Federal Employees Union. They went all out, going to every Democrat in the Senate, and stopped the creation of this new cabinet department, dedicated to protecting our country and its citizens, dead in its tracks. The debate in Congress over the protections to be afforded Federal employees in the new department lasted nearly six months, delaying the creation of the new agency by the same amount of time. To the Democrats in Congress, not upsetting the unions was far more important than protecting our country from terrorist attack. Those same Democrats later shoved Barack Hussein Obama's health care bill down our throats so fast most of them hadn't even read the bill. But defending our country at its most vulnerable could wait six months. That was less important to them than taking care of their precious unions so they could get re-elected.

The Department of Homeland Security was created with modified personnel rules but the Federal Employees Union, and its friends, refused to give up the fight. In 2006 a liberal Federal judge ruled that union rules and collective bargaining that existed in the agencies before they were merged into the new Department had to stay in place. The Bush administration caved. Now, the shop stewards run the show again. If the unions can destroy American industry, like they have in Detroit, why not let them take a crack at the Department of Homeland Security too?

Being on loan from the State Department to the Office of Homeland Security, my one year "detail" ran out so I had to go back to the State Department. General Williams, being the guy he was, gave my job to someone else. His personal secretary informed me he was telling people he had advised me not leave OBO to work for Tom Ridge. This was completely untrue. Because I was leaving what he called his "team," General Williams felt the need to make false statements about me, and refused to allow me back to OBO. Being a political appointee, which meant I was employed at the "will of the President," in this case at the will of General Williams, I found myself on the street. Thus ended my career as a political appointee in the administration of George W. Bush.

I left the administration after working there for two years, both at the State Department and the Office of Homeland Security in the White House. By the time I left, the new Department of Homeland Security was just getting started, but it has taken years to get on its feet. To the Department's credit, and that of President Bush, our nation has not had another attack on its soil. This alone speaks volumes for the new Department, and for the administration. They have done a commendable job in this area. Regardless, however, the Department of Homeland Security is way too large and involved in too many areas it has no business in. But once an agency is created, it can't be dismantled. DHS is here to stay.

Of course, liberal federal judges won't allow DHS to protect us as well as it could. A perfect example was the decision by U.S. Judge Charles Breyer (the brother of the Supreme Court Justice) of the Northern California District, who ruled against DHS in its effort to send out letters to business owners notifying them of the *possibility* they might be employing illegal aliens. The intent of the DHS letter was to notify employers of the requirement to ensure their employees were in the country legally. It was a way for employers to assist DHS in doing its job. What could possibly have been wrong with doing this, especially when it would have required at least ten suspected illegals at the place of employment for the letter to be sent? What are the odds an employer would have that many workers who were illegal aliens and not know about it? It appeared Judge Breyer let his personal prejudices cloud his legal judgment. Striking down the letter would allow more illegals to work in this country, clearing the way to their becoming "legal" by way of amnesty, and voting Democrat the rest of their lives. The legal interpretation of the law was the last of his concerns.

One of the most vocal opponents of the letter was Hector Figueroa, secretary-treasurer of Local 32BJ of the Service Employees International Union, who called Judge Breyer's ruling "a victory that will halt unnecessary discrimination against workers and turmoil in our economy." He went on to say, "The court recognized that implementing 'enforcement only' policies based on a backlogged and inaccurate database will not fix our broken immigration system. The notion of making immigrant workers miserable—by targeting and scaring them through no-match letters, raids and other punitive measures—is not only inhumane, it's irrational."[26]

Needless to say, the SEIU didn't want the letters sent. That would have meant the U.S. was on to employers who weren't doing what they were supposed to do—not employ illegal aliens.

---

[26] Jerry Seper, "Judge blocks crackdown on hiring of illegals," *Washington Times*, October 11, 2007.

If the letters were sent and employers complied, the illegals would be detained and sent back home. They were here illegally, weren't they? Isn't that the law? Isn't Judge Breyer supposed to enforce the law? But the SEIU won and the Department of Homeland Security lost.

The Department of Homeland Security's woes never seem to end. Thirteen years, almost to the date after the Twin Tower attacks, *The Washington Post* ran a front page story describing the "exodus" of top-level officials from the Department of Homeland Security. Current and former officials say this is undercutting the agency's ability to stay ahead of emerging threats, to include potential terrorist strikes and cyber-attacks. Employees describe a dysfunctional work environment, abysmal morale, and the lure of private security companies paying top dollar that have proliferated in Washington since the Sept. 11, 2001, attacks.[27]

The atmosphere at the DHS was so low that in 2014 it retained a private consulting firm, Deloitte, to develop recommendations to improve morale. Deloitte is where Janet Hale went to work after she left DHS. It's interesting she works for the firm that consults to the same Federal agency where she had been the first Undersecretary for Management—responsible for, among other things, personnel. Ms. Hale was in that job for five years, so she had plenty of time to get things such as personnel and staffing off the ground.

According to the *Post*, Deloitte's contract is to "improve morale" at DHS. I can say from personal experience that one reason morale stinks at DHS is because of the senior people who were first put in charge of running it. If an organization starts off on the wrong foot, especially the senior people it brings on, it is going to stay that way for a long time. The government's solution is to always hire consultants to fix what is screwed up. Sometimes the consultants are the same people who were in charge of the screwed up organization before they left the government.

After just a few years of existence senior-level vacancy rates at DHS are high and many top officials are leaving for jobs with

---

[27] Jerry Markon, Ellen Nakashima and Allen Crites, "Turnover at the top has DHS unsettled," *The Washington Post*, September 22, 2014, p. A1.

private security companies, to include The Chertoff Group. Led by former DHS Secretary Michael Chertoff, the firm employs so many former officials it is known in homeland security circles as a "shadow DHS." Employee frustrations reflect the fundamental organization of the department, and the inherent difficulties of merging 22 government agencies.[28]

The personnel problems at DHS aren't going to get fixed anytime soon. This is because DHS is dysfunctional by design, and its senior managers are incompetent.

> Today, employees describe a stifling bureaucracy made up of agencies with clashing employee cultures and overtaxed by high-pressure responsibilities and relentless congressional carping. It can take many months to hire someone and weeks to get supplies as basic as a whiteboard.[29]

There was no reason to merge 22 agencies into one department. For example, Immigration & Customs Enforcement (ICE) was created using the former Immigration & Naturalization Service (INS) and the investigations division from the former Bureau of Customs. The two major components of ICE are Enforcement& Removal Operations (which is the former INS), and Homeland Security Investigations (which is the former Customs component). These two branches of ICE don't get along, and never will, because they came from two different organizations and cultures. They should have stayed where they were. The only thing accomplished by the creation of DHS has been more government dysfunction.

> "If you look at the last six, seven years, there's been enormous turnover," said Michael Brown, a former Navy rear admiral and high-level DHS cyber security official who retired in 2012. "Absolutely, it's a problem for consistency and continuity."

---

[28] Ibid.

[29] Ibid.

Those who have left also say they grew weary of fighting to get the simplest things done.

"My cyber folks were spending more time on human resource issues and acquisition than they were analyzing technical data to defend and protect networks," a former senior official said.[30]

The last sentence highlights the same employee issue the law creating the department tried to solve—being able to get rid of poor performers. As described previously, the Federal Employee Unions fought tooth and nail to get this provision removed from the statute, and succeeded when the Bush administration caved. A dozen years later this same issue, combined with systemically abysmal senior management, has made DHS a department whose dysfunction threatens the security of the entire country.

DHS is a component of the Executive Branch, therefore it reports to President Obama. If the Department of Homeland Security is a ship without a rudder, this is in large part due to Obama's failure to pay any attention to it. From what is happening at the U.S.-Mexican border, with floods of illegal aliens from Latin American (and other countries) entering the country, one could be forgiven for thinking he doesn't want DHS to do what it was created to do—defend our homeland, starting at our borders. If Obama wanted DHS to function as it is supposed to by law, he'd figure out a way. The fact that he isn't doing anything to get DHS functioning as it should, when he could easily do so, gives the distinct impression he doesn't care to. Actions speak louder than words.

---

[30] Ibid.

PART II: OPERATION IRAQI FREEDOM

4—A Slam Dunk

By the time President Bush started talking his nonsense about granting amnesty to illegal aliens, just months after 9/11, another pot was brewing—Afghanistan. After 9/11 President Bush declared to the nation and the world he would pursue Osama bin Laden wherever he was, and it turned out he was in Afghanistan, hiding in the mountains of Tora Bora near the border with Pakistan. The assault on Al-Qaeda in Afghanistan has been debated at length but the prevailing wisdom is that it was necessary, that bin Laden was there, and that he needed to be pursued and destroyed. But it is this last point that has proven elusive, and has created as many questions as it has answered.

General Tommy Franks was at the time the CENTCOM Commander. The United States armed forces are located around the world. The globe is divided into regions for purposes of designating who is the military commander in the event of hostilities. Therefore, anything that involves U.S. forces in the Middle East falls under the CENTCOM Commander, whose offices are actually located at MacDill Air Force Base in Tampa, Florida. When Bush declared he was sending forces into Afghanistan, which lies within the geographic region of CENTCOM, it meant the operation fell under the command of Tommy Franks.

Franks is an affable fellow. Adopted by two loving parents of simple means, he lived a hardscrabble life in Midland, Texas, driving pickups and chasing girls, like any normal good ol' boy. He went to the University of Texas at Austin (UT), flunked out and enlisted in the Army. This was at the height of Vietnam. He was a good enough soldier to be asked to go to Officer Candidate School, meaning that he could add 2+2 and polish his belt buckle, and off he went to Vietnam as a Field Artillery Second Lieutenant and forward observer. In his book *American Soldier*, Franks describes the highlight of his service in Vietnam as his ability to handle multiple radios at one time to call in artillery fire on enemy positions while flying passenger in an observation helicopter. He took great pride in devising a method by which he rigged the headphones and the radios in the aircraft to be able to do this, almost as if he wanted to patent the improvisation. That was the highlight of his Vietnam experience. He served proudly, came home, got married, and began a rise to the highest levels of Army service. He never mentioned in his memoir if he ever graduated from college.

There is no way to make four-star general in the United States Army without 'being connected.' Tommy Franks had friends in all the right places. He and Laura Bush went to the same high school in Midland, Texas. But for Franks to have gotten where he did, being a university dropout, is truly amazing. Franks surely must have been an adequate officer, but he must have also mastered a particular skill absolutely essential to advancement in the Army. He must have been a true "yes man." The fact is, military officers will not do or say anything as they advance up the ladder that they think might piss someone off, thereby jeopardizing their career.

Tommy Franks was groomed to be the successor to then-CENTCOM Commander Tony Zinni, a Marine Corps four-star general who had spent years in the Middle East and knew the people and their culture. Franks had been Zinni's deputy commander, groomed to be his successor by simply showing up for work with the right boot on the right foot. When Zinni retired, Franks took over and turned out to be at the right place at the right time. It's a funny twist of fate that in both the Gulf War of 1991 and this recent conflict, the previous CENTCOM Commanders had been Marines, but then left the job to their Army replacements, who then got all the glory for leading the subsequent attacks. The Marines must have gone nuts over this. The CENTCOM Commander before Schwarzkopf was Marine General George Crist, who resigned because he got upset when he didn't get promoted to Commandant of the Marine Corps after the CENTCOM job. I guess retiring as a mere four-star general just wasn't good enough for him. He had to retire as Commandant of the Marine Corps or his career was a flop.

The planning for operations in Afghanistan began in earnest soon after 9/11, with Tommy Franks at the forefront. He describes in detail in *American Soldier* how he did this. But the main point was that everything he did was done at the request of, and to the specifications of, Donald Rumsfeld. The entire operation was Rumsfeld's, from soup to nuts. It was Rumsfeld who pulled all the strings and demanded that the war be conducted the way he wanted. Franks was more than a willing water boy, carrying whatever Rumsfeld wanted, and dumping it all on his poor staff officers in Tampa. My heart goes out to those poor souls on the CENTCOM staff right after 9/11. If they still have their sanity it's nothing short of a miracle.

The planning for operations in Afghanistan was thorough. The numbers and types of our forces seemed to match the terrain and the size needed to destroy the enemy's. And most important, the original successes we achieved were substantial. But two things went wrong. The first was not capturing Osama bin Laden, and the second has been our inability to maintain the successes we initially achieved in Afghanistan, at great loss of life.

During December of 2001, U.S. intelligence identified Osama bin Laden's location in the mountain range called Tore Bora, in the east of Afghanistan along the Pakistan border. Not only did the mountainous terrain provide ideal protection for bin Laden, but the location was very close to Pakistan, offering a quick escape route from approaching forces from the west. Tommy Franks knew where bin Laden was, but instead of sending in U.S. forces to capture or kill him, he went the 'politically correct' route and sent in Afghani warlords to make it look like the locals were pulling their weight, when in reality they were worthless and just wanted American money for their own gain. Their only allegiance was to the U.S. dollar bill. The attack was a flop, and bin Laden escaped. That was the closest we came to capturing or killing him for another 10 years.

When I heard what had happened I was as shocked as I was the night Bush the First announced the cessation of hostilities at the 'end' of the Gulf War a dozen years before. How could Franks let bin Laden go? Could Franks be that inept? I heard a first-hand account from a West Point classmate who was at the command center in Afghanistan when the radio traffic came in the night bin Laden's location was pinpointed. U.S. Army officers in the field were requesting everything higher headquarters could give them to throw at bin Laden, yet their requests went unanswered. The radio had not gone dead. Higher headquarters, CENTCOM Command, refused to answer their requests for support. Why? Did the administration want bin Laden to get away? No one knows. But he did, and the war went on, and the military-industrial complex (i.e., defense contractors) kept grinding away. I am not a conspiracy theorist, but one has to wonder how this could have happened.

While Afghanistan was in full swing, the plans for invading Iraq were being worked on as well. (The evening of September 11, 2001, Donald Rumsfeld was quoted saying, "You know, we've got to do Iraq—there just aren't enough targets in Afghanistan.")[31] Again, Franks was actively involved in this, soon to become the commander of two major military operations at the same time. This is a commanding general's dream. During all of this Franks would fly back and forth from the States to the Middle Eastern theater of operations on his jet with his close personal staff—and his wife! Did Franks think he was a movie star? A commanding general in wartime simply does not travel around with his wife on his official aircraft, but that's exactly what Tommy Franks did. Not only was his wife everywhere he went, but she sat in the middle of classified briefings given to her husband when she had no authorization to be present. No one said a thing, certainly not to the general's face. Eventually, one of his staff officers had the courage to file a complaint with the Army Inspector General. Of course, Franks was completely exonerated. He was, after all, the commander general.

The higher one goes, especially if they are politically connected, the more they can ignore the law and get away with it. Sandy Berger, Bill Clinton's former National Security Advisor, stole a classified document from the National Archives while he was Clinton's representative to the National Commission investigating the September 11, 2001 terrorist attacks. The stolen document, written by former National Security Council terrorism expert Richard A. Clarke, was an "after-action review" prepared in 2000 detailing the Clinton administration's actions to thwart terrorist attacks during the "millennium" celebration.

The Clark report discussed the Clinton administration's knowledge of the rising threat of attacks on U.S. soil. The question of what Clinton knew, and what he did about the

---

[31] Cullen Murphy and Todd S. Purdum, "Farewell to All That: An Oral History of the Bush White House," *Vanity Fair*, February 2009.

emerging threat from al Qaeda before leaving office in January 2001, was of major concern. This concern was highlighted by Berger spending hours poring over the Clarke report before his testimony in front of the Commission. Berger stuffed five copies of the document in his socks and down his underwear, underneath a construction trailer outside the building during a 'break,' made numerous trips to the bathroom, and demanded to be left alone by the guards, who were not allowed to leave, while he 'reviewed' the different copies of the document in the reading room.[32]

The obvious question was whether Clinton ordered Berger to steal the document to preserve his (Clinton's) legacy. Why else would Berger stoop so low and behave like such a fool? But what would Clinton care if one of his minions took the fall for him? In the end nothing happened to Berger other than a misdemeanor and a fine. Yet he stole, and later shredded with a pair of scissors, a classified document out of the National Archives, while at the same time holding a Top Secret security clearance. If Clinton did nothing wrong, what was he afraid of?

John Deutch, Clinton's former Director of Central Intelligence, was caught with classified information on his unclassified computer at home. The computer had been issued by the CIA, but wasn't supposed to be used for any classified work. This was bad enough, but he had connected the computer to the Internet at his house, and used it to watch porn! The computer had been loaded with classified information he had taken from work, improperly stored while at his home, downloaded onto his unclassified home computer, and then connected to the Internet and the world. The information that was found on his unclassified home computer included "…magnetic media related to covert action, Top Secret communications intelligence and the National Reconnaissance Program budget."[33]

What happened to John Deutch? Clinton's new Director of Central Intelligence, George Tenet, did nothing. The CIA's

---

[32] John F. Harris and Allan Lengel, "Berger Will Plead Guilty To Taking Classified Paper," *The Washington Post*, April 1, 2005, p. A01.

[33] L. Britt Snider, "Improper Handling of Classified Information by John M. Deutch," *CIA Inspector General Report of Investigation*, February 18, 2000.

General Counsel declined to refer the matter to the Justice Department. And then, when the CIA Inspector General finally opened a formal investigation and referred the matter to the Justice Department, Janet Reno refused to prosecute. It was confirmed by the CIA Inspector General that Deutch knew he was committing a violation, and that senior CIA officials raised "anomalies" in the way they answered questions about their investigation of the incident. In short, it was a huge cover-up by the Clinton administration of a senior Clinton administration official who knowingly broke the law—at the time he was breaking it. Deutch got away with pleading to a misdemeanor and paying a $5,000 fine. On his last day in office Bill Clinton pardoned him. Senator Richard Shelby, Republican from Alabama and the Chairman of the Senate Intelligence Committee said, "Deutch essentially walked away from what is one of the most egregious cases of mishandling classified information that I have ever seen short of espionage."[34]

As the planning for the invasion of Iraq progressed, it became clear to all involved that Donald Rumsfeld wanted it to be as lean and mean as humanly possible—I call it "Invasion Lite." He initially wanted around 35,000 soldiers to invade Iraq! That was soon discarded for a higher number, but not nearly enough. When I was at West Point I took a course during my last year called "History of the Military Art." It was mandatory for all cadets to take during their First Class (senior) year. It was a fascinating course, starting with the Trojan and Greek wars, went through the Roman conquests, Napoleon, the American Civil War, and the major world wars. We studied strategy (the big picture) and tactics (the little picture). One of the founding principles of warfare is this: when on the offensive (i.e., attacking) never attack with less than a 3/1 advantage in soldiers and overall force.

From the results of our invasion it appears this principle never came up. It can only be assumed that Tommy Franks had West Point graduates on his staff, but these would be officers of full colonel rank and higher who would never have the courage to tell Tommy he was out of his mind. If they did he would start

---

[34] "Senate Looks into Former CIA Head's Pardon," *Dallas Morning News*, February 16, 2001, p. 6A.

one of his Texas cussing sessions, after which they would have had their heads handed to them. (Franks had one of the foulest mouths in the United States Army, a trait he was quite proud of. This is proof again that he must have been connected, otherwise his mouth would have gotten him booted out of the Army decades earlier.) But it wasn't up to the officers on Tommy Frank's staff to be aware of this military doctrine, it was up to Franks himself. Any officer who had risen to the rank of four-star general and didn't know of this military principle, going back to the beginning of modern warfare, was not deserving to wear the uniform of the United States Army. Franks must have thought that all of the sudden warfare had changed and Infantry soldiers on the ground were obsolete and no longer required—that we could win based on our superior technology alone. Warfare hasn't changed at all. We just have more technology available to support the foot soldier who is the one who fights the fight on the ground, where it matters.

Why this 3/1 ratio when on the offensive, when attacking? The force being attacked is stationary, and if led by competent commanders it is dug-in and doesn't have to move long distances like the attacking force does. It has "central position," whereas the attacking force has to come from multiple directions, with different forces attacking from different places. It is in fortified positions in the ground in the form of fox holes, or well placed inside fortifications using earth, wood, steel and concrete to improve its positions. In the case of Iraq, the enemy was "dug in" by being hidden in buildings in every town, and with large man-made sand and dirt earthworks to hide and protect their tanks and other crew-served weapons. Multiply this on a scale covering the entire country and you have hundreds of thousands of troops, with their tanks and other crew-served weapons, hidden in every conceivable place, hidden from plain view, and protected by earth, steel and concrete. The Iraqi army under Saddam Hussein was estimated to be as large as a million men, yet Rumsfeld was initially planning to attack this force with about 35,000 soldiers. At the very most 20,000 of this attacking force would have been actual combat Infantry and Marines, but it was probably closer to 10,000. Granted, the Iraqi army had its ass handed to it by the U.S. Army during the Gulf War, but that was because we went into that conflict after a 37-day aerial bombardment that was equal to some of the bombings during World War II, and then we attacked with 500,000 soldiers supported by the Army's new M1A1/2 tank. The Iraqis didn't have a chance. This time things would be different.

Rumsfeld continued to plan for "Invasion Lite," and Franks continued to suck up and do whatever "Rummy" wanted. The facts spoke undeniably against going into Iraq with anything less than half a million men, but who cares about facts? Besides, it had been so easy in 1991, why would it be any different now? Who would expect the Iraqis to adapt to the beating they had received then and come up with new tactics now? But even George W. Bush expressed his doubts. At one point during the planning for the invasion he asked Tommy Franks: "Is this good enough to win?"[35]

According to Bob Woodward in his book *Plan of Attack*, when asked by the President for his assessment of the situation in Iraq, George Tenet said it was "a slam dunk" that Saddam possessed Weapons of Mass Destruction (WMD).[36] This gave the President additional justification to invade. Not only should Tenet have been fired by noon on September 11, 2001, he was still around and able to give these nifty little intelligence assessments to his boss. But he was telling Bush what he knew Bush wanted to hear. They were acting like they were under some kind of trance. By the time the planning for Iraq had reached this point reality was out the window, and Bush was out to lunch. Rumsfeld was running the show. And Tommy Franks did whatever he could to please his boss, all at the risk soldiers' lives and the assurance of victory on the battlefield. Sounds like Powell and Schwarzkopf the night Desert Storm ended—"déjà vu all over again."

Senator Bob Graham, Chairman of the Senate Intelligence Committee, went to visit Franks at his Central Command headquarters on February 19, 2002:

---

[35] Bob Woodward, *Plan of Attack*, (New York: Simon & Schuster, 2004), p. 22.

[36] William Hamilton, "Bush Began to Plan War Three Months After 9/11," (excerpts from Bob Woodward's book, *Plan of Attack*), *The Washington Post*, p. A1, April 17, 2004.

> He [Franks] told me that we were no longer fighting a
> war in Afghanistan and…some of the key personnel,
> particularly some special-operations units and some
> equipment, specifically the Predator unmanned drone,
> were being withdrawn in order to get ready for a war
> in Iraq. That was my first indication that war in Iraq
> was as serious a possibility as it was, and that it was in
> competition with Afghanistan for materiel. We didn't
> have the resources to do both successfully and
> simultaneously.[37]

An Army general told a United States Senator that "we were no longer fighting a war in Afghanistan." The senator was hearing this for the first time, and was Chairman of the intelligence committee.

Richard Clarke, the same guy whose report Sandy Berger stuffed down his underpants, had this to say about invading Iraq based on a link between Saddam Hussein and al Qaeda: "Having been attacked by al Qaeda, for us now to go bombing Iraq in response would be like our invading Mexico after the Japanese attacked us at Pearl Harbor."[38] After hearing Rumsfeld, Wolfowitz and Bush discussing the link between Saddam and al Qaeda after 9/11, and their plans to attack Iraq as a result, Richard Clark said it was: "a little disgusting that they were talking about it while the bodies were still burning in the Pentagon and at the World Trade Center."[39]

For his part the President allowed all of this to go on without the slightest show of stopping it or caring where it went—like Lyndon Johnson during Vietnam, who had no ability to control the disaster McNamara had created. Harry Truman had a sign on his desk in the Oval Office that read, "THE BUCK STOPS HERE." It is the President who is ultimately responsible for all that goes on in the government and what the government does. He has been elected to run it. He is the Commander-in-Chief.

---

[37] Cullen Murphy and Todd Purdum, op. cit.

[38] Richard A. Clarke, *Against All Enemies,* (New York: Free Press, 2004), pp. 231–232.

[39] Cullen Murphy and Todd Purdum, op. cit.

Rumsfeld would not have been allowed to do anything if Bush hadn't approved it, or had told him to come up with a better plan. As they say, "You don't know what you don't know." This applies to Bush. He didn't know a good plan from a bad one, but Franks should have because he was the career soldier in the bunch. The fact is this: Bush knew nothing about waging war, being a de facto draft dodger himself, nor did one of the chief architects of the war, Vice President Dick Cheney. Both had avoided the Vietnam War, Bush by joining the Texas Air National Guard, and Cheney by getting at least five draft deferments and ultimately hiding behind his wife's maternity dress. Yet both of these men had absolutely no problem waging a war that was fraught with failure—from the lack of troops, to the lack of intelligence about the enemy we were going to fight.

With the intelligence capability our country has, it is inexcusable that we did not know more about the enemy we were going to attack. However, with Clinton's watering down of our intelligence capabilities, specifically our human intelligence (our spies working with 'bad people'), this failure isn't surprising. George Tenet, Director of the CIA, must have known these intelligence gaps existed. He had been around the CIA as a Senate staffer, and then as Director, for years. How then could he tell the President that the case for WMD was "a slam dunk?" The only conclusion is that George Tenet didn't have a clue if Saddam possessed WMD or not.

Either Tenet thought he had enough intelligence, but didn't, or he was pulling that assessment out of thin air. Personally I think the latter. He didn't have a clue what we were going up against or getting ourselves into, but wanted to say what he thought his boss wanted to hear. Just like Tommy Franks telling Rumsfeld what he thought Rummy wanted to hear. And these were "the best and the brightest" people we had at the absolute highest levels of our government and military. It's scary to think about. They all fell to the belief that the war would be a cakewalk like the Gulf War, which started with a 37-day aerial bombardment preceding a ground attack by 500,000 troops. Rummy thought the results would be the same with an aerial bombardment the opening night of the invasion and an attack by around 125,000 total troop strength (US and Coalition), which the number eventually rose to. In reality no one had done any homework on the enemy, its capabilities, or even what the enemy looked like.

One of the most revealing and prescient statements about our invasion of Iraq, and the possible links that Saddam Hussein may have had to 9/11, was made by Vincent Cannistraro, a former CIA counterterrorism expert:

> ...we are in grave danger of overreaching. Having failed to uncover any solid evidence linking Iraq to the attacks of Sept. 11 or to the succeeding anthrax threats, the anti-Iraq war party...is resurrecting the argument that Saddam Hussein's presumed accumulation of weapons of mass destruction poses an imminent threat. It is a dubious proposition, supported by little validated intelligence. Indeed, Iraq may be one of the least appropriate targets for the antiterrorism campaign ...we will diminish our ability to deter new rounds of violence against America— and we may create new threats rather than containing immediate ones.[40]

Mr. Cannistraro made his comment on December 3, 2001.

---

[40] Vincent M. Cannistraro, "Keep the Focus on Al Qaeda," *The New York Times*, December 3, 2001.

5—Operation Iraqi Freedom

To get public support and buy-in for the war, the President told the country that Saddam Hussein possessed weapons of mass destruction, the "WMD" that has become a part of our vernacular. The President had established the doctrine of "preemptive attack," attacking the foe before the foe had the opportunity to attack us. This is what we were told. Yet, after the war began the President said the case for invading Iraq, based on the premise that Saddam possessed weapons of mass destruction, was all a big mistake. But he would have invaded anyway! He even had the nerve to joke about not finding any WMD in Iraq, showing a video of him looking for WMD under his desk and behind the curtains in the Oval Office at a White House Correspondents Dinner. Ha, ha, ha, a real knee slapper. Like the day his father stopped the Gulf War those years before, I couldn't believe it.

I know what I heard before we invaded Iraq: It was the President of the United States telling me, and the world, that Saddam Hussein possessed weapons of mass destruction and that he was just about to start using them, with the implication he would start using them against us. "We know he [Saddam Hussein] is developing weapons of mass destruction..."[41] We were even told he had small planes that were equipped with spray nozzles under their wings that might be used to emit poison gas and nerve agents over our cities. Was Saddam going to fly them across the ocean and then start spraying gas over our heads? How was he going to get them that far, ship them Federal Express so they would be here in time for his "attack!" I never felt the case for invading Iraq was solid or had been proven, yet I supported my President because I had worked on his campaign, and because he was a nice guy. He wouldn't lie to me would he? Nice born-again guys who go to church don't lie—do they?

President Bush told us we were going into Iraq to eliminate Saddam's weapons of mass destruction and to overthrow his regime. We were told the United Nations sanctions and the

---

[41] "Bush on State of War" (text), *The Washington Post*, October 11, 2001.

inspections of potential WMD sites after the Gulf War had been complete failures. The President told us that Saddam Hussein had left him no choice but to invade. Many of us believed him, and the President got the required number of votes from the Senate to attack. Many of those votes were cast by liberal Democrats wanting to be seen by the American people as being tough on national defense. John Edwards at least had the courage to say he made a mistake voting for the war, but of course by doing that he also implied that he was disingenuous and voted for the war when he really didn't want to. He had the choice and he took it, and for that he will be remembered and judged. If he had any integrity he would have voted his conscience (which is why people elected him), and voted against the war. But he wanted to be looked upon as a hawk to get votes for his next run at the White House. Since then he has been exposed for his affair and his love child, a big fall for a former U.S. Senator. The little head was doing the thinking for the big head once again. Clinton could pull that off, but he already had the job. And why all the fuss, anyway? It's only sex. Who cares if Edwards' wife is fighting cancer while he's nailing a young blonde?

As the invasion plans were getting more defined, the sanctions were mentioned by Donald Rumsfeld, but in an off-hand manner. He didn't care about them any more than George H.W. Bush did, or his son George W. Bush, for that matter. As far as Donald Rumsfeld was concerned: "Sanctions are fine, but what we really want to think about is going after Saddam …. Imagine what the region would look like without Saddam and with a regime that's aligned with U.S. interests. It would change everything in the region and beyond it. It would demonstrate what U.S. policy is all about."[42] This followed the sentiment made by Madeleine Albright in 1998: "But if we have to use force, it is because we are America; we are the indispensable nation. We stand tall and we see further than other countries into the future, and we see the danger here to all of us."[43] A little arrogant, perhaps?

---

[42] Ron Suskind, *The Price of Loyalty,* (New York: Simon & Schuster, 2004), p. 72.

[43] *Today Show: Interview with Madeleine Albright,* NBC, February 19, 1998.

Could there have been another reason for invading Iraq the American people were kept unaware of? Douglas Feith was the Under Secretary of Defense for Policy under Donald Rumsfeld and Paul Wolfowitz, and a leading proponent of the invasion. Richard Perle was another Rumsfeld advisor. Both were members of an American study group on Israeli strategy, which issued a statement in July 1996:

> Israel can shape its strategic environment....This effort can focus on removing Saddam Hussein from power in Iraq—an important Israeli strategic objective in its own right....As a senior Iraqi opposition leader said recently: 'Israel must rejuvenate and revitalize its moral and intellectual leadership. It is an important—if not the most important—element in the history of the Middle East'.[44]

This sentiment was echoed by The Jewish Institute for International Affairs, which stated on September 13, 2001:

> A long investigation to prove Osama Bin Laden's guilt with prosecutorial certainty is entirely unnecessary. He is guilty in word and deed. His history is the source of his culpability. The same holds true for Saddam Hussein.[45]

On September 10, 2002, by Philip Zelikow, a member of the Presidential Foreign Intelligence Advisory Board, stated:

> Why would Iraq attack America or use nuclear weapons against us? I'll tell you what the real threat is and actually has been since 1990. It's the threat against Israel....The American government doesn't want to lean too hard on it rhetorically, because it is not a

---

[44] "A Clean Break: A New Strategy for Securing the Realm," Institute for Advanced Strategic and Political Studies: Study Group on a New Israeli Strategy toward 2000, July 1996.

[45] "This Goes beyond Bin Laden," Jewish Institute for National Security Affairs (press release), September 13, 2001.

popular sell....The Iraq problem is a peculiar combination at the moment, of being exceptionally dangerous at a time when Iraq is exceptionally weak militarily. Now that's an appealing combination for immediate action.[46]

There was a pattern of thought in influential Washington circles that Saddam Hussein had to go, and the security of Israel was the major driver. But the supply of oil was the elephant in the living room. Dick Cheney said as far back as 1998: "You've got to go where the oil is." As the CEO of Halliburton, he would know. It appears Rumsfeld was firmly sold on this line of thought based on his statement of July 27, 2001: "If Saddam's regime were ousted, we would have a much-improved position in the region and elsewhere...A major success with Iraq would enhance U.S. credibility and influence throughout the region."[47]

The biggest boost for the war's go-ahead came when Colin Powell was ordered by Bush to go to the United Nations to show that esteemed body of diplomats that Saddam had weapons of mass destruction—and was about to push the button. For several days before he went to the UN, Powell poured over documents at the CIA and asked hundreds of pointed questions of the staff. We are told by his adoring media that he did this to get all the facts. I tend to think it was for another reason—to make sure he was not going to put his foot in his mouth at the UN. The media plays this out like Powell was performing his due diligence and pouring over everything in order to be prepared to do a good job. Since then Powell's testimony has been proven to be completely bogus, and he has been relegated to the dustbin of credibility.

When Powell presented his so-called evidence before the UN Security Council, it was pretty clear he was grabbing any straw he could to make a case to invade Iraq. He no doubt suspected we didn't have a case to make. He knew Bush wanted to go to war and he was serving Bush's cause, even though he likely didn't

---

[46] Emad Mekay, "Iraq Was Invaded 'to Protect Israel'—US Official," *Asia Times Online*, March 31, 2004, and "Letters," *London Review of Books*, May 25, 2006

[47] "Iraq," U.S. Department of Defense Memo from Donald Rumsfeld to Condoleezza Rice, July 27, 2001.

believe in the cause himself. But if Colin Powell is so brilliant, why did he have so many doubts about our reasons for going to war up until the day before he flew to New York? This was evident by the unusual amount of time he spent at the CIA asking all his questions and going over all the documents they had. It is clear now that the President and Powell were pulling the case for war with Iraq out of thin air.

I recall Powell's testimony that day at the UN. He played the translation of a recorded cell phone conversation between two Iraqi army officers that had been intercepted by the National Security Agency (NSA). This is the agency located at Fort Meade, Maryland that has the electronic capability to tap anyone's phone and look at objects the size of a postage stamp from miles in space. We were told this information was so secret that Powell had to insist on the phone call being "declassified" so he could share it with the world! The call didn't prove squat. The conversation didn't say anything. It was a couple of Iraqi clowns jabbering over the phone about a "weapon."

As he held up a little vial of powder, he told the Security Council: "less than a teaspoon full of dry anthrax in an envelope shut down the United States Senate in the fall of 2001." Yes, the U.S. Senate was shut down because anthrax had been discovered in an envelope mailed to a senator. But other than the powder being fake, it didn't prove that Saddam had WMD. This was fear-mongering by Powell to implicate Saddam by vague reference, nothing more.

Regardless of the holes in Powell's testimony and logic, the UN approved a resolution authorizing the U.S. to invade Iraq. The reason the UN did so was not because of any proof it had received by Colin Powell of Saddam's possession of WMD, but because they heard words coming out of Colin Powell's mouth asking them for something. If he said the sky was falling everyone in the Security Council would have run out of the building. No matter what Colin Powell said everyone believed it to be the Gospel, the word of the Messiah himself (that would come later with the election of Barack Hussein Obama). So much power was placed in the hands of this one man, way too much power. No one ever questioned anything Powell said. If Powell said it, then it must be true. It had to be true! Like the

Gulf War twelve years before, Colin Powell sold our country down the river—again.

With UN authorization (i.e., permission) the plans for the invasion of Iraq continued. George Tenet said the case for WMD was "a slam dunk," and we know now how worthless his assessments were. Colin Powell had succeeded in blowing smoke in the UN's face, and Tommy Franks continued with his plan for "Invasion Lite," based on what Donald Rumsfeld told him to do. (On December 4, 2001, Rumsfeld responded to questions about troop levels for the invasion of Iraq: "I'm not sure that much force is needed [500,000 troops] given what we've learned coming out of Afghanistan.")[48] Not allowing for anywhere near a ratio of 3/1 in the invasion plans, the number of forces was slowly increased to around 125,000 U.S. Army soldiers, Marines and Coalition forces. The plan called for the land transit across Turkey of the 4th Infantry Division, commanded by a Raymond Odierno.

Ray Odierno graduated from West Point in 1976, a year ahead of me. A glance at his uniform shows he doesn't have Airborne (parachute) wings or a Ranger tab. In the 1970's, when we attended West Point, probably 95% of all cadets went to Airborne School at Ft. Benning, Georgia. If they didn't go as cadets, they went right after graduation. If you were an Infantry officer (which I was), you went to Ranger School too. These courses weren't mandatory, but not to attend was taken as a sign of weakness. Ray Odierno was a Field Artillery officer, but in those days most of them went to Ranger School, and all of them went to Airborne School unless they were physically unable to. Did Ray Odierno have chronic injuries as a cadet or as a new Second Lieutenant that prevented him from at least attending jump school, or was he just lazy? When I look at his uniform as the Chief of Staff of the United States Army, and consider the time period when he graduated from West Point, I find it very odd that Ray Odierno doesn't at least have jump wings from the Airborne School at Ft. Benning, Georgia. This may not seem like a big deal to the average person, but to guys like me it's a very big deal. It's an indicator of how serious a cadet or junior officer was

---

[48] Bob Woodward, *Plan of Attack*, p. 41.

about serving in the U.S. Army. Did Ray Odierno care about the absence of these military decorations on his uniform, badges that signify the successful completion of two very difficult courses of Army training? Or maybe he knew he wouldn't need them. Maybe he had connections that would take him to the top anyway. We know David Petraeus didn't need a thing on his uniform to make it to four-star general because he married the daughter of the Superintendent at West Point. Ray Odierno has a lot of ribbons, but the vast majority of them are "service" ribbons handed out for being at certain places at certain times. One or two of them might be for heroism or valor, the rest are eye candy.

Because Turkey screwed its "ally" the U.S., and would not allow transit across its territory, the 4th Division sat in boats in the Mediterranean for weeks while the initial invasion of Iraq, and the real fight, went on without it. Odierno must have been climbing the walls in his transport ship. Later, when his division finally got involved the initial fighting was already over, so he may have felt the need to catch up. There is speculation that many Iraqis were needlessly killed because Ray Odierno and his division had been left out of the initial stages of the fight. He probably felt he had to mix things up when he got there so he could say he hadn't missed all the action.[49]

When the invasion and the initial ground fighting began it consisted primarily of two main attacks, one Army and one Marine, coming northwest from Kuwait. The ground commander of all U.S. forces who reported to Franks was U.S. Army Lieutenant General (three-star) David McKiernan. Because the Marines can't stand being under the command of an Army general, they sent Lieutenant General (three-star) James Conway over. He was there so the Marines would have a general in Iraq of equal rank to the Army general in charge, so they wouldn't have to take direct orders from him. Whenever McKiernan wanted to say anything to the general in command of the Marines on the ground, Major General (two-star) James Mattis, he had to go through LTG Conway, thereby creating another layer of military bureaucracy in the middle of a war. But the Marines didn't care.

---

[49] Thomas E. Ricks, *Fiasco* (Penguin Group, 2006), pp. 232–233.

Their Marine ego is far more important than any military efficiency that might result by cooperating with the other services in the midst of a war fight.

Conway eventually became the Commandant of the Marine Corps, having done such a great job as a messenger between McKiernan and Mattis. This arrangement flew in the face of another military doctrine of warfare, "unity of command." The Marines didn't want to report to an Army general, so they slid in a three-star of their own. That meant Mattis had two people to report to, Conway and McKiernan. Reportedly, McKiernan was very upset about this, but Franks didn't have the courage to correct it and kick Conway out the door, which is exactly what he should have done. In the military, politics is as important as it is in Washington.

Of note is the fact that LTG Conway was later responsible for the creation of the Fallujah Brigade in April 2004. This neat little operation, where the Marines would pull out of the area so the place would quiet down on its own, turned out to be a complete disaster. Instead of everything quieting down after the Marines left Fallujah, the insurgents jumped on the golden opportunity Conway gave them. He wanted to negotiate with the enemy instead of kill him. The insurgents took advantage of Conway's "kumbaya" crap to kill more of his Marines. That's what happens when generals lose their focus: their soldiers get killed and the enemy gets away. More often than not the general gets a promotion because he's got such a keen grasp of "the complexities of the situation," and he's "thinking outside the box." From the opening days of the Iraq conflict, once a senior military officer was selected for advancement it didn't matter how bad he screwed up, he was on his way up. General Conway was no exception.

(On October 17, 2014, General Conway's successor, General James Amos, retired as the 35th Commandant of the Marine Corps. Shortly before he retired news sources reported he lied on his resume when he claimed to have graduated from The Basic School for new Marine Corps officers. His resume was included in his biographical information submitted to Congress for his nomination hearings to become the Marine Corps Commandant, which would constitute perjury.[50] News stories also reported how he tried to exert command influence in the court martial of Marines charged with urinating on dead Taliban bodies in Afghanistan, a direct violation of the Uniform Code of Military Justice.[51])

On the very first day of the invasion the first casualty was an Army soldier killed in a drive-by shooting from a mini pickup truck. He wasn't killed in a conventional fight against regular Iraqi army soldiers. He was killed by a guy dressed in civilian clothes driving by in a pickup truck. This would be the case throughout the ground battle leading up the road to Baghdad: no conventional Iraqi forces or soldiers in uniforms like the Gulf War, no Iraqi tanks like the Gulf War, no conventional lines of defense by the Iraqi army like the Gulf War. Yet our commanders, most of all Rumsfeld and Franks, never got the hint that this was their new enemy. They never figured out that we were up against guerrillas in a street-by-street, building-by-building fight, who wore civilian clothes and road in civilian cars. Instead, the entire campaign all the way to Baghdad was fought by the U.S. with M1A1/2 tanks blowing up anything firing at them with a bullet or an RPG (rocket-propelled grenade), and continuing the move forward without killing the bulk of the enemy's ground forces—the insurgents.

The United States M1A1/2 tank is the most powerful tank ever made. Nothing can stop it except another tank, which the Iraqis didn't have, or an anti-tank rocket fired from the shoulder of a man hidden behind an obstacle, which they did. If you have enough M1A1/2 tanks, you are likely going to get where you want to go. There is only one problem with a concept of warfare that relies completely on tanks, as this concept did. With enough M1A1/2 tanks you will reach your objective, but you won't kill individual enemy soldiers you pass along the way if you don't have Infantry forces moving in coordination with your tanks. The enemy will still be there after the tanks roll through. In Operation

[50] "Semper Lie: Marine Corps Commandant James Amos padded resume," Rowan Scarborough, *The Washington Times*, October 14, 2014.

[51] "Retiring Marine Corps commandant accused of padding resume," Barnini Chakraborty, *Fox News.com*, October 15, 2014.

Iraqi Freedom, the assault of M1A1/2 tanks moving up the road from Kuwait to Baghdad was like a car driving through a puddle of water. The car will drive through the puddle, but the water will go right back into the puddle where it was before. Because we didn't kill the insurgents as we advanced north to Baghdad, they were still there as we continued up the road toward the next town. All they did was pick up their weapons and ammunition and follow our tanks. The U.S. was in such a hurry to get to Baghdad that all mopping up (killing the enemy in house-to-house fighting by Infantry soldiers) was avoided because Rumsfeld and the President wanted to declare "Mission Accomplished" as fast as possible. Tommy Franks just went along for the ride.

The cause of the problem was that we invaded with too few Infantry soldiers. The problem existed when we first invaded Iraq in the spring of 2003, and it remained for years afterward. The United States invaded Iraq in the spring of 2003 with a fraction of the number of ground combat soldiers needed to do the job right the first time, all because Donald Rumsfeld thought he was smarter than Sun Tzu, Clausewitz, and all the military scholars who have studied warfare throughout history. He thought the U.S. could defeat any enemy, of any number, anywhere, and at any time regardless of the number we brought to the fight. We can only do this with the right number of soldiers and equipment to do it with. Rumsfeld's plan for the invasion of Iraq was wrong, and we will be paying the price for his incompetence, and his arrogance, for years.

But Tommy Franks was equally to blame. He was the four-star general in command, a veteran of Vietnam who had attended all the U.S. Army's staff colleges where they do nothing but study the art of warfare, from the Greeks through Vietnam and Desert Storm. These courses look at planning attacks on a major scale, because the students are being groomed for the senior commands in the next war. What did Franks do when he attended the U.S. Army War College in Carlisle, Pennsylvania— party like he did at the University of Texas? What was Franks thinking, or was he thinking at all? Did he ever stand in front of Rumsfeld and say the plan was risky? Did he ever say the plan had holes in it? Did he ever say to the Secretary of Defense that his plan to invade a country with an army as large as a million men, albeit a crappy one, with 125,000 U.S. and Coalition forces was taking a chance? Did the attack include a 37-day bombardment like the Gulf War? And who was the enemy? Did the CIA have a real grasp of who we were going up against? It would seem the answer to all these questions would be no. And if Franks didn't ask any of these questions, did he even think of them? How could he not think of these things with his years of military experience, the training he had, with his rank and the high level of responsibility he had been entrusted with? Or, did Tommy Franks put himself ahead of his country and his soldiers because he was afraid of getting fired by Rumsfeld if he opened his mouth?

To invade a country without using all the forces at our disposal was a crime. We obviously didn't plan for the enemy we would be fighting against, or the fight itself. How could we have with the results we got?

We never went up against the Iraqi army. Instead, we were up against the insurgents from the first day of the war. Yet our leaders and military commanders never adapted to a situation they hadn't foreseen or planned for, and as a result they never changed their strategy. If they didn't plan for it, then it was treated as though it wasn't happening, as though it couldn't happen. Other than invading in the first place, this was the biggest mistake of the war. The entire administration from the President on down, including Rumsfeld, Powell, Tenet and Franks, thought it would be a pushover without taking the time to find out what they were getting our country into, or what would happen after we got there.

The United States failed for far too long to adapt to the changing situation on the ground once the fighting got underway. Getting the United States into the war on flimsy grounds was one thing, coming up with a flimsy invasion plan was another, but not adapting to the changing environment and the realities of the war on the battlefield was inexcusable.

As the advance progressed towards Baghdad, the soldiers and Marines were taking a real beating. The only reason we made it to Baghdad at all was because we had the M1A1/2 tank and the Iraqis didn't. But what about the unconventional plain clothed forces we were up against, the insurgents? Who were they and where did they come from? And where was the Iraqi army, the guys whose butts we handed them 12 years before? They were gone. It was just insurgents now, yet our tactics never changed. Like the car driving through a puddle of water, what good was it to blow through a small Iraqi town with tanks, fighting every inch of the way, only to leave the insurgents behind as we drove up the road toward Baghdad at 40 miles per hour? We didn't kill the enemy. We just pushed him out of the way and left him there to fight us another day in another Iraqi town closer up the road to Baghdad.

And where were the insurgents getting their weapons and ammunition? Saddam had been hiding tons of it in small towns all over Iraq just for this occasion, yet when we found these caches we left them in place instead of destroying them because we were afraid there might be WMD inside the stockpiles that would spread contamination if exploded. Without human intelligence from the CIA, there was no way for us to know the caches were there before we invaded. And if we didn't know the caches were there, we certainly didn't know if there were WMD buried underneath them. It was all a big surprise to everyone, probably George Tenet most of all. But if we were going after WMD, as the President and Colin Powell told us, why didn't we have the chemical and biological experts with the advancing troops to detect WMD if and when we came across these weapons caches? There is only one plausible explanation: the invasion was planned so fast and so poorly that the basics were never considered, such as specialized soldiers to send with the combat troops for these very occasions. The stockpiles of weapons and ammunition were left where we found them, for the insurgents to grab as they followed behind us up the road to Baghdad.

If the President's reason for invading Iraq was Saddam's WMD, why didn't we have WMD experts with the advancing troops to deal with these weapons stockpiles? The only possible answer is President Bush used the WMD threat as an excuse to attack Saddam Hussein. Once he got the votes needed from the Senate, and the approval (i.e., permission) from the UN, Bush didn't bother to staff our invading units with WMD experts because that wasn't the reason we were invading. The WMD claim was a ploy to get us into the war, just like the attack on Pearl Harbor was the excuse FDR needed to get the U.S. into World War II.

This proves the fallacy of the WMD reason to invade Iraq. We were told we were attacking Saddam because he possessed weapons of mass destruction, but we didn't have WMD experts with the advancing units to make the WMD determination if and when we thought we may have come upon some. Tons of weapons, ammunition and explosives were left where they had been found, with thousands of insurgents still alive because we didn't have enough Infantry with our tanks, whose job it would be to kill them.

The result was insurgents following our tank columns as they advanced toward Baghdad, with more insurgents waiting for them up the road, all armed with weapons and ammunition caches we had left behind because we were afraid to destroy them. As we got closer to Baghdad we were hit from the front, rear, and flanks by insurgents we had already passed by in towns as our tanks rolled through. We had no Infantry to mop-up, so they were shooting at us with the same ammunition our forces had left behind in those same towns, all because we didn't have WMD experts to make the decision to destroy it.

This was utter incompetence. As the title of Colonel H.R. McMaster's book so aptly puts it, this was gross "dereliction of duty." It placed the lives of our soldiers at tremendously greater risk than they should have been in. Our commanders, from the President on down, are to blame. This is not the way to fight a war. But this is the way Rumsfeld and Franks planned and fought it, and then bragged about it to a fawning media looking for a story.

As our tank columns approached Baghdad the fighting got incredibly intense. The insurgents put up a fierce battle on the outskirts of the city. One tank brigade commander, Colonel David Perkins, decided he would plow his way into the heart of the city, without approval from his higher command. On his own, Colonel Perkins sent his units forward on what would be known as the "Thunder Runs." The enemy casualties caused by these swift advances were immense. But so were ours. The American units achieved their objective, reaching the center of the city where Saddam's government buildings were located, and which would later be called the "Green Zone." These advances also reached Baghdad International Airport, where the headquarters of all Coalition forces in Iraq would be located. It was soon after these advances reached Baghdad the words "Mission Accomplished" appeared on the deck of the aircraft carrier USS *Abraham Lincoln* as the backdrop for Mr. Bush's famous speech.

But all that had really been achieved was the presence of U.S. forces on the ground in the center of Baghdad. That was it. We no more had command of the situation on the ground in Iraq than we had a prayer of finding any WMD. We were stuck there, holding onto a few city blocks in the middle of Baghdad with our fingertips, and calling it "Mission Accomplished."

From the day the first U.S. casualty was killed by a plain clothed civilian in the back of a pickup truck, until the day the President declared that our mission had been accomplished, we had not come across any regular Iraqi army units of any size. Yet our tactics never changed. We were using *half* the armored tactics the Germans had used during the Blitzkrieg in the opening days of the war in Western Europe. During the Blitzkrieg the Germans had Infantry to kill any dismounted (not in tanks) enemy they came across, and hold onto everything their advancing tanks captured and destroyed. When the tanks got too far ahead of the Infantry they were ordered to stop to let the Infantry catch up. They coordinated their forces, a concept beyond the comprehension of Rumsfeld and Franks. We were fighting with tanks, but without Infantry to kill the insurgents the tanks had missed, and to maintain control of the locations the tanks had reached. So tenuous was our "victory," it could have been achieved if we had simply conducted an airborne (parachute) assault on the same locations in the center of Baghdad. We would have had Infantry to maintain control of it, and the President could have declared "Mission Accomplished" just the same.

Armored soldiers don't do what Infantry soldiers do. They like to ride and shoot big projectiles and blow things up, and they do this very well. Infantry are the foot soldiers on the ground, who go house-to-house and door-to-door. That's the only way to fight a war and to win a war. Every other part of the military, including tanks, planes and boats, exists to support the Infantry. Without an Infantry soldier holding a piece of ground you haven't "accomplished" anything. Tanks only have a crew of four. They may arrive somewhere, and even blow the place up, but then what? They're not going to get out of the tank. But if they did they would be too few in number to accomplish anything other than getting themselves killed. Infantry units hold ground the tanks have helped them capture because they have the manpower. Then again, if you're executing "Invasion Lite," you don't go in with tens of thousands of Infantry soldiers. The Infantry is heavy with soldiers, and Rumsfeld didn't want that. He wanted the smallest number of soldiers in the invasion force for political reasons, so he could claim he was invading with just enough forces to do the job, not alarming the American people that we were getting involved in another Vietnam.

Today, Obama fights America's wars with drones, un-manned aircraft flown from the other side of the world. These are extremely effective weapons, but they aren't soldiers on the ground. With drones we don't have "skin in the game." A 'pilot' flying a drone from Arizona isn't the same as an Infantry soldier in Iraq or Afghanistan pointing his rifle at a man, pulling the trigger, and watching him fall to the ground. Drones are like speed cameras: they are accurate as hell, but not the same as a cop.

Rumsfeld invaded Iraq on the cheap, with tanks that could cause a lot of damage and make it to their objective, only to sit there getting shot at with rocket propelled grenades. He thought the tanks would destroy everything, even soldiers dug into holes in the ground and hiding behind every wall. That's because he didn't know how to wage war. Tommy Franks, who was supposed to, sat there and did nothing. Holding onto his four-star job and taking his wife for joy rides in his plane were more important to Tommy Franks than planning an attack that would work, and protecting his soldiers from unnecessary harm and high casualties.

Rumsfeld never bothered to find out what or who his enemy was. This is inexcusable in modern warfare, especially with our intelligence capability. But after Bill Clinton's decimation of our human intelligence capabilities we went into Iraq blind. If Rumsfeld and Franks knew who and what their enemy was, they wouldn't have planned this war as they did. They didn't know. They couldn't have known. Yet they went in anyway. As bad as that was, they failed to adapt to the realities of the situation on the ground once they must have realized they were up against an enemy they hadn't planned for, who used tactics and had stores of weapons and ammunition we left in place and didn't have the soldiers to fight against. But they still refused to change the way they fought the war regardless of the facts they were up against.

A tank can't kill a soldier in a hole. All it can do is fire a projectile over his head. A tank can't kill a man hiding behind a wall, unless it has infrared vision to 'see' him. Tanks can only destroy so much. They can't destroy what they can't see. Thousands of insurgents hiding in buildings in every small Iraqi town can't be seen as the tanks roll by. Rumsfeld just planned on there being no enemy left after the tanks rolled through towns on their way to Baghdad. He thought they would drop their weapons and run away at the first sight of our tanks. And Tommy Franks went right along, even though he had to know our tanks should be coordinated with large Infantry forces to clean up what insurgents were left. They were both wrong. It's OK to be wrong as long as you have the capacity to change your plan and adapt to the situation. But Rumsfeld's ego wouldn't allow him to do that, and Franks was afraid to say anything, assuming he had anything to say. What makes a real warrior is the ability to do this. Rumsfeld wasn't one. Franks was supposed to be, but wasn't one either.

This is the way Franks fought the war Rumsfeld told him to fight. Franks probably knew better, but allowed Rumsfeld to go on with his ridiculous plan when he should have refused to buy into it, cost what it may to his career. But that would have taken courage, the kind of courage General Eric Shinseki, the Army Chief of Staff had. General Shinseki was the only general officer who told Rumsfeld the war could be fought, and won, with half a million men. At one point in the planning for invasion Rumsfeld said, "Absurd. We don't need nearly that many. Not very many. Certainly no more than 125,000."[52] How on earth would Rumsfeld know what was needed? It was Shinseki's job to tell him. For doing just that, Rumsfeld fired him.

---

[52] Andrew Cockburn, *Rumsfeld: His Rise, Fall, and Catastrophic Legacy*, (New York: Scribner, 2007), p. 152.

Tommy Franks will be remembered as one of the worst field commanders in our country's history. He rose to the position of CENTCOM Commander, and then blew it. Franks got to the level he did because he was a "yes man." We have paid dearly for Franks' poor planning and execution of the battle, primarily because we didn't have enough Infantry soldiers in the attack. But the ones who have paid the most are the Iraqi people caught in the crossfire.

If we had gone to Iraq with overwhelming force, which to his credit Colin Powell had done during the Gulf War, the results of our invasion of 2003 would not have happened. I have West Point classmates who were involved in the planning of Desert Storm, the first Gulf War. The Iraqi army was so bad we had parity against them with a ratio of 1/3 *against* us. That was when Iraq had a real, conventional army numbering as much as a million men. We still bombed them for over a month before we invaded. Given these numbers, the worst planning for the 2003 invasion would have justified at least 300,000 soldiers. Rumsfeld initially wanted to invade with less than 35,000!

After the first Gulf War we had a force of 400,000-500,000 soldiers in Iraq but sent them home. Imagine what the results would have been having that many during, and after, our invasion in 2003? The belief that the more soldiers you send into a fight the more casualties you will have is not always true. In Iraq we had just enough troops on the ground to be easy targets, but not enough to mount an offensive campaign against the insurgency. If we had 500,000 troops in Iraq the insurgency wouldn't have gotten off the ground—there would be too many U.S. and Coalition forces there to start anything. Whatever the insurgency tried would have been put down immediately. This is not just theory. What has happened in Iraq for the past ten years? We invaded Iraq without enough forces, and would not adapt to the changing situation in the field as things started to deteriorate. As soon as the situation in Iraq started to fall apart, which the world saw happening on cable news, the President could have made a decision to pull out completely, or send in more forces to address the situation. Instead, George W. Bush did nothing.

War is a confusing business. The one thing that can be counted on is that it will not go as planned. Tommy Franks would have known this, yet he planned our invasion without enough forces in case things went wrong, which of course they did. Our soldiers became targets. By2005-2006 the insurgents were picking off our soldiers in droves. In effect, the U.S. was stuck in another "quagmire" just like Vietnam. But if we were staying, at least we could increase our troop strength. We didn't do anything until the "surge" of January 2007, almost three years later.

The chart below from iCasualties.org provides a yearly count of American deaths in Iraq since our invasion:

Iraq Coalition Military Fatalities By Year[53]

Year	US	UK	Other	Total
2003	486	53	41	580
2004	849	22	35	906
2005	846	23	28	897
2006	823	29	21	873
2007	904	47	10	961
2008	314	4	4	322
2009	149	1	0	150
2010	60	0	0	60
2011	54	0	0	54
2012	1	0	0	1
2014	3	0	0	3
Total	4489	179	239	4807

---

[53] Casualties.org, "Iraq Coalition Casualty Count."

The question remains: why did it take Bush so long to increase our force strength if we were still in Iraq, but not in sufficient numbers to fight back? It has never made sense that Bush (and Rumsfeld) made the decision to stay after we had captured Saddam, but didn't increase the number of troops after the situation got worse and our casualty list started to go up. If we were staying in Iraq to finish off the insurgents, we weren't doing a very good job. The more we pushed the insurgents with our minimal forces, the more of our soldiers they killed. From 2003-2006, the U.S. had just enough soldiers on the ground to be targets, but not enough to mass a strategic offensive and destroy the insurgency. This was all because of the abysmal planning of the war before the invasion, followed by the lousy handling of the war from its opening day—all of which was the work of Donald Rumsfeld, with the approval of George W. Bush.

By 2004 the civil war between the Sunni and Shi'a, and the terror being inflicted upon Iraqi society by the forces of Al-Qaeda in Iraq (AQI) and infiltrators from Iran, Syria and Saudi Arabia, was in full swing. Instead of local Saddam zealots killing our soldiers, we had forces that were better trained and equipped coming from other parts of the Arab world, using the Sunni and Shi'a factions within Iraq as surrogates.

We were now committed to a whole new war that we hadn't planned for, but we still didn't change our tactics in order to fight it successfully. The fact we had been fighting insurgents and not regular Iraqi army forces from the opening day of the war should have been a huge red flag that the plan of Tommy Franks and Donald Rumsfeld had to be re-worked. A year later we were up against the same insurgents, where all indications showed they were being equipped, supported and trained by the Shi'ite Iranians from the east, the Sunni of Syria and Saudi Arabia from the west, and Al-Qaeda forces from the Balkans and Central Asia from the north.

Yet our leaders still refused to send more troops to meet the demands of the situation. Instead, all we've heard since 2004 is "The Iraqis are doing better," "They're doing a good job," and "Our strategy is working." It was, and still is, pure nonsense.

We should have left Iraq after declaring that our objectives had been accomplished: we captured Saddam and, despite wanting to, found no WMD. Or, if we were staying, we should have poured in at least 200,000-300,000 more troops to adapt to the situation on the ground. Instead, Bush did neither.

Is this hindsight or Sunday morning quarterbacking? No, it is not. These events were occurring right before our eyes. The President and the Secretary of Defense had all the information they needed at the time to make the right decisions, and all the manpower and forces needed to implement them, yet they never did a thing to address the problems they faced. People at the highest levels of our government are supposed to have the capacity, cerebrally and otherwise, to do this. Instead, Bush and Rumsfeld waffled and procrastinated just like Johnson and McNamara did during the Vietnam War. Our national leadership should know better by now, but it doesn't. It probably never will.

The members of this cabal completely failed at their jobs. This assessment includes George W. Bush more than anyone else. It has to because they all worked for him. The irony is that his father, George H.W., pulled out in 1991 when he should have stayed, while George W. stayed when he should have pulled out!

The combination of the following factors created the situation in Iraq:

1. Not invading Iraq with enough ground forces to kill the enemy, and trying to finish the mission too fast. We went in with plenty of armored units, but not enough Infantry to mop-up (i.e., kill) every enemy soldier (insurgent) in every village and town the tanks were going through. In addition, Bush and Rumsfeld were in such a rush to declare victory the advancing units were practically sprinting to Baghdad, passing insurgents every step of the way.

2. Not adapting to the realities of the situation on the ground. We should have added more forces as soon as it became clear we were not up against conventional Iraqi army units—as it had been assumed we would be. Instead, our forces were up against thousands of plain clothed guerilla fighters who were hiding behind every tree, rock,

wall and doorway. This would have required 200,000-300,000 more troops than Rumsfeld had planned for. But if he didn't plan for them, it would appear they simply weren't needed. The war would be won with what Rummy had planned, and that was that.

But the generals had to know better. If they didn't they should have been fired. If they did know but didn't say anything they should have been fired, or simply quit. But "Invasion Lite" was all Rumsfeld wanted, so they would have been fired if they said anything that didn't follow that line, like Shinseki. Rumsfeld still wouldn't have changed his plan. At least these generals would be able to look themselves in the mirror. But getting that next star was more important.

3. Paul Bremer's decision to eliminate the Iraqi Armed Forces and the Iraqi National Police. Doing this, combined with not having enough Coalition forces on the ground already, was a recipe for disaster. This was the icing on the cake needed to create a completely unsecure and unstable Iraq, an Iraq wide open for any terrorist organization to walk right through the front door and do what they do best—murder people.

This combination of factors created the situation in Iraq after the initial invasion, but this beast has continued to be fed up to the present day. In later chapters I will describe some of the ways this has been done. Suffice it to say, the situation in Iraq couldn't have been planned or executed worse than it was. Inept leadership from the President on down through Rumsfeld, Franks, Tenet, Bremer, Wolfowitz, Cheney, Feith, and a host of military advisors led our country to this point half a world away. I didn't include "a host of civilian advisors" because I wouldn't expect them to know any better. But senior military advisors should. It was shameful of any general officer, specifically Tommy Franks who fought in Vietnam, to allow our civilian leadership to enter upon this disastrous course without trying to stop it, or drastically alter the plan. Didn't he learn anything from that experience? How can a country invade another if it does not go all out with overwhelming force to achieve its objective and, yes, occupy it if that is what is needed to protect and secure the population? What was Franks doing in Vietnam, or was he too young and naive to understand what was happening? One thing that's obvious from our invasion—the lives of the Iraqi people are not important to our national leadership.

The only senior ranking officer who said the correct thing was the Army Chief of Staff, General Eric Shinseki, who told Rumsfeld it would take several hundred thousand soldiers to invade Iraq successfully. He knew this because he studied military history at West Point, and remembered what he had learned in Vietnam. He knew it takes a 3/1 ratio to attack an entrenched enemy. He knew you always attack with more forces than you think are needed in case the unexpected comes up—which is to be expected in warfare. If you have more forces than what is actually needed, send them home. He knew our intelligence gathering capability stank, and that whatever intelligence estimates we were getting couldn't be relied upon. After eight years of the dismemberment of our human intelligence resources by Bill Clinton, executed by George Tenet, and the continuation of that policy by Tenet as Bush's CIA Director, our intelligence on Iraq was worthless. Look at what Powell went through trying to get straight answers from the CIA the night before he went to the UN. On the other hand, General Shinseki was trained to expect the unexpected.

Tommy Franks' book *American Soldier* was written at the same time he was leading us into the quagmire in Iraq, and he retired to publish it and cash in. *American Soldier* was co-authored with Malcolm McConnell, which means it was written by Malcolm McConnell. Nearly every page of the book has direct quotes by dozens of individuals, going back decades, without notes at the back of the book attributing the sources. Unless Franks had a stenographer or a recording devise with him his entire adult life, how can he pull that off—unless he just pulled the quotes out of his ass like he did the plan for the invasion of Iraq? Without notes at the end of it, Tommy Franks' book is more a fiction novel than a factual historical account.

By the time Franks' book had been out six months the situation in Iraq was heading down the toilet. Who's the one who didn't know what he was talking about, Franks or Shinseki? General Shinseki knew what would be needed, and he advised Donald Rumsfeld accordingly, which was his job (i.e., to advise the Secretary Defense and the President). For his advice Rumsfeld fired him, and didn't even have the professional courtesy to attend his retirement ceremony. But I don't blame Rumsfeld for this. I blame the Commander-in-Chief. If George Bush had a grain of decency and respect, he would have ordered Rumsfeld to knock off his childish crap and attend Shinseki's retirement ceremony. Instead, we just got another example of the hands-off leadership of George W. Bush. Whatever Rumsfeld did the President didn't stop him. Their relationship turned out to be exactly like the one between Johnson and McNamara. Rumsfeld even looks like McNamara.

The one thing the Bush administration did right (partially right, that is) was the "surge" of 2007. The surge contributed an additional 25,000 troops to the fight. The reason the surge was successful was the same reason the initial phases of Operation Iraqi Freedom were a dismal failure—the surge consisted of INFANTRY SOLDIERS! U.S. Army soldiers will destroy any foe in their path, if there are enough of them to do the job. There is no enemy force on earth that can stand up to the right number of American soldiers who are given a clear objective and a mission to accomplish. But the surge was too little, too late. It only had enough strength to contain a relatively small geographic area. When the surge went into Baghdad it was immediately successful because it was doing what the initial invasion forces should have been doing as the armored columns drove up the road to Baghdad. The surge was a mission that called for its soldiers to go house-to-house and door-to-door and kill insurgents. We should have been doing this all along instead of going on meaningless "presence patrols" to show the people we were still around in cities and towns, but not concentrated enough or massive enough to constitute a meaningful fighting force, resulting in our soldiers getting constantly picked off. The surge clearly showed we had finally started to learn from these lessons and it successfully cleaned up parts of Baghdad. But the enemy simply moved northeast to Baquba and outlying areas, and continued to do the same thing there it had been doing in Sadr City for nearly four years by that time. The surge was a good move, but all it did was move the fight somewhere else that had been relatively peaceful.

By being successful but too little, too late, the surge showed there had to be much greater numbers than a mere 25,000 more soldiers. With only 25,000 troops we could clean up a small area and then move on. Once we left that area, the insurgents moved right back in. Or, we could have cleaned up an area and stayed there. That area would have been the safest place in Iraq, but the size of a postage stamp in the middle of a country that was falling apart. The only way to really clean up Iraq was to "surge" the entire country, which would have taken at least 250,000 soldiers, 150,000 of which would be Infantry. The surge was a good operation, but it couldn't sustain the successes it achieved because it was too small to secure more than a part of Baghdad at one time. It was great for that part of Baghdad, but what about everywhere else it had no presence? What about when the surge forces left?

After the Second World War the United States, along with its other major allies, occupied Germany for decades. After the war there were thousands of pro-Hitler sympathizers who wanted to continue the fight in his memory. In addition, there was the very real fear of the Soviet Union invading Western Europe and overwhelming the entire continent, as Hitler had attempted to do just a few years before. The United States had to remain in Germany for years to prevent all these events from occurring. As the years went by the pro-Hitler sympathizers dwindled, and about 40 years later the Berlin Wall came down. It took a while, but our occupation of West Germany was successful.

After our invasion of Iraq 50 years later, we faced an almost identical situation, but our leadership never bothered to look back at our experience—and success—in post-war Germany. Like Germany, there exist thousands of pro-Saddam sympathizers in Iraq who believe he had the right idea about the Kurds and the Shi'ites. And like Germany, Iraq stands to be overrun by its neighbor to the east, Iran, and now by its neighbor to the west, Syria. Yet, because our leadership was weak, we waffled. Instead of formally occupying Iraq, which we should have done in order to maintain peace, we refused because of the political implications. Our troops suffered because we didn't have the draft to replace them. An occupation would have required thousands of soldiers to serve in Iraq, but would have resulted in fewer casualties because of their overwhelming numbers. Bush wouldn't do this because of the political uproar that would follow. But he received the votes he needed from the U.S. Senate to invade Iraq, so what was he afraid of? By 2004-2005 he was afraid to increase our forces in Iraq. He had the votes and had the chance to do it right in 2003, but Rumsfeld wanted "Invasion Lite," so the opportunity was lost.

We saw this in Afghanistan. It was a great operation in 2002-2003, but as soon as we drew down our forces the Taliban and Al-Qaeda came right back. Military success only works if maintained. That's why nothing happened in Western Europe after the Second World War. We stayed there at high troop levels for the purpose of keeping the peace in Germany, and prevented the Soviet Union from invading. Does anyone think for a moment it would not have invaded if the U.S. and its allies didn't have a million men in Germany for 40 years? There isn't that much difference between Germany after World War II and Iraq after we invaded in the spring of 2003. The size and scale are different, but not the strategy. Without a large force in Iraq we couldn't maintain what security we had achieved (like we did in Germany), nor could we prevent an attack from the outside (like we did from the USSR) if one of Iraq's neighbors chose to do something by seizing the opportunity.

The low levels of our forces also created a terrible strain on our soldiers. All of the fighting in Iraq was done by an incredibly small a number of soldiers and Marines because we didn't have enough replacements to give them the needed rest. We kept sending our soldiers back to Iraq tour after tour, but never brought in enough new recruits because we didn't have a draft. Why would someone volunteer for combat if they don't have to? It takes a very brave young man or woman to do this, even with the money that's thrown at them. They may be brave, but we simply didn't have enough of them. The few volunteers we had did all the work, with the help of the Reserves and the National Guard, but all of them combined aren't enough. The actual fighting was done by combat soldiers, which is a small fraction of the total strength of our armed forces. The surge was successful where it operated because it was a concentration of combat soldiers in one area. But we never had enough soldiers to do throughout Iraq what the surge did in parts of Baghdad.

Has the fighting ended in Iraq, or was the invasion the first of several phases? Was there complete and unconditional surrender like we used to demand of our enemies after we defeated them, leaving no room for doubt about who was victor and who wasn't? Were our soldiers ever greeted as conquering heroes everywhere they went, with Iraqi children waving little American flags that we were actually going to give to them when we invaded? The answer to all of these questions is a clear and resounding "no." We were not welcome in Iraq, and never were. The only thing about our invasion the Iraqis liked was taking out Saddam Hussein. Our soldiers were in firefights every day for years after the invasion. There is no end in sight, and never has been for the past 11 years through the end of the Bush administration and into the first 6 years of Obama's. The streets of Baghdad aren't any safer today than they were the day "Mission Accomplished" was shown behind President Bush on the deck of the *USS Abraham Lincoln*. As a matter of fact, in 2014 they are worse because the insurgency has had a decade to form and plan it strategy. The United States is no closer to victory now than the day our invasion began, when a soldier was killed by a man in plain clothes firing from a pickup truck.

The initial phase of Operation Iraq Freedom ended in this manner. We had reached the center of Baghdad and had been severely banged up on the way there. In the months and years that have followed, the U.S. and the Iraqi government of Nouri al-Maliki have battled against an insurgency that is fierce, has plenty of firepower, is made up of men willing to die for their cause and blend into the population. They *are* the population! This is what waited for us the day the "Mission Accomplished" appeared on the deck of that aircraft carrier. We were sold down the river by George W. Bush, and I helped him get elected.

6—Paul Bremer

The first senior American official to oversee the reconstruction of Iraq was retired U.S. Army Lieutenant General Jay Garner. He had been recruited for the job by Douglas Feith, Under Secretary of Defense for Policy, and one of the principle architects of the war. Just as the initial invasion was coming to a close LTG Garner was sacked by Rumsfeld, who replaced him with Paul Bremer, a former State Department Foreign Service Officer.

Jay Garner told PBS's *Frontline* during an August 11, 2006 interview:

> The phone rings, and I pick it up, and it's Secretary Rumsfeld. He says: "Hey, I'm calling just to tell you what a great job you're doing. It looks like things are really moving. Watched everything going on, and just keep up the good work and all that. And by the way, I wanted to let you know that today the president chose Jerry Bremer to be his presidential envoy, and he'll be coming over there." And he said, "I don't know when the president's going to announce that, but it could be today, or it could be tomorrow. It can be next week."…
>
> Sun Tzu says you don't want to go to bed at night with more enemies than you woke up with that morning. [After disbanding the army] we went to bed with a whole lot more enemies that night than we had begun the day with.[54]

Paul Bremer has had a very interesting career. In 1983, he was appointed by Ronald Reagan as Ambassador to the Netherlands, even though he didn't know how to speak Dutch. In 1986 he was appointed Ambassador-at-Large for Counterterrorism and Coordinator for Counterterrorism, the same job my West Point classmate Mike Sheehan held several years later. Bremer retired from the Foreign Service in 1989 and went to work for Kissinger

---

[54] "Interview with Lt. Gen. Jay Garner (Ret.)," *PBS Frontline*, August 11, 2006.

and Associates, a worldwide consulting firm founded by Henry Kissinger. Then Bremer became Chairman and CEO of Marsh Crisis Consulting, a risk and insurance firm, and subsidiary of Marsh & McLennan Companies, whose offices were in the North Tower of the World Trade Center. After the September 11 attacks, Bremer claimed his office was above where the second aircraft hit.

Paul Bremer was truly at "ground zero" as far as the events of September 11, 2001 were concerned. His office was in the North Tower, but he was fortunate not to be there when the plane hit. He was well-versed in counterterrorism, so one would assume he knew everything there was to know about Osama bin Laden and al Qaeda long before the events of 9/11. He was also very high up in the global financial world, working for Marsh & McLennan Companies up to the day of the 9/11 attacks. Marsh & McLennan was the world's largest insurance broker at the time. Bremer knew all the key players at the top of our nation's political and economic universe. Therefore, it is very interesting he was given the job of running Iraq after our invasion of March 2003.

Jay Garner was a professional soldier. His experience would have been an asset in keeping peace in Iraq while the country turned itself around. With his diplomatic experience, especially in his work in counterterrorism, Paul Bremer should have had a good idea how to maintain order in Iraq as well. Things didn't work out that way, however. Instead of getting the job in Iraq because he was the best fit for it, he got it because he knew all the right people. This change of personnel from Garner to Bremer shows how totally unaware the people in Washington were of the situation in Iraq, and would haunt our national leadership as the years went by.

The inability to face reality on the part of senior U.S. officials, especially to admit they made gross mistakes and errors in judgment with their invasion of Iraq, led to a quagmire there just like Vietnam in the late 1960's and early 1970's, and for the same reasons. As bad as Iraq was getting by 2004, if Bush and his administration had taken a realistic approach, the situation might not have gotten as bad as it soon did. However, to acknowledge their mistakes would have implied Bush had screwed up with by invading, so this was off the table. Maintaining 'face' was far more important than saving the Iraqi people from genocide. By 2004-2005, George W. Bush and his team were stuck, and couldn't get out.

Charged with all aspects of reconstruction and governance Paul Bremer proceeded to reinvent Iraq, in effect creating a new Iraq complete with a constitution, a rule of law, civil works, and something resembling a democracy. Bremer was placed in charge of the Coalition Provisional Authority, the CPA, to accomplish all this. Many of the steps Bremer took were well intentioned, did a lot of good, and helped a lot of Iraqi people. But everything he did went down the drain when he made two decisions. These decisions have led directly to the deaths of tens of thousands of Iraqis:

1. In the effort to cleanse Iraqi society of any vestiges of Saddam's regime, Bremer dissolved Saddam's personal political party, the Ba'ath Party. Anyone of consequence in Saddam's regime, and in Iraqi society, was a member of the Ba'ath Party, similar to being a member of the Communist Party in the former Soviet Union. A "Who's Who" of Iraqi society, one had to belong to the party to get ahead. To rid the country of this cancer, Bremer "de-Ba'athified" it. When he did so, he purged everyone in the country down to its lowest civilian ranks. This resulted in the firing of everyone who had any knowledge of the basic functions of government, e.g., the mid-level bureaucrats who ran the governmental institutions throughout the country, to include the provinces and towns.

2. But the other decision Bremer made was far more critical, making the one described above appear inconsequential by comparison. Without public notification, and in the face of overwhelming opposition from anyone aware of his plan, he dissolved the Iraqi Ministry of Defense and Ministry of Interior, the parent organizations of the Iraqi Army and the Iraqi National Police.

With the stroke of a pen Paul Bremer eliminated the two ministries responsible for the security of the country and the Iraqi people. These decisions would result in the deaths of as many as half a million people. Getting rid of Saddam Hussein after our invasion we chopped off the head of the beast. Doing this we created a tenuous situation in a country that has a history of being run by a "tribal" leader. By disbanding the entire Iraqi Armed Forces and National Police, Bremer chopped off both its arms and legs. What was left was a country with no head to lead it, and no arms and legs to get anything done. In time Iraq became the perfect breeding ground for the rise of one of the most violent and fanatical terrorist organizations in mankind's long and violent history—the Islamic State. Without enough American forces to protect and secure the country because of Rumsfeld's inept plan to invade with minimal force, and no Iraqi army or national police thanks to Paul Bremer, the country was wide open for the violence and civil war that was to follow.

With his years of experience in diplomatic affairs and counterterrorism, how could Paul Bremer not know Iraq was in a very bad state of affairs? He had to see there were scant U.S. forces to protect Iraq, and that we had destroyed Iraq's critical infrastructure. He must have been aware of the insurgents and the violence they had been causing since the first day of the war. As a career diplomat and supposed expert in counterterrorism, he had to know of the civil unrest between the Sunni and Shi'ite factions of Islam during the 25 years of Saddam's rule. Or did Paul Bremer spend his years as a career diplomat just attending cocktail parties?

This is tough language, but these two decisions of Paul Bremer's were insane. It would have been enough if Paul Bremer fired all the senior ranking generals and members of the Ba'ath Party, but to fire every member of the Iraqi armed forces and every member of the national police made absolutely no sense in light of the extreme circumstances facing the country. In addition, Bremer fired nearly every government official. Who would patrol the streets, man the border crossing stations, and defend the country from outside attack from Iran or Syria? The Iraqi government couldn't do it because they no longer had a Ministry of Defense or Interior. Paul Bremer disbanded them.

The U.S. Army couldn't do it because it was only part of the total Coalition force of 125,000 soldiers, two-thirds of them support troops who don't fight. That left roughly 30,000-40,000 U.S. combat troops to do what had previously been done by about one million Iraqi soldiers and around the same number of Iraqi national policemen. Even if you cut those numbers in half to account for their non-fighting elements, that's around half a million each. Paul Bremer shifted the odds against the Iraqi people and the Coalition forces, and turned them in favor of the insurgency, all with his signature. For this George W. Bush awarded him the Medal of Freedom.

With his elimination of Iraq's internal and external security forces, Paul Bremer eliminated the external and internal security of the country. In addition, he fired all of the government employees who knew how to operate the dams, the electrical power systems, the water purification plants, the sewer systems, the streets and highways, the stop lights, and the schools. But worse, Paul Bremer provided the insurgents with fresh recruits— the newly fired soldiers and policemen he had just sacked, all with their own weapons and ammunition, who now had a reason to hate the United States and our presence in their country.

For a period of time after the initial fighting stopped Iraq was calm. I knew people who said they went to dinner at restaurants in downtown Baghdad after the invasion. But when Paul Bremer made the decision to disband the Iraqi army and national police, he made sure things wouldn't remain this way for long. All calm went out the window. By 2004 the violence began to escalate as a direct result of his decisions. Insurgents were going after Iraqi civilians and Coalition forces like ducks in a pond. American casualties were mounting every day, and the word "Vietnam" was being heard on the streets of every city and town in America. But why were we still there? Saddam had been yanked out of a hole near his home town of Tikrit, and we couldn't find any weapons of mass destruction, although that was the reason we were given by the President for invading. If we couldn't find WMD, the entire operation was in question.

Around this time Cindy Sheehan became national news. She was a mother from California whose son Casey was killed in Iraq in 2004. She gained national attention when she camped outside the entrance of George W. Bush's Texas ranch, protesting his invasion of Iraq. Cindy Sheehan became a symbol of parents who were angry their children were being killed trying to find WMD when there were none. She also became an icon for the liberals who were against the war. At first I thought Cindy Sheehan was annoying, but then I thought of how would feel if I lost a child under the same circumstances, especially after having lived through the debacle of Vietnam. Just like Cindy Sheehan, I would be furious if I lost my child for nothing. (By the way, Cindy Sheehan does not support the foreign policies of Barack Hussein Obama.)

If only we could have found some WMD then all would be well. But it was not to be. I remember talking with my mother about this. She was such a staunch Bush supporter that she would simply say we would find the WMD, that Saddam had hidden them all. But as the months went by and we weren't finding anything, the best we could hope for was the occasional discovery of a few hundred artillery rounds with a chemical symbol stamped on them. They would flash the discovery of this "massive trove of WMD" on TV, yet they would all be rusty and not usable. Just old discarded mortar and artillery rounds from Iraq's war with Iran, or when Saddam used them against his own people after the Gulf War, all with our knowledge of course.

So why were we still there after 2004? At this time the tension between the Muslim Sunni and Shi'ite factions in Iraq started to pick up. By 2005 we found ourselves right in the middle of an all-out civil war. We never should have stayed after we captured Saddam, and it was obvious by then we wouldn't find any weapons of mass destruction. But we stayed anyway. We had to stay because we had created the very "power vacuum" Bush the First was supposedly trying to avoid in 1991. When Paul Bremer fired every single Iraqi soldier and national policemen (the Iraqi provinces have their own police forces), he created a "power vacuum," but this one is on steroids. However, Paul Bremer couldn't have done a thing without the permission of George W. Bush.

Thanks to Paul Bremer there was no Iraqi army, so there could be no national security, and there was no national police, so there was no civil security. In his effort to wipe the slate clean and start from scratch, Paul Bremer went way beyond what was needed. He eliminated all the country's security infrastructure, and along with it the security and safety of the Iraqi people. Throw in the fact that we invaded with barely enough force to roll into central Baghdad, and you had a recipe for disaster that had been scripted in the White House and the Pentagon. I don't believe for a minute this was done purposely. Bush and his team weren't that smart. It was done out of pure arrogance, ignorance, and to satisfy the agendas of a handful of senior officials in the Bush administration. And it was all done with the acquiescence and the approval of George W. Bush.

Even though he was not a soldier, Paul Bremer had to know that we didn't have enough forces when we invaded Iraq, and therefore not enough forces to protect the county after he disbanded the Iraqi Army and National Police. He was surrounded by military and former military advisors who should have known this. One of these was retired U.S. Army Colonel Paul Hughes, who I've met and spoken with at his current place of employment, the United States Institute of Peace. Colonel Hughes was interviewed in the documentary *No End in Sight*. He describes his disbelief upon hearing the news that Paul Bremer had disbanded the Iraqi Army, even though he worked down the hall from Paul Bremer and saw him many times each day.[55]

Rather than consult with his staff, Bremer never asked anyone for their opinion of his plans because he didn't want anyone to disagree with him, which is insecure behavior. He was afraid of any feedback that did not conform to his plan. Instead of being open to other ideas, he made up his mind without consultation with others, and then implemented his decisions with his staff unaware of what was coming and ill prepared to act upon it. The Coalition Provisional Authority, the CPA, became an organization famous for employing young people in search of adventure, old military retirees in search of something to do, and State Department civilians looking for advancement. All of them were looking for money.

There are theories put forth by his apologists that Paul Bremer was ordered by Donald Rumsfeld, or someone else, to dissolve

---

[55] *No End in Sight*, Charles H. Ferguson, 2007.

the Iraqi Ministries of Defense and Interior—that Bremer was just following orders. I haven't seen any evidence of this. But if that happened, it would imply that Bremer didn't want to dissolve these two ministries, but was doing what his superiors told him to do. This would be the "Nuremburg defense," and it doesn't pass the smell test. Either Bremer dissolved these ministries on his own, or he dissolved them at the order of someone else. Either way, he still comes out looking bad: 1) he was ordered to, agreed with the order, and executed it, or; 2) he was ordered to, disagreed, but did as he was told, regardless of the consequences. This is not hair-splitting.

Other than Bush's decision to invade, no other decision has been responsible for the deaths of so many thousands of Iraqis, military and civilian, and the destruction of Iraq than the decision by Bremer to dissolve the Iraqi Army and National Police. If Paul Bremer was ordered by Donald Rumsfeld to dissolve these two Iraqi ministries, but he didn't want to, then he's just as guilty as if the whole thing was his idea. Actually, it's worse if he thought it was a bad idea but still went along with it. This is like Robert McNamara claiming that he executed the Vietnam War even though he didn't think it was right and we couldn't win it—but he did what he was ordered by his President and 58,000 American lives were lost. If that's true, why did McNamara wait until he was on death's door before he told the American people the truth? Probably because it wasn't true, or he was afraid he would get lynched. In the end, whose signature was on the CPA orders dissolving the Iraqi Ministry of Defense and Ministry of Interior? It wasn't Donald Rumsfeld's. It was Paul Bremer's. The signature on the documents is all that counts.

Where did many of these Iraqi soldiers and policemen go, with their weapons and ammunition, and a new-found hatred of the Americans who took away their job and the capability of feeding their families? We destroyed the Iraqi economy with the UN sanctions after the Gulf War, and then we did this? Many went directly into the insurgency as new members of the same forces that were already killing American soldiers. By maintaining the Iraqi Army and National Police, we could have at least kept an eye on these men, trained them in ways we felt would be best for their country, and kept them busy instead of going off to join the insurgency. But Paul Bremer's incompetence stopped any chance of that ever happening.

Paul Bremer was the primary cause of the insurgency, but without the invasion history would barely have recorded him. It all starts at the top, and ends there too. George W. Bush was the President, and nothing could have happened without his approval. In his excellent book *Embracing Defeat,* John Dower details the American occupation of Japan after the war. One of the biggest issues in his book was is the status of Emperor Hirohito, especially as it related to the war crimes trials. The Japanese people worshipped the emperor, and everyone knew he had approved the attack on Pearl Harbor. The Japanese people claimed he was their supreme leader, but they didn't want him to be tried for war crimes. This created a dilemma until Douglas MacArthur decreed the emperor was off-limits. MacArthur wanted the emperor to live to prevent revolt, and to help the people of Japan recover emotionally from their defeat.

Japan is not the United States, however, and the president is not an emperor, but you wouldn't know it if you just arrived from another planet. When the President of the United States commits what could be considered a "war crime," nothing happens. Article 5 of the charter establishing the jurisdiction of the International Military Tribunal for the Far East (the Tokyo war crimes trial), read as follows:

> The following acts, or any of them, are crimes coming within the jurisdictions of the tribunal for which there shall be individual responsibility:
>
> a. *Crimes against Peace:* namely, the planning, preparation, initiation or waging of a declared or undeclared war of aggression, or a war in violation of international law, treaties, agreements or assurances, or participation in a common plan or conspiracy for the accomplishment of any of the foregoing:.......[56]

---

[56] John Dower, *Embracing Defeat* (W.W. Norton & Company/The New Press, 1999), p. 456.

The definition of other acts that fell under the jurisdiction of the Tokyo tribunal followed later in the document, but this was right at the top. Based on this description, there is no difference between what senior Japanese officials were being charged with after the war, and what George W. Bush did when he invaded Iraq in March 2003. Dower elaborates at length about the double-standards shown in the trials. The victors did many things they accused the losers of doing. The one area where they differed, and differed greatly, was their respective treatment of captured prisoners of war, or POWs. No one disputes the good treatment of POWs by the American and British. But what of the treatment of POWs by the Soviet Union, whose representative sat in judgment over the Japanese? No one said a thing about this.

If the United States didn't commit a crime against peace when it invaded in Iraq on 2003, what did it do? Because the invasion was sanctioned by the UN, no charges will ever be filed against George W. Bush. He's off the hook. Maybe that's why getting UN permission was so important to him. Colin Powell may have kept *"W."* out of jail.

Then there was Hirohito. So much effort was expended by the American occupation to hold him above reproach that the chief prosecutor, an American jurist named Joseph Keenan, coached many of the accused to ensure they did not implicate the emperor. On December 31, 1947, former Prime Minister Hideki Tojo:

> ...frankly testified that it was inconceivable for him or any subject to have taken action contrary to the emperor's wishes. In response to this unintentionally candid and damaging observation, Keenan immediately arranged, through the emperor's own close advisors, that Kido [former Privy Seal] be contacted in prison and urged to tell his fellow defendant to rectify his potentially incriminating comments as soon as possible. Other intermediaries were used as well. Tojo was happy to comply, and the opportunity to do so arose in the courtroom a week later. On January 6, [1947] in the course of an

exchange with Keenen, Tojo retracted his earlier statement.[57]

The circumstances at the end of the Second World War were different than they are today, but individual responsibility hasn't changed a bit. George W. Bush's invasion of Iraq in 2003 is very similar to the "unprovoked" attack by the Japanese at Pearl Harbor (although FDR had to know this was coming), or Germany's various invasions which eventually led to war in Europe. Yet, because it was the President of the United States who attacked Iraq—without provocation—everything's OK. It may be so to many Americans, but it isn't to the rest of the world, which is why so many hate us.

Personal responsibility, that quality George W. Bush talked about so much during his 2000 presidential campaign, went out the window the day he was inaugurated. Not only has he never been held accountable for his unprovoked invasion of Iraq in 2003, no one in his administration was ever held accountable by him for their many screw-ups before and after. Paul Bremer is tied with Rumsfeld, Franks, Cheney, Tenet, Wolfowitz and Feith for position at the top of the list.

---

[57] Ibid, p. 468.

7—MNF-I

During the initial phase of Operation Iraqi Freedom the coalition forces were called the Coalition Forces Land Component Command, or CFLCC. CFLCC was commanded by Lieutenant General David McKiernan, who reported directly to Tommy Franks in Tampa, Florida. All Coalition forces in Iraq were under the command of LTG McKiernan, comprising not only all the American forces but British, Australian, and all other allied forces who had joined the United States in what President Bush referred to as the "Coalition of the Willing." As time went by the Coalition dwindled down from around 25 countries to at most 10 on a good day, and more like five on a bad one. Great Britain and Australia finally pulled out because they were hard pressed by their people back home. Only Tony Blair's strong support of Bush during most of the ordeal kept the Commonwealth nations involved as long as they were. By the time I left Iraq in September 2007, the only countries left were El Salvador, Mongolia, the Republic of Georgia, Korea and Japan. Not much of a fighting force.

The United States, as always, made up about 98% of all forces in Iraq until Obama's troop withdrawal of 2011. When Australia decided to pull out all of its forces Kevin Rudd, the Prime Minister at the time, said former PM John Howard "misled" the Australian people into joining the conflict alongside the United States.

All Coalition forces were part of the Multi-National Forces-Iraq, or MNF-I, which was commanded by General David Petraeus until the fall of 2008. His successor was General Raymond Odierno, the current Chief of Staff of the Army. The previous MNF-I commander was General George Casey, who held the position for approximately two and a half years. The various subordinate commands that fell under MNF-I were:

1. The Multi-National Corps-Iraq, or MNC-I, formerly under the command of Lieutenant General Raymond Odierno prior to his assuming command of MNF-I.

2. The Multi-National Security Transition Command-Iraq, or MNSTC-I, under the command of Lieutenant General James Dubik, and which was formerly under the command of LTG Martin Dempsey.
3. Task Force 134, formerly under the command of Marine Corps Reserve Major General Douglas Stone.
4. The Joint Area Support Group, or JASG.
5. The Joint Special Operations Command-Iraq, or JSOC-I.

These commands and their missions will be described individually.

The Multi-National Forces-Iraq was the overall command of all forces in Iraq, including U.S. and other Coalition forces. As mentioned above, it had been commanded by General George Casey. During the time that General Casey led MNF-I, the situation in Iraq deteriorated to the point where U.S. casualties grew to weekly rates reminiscent of the Vietnam War, and Iraqi civilian deaths went into the tens of thousands. It was while General Casey was in command of MNF-I that the civil war within Iraq between the Shi'ite and Sunni factions of Islam escalated, and the outside influence of Al-Qaeda in Iraq (AQI), Iran, Syria, Saudi Arabia and others increased. Also during Casey's command we witnessed the rise of the cleric Muqtada Al Sadr, whose shenanigans went untouched, even while he taunted the United States and his Mahdi Army killed American soldiers by the hundreds. All of this occurred during General Casey's command, "on his watch" as they say, leading anyone to wonder how he held onto the job as long as he did, similar to George Tenet.

What happened to General Casey when he left this position? Rather than be allowed to 'retire' like General Shinseki, he was promoted to the highest job in the United States Army, its Chief of Staff. How could this happen? It was highly probable he was given this job in order to avoid the embarrassment (to him or the administration?) of being ushered out of the Army, which is what should have happened. Instead, he was promoted—most likely so the President could say he was given this new job as a reward for having done such a great job back in Iraq. General Casey's promotion to Army Chief of Staff was an implicit way for the President to say things in Iraq had to be going pretty good, so why wouldn't the outgoing commander get promoted. It was another example of the smoke and mirrors the Bush administration subjected the American people to.

Instead of saying things weren't going well in Iraq and the commanding general there was going to "step aside," the President promoted that same general who did nothing during the period of turmoil described above. General Casey kept telling the White House the situation in Iraq was improving, and the Iraqis were doing a great job. Nothing could have been farther from the truth during General Casey's tenure, but he got promoted as if that was reality. Instead of refusing the job because his time in command was a disaster, General Casey gladly stepped in and watched soldiers get killed because he let two and a half years go by without asking for more troops to deal with the deteriorating situation on the ground.

His replacement was General David Petraeus, the former commander of the 101st Airborne Division during the initial phases of OIF and later commander of MNSTC-I. (The 101st used to be an "Airborne" unit, gaining fame at Bastogne during the Battle of the Bulge near the end of World War II. Since the Vietnam War, it has been an "Airmobile" division, meaning it no longer parachutes into battle, but rides in helicopters. The "Airborne" on the shoulder patch is for nostalgic reasons only.) After leaving Iraq, General Petraeus came back to the States, got his third star, and took command of Fort Leavenworth, home of the famous federal prison and the Army's Command and General Staff College. While there General Petraeus advanced the training in Middle Eastern studies to better indoctrinate mid-level Army officers to the ways of fighting in this area of the world in the years to come.

When General Casey left for his nice new office in the Pentagon, General Petraeus, now a brand new four-star general, stepped onto center stage in Iraq with a new vision and new ideas, a welcome change to the narrow vision of Casey, who was afraid to ask for more troops to do what was needed. (Or, being so out of touch with the realities on the ground in Iraq, General

Casey didn't think anything was needed.) It was widely believed at the time that General Petraeus agreed to take the job only if the surge was implemented. It is not known how many soldiers Petraeus asked for, or if it was the 25,000 sent over. We do know the President said he would give Petraeus whatever he wanted. It's too bad Petraeus didn't ask for more, but 25,000 was better than nothing. Anything was better than what we got out of George Casey.

It has now come to light that the surge was not even General Petraeus' idea, or that President Bush was really "giving the generals whatever they asked for." In his September 2008 *Washington Post* series on the turmoil inside the Bush White House in 2005-2006, Bob Woodward has described how it was Meghan O'Sullivan, Deputy National Security Advisor, and Steve Hadley, the National Security Advisor, who realized the war was at a complete standstill and told the President so. (They were two of the few civilians in the Bush administration who had a clue about the war.) In a couple of satellite video teleconference calls, Hadley and others on the NSC staff asked General Casey, with Bush's permission, direct questions about the war and its current state at the time. Woodward reports that Casey was livid at being asked the questions at all, and furious at the insinuation he didn't have the situation in Iraq under control. The body count of U.S. soldiers and Iraqi civilians must have meant nothing to him, but it certainly did to Hadley and the President.[58]

The arrogance and attitude of Casey, as portrayed in the Woodward series, say it all. Not only was Iraq going down the tubes on Casey's watch, but that someone would dare ask him legitimate questions about it was more than he could handle. For the previous year he had been telling the President that Iraq would be able to stand on its own in 12 months, which was preposterous. In addition, he was telling the President we should be withdrawing troops, not adding more. It is clear from the Woodward series that General Casey was concerned only with his own reputation, nothing more. It is also clear where the ego, arrogance and incompetence of senior officers and government officials can lead our country, and what they can get us involved

---

[58] Bob Woodward, "The War Within, Part I – Doubt, Distrust, Delay," *The Washington Post*, September 7, 2008.

in. It is amazing General George Casey was promoted to U.S. Army Chief of Staff. That single act by the President, and agreed to by the Senate, was a slap in the face of every American soldier and Iraqi killed while General Casey was in command of MNF-I. He was as clueless of the realities of the situation in Iraq as Donald Rumsfeld and Tommy Franks were in planning the invasion.

- Lousy plan before the invasion.
- Lousy execution of the battle theater afterwards.

When General Petraeus came into the job as Commander of MNF-I, the President went out of his way to tell the media that he was "listening to his generals," and "giving the generals in Iraq everything they ask for." Great, but why didn't he do that before we went over there when General Shinseki, the Army Chief of Staff, said we would need half a million troops? The President's statement that he was listening to his generals was too late—about three years too late. He should have listened to them before he ever went over there. He should have listened to his senior U.S. Army military advisor, his expert on land warfare. Instead, all he listened to was Rumsfeld, who wanted the war fought his way (i.e., "Invasion Lite"), and there was no other discussion about it. Tommy Franks was Rumsfeld's water boy who implemented Rumsfeld's plan when everyone, including the President, should have listened to Shinseki who was the President's senior ground warfare advisor, not Franks. They were all listening to the wrong guy, who was not the senior ground warfare advisor to the President. Franks had only one thing going for him, and it was not the fact that he was the CENTCOM Commander. It was the fact that he was a "yes man" who did whatever his boss told him to do in the face of overwhelming historical evidence the plan he was executing was completely bogus.

If the two generals, Franks and Shinseki, had gone to Rumsfeld as a team and laid out a viable plan for the invasion and occupation of Iraq (which is what they should have done), none of this would have happened. Instead, in his autobiography Franks calls the Chiefs of Staff of the major armed forces of the Unites States "Title Ten motherfuckers" (referring to Title 10 of the United States Code, which addresses the role of the armed forces).[59] In Tommy Franks' opinion, the Chiefs of the Army, Navy, Air Force and Marines weren't real field commanders like him, and didn't know what was happening on the field of battle. He admits in his book he had no respect for the Chiefs of Staff, implying Shinseki, so working together for these two officers was out of the question. Franks sold Rumsfeld on his 'leadership,' and probably torpedoed Shinseki at the same time. Look where we ended up. Well, Tommy Franks had it the other way around. He thought he knew what was going on in the real world of warfare, when he was better at playing war games on computers than in real life. Tommy Franks should have stayed home in Midland, Texas pumping gas.

General Petraeus brought with him to Camp Victory (the name of the base where NMF-I was located on the western side of Baghdad, near the airport) a group of "young Turks," army colonels with PhDs who would transform the fight in Iraq into something better. One of these colonels was H.R. McMaster, who wrote the well-known account of Vietnam entitled *Dereliction of Duty*. The book is a well-documented account of the abominable planning and escalation of the Vietnam War, specifically the insanity of the McNamara policies of "limited warfare" and "limited engagement," which led to the deaths of 58,000 American soldiers. The amazing thing about Colonel McMaster's book is that it was written in 1998, five years before the invasion of Iraq. One wonders if Tommy Franks or Donald Rumsfeld ever read it. The similarities between Vietnam and Iraq are so numerous they are hard to count. Colonel (later Brigadier General) McMaster could write another book about the Iraq conflict, but he has to be careful because he served in it.

Dereliction of Duty described how the Joint Chiefs of Staff acquiesced in almost every meeting with McNamara (that he bothered inviting them to) and "the best and the brightest" of the day. It was only General Greene, the Marine Corps Commandant, who plainly told President Johnson and Secretary of Defense McNamara what it would really take to win in Southeast Asia. General Greene gave them the number of

---

[59] Tommy Franks with Malcolm McConnell, *American Soldier*, (HarperCollins, 2009), p. 277.

soldiers and Marines that would be needed, and also the amount of time the war would last and the expected number of casualties. But no one listened to him, just as no one listed to General Shinseki, who said the same thing to his Secretary of Defense 40 years later.

The Chairman of the Joint Chiefs of Staff during Vietnam, General Earle Wheeler, was a career Army officer who never fought in combat, but instead sat out the entire Second World War in the States as a training officer, sending soldiers to battle, and in many cases to their death. Wheeler was a complete desk jockey, going along with everything McNamara wanted and never saying a thing. The war was going so bad, however, that General Wheeler and the entire Joint Chiefs of Staff planned to resign 'en masse' in protest of the way it was being waged. But they never had the chance. Just when this was about to happen General Wheeler suffered a heart attack. That was the end of it. The idea never went any further. Then again, it's likely that it never would have. General Wheeler's heart attack was probably just what the rest of them needed to back down, not having the courage to act on their own. Like Wheeler, General Franks went along with everything his Secretary of Defense wanted, in the face of overwhelming evidence that the plan would not work.

McNamara's strategy of "limited engagement" in Vietnam is eerily similar to Rumsfeld's strategy of "Invasion Lite" in Iraq. Rumsfeld invaded a country half a world away that had an army estimated to be as large as a million men, and did it with only 125,000 Coalition forces, the vast majority of them support troops and not combat soldiers. The United States didn't lose the Vietnam War. We were never beaten. Our national leadership chose not to win it. They wouldn't allow us to. In Iraq we chose to invade a country that had not attacked us, or anyone else, with a fraction of the forces needed to do it successfully. We wouldn't allow ourselves to win in Iraq, just like we wouldn't allow ourselves to win in Vietnam—because we never destroyed the enemy. The end result of both wars will be the same, unless something is done about this one before it's too late, which it looks like it already is.

Throughout 2014 a spinoff of al Qaeda in Iraq (AQI) called the Islamic State of Iraq and Syria, or ISIS (also called the Islamic

State of Iraq and the Levant (ISIL), the Islamic State of Iraq and al-Shah, and the Islamic State) was on the verge of taking over Baghdad. Rumsfeld's "Invasion Lite," followed by Paul Bremer, followed by General Casey, followed by Obama's drawdown, followed by his withdrawal of all combat forces, followed by Prime Minister Nouri al-Maliki's inept Shi'ite government, have all led Iraq down the road toward complete collapse.

Under MNF-I was the Multi-National Corps-Iraq, or MNC-I, at one time under the command of Lieutenant General Raymond Odierno, who later became MNF-I commander, and then Army Chief of Staff. MNC-I was the command element that comprised all Coalition combat forces in Iraq. The Coalition forces involved in the fighting were broken down by regions of the country, such as MND-North, for Multi-National Division-North. As the name implied, this described the forces in the northern part of Iraq that fell under the U.S. Army division commander in that part of the country. As time went by these divisions rotated out of combat, to be replaced by others coming from the States, but the designation remained the same. Therefore, if the 82nd Airborne Division, as well as a smattering of other token Coalition forces, were located in the operational area in northern Iraq, this combined force made up the Multi-National Division-North. When another U.S. Army division came in to replace the 82nd, that unit was also called "MND-North." The same went for the forces to the south (MND-South), the east (MND-East), and central Iraq, or MND-Central. Because there was so much action near Baghdad in the center, this area was broken up into two sub-areas. All of these combat forces made up MNC-I.

What about the western part of Iraq, Anbar Province? Shortly after the initial phases of the conflict, the Marines replaced the Army in the area around Fallujah and Ramadi, two of the main towns in eastern Anbar Province along the Euphrates River, 40-50 miles west of Baghdad. The Army had been having a tough go of it for months, but the real problems were dealing with the local tribal leaders, most of them Sunni. When the Marines were directed to replace the Army in Anbar Province they publicly announced that they would do what the Army had failed to do, i.e., turn things around and clean things up. This was a professional slap in the face by one service of the other, and was an open show of dislike of the Army by the Marines. But the history of animosity between the Army and the Marines goes back a lot farther than Operation Iraqi Freedom.

The Marines are jealous of the Army because they aren't their own service. The Marine Corps is part of the U.S. Navy. As a result it doesn't get as much funding or equipment as the Army does. And it has to do what the Navy tells it to do. The result is a lot of frustrated Marines. Not being its own service the Marine Corps has to go out of its way to be noticed and get attention. The Marines have great looking dress uniforms and neat commercials on TV. That's how they get attention, recruits, and the public thinking they are the only combat force this nation has. It's all good PR, just like a major corporation. But the Marine Corps is barely 200,000 strong. The U.S. Army is over half a million strong, with 546,000 active duty soldiers. Yet, the average person (and most of the ever-alert media) see an American in uniform and think he's a Marine, even if the soldier has "U.S. Army" on his shirt. I've seen this in the papers countless times. The media regularly captions a photograph of a U.S. Army soldier and refer to him as a "Marine." The Marines eat this up.

> The Marine Corps' combat capabilities in some ways overlap those of the United States Army, the latter having historically viewed the Corps as encroaching on the Army's capabilities and competing for funding, missions, and renown....Most significantly, in the aftermath of World War II, Army efforts to restructure the American defense establishment included the dissolution of the Corps and the folding of its capabilities into the other services. Leading this movement were such prominent Army officers as General Dwight D. Eisenhower and Army Chief of Staff George C. Marshall.[60] While the rivalry is still

---

[60] Krulak, Victor H., *First To Fight: An Inside View of the U.S. Marine Corp*, Chapter 7, *The Marines' Push Button*, (Naval Institute Press, Annapolis, Maryland, 1984), pp.113–119.

present today, most Marines and soldiers adopt a more cooperative attitude when operating jointly.[61]

Doctrinally, Marines focus on being expeditionary and independent, while the Army tends more toward overwhelming force with a large support element....The Army operates a great many different types of units, while the "Every Marine's a rifleman" creed shows the Marines' focus on standardized infantry units with the other arms in support roles....The Marines often utilize the Army for the acquisition of ground equipment (as well as benefiting from Army research and development resources), training resources, and other support concepts. The majority of vehicles and weapons are shared with, modified, or inherited from Army programs.[62]

If the Marines are effective when operating independently and in an expeditionary role, it's because when they're in this mode they don't have to cooperate with anyone else. But no service is "independent" if it has to rely on another for its equipment and supplies when deployed for anything beyond a few weeks or months, which is the case with the Marine Corps. It has to rely on the Army for almost everything if it is deployed in a land combat role beyond a very short period. It doesn't have the capability to sustain itself beyond that, so how effective can it be? By having robust logistics support, as well as every other land combat capability, the Army is the service that has true independence and the capacity to operate for extended periods of time, to include conducting amphibious operations, which are not unique to the Marine Corps. The Army has the ability to attack with overwhelming force, not the Marine Corps. The Marines Corps has its own fighter jet aircraft, which the Army doesn't have. But the United States Air Force makes that point rather

---

[61] Baron, Kevin, "Gates: Time has come to re-examine future of Marine Corps," August 12, 2010.

[62] Priddy, Maj. Wade, "Marine Detachment 1: Opening the door for a Marine force contribution to USSOCom," *Marine Corps Gazette*, (Marine Corps Association, 2006), 90 (6): 58–59.

mute. If the Marine Corps' creed is, "Every Marine's a rifleman," this is most likely because they have all the other services to provide support for them, so they can focus on combat functions and not much else. This is the value of the Marine Corps. But this value is nullified by the Marine Corps' inability or desire to work in true collaboration, and cooperation, with the U.S. Army that supports it. As the saying goes, "don't bite the hand that feeds you." The Marines do this to the Army every day.

Does the Marine Corps really work, or just look nice? The Marines are good, but they're not better than the Army, even though they think they are. In the "joint forces" nature of warfare today the Marine Corps needs to check its attitude of superiority and arrogance at the door and work with the Army to get the mission accomplished, rather than making every effort not to. This hasn't happened in Iraq since the opening days of the war, and the results speak for themselves. Without the U.S. Army the Marine Corps wouldn't be able to function past a few months of deployment. It would cease to be "independent and expeditionary" very quickly. The Marine Corps is the smaller of the two land forces in our country, not the only one, and is dependent on other branches of the service to function, whereas the Army is fully autonomous.

We have two land forces that essentially do the same thing. The redundancy constantly causes problems because the Marines refuse to work with the other branches of the service, primarily the Army, the other land component. If both Eisenhower and Marshall wanted to dissolve the Marine Corps after World War II, there had to be a good reason. It's highly probable they experienced the redundancy and overlap, as well as attitude, when operating jointly with the Marine Corps throughout the war. Their logic and expertise of military doctrine and history would have told them the arrangement didn't work, any more than it does today. Unfortunately, Eisenhower and Marshall failed to have the Marine Corps disbanded, most likely having been overruled in the White House by Marine Corps supporters. The problems between the two services continue, and are no closer to being worked out than the problems between the Sunnis and the Shi'ites.

If the Marine Corps' unique area of expertise is amphibious warfare, where does it fit into our nation's war fighting capability if we don't do these operations anymore? The Marine Corps has a lot in common with labor unions—they both served a useful purpose when they were created, but that was a long time ago. The U.S. Army executed as many, if not more, amphibious landings during World War II as the Marine Corps, but you wouldn't know that talking with a Marine. To a Marine, they're the only force that does these, or ever has. Where was the Marine Corps on D-Day, the biggest amphibious operation in the history of warfare? The Marine Corps should do what its name implies: serve as a "marine corps" that is deployed with the U.S. Navy's surface fleet. That is what the Marine Corps does that is truly unique, and is still needed to this day. Beyond this role, the Marine Corps isn't needed as a land force. We already have one of those. It's called the United States Army.

A good example of the problems between the Army and the Marines took place in Afghanistan. So intent were the Marines to be in charge of their own theater of operations, without the Army meddling in their business, they begged to be given complete responsibility for Afghanistan. This never got off the ground, likely because everyone knew they wouldn't be able to support themselves. Within weeks the Marines would have needed the support of the Army, which is stretched so thin it can hardly support itself. The Marine Corps' notion that it can do all things anywhere and at any time, on its own, is based on fantasy not reality. It's partly based on the fact the Marine Corps has its own fighter aircraft. That's great, but only means it doesn't have to call up the Air Force. As a land fighting force the Marine Corps can't sustain itself, and that's all that matters. The Army remains in charge of operations in Afghanistan, much to the chagrin of the Marines.

The on-going conflict between the U.S. Army and the Marines gets our country nowhere. We end up fighting two wars whenever the Marines and the Army are placed in the same theater of operations—one war against each other because the Marines refuse to work with the Army, and the other war against the enemy we're supposed to be fighting.

One of the Marines' main issues in taking over Anbar Province was their image and their professed ability to deal with any situation, be it fierce combat or delicate inter-personal negotiations, with whoever had the honor of being in their presence. They even went so far as to announce that their combat uniforms would look radically different than the Army's, in order to show the Iraqis they were so different and things would be so much better. This last point finally got under the Army's skin so much the Marines had to back down and go in with their normal desert camouflage.

The Marines entered Fallujah in eastern Anbar Province, and within a short time the situation went to hell. The primary flash point was the famous, and very tragic, incident where four Blackwater security contractors (i.e., mercenaries) were slaughtered by local militia. Their bodies were set on fire and dragged down the street, then hung from the steel beams of a bridge, all of it broadcast around the world later that same day. I was told while I was in Iraq that the Blackwater contractors had pissed off the locals in Fallujah in the days preceding the incident by running people off the road and shooting toward anyone who looked at them the wrong way. I was also told that the day before the incident the Blackwater team asked for directions through the town, saying they needed it for a convoy the next day. This was a gross security violation on their part. It alerted the locals in the town of their intentions and their direction of travel, and also the time they would be doing it. They set themselves up by acting like jerks, alienating the local population, and then nailed their own coffins by committing security violations and broadcasting their intentions. The Blackwater contractors acted cocky and arrogant, and it cost them their lives. After this incident the Marines, rightfully so, replied in kind and started kicking some insurgent ass, leading to months of some of the worst house-to-house and door-to-door fighting of the war.

Toward the end of our troop presence in Iraq the Marines had responsibility for Anbar Province. But not to be just like everybody else (i.e., the U.S. Army) their geographic area of responsibility was referred to as MEF-West, for Marine Expeditionary Force-West. The Marines did not want their sector to be named the same way as the Army's. But the Marine's disdain for the Army goes much farther than just a name.

For example, when I first travelled to Al Asad, one of the main Marine bases in Anbar Province, I flew there on a U.S. Army Blackhawk helicopter, a UH-60. This is the primary helicopter of the Army, having replaced the famous "Huey," or UH-1 helicopter of the Vietnam War. The flight was uneventful, and we flew directly from the International Zone (formerly the "Green Zone") to Al Asad and back. It was about an hour each way, during daylight going out there from Baghdad, and in the middle of the night coming back. I did this a couple of times. A few months later the Marine units rotated out, and the 1st Marine Expeditionary Force (MEF) was replaced by the 2nd MEF, whose commander must have really hated the Army. When this happened the 2nd MEF Marines stopped all U.S. Army aircraft flights into Al Asad. They wouldn't let the U.S. Army fly helicopters into a Marine base! I was amazed, but what really got me was they were allowed to get away with it. In order to get to Al Asad, a trip that lasted about one hour, we had to get on a Marine CH-46 twin rotor aircraft that made a round-robin trek from Marine base to Marine base. The entire one-way trip lasted 2-3 days because we had to spend the night at Taqadem, or "TQ," and then continue on our trek the following day to Al Asad on an Air Force C-130 transport. It was absurd, yet that's the way the Marines wanted it, and that's what the commander of MNC-I, Ray Odierno, let them get away with. When you consider we were at war, childish behavior like this was unacceptable. It showed the complete breakdown of command and control, simplicity, combat effectiveness, and rational thought going on over there. It's no wonder operations in Iraq were such a mess.

Task Force 134 was the element responsible for all the detainees captured by Coalition forces. A distinction has to be made, because detainees were captured by Iraqi forces too, yet they didn't fall under the control of TF-134. There were so many detainees, especially after the surge in February 2007, that housing and feeding them had become a monumental task by the spring of 2007. Facilities had to be constructed and contracts for food service needed to be put in place. TF-134 had this responsibility, and was working on these issues when I left Iraq in September of 2007.

The Joint Area Support Group, or JASG, was the command element responsible for the International Zone (IZ), formerly called the Green Zone. The International Zone was the area of central Baghdad where all of the former Iraqi government headquarters buildings were located. Essentially, the JASG Commander was the "Mayor" of the IZ. After the United States and the Coalition 'secured' central Baghdad, the Green Zone was established to protect all coalition personnel and facilities, not the least of which was the Republican Palace, the former headquarters of Saddam's government. Because the United States didn't have an embassy before our invasion in 2003, we made the north wing of the Republican Palace the U.S. Embassy in Baghdad. Having spent time with the State Department in Overseas Buildings Operations, I found this solution to be interesting. The rest of the building was used to house the Iraq Reconstruction Management Office (IRMO), a Green Beans gourmet coffee shop, a short order deli, an internet café, and other facilities for the soldiers' (and contractors') morale. The Army calls these "MWR" facilities for "Morale, Welfare and Recreation."

The Joint Special Operations Command-Iraq, or JSOC-I, was the Coalition-trained (i.e., US-trained) Iraqi equivalent of our Special Forces, their most elite soldiers. It was basically a joke. JSOC-I wouldn't have been able to fight its way out of a wet paper bag. They just had fancier uniforms than the rest of the Iraqi army's.

Half way through my tour in Iraq the Embassy changed the rules for entry onto the compound. They would no longer allow contractors who didn't live in a trailer on the embassy compound access through the checkpoint. Any soldier could walk right in, even if he or she didn't live there, but we contractors couldn't. Then there was hardly anything to do with our free time. Things got worse from that point on for those of us who lived on the other compounds in the IZ, to include me.

In addition, we were going to have our privilege to use the embassy infirmary taken away as well. Contractors would no longer have access to medical treatment at all, meaning we would have to fly back to the States or to Dubai if we really got sick. In other words, we were sent to Iraq on a Department of Defense contract, but medical services were soon going to be pulled by DoD and the State Department. As far as they were concerned we weren't worthy of receiving adequate medical care. But DoD had no problem awarding contracts and sending us over there. Fortunately, I didn't get sick during the latter part of my tour.

I lived at FOB (Forward Operating Base) Blackhawk, across the street and down a block from the embassy. This was where "Believers Palace" was located, which was completely destroyed by our guided bombs the opening night of the war. It was beneath this palace that Saddam had his famous bunker. The bunker was amazing, having been designed by the granddaughter of the same German engineer who built Hitler's bunker in Berlin, the one where he spent the last days of his life before killing himself. Saddam's bunker was so well designed and constructed our bombs didn't make a dent in it, and we tried. The palace was completely destroyed above ground, but the bunker wasn't touched. It was the looting after Saddam left Baghdad that destroyed it. The entire bunker, about the size of a floor in a large office building, sat on shock absorbers surrounded by yards of reinforced concrete. Saddam and his immediate staff could live there for over a month.

Mid-way through my tour in Iraq, I began to hear about the "Negroponte Memo." John Negroponte, a career Foreign Service officer, was the U.S. Ambassador to Iraq from June 2004 to April 2005. For whatever reason, he found himself at the top of the heap and got huge jobs after 9/11. How a guy who made his career attending cocktail parties got the position as National Intelligence Czar, I don't know. But then again, what does a retired Navy admiral know about securing diplomatic facilities? It doesn't have to make sense. When I was in Iraq, from July 2006 to September 2007, the place was falling apart, but I heard the Coalition (i.e., the US) was going to give the IZ back to Iraq! In other words, we were all dead. I couldn't believe this, but then I heard when he was ambassador, Negroponte had written a memo stating that in the future the Coalition (again, almost solely the US, with some window dressing from smaller states) was going to disband the IZ. That point in time was approaching and meant no barricades, no checkpoints, no security, nothing. The portion of Baghdad where the IZ was would be just another part of the city.

For a while after the initial fighting ended in the spring of 2003, Baghdad was relatively quiet. The shit hadn't hit the fan yet, which meant the full effects of Bremer's actions hadn't taken hold. By the time I got there the only thing keeping us alive was the security of the IZ. If I had walked outside any of the IZ's gates, I wouldn't have made it 50 feet before getting killed. This is not an exaggeration. When the Negroponte memo was written the situation in Baghdad may have been better, but it wasn't any more. The Bush administration was in such a rush to make everything look great and completely under control, it wanted to turn everything over to Iraq as fast as it could. The purple thumbs after the "free democratic elections," were supposed to make it look like just another day in good ol' Baghdad. The only thing missing was the apple pie. Thankfully, someone with a brain decided the IZ wasn't going anywhere anytime soon. The Negroponte memo, that stellar piece of diplomatic nonsense, was stuffed in a filing cabinet.

Most of Saddam's old palaces were constructed during the period of the UN sanctions imposed after the Gulf War. He built them primarily to show the world the sanctions weren't working, which they weren't, and to thumb his nose at George H.W. Bush, who let him get away. It isn't difficult to understand why Saddam did this. After all, he was allowed to remain in power (i.e., alive) by Bush the First, and the sanctions had absolutely no impact on his lifestyle or his authority over the Iraqi people. Bush let him get away with his invasion of Kuwait, and let him remain in power in Baghdad, so why shouldn't Saddam show the world he was alive and well, and able to build however many palaces he wanted. To do otherwise in his culture would have made him look like he had been defeated in the Gulf War and was nothing more than a puppet of the US.

But we were too dense to see what he was doing during the intervening years between the two wars fought by father and son. One war was fought with a terrible end, and the other fought with a terrible beginning, and without an end in sight. The ones who have suffered the most throughout all this were the Iraqi people. The sanctions were a joke, a waste of time, and hurt the people we said we were trying to help. What would have really helped the Iraqi people was not ruining their economy with the sanctions, but killing Saddam Hussein during the Gulf War in 1991 when we had half a million soldiers there to deal with any situation, such as the "power vacuum" we heard so much about. None of this happened, making Saddam Hussein a target for George W. Bush 12 years later.

The other primary element of MNF-I was the Multi-National Security Transition Command-Iraq, or MNSTC-I.

Graduating from West Point, June 8, 1977.

A lieutenant assigned to A "Alpha" Company (Airborne), 3rd Battalion,
5th Infantry, 193rd Infantry Brigade, Fort Kobbe, Canal Zone,
Republic of Panama.

First Classman (senior) at West Point. I am receiving an award from my cadet regimental commander, Ricky Lynch. Ricky is now a three-star general and the former military spokesman in Iraq, and also a former division commander there. He is now the III Corps Commander at Fort Hood, Texas.

To Mike
With Best Wishes,

Shaking hands with President George W. Bush when he visited the remote headquarters of the Office of Homeland Security (OHS) in Building #3 on the U.S. Navy's Nebraska Avenue Complex (the "NAC"), across from American University at the intersection of Massachusetts and Nebraska Avenues in northwest Washington, DC. The author was Governor's Ridge's Senior Director for Administration at OHS.

With a friend and President George W. Bush, and his wife Laura Bush,
at the White House Staff Christmas Party, 2002.

WHITE HOUSE OFFICE OF HOMELAND SECURITY
OCTOBER 8, 2001-2002

To Mike O'Brien
With Best Wishes,
Tom Ridge

Thank you Mike!

The Office of Homeland Security staff with Governor Tom Ridge on
the east steps of the Old Executive Office Building across the driveway
from the West Wing of the White House. Governor Ridge (called "Governor"
out of respect for when he was the Governor of Pennsylvania before
coming to Washington) is front center. The author is standing two
rows behind Governor Ridge's left shoulder.

The Kuwait Hilton, Kuwait City, on the Persian Gulf. This is where contractors stayed before they took off for Baghdad. It looks nice, but the accommodations inside the 'villas' along the beach were nothing to write home about. They were extremely plain inside, almost dismal. Wealthy Kuwaiti families would rent a villa for a week and hang out with their kids. They had money to burn. The best part was the restaurant, which we were given vouchers for.

Inside a U.S. Air Force C-130 transport, ready to take off from Ali Al Saleem U.S. Air Base in Kuwait for Baghdad. We would sit in these for what seemed like hours, usually baking. If you had to go to the bathroom, you were out of luck, unless you were willing to piss in a tube near the cargo ramp while everyone watched. I learned right at the beginning of my tour that getting anywhere in the Iraqi theater of operations was a complete nightmare. On these flights we were practically sitting on top of each other, and we had to carry everything we had with us.

In a C-130 cargo plane flying from Ali Al Saleem Air Base in Kuwait to Baghdad International Airport (BIAP).

With my co-worker. Everywhere she went Iraqi men would just stare at her because of her blonde hair.

With Col. Craig Agena on board a U.S. Blackhawk helicopter on our way to Diwaniyah, near al-Hilla, south of Baghdad.

The walkway between Phoenix Base and the Ministry of Defense building, which can be seen in the background. Just beyond the MOD building was the wall separating the IZ (International Zone) from the city. The 12 foot high pre-fabricated concrete "T-walls" were the most common sight in Iraq. They were virtually everywhere the Coalition was. I walked down this sidewalk about three times a day.

Closer down the walkway to the Ministry of Defense building. The Al-
Mansour Hotel can be seen in the background. One day a sniper shot a bullet
from the hotel through the window of General Babakir's (the Iraqi Chief of
Staff) office on the side of the MOD building facing the hotel, a distance of at
least 1,500 meters. The sniper not only knew which window was Gen.
Babakir's, he was also a very good shot. No one was hurt, and the bullet
dropped into a trash can after bouncing off the wall in the office.

Believers Palace, up the road and across the street from the Republican Palace. This was the Ba'ath Party headquarters, with Saddam's bunker underneath. It was destroyed by JDAMS—Joint Direct Attack Munitions, or guided bombs— the opening night of the war. The compound surrounding Believers Palace was called FOB (Forward Operating Base) Blackhawk, where I lived for 14 months. Some trailers are visible to the upper right.

Home sweet home, Believers Palace.

Close-up of the front of Believers Palace. The main hall is just inside. It can be seen through the debris because there is no longer a roof, allowing sunlight in.

Just to the left of the front door of Believers Palace. At different times I lived in the two trailers in the center of the photograph, under the front overhang of the palace. The air conditioners would go out all the time due to constant use. When that happened it would be too hot to sleep, so we would have to sleep inside the palace on cots. Inside the palace on the top floor was a private bar for Saddam's parties.

Outside of my trailer at FOB Blackhawk. Sandbags were everywhere, most of them in disrepair and leaking sand all over the place. There was almost more sand outside the bags than in.

A trailer that went up in flames near mine. The Iraqi contractors hired to install all of the trailers for the U.S. personnel on FOB Blackhawk didn't bother to use a ground wire when connecting the electrical power to the trailers. A wire in, a wire out. Who needs a third wire? Where was the U.S. supervision? These were going up all over the place like match sticks. The DFAC (dining facility) on FOB Blackhawk lit up like a candle one night and was completely destroyed, but not from bad wiring. Anti-aircraft flares from a U.S. helicopter landed on its roof and it went up in flames.

More damage inside.

A sergeant shows the entrance to Saddam's bunker complex at
Believers Palace. We had to go up a flight of stairs, and then
down several flights to get to the bunker.

Inside Believers Palace.

Believers Palace.

The main conference room in Saddam's bunker.

Saddam's old communications tower on FOB Blackhawk, next to Believers Palace. This could be seen for miles. All anyone had to do was aim at it and have the right distance, and they could drop rocket and mortar rounds near it all day. I lived 25 feet from where the picture was taken. I complained to JASG about the tower, asking why it couldn't be taken down for our safety at FOB Blackhawk, and was told it wasn't going anywhere.

The Republican Palace in the International Zone, formerly called the Green Zone. This was Saddam's main palace and the seat of the government. The far end (the north end), was the U.S. Embassy. The near end (the south end), housed the offices of IRMO (Iraqi Reconstruction Management Office) as well as the MWR, Green Beans coffee bar, and other amenities. Contractors who did not live in trailers on the Embassy compound were barred from getting onto it half way through my tour. The row of cars behind the building, to the far right of the picture, is where the mortar round killed the woman from the KBR housing office.

The Republican Palace as seen from a Blackhawk helicopter on final approach into LZ (landing zone) Washington across the street. This is a good view looking north across the Tigris River to the other side of Baghdad and Sadr City. It was on the other side of the Tigris River, in the area shown here, that most of the suicide bombings in the markets happened. The markets were where the insurgents got the highest number of kills.

Inside the IZ looking toward the Tigris River and Baghdad. The tent-like structure is where the main swimming pool was for the IZ. The pool was built by one of Saddam's sons for his parties. A mortar round landed on the edge of it one afternoon, and it had to be closed for repairs. Sadr City is the farthest part of the picture. It is home of Muqtada al Sadr's "Mahdi Army," the biggest anti-American militia in the country.

Trailer park inside the U.S. Embassy (Republican Palace) compound.

The Ministry of Defense in the background with parts of Phoenix Base
in the foreground. Phoenix Base was the home of MNSTC-I, and
is about a mile north of the Republican Palace. We are about to land
at the LZ inside Phoenix Base.

A good look at the front of the Ministry of Defense building. The United States spent $58 million dollars renovating it. It had no air conditioning for over a year because LTG Dempsey refused to pay $48,000 for a longer cable to connect a brand new generator to the building. The building in the background was the former Iraqi Ministry of Planning.

Iraqi soldiers ready for a parade in front of the Ministry of Defense.

All of the military in the Iraqi armed forces had to swear an oath to the new government and constitution.

The Iraqi Army Band.

The ziggurat-shaped Council of Ministers Hall that was destroyed the opening night of the invasion on March 20, 2003. This building was seen around the world engulfed in flames.

Shock and Awe!

Damage to one of the 19 new (and still unoccupied) buildings that MNSTC-I J-7 constructed for the 5th Brigade, 6th Division of the Iraqi Army at FOB Honor, located in the IZ. Anywhere within the IZ was an easy target for 122mm mortars fired from anywhere outside the IZ.

The Hall of Meetings at FOB Honor destroyed during the invasion. The 5th Brigade of the Iraqi Army 6th Division occupies sections of it for living quarters.

The Crossed Swords at Saddam's parade field in Baghdad. The hands holding the swords were molded from his own. There was a matching pair of swords at the other end of the field. The Iraqi flag has Arabic script in Saddam's handwriting. He even had inscriptions on monuments with ink made from his blood.

Tomb of the Unknown Soldier in Baghdad. Some of the architecture in Baghdad was very impressive.

The Baghdad Sheraton.

The radio tower in Baghdad. This is a good view of Baghdad and how large it is. The weather was always perfect. Great place for a resort!

Camp Victory, west of Baghdad and next to the International Airport. This was a resort built by Saddam—many were built during the 'sanctions' after the Gulf War—where he had numerous palaces for himself, members of his family, and guests. The water was stocked with fish for their pleasure. It was taken over by the Coalition (the US) and was the headquarters of MNF-I, the Multi-National Forces-Iraq. General George Casey lived in one of the palaces for two and a half years while Iraq went down the toilet.

The Tigris River flowing through Baghdad.

Baghdad from the air.

Baghdad from the air.

After an explosion, quite possibly a suicide bomber, somewhere in Baghdad. We would hear these explosions all the time, and often feel their concussion. They would be followed by the plume of black smoke afterwards that would last all day.

The Al-Askari, or "Golden Mosque" in Samarra, north of Baghdad. It was blown up twice by Sunni extremists. An Iraqi infantry brigade was going to be placed along the highway between Baghdad and Samarra to protect travelers on the way to and from the mosque for worship.

The mosque became a focus of the civil war between the
Sunni and Shia, and the new Iraqi government's inability to
do anything about it, or to rebuild the mosque.

Typical view of the Iraq countryside and one
of its thousands of irrigation canals.

The Euphrates River.

Date palms.

The Blackhawk had a machine gun on both sides.

A wealthy man's house.

Waiting for the helicopter to be re-fueled. We would have to
get off the aircraft and walk 100 feet away from it whenever it
re-fueled in case of an explosion.

Defensive tank emplacements. A hole is dug and the tank rolled in, while a
"berm" of dirt from the hole is built around the tank in the direction of the
approaching enemy, shielding it from view. The main gun of the tank sticks
out over the berm in the direction of the enemy. This is how all armies set up
a tank in a defensive position.

One of thousands of tank and infantry trenches dug by the Iraqi army during the last war, or possibly the Gulf War. These could be seen everywhere from the air. The trench was designed to allow Iraqi soldiers to move along its length and not be seen, while not being at a parallel or perpendicular angle to an approaching enemy. I doubt its shape ("W") had any political significance.

Al Asad Air Base in Anbar province. Built by the Soviets, the air strip is on a plateau, while the hangers for the aircraft are in the sides of the hills that slope down from it. The main base is at the bottom along a waddie.

Hulks of old Iraqi Air Fore Soviet era jets, in desert camouflage.

The head cook for the Iraqi army brigade headquarters at Al Asad, in his 'field kitchen.' The Iraqi unit was at the far end of Al Asad, while the Marines occupied the main part of the base with all of the buildings and roads.

The kitchen and staff.

Preparing dinner.

The 'field stove,' which has multiple uses. It can also be used as a mattress spring, after it cools down.

Dinner with the Iraqi Brigade at Al Asad. I loved the bread, and it started to show.

Old farm house on the corner of the base at Al Asad. J-7 was building a new camp for the Iraqis on this spot. Of course the entire base belonged to the Iraqis, but not according to the Marine major who thought the camp belonged to him and his Marines.

The oasis at Al Asad, where Abraham stopped to rest on his journey across the desert.

An archaeologist's dream.

With my roommate, the retired U.S. Army colonel who thought the culture of
the Iraqi people didn't mean a thing. He retired from the Army with one
month's notice to go to Iraq and make the big bucks. This is hardly any notice
after serving 29 years on active duty.

8—MNSTC-I

Author's note: The descriptions of the various staff sections of MNSTC-I can be confusing and difficult to follow, and for this I apologize. However, this shows the inherent confusion in the structure of the organization, resulting in its ineffectiveness.

The Multi-National Security Transition Command-Iraq (or MNSTC-I, pronounced "min-sticky"), was the only other element commanded by a U.S. Army three-star general in the country. It was at the same command level as MNC-I, and was responsible for 'standing up' the Iraqi Ministry of Defense (MOD) and Ministry of Interior (MOI). In effect, this meant getting these two Iraqi ministries started again from nothing, to the point where they could stand on their own to protect and defend the entire country without any outside assistance. This was not possible for reasons I shall explain in detail. Paul Bremer disbanded these same two ministries when he was in charge of the Coalition Provisional Authority. Logic follows that the sole reason for the existence of MNSTC-I was to reverse what Bremer did. Instead of just "de-Ba'athification" of the senior generals in both the Iraqi army and the national police, and then training and promoting the next senior officers in line who had been vetted and their loyalty to the new Iraqi constitution verified, Bremer fired everyone. Had he left the core institutions in place, with their mid-level managers and commanders, there would have been an Iraqi army and national police the Coalition could have worked with and trained to defend and secure the country. Instead, Bremer left Iraq with no security forces of its own, and the Coalition with little to protect the country and mold into an effective fighting army and police force. It fell on MNSTC-I to do this herculean task.

Before MNSTC-I was fully in place to take on these roles and duties, a 'food fight' occurred between the U.S. Department of State and the Department of Defense, long time institutional rivals. To begin, State is a liberal/pacifist department, while Defense is hawkish. State is about the use of diplomacy, while Defense is about the use of force (at least it's supposed to be).

From these different views organizational disputes arise every day. These disputes fall over into budget battles, and it is usually up to the President to resolve them. If the President is a hawk, such as Reagan was, Defense will get the lion's share of the money. If the President is a dove, like Bill Clinton was, State will get it. However, when George W. Bush brought Colin Powell on as Secretary of State and Donald Rumsfeld as Secretary of Defense, the fight became far more intense. Both men had the President's ear and respect, and the country's attention and admiration. Yet, after 9/11 it was Rumsfeld who prevailed, while Powell took a back seat, which he had not bargained for. This is understandable in light of the attacks of 9/11, whereby national defense and the protection of our country was paramount on everyone's mind. Rumsfeld had an easy argument to prove. This is probably one reason why Powell went to the UN, even though he must have known the case for war (e.g., WMD) was weak. He went there because he still wanted to be a player on the world and domestic scene. His days in Washington, however, were numbered. He was not in the mainstream of a neocon administration that wanted to preemptively go after anyone who opposed the United States, and he had completely blown his reputation and his credibility with his bogus and futile UN appearance. He later became a sock puppet for Barack Hussein Obama.

It is said that what goes around comes around. If Colin Powell had done what he should have done during, and at the end of, the Gulf War he would have been the hero of the age along with the first President Bush and General Schwarzkopf. Instead, he ended up being a dupe for the second President Bush and his hatchet man, Rumsfeld. Fortunately for our country Powell is out of the limelight and we don't have to listen to his bogus advice and counsel anymore. It wasn't any good in the first place.

After the initial phases of Operation Iraqi Freedom (OIF) ended, it was left to the State Department to sort out the new Iraqi government and draft its new constitution. The State Department created the Iraqi Reconstruction Management Office, IRMO, to do this. The task of IRMO was to advise, train and equip the new Iraqi government and its respective cabinet ministries. It all looked good on paper, but it never worked in Iraq. Instead of a smooth transition to a democratically-elected government, the effort was a disaster. The primary reason was because we wanted the Iraqis to do things our way, which was simply not possible. That was never going to happen—not then, not today, not tomorrow, never. They are Iraqi, they are Middle Eastern, and we aren't. We can't expect Iraqis to do anything the way we do it, including going to the bathroom. (Westerners go to the bathroom sitting on a toilet. Iraqis, all Middle Easterners, and most of the world squat over a hole in the ground or in the floor. I once saw someone's footprints on a toilet seat!)

The IRMO plan could have worked if the insurgency hadn't happened. Its job was for State and the other U.S. Cabinet departments to advise their new Iraqi counterpart ministries. However, the insurgency that began in 2004-2005 between the Sunnis and the Shi'ites turned all that around. Much of this insurgency was fueled by the Shia from Iran to the east, and the Sunni from Syria and Saudi Arabia (where most of the 9/11 hijackers were from) to the west. But now, without its army or national police and a skeleton U.S. Army to defend the country, who was there to protect the people and the country whose dictator was in prison awaiting execution? (The trial was a formality, everyone knew Saddam was not long for this world.) The State Department was ill-equipped to deal with Iraq's two "security ministries," as their Ministries of Interior and Defense were called, so our Defense Department stepped in and said it wanted the job. State still wanted to keep it, but Defense won out and created MNSTC-I.

The first commander of MNSTC-I was none other than David Petraeus. He was a two-star general at the time, not yet having gone back to the States to take over Fort Leavenworth and get his third star. From all accounts I heard in Iraq, General Petraeus did a decent job running MNSTC-I and made a lot of progress. More will be discussed about this later. That is about the best that can be said for his command, and for the organization itself. MNSTC-I was the most convoluted and dysfunctional organization, military or otherwise, I have ever been associated with. I know because I served as a member of its staff for 14 months. Everyone joked about it constantly and talked about how bad it was. This included retired military people, as most of the civilian contractors were. The only ones who didn't were the senior ranking officers, who would never say anything negative about the organization, including its dysfunction, for fear of getting into trouble. Speaking one's mind the higher one goes in the military is not going to happen, so fresh ideas and new ways of doing things never get to the table and get implemented. It was only the contractors who had the courage to say anything, because they didn't have to worry about their next promotion. But if they did they got fired and sent home on the first flight out. This was because the firms they worked for wanted to keep getting government contracts in Iraq (and Afghanistan), and the only way to maintain this was to say nothing, do what the military wanted, and keep their mouths shut. Nearly all the managers of these companies were retired military officers themselves, so they just continued with the same behavior as they had while on active duty. Employees of these companies who spoke their minds were let go and replaced by new people who were strongly encouraged by their managers to keep their mouths shut when they got to Iraq. This way the firm could keep getting hired by the military to support it.

To prove the point my employer in Iraq had a form it asked all of its employees to sign. The form was a waiver of our right to say or write anything we saw or heard in Iraq after we returned. I was asked to sign the form the day before I left, and refused. Why would I sign something that allows my former employer to sue me if I say (or write) something it doesn't like. I wanted to write this book, so I didn't sign it. Everything here is true, and my former employer wouldn't like seeing it in print because the truth would make it look bad, as well as its client, the U.S. Department of Defense. I didn't sign the form, but I'm not mentioning the name of my former employer either.

When I arrived in Iraq in July of 2006, MNSTC-I was commanded by Lieutenant General (three-star) Martin Dempsey, a 1974 graduate of West Point. General Dempsey was a very likable guy, and took pride in his singing voice, which he liked to show off. He sang at the West Point "Founders Day" dinner at Camp Blackhawk, one of several camps or FOBs (Forward Operating Bases), inside the International Zone in Baghdad. The

West Point Founder's Day dinner is held on the anniversary of the founding of West Point in 1802. It is held in cities around the world and every military installation where West Point graduates are. It's a great opportunity for gathering together and telling "war stories," but mostly to reminisce about cadet life.

One of the limitations of life in Iraq was General Order #1, which stipulated there would be absolutely no drinking by all Americans in the CENTCOM theater of operations, (e.g., Iraq and Afghanistan), also no pornography, adultery, etc. It was a standing order from the CENTCOM Commander located in Tampa, Florida! It was a joke. No one followed it, but it was an order just the same. If you didn't follow it and got caught, you could be subject to disciplinary action and court martial if you were in the military. If you were a civilian you could be sent home. The State Department, specifically the U.S. Embassy and its staff in the IZ, took the position they didn't have to adhere to General Order #1. So they didn't. State Department employees could be seen drinking in front of military personnel all the time, not giving a hoot about the consequences. The U.S. Ambassador, Zalmay Kahlilzad, didn't enforce General Order #1 because it was issued by the CENTCOM Commander and not the Secretary of State.

There has always been dispute over who is the higher ranking U.S. official in a foreign country, the U.S. Ambassador or the U.S. Commanding General if he is a full four-star. Usually they split the difference and say they are equally in charge and everyone is happy. But in the case of General Order #1, the State Department employees were not going to follow it because that would mean they couldn't drink and screw around. The result was the military and all its civilian contractors were subject to it, while the State Department staff and all its contractors weren't. They were all very happy, while the military and its contractors couldn't stand it. One Air Force Captain at MNSTC-I, who was clearly an alcoholic, got drunk and ran into a barricade with a Ford Explorer. He was going to be court-martialed, or given a lesser punishment, an Article 15 issued by a U.S. Air Force general. Either way his career was over. He went to the office of the general who was going to issue his punishment. The office was in the Republican Palace, where the U.S. Embassy was located. While he was waiting a couple of young female Embassy staffers walked by him talking about the party they had the night before and that everyone had gotten drunk out of their skulls. Nothing was going to happen to them, but this poor guy was going to be kicked out of the Air Force with nearly 15 years of active duty. He had a serious drinking problem, and maybe it was the best thing that could have happened to him. Maybe it steered him toward getting some help.

The DoD people with alcohol or drug problems didn't bother going crazy because of General Order #1. They simply defied the order and drank and/or drugged anyway. The Air Force captain's problem was that he got caught. Many people, military and civilian, were sent home because their drinking got out of control. I heard a story about a reserve Army lieutenant colonel during the initial phases of OIF. While flying back to the States he got so drunk the plane was forced to make an emergency landing because the crew thought he was dying. When the incident got back to his military unit he was discharged from the Army Reserves. As a reservist he had a full time civilian job—as a social worker specializing in addiction treatment.

I would walk into IRMO offices in the embassy wing of the Republican Palace and see full blown bars. Staff would walk to the free deli downstairs and load up with as many sodas as they could carry to use as mixers for the after-work party at the end of the day, which was any time they decided the day was over. This went on all the time because there wasn't anything else to do, unless one had a partner for casual sex. There were many heavy drinkers in Iraq who got away with it because their spouses weren't around. Many contractors were in Iraq because they were free to drink (and do drugs) without their spouse coming down on them. If someone had a drinking problem before they went to Iraq, they had a much bigger one by the time they left. Of this I had no doubt at all. The situation was ideal for this. As for extramarital sex, that's all the Catholic chaplain talked about during his sermons. He was obviously doing a lot of counseling in that area and knew it was going on all the time. A lot of contractors stayed in Iraq for two, three and four years, and in a few cases even five, because they enjoyed the freedom of drinking and drugging away from their spouse, and probably the sex too. Of course, the money was fabulous. So if someone had an alcohol or drug issue, wanted to screw around outside their marriage, and get paid great money all at the same time, Iraq was the place to be.

One place that people figured General Order #1 didn't apply was the British Embassy because it was 'foreign soil.' The first time I went there I couldn't believe how nice it was. The swimming pool was on par with any four or five-star hotel, with a full bar right next door on the "veranda." I went there for a function once and saw several U.S. Army officers, including CPATT Commander Major General Kenneth Hunzeker, drinking like it was no big deal—in his uniform. Seeing the general was a shock because General Order #1 was a very big deal. Even though we were at the British Embassy, that didn't mean we were beyond the intent of General Order #1, which applied to the entire CENTCOM theater of operations. The order didn't say it was OK to drink at a foreign embassy. I know because I read it. We were told to read it. I'm sure MG Hunzeker read it too. People like the general were splitting hairs with the order just like the embassy staffers were, only using different excuses. He should have been above that. If U.S. Army soldiers or contractors saw a general drink at the British Embassy, they were certainly going to drink too. Why shouldn't they? If they did it there, they would do it other places too. Where would it stop?

MG Hunzeker was later promoted to three-star general. For a large part of his one-year tour in Iraq he was back in the States for medical treatment. If he was medically unable to perform his duties how did he get assigned to Iraq, which was very demanding physically? How did he get promoted? I know an active duty four-star general who's had a pacemaker in his chest for over 15 years. How has he pulled that off? The Army is a tough life, and I knew guys who were discharged for the slightest medical condition. But once a senior officer was selected for assignment to Iraq, it didn't matter if he could do his job or not. There were many general officers who didn't serve in Iraq, and I would bet most of them didn't get their next star. But if one was sent to Iraq it was tantamount to being promoted. Iraq was simply a rubber stamp on their resume. Once MG Hunzeker got sent to Iraq, his third star was in the bag. However, there was one thing I found very impressive about MG Hunzeker: he was the only general officer in Iraq who rode in a HUMVEE and not a Suburban, and the only one protected by U.S. Army soldiers and not security contractors. I hope his health is better.

My manager would get all bent out of shape when people wouldn't follow General Order #1 simply because it had been issued by a four-star general. It didn't have to make sense, it just had to be followed. I once told him if someone wanted to drink while they were in Iraq they were going to, and no order issued from a general in Tampa, Florida was going to stop them. He was trying to be righteous and show how much he followed orders. He was a buffoon who would have walked off a cliff if a general told him to. After I saw General Hunzeker drinking at the British Embassy, colleagues told me they had seen General Dempsey drinking there too. If Dempsey was doing it, Hunzeker was OK because Dempsey was his boss.

Even though I thought the enforcement of General Order #1 was a joke, I was disappointed when I heard about Dempsey. How could a general who drank at the British Embassy enforce General Order #1 against a soldier who had gotten smashed, but not at the British Embassy? These generals had no problem with this double standard. If the generals, or anyone else, wanted to drink that bad why couldn't they just do it in the privacy of their room and not in front of the people who worked for them? This was another example of the arrogance of high ranking officers who think, because they have risen to the level they have, they can get away with anything. If you look at Tommy Franks letting his wife sit in on classified briefings, or Norman Schwarzkopf rising to the rank of four-star general when he was over the Army's weight limit by probably 100 pounds, then it's easy to see why they think this way. People will do whatever others allow them to get away with doing. If no one above these generals says anything, they'll do whatever they want. Then again, no one should have to say anything to them. They should have the integrity to follow the orders of their superiors on their own. But don't let the common soldier get caught doing the exact same thing. He's screwed. Generals who drank, no matter where they did it, were not only violating General Order #1, they were thumbing their noses at their four-star commander in Florida, right in front of everyone else, soldier and civilian. Great examples of leadership. Both Generals Hunzeker and Dempsey have been promoted to the next higher rank of three- and four-star general, respectively.

The mission of MNSTC-I was to get the Iraqi Ministry of Defense and Ministry of Interior up and running from scratch. The Ministry of Defense was responsible for the Iraqi army, navy and air force (its national protection), while the Ministry of Interior was responsible for the national police (its internal protection). When Paul Bremer disbanded both ministries he created the void in security that has been mentioned. When added to the minimum number of U.S. forces Rumsfeld and Franks used in the invasion, Bremer's actions created a huge pool of newly unemployed soldiers and policemen, many still carrying their weapons, who became potential recruits for the insurgency. After our Defense-State battle ended, MNSTC-I was tasked with the mission of getting these two ministries started again, essentially from nothing, all thanks to Paul Bremer.

MNSTC-I was made up of so many organizations it took the average person months to figure out all its different parts. Whenever I tried to explain MNSTC-I to new arrivals I would be working with, their eyes would glaze over because it was too complicated for them to follow. I realized it was better to let them figure it out on their own. The MNSTC-I organization consisted of its own staff, called the "J" staff because it was comprised of "joint forces" from the different military components. (Staff elements have different designations based upon their level in the Army hierarchy. For example, all the staff sections in a battalion are called the "S" staff, with the "S-1" being the Personnel Officer, the "S-2" the Intelligence Officer, the "S-3" the Operations Officer, and so on. As the levels of command go higher, the letter designations of these same staff functions change. If the unit is commanded by a general, the staff sections begin with the letter "G.")

The various "J" staff sections of MNSTC-I performed a variety of missions, primarily for the Iraqi Ministries of Defense and Interior, and also for MNSTC-I itself. In reality MNSTC-I was the *de facto* headquarters staff of MOD and MOI. The staff section I had the most dealing with was J-7, the Construction Branch of MNSTC-I.

The only mission of J-7 was to build facilities needed by the Ministry of Defense and the Ministry of Interior. The other parts of the MNSTC-I performed staff functions needed by MNSTC-I, as well as the Iraqi Ministries of Defense and Interior. In this sense J-7's function was strictly for the MOD and MOI, making it the *de facto* construction unit of the Iraqi Ministry of Defense and Ministry of Interior. J-7 was totally responsible for the physical infrastructure of the security ministries of Iraq, a huge responsibility that I will describe in a separate chapter.

The organization of MNSTC-I was critical. It was as though MNSTC-I was a part of these two Iraqi ministries, or an extension of them. But because MNSTC-I's dysfunction and the lack of coordination and control of its various staff elements, the Iraqi Ministry of Defense and Ministry of Interior were years away from being capable of standing on their own. MNSTC-I's dysfunction was passed on to both the Ministry of Defense and Ministry of Interior, leading them to be just as bad. In later chapters I will detail what this means to Iraq's capability of defending itself, and the implications for its future security. Suffice it to say, MNSTC-I's failure regarding MOD and MOI was a microcosm of America's failure regarding Iraq in general.

There were more parts to MNSTC-I than just its primary J-staff sections. MNSTC-I was made up of many other functional areas, all under the command of its three-star general, all having different missions. The organization was hard, if not impossible, to make any sense of. It was also impossible to effectively manage. In addition to the primary J-staff elements described above, MNSTC-I was made up of "transition teams" and "training teams," or "TT's," each addressing different parts of the Ministry of Defense and Ministry of Interior. MNSTC-I's other components were: the Ministry of Defense Transition Team (MODTT); the Ministry of Interior Transition Team (MOITT); the Coalition Police Assistance Training Team (CPATT); the Joint Headquarters Transition Team (JHQTT); the Ministry of Defense Logistics Transition Team (M-4-TT, which was part of JHQTT); the Health Affairs Transition Team (HATT); the Coalition Military Assistance Training Team (CMATT); and the Coalition Air Force Transition Team (CAFTT). Needless to say, the workings of these various staff elements proved difficult at best. The worst thing was getting any of it to make sense to the Iraqis we were there to advise.

From MNF-I down, the entire organizational structure of the Coalition was dysfunctional and impossible to make sense of to the Iraqis we were there to advise and help get on their feet. We couldn't even figure it all out ourselves and make it work, so how could it be made to work for them? But nowhere was MNF-I more dysfunctional than MNSTC-I, an organization of around 2,500 people including American military, Coalition (non-American) military, American civilian contractors and advisors, and non-American civilian contractors and advisors. Critical factors were the roles and relationships of, and between, the U.S. military and the U.S. civilian contractors in Iraq, which are described in later chapters. These roles and relationships are directly related to our nation's growing dependency on the "military-industrial complex" President Eisenhower warned us about in 1962.

Suffice it to say, the military didn't want us contractors there for several reasons, not the least of which was their envy of the money we were making. Another reason was all the experience we had in our subject areas, which the military felt made them look bad, and in many cases it did. As things turned out we were not only advising the Iraqis, we were keeping tabs on the MNSTC-I staff doing work for the Ministries of Defense and Interior, who were our customers. We wanted to make sure work done on behalf of MOD and MOI was satisfactory, and why not. That's what we were there for. The last thing MNSTC-I's military wanted was us contractors commenting on how they were doing their job, or the quality of their work. This is where I got into trouble.

Just as the U.S. Department of Defense has two sides, the military and the civilian, so did the Iraqi Ministry of Defense. We designed it that way. The military side of the U.S. Department of Defense is composed of the Joint Chiefs of Staff. The civilian side is composed of the various Under Secretaries and Assistant Secretaries for Personnel, Logistics, Finance, etc. The civilian side provides support to the military side of DoD, allowing our military to wage war. The same basic structure exists in the Iraqi Ministry of Defense, which I advised. MOD had its military side, the Joint Headquarters Staff, and civilian side, the Directors General, or DGs. These were equivalent to our Assistant and Under Secretaries in the Department of Defense.

I worked in the Ministry of Defense Transition Team (MODTT), an organization of about 50 civilian advisors. Our job was to advise the civilian side of the Iraqi Ministry of Defense. There was also the Joint Headquarters Transition Team (JHQTT), whose job it was to advise the military side of the Ministry of Defense. In theory it all made sense. In reality it didn't work at all. Because so much emphasis was placed on "coalition building," the head of my team was a British civil servant from his own Ministry of Defense in London. A nice fellow, but he had no business running an organization made up almost completely of Americans, especially when the United States was paying the freight for everything and providing 95% of the soldiers in Iraq.

Due to political correctness, there were non-Americans running key parts of the MNSTC-I organization. They were all over the place. The British and Australians actually took "cultural awareness" training before arriving in Iraq to learn how to deal with Americans! Because the head of my team was British, his main concern was for the Commonwealth members of his staff, and not the Americans. The Joint Headquarters Transition Team was headed up by an Australian Brigadier General. Whenever these people rotated out, they would be replaced by another person of the same rank or civilian grade from the same country. When the head of MODTT, David Murtagh, left Iraq he was replaced by John Cochrane, who also came from the British Ministry of Defense in London. Therefore, the two senior advisors to the military and civilian sides of the Iraqi Ministry of Defense weren't Americans.

I was hired to be the Real Estate Advisor to the Iraqi Ministry of Defense. I was employed by a firm in Alexandria, Virginia, which was a division of a major U.S. corporation. After I returned home, whenever I told someone my job title they would ask what I was doing selling houses in Iraq! When the average person thinks of real estate, all that comes to mind is a "FOR SALE" sign on someone's front lawn. Most people have no idea there's difference between residential and commercial real estate.

Unless they're in the business, they don't have a clue what commercial real estate is. On the slim chance someone did know, they would usually ask me what real estate had to do with the war. My job was to advise the Iraqi Ministry of Defense on everything relating to its land and buildings, include its military installations. That's why I had to work with J-7.

When I arrived J-7 was headed by an active duty U.S. Navy Captain, the equivalent of an Army full Colonel. He was responsible for about twenty military personnel, most of them reservists, and a few civilians. His deputy was a U.S. Army Lieutenant Colonel, who was a reservist from Mississippi. His full time civilian job was teaching high school. All construction for the Iraqi military and national police was being supervised by a single active duty U.S. Navy captain, who had been in the Pentagon for five years before coming to Iraq. At his going away party before leaving Iraq, the captain admitted he had never been responsible for a construction project over $12 million dollars during his entire career. By industry standards this is peanuts. Based on his responsibilities as the chief of J-7, this was a comparison between a one-car garage and the Bellagio in Las Vegas. Yet, in Iraq he was the sole person responsible for the oversight of billions worth of construction for these two Iraqi ministries. And most of his senior staff were reservists who hadn't put on their uniform in years, other than one weekend a month and a couple of weeks during the summer.

The results of this poorly staffed and poorly run organization showed. The captain never made an effort to determine who owned the land upon which he was constructing new Iraqi army camps, or the land on which new police or border stations were located. I asked him once if he would build a house on land he didn't own back in the States, and he just grunted. He simply didn't care, and he certainly wasn't going to listen to some civilian contractor. After all, he was a U.S. Navy Captain. To him, I was nothing. I would get this same treatment the entire time I spent in Iraq, to include getting it from the captain's replacement, a U.S. Navy Captain, as well as the new deputy, a U.S. Navy Commander.

I went to my boss, David Murtagh, the British Ministry of Defense civil servant, and told him what was going on regarding title to the land J-7 was building on. He couldn't have cared less. At one point I asked to have a meeting with him and the navy captain to discuss the issue. The meeting began with the Navy captain talking directly to David Murtagh, leaving me completely out of the conversation, yet I was the one who asked for the meeting. Finally, I had to force myself into the conversation. I started with the issue of finding better ways to determine ownership of land where the captain was building Iraqi military camps. This was for the captain's benefit so he wouldn't be in any land title trouble. He simply refused to listen to anything I had to say. I tried to explain the difficulty traveling to the Land Registration Office in each province where the land records were kept. The only way to determine who owned land the captain wanted to build camps on was to get to these offices. I had previously given him the complete list of these offices, which he claimed he had never seen before I gave it to him. With the list he could identify who owned these properties and compensate them for their land. He didn't care.

The captain had staff who could travel to these offices, and who had gone to some of them already. But the ones who really needed to travel to these offices were the real estate staff from the Ministry of Defense, who the captain was building the camps for. When I finally got a chance to speak, I explained all of this to the captain and David Murtagh. I explained the problem the Coalition was creating by violating the private property rights of Iraqi citizens when their land was taken without their permission or just compensation. I asked the captain for his help getting MOD real estate staff to the land registration offices because they had no way of getting to them on their own. I got nowhere with the captain, and David Murtagh started talking about "geopolitics." The meeting ended with nothing resolved other than the captain being pissed off at me.

My intention was to prevent a situation where the Iraqi Ministry of Defense, and the United States Government, could be held liable for taking private property without the owner's permission. No one cared. The captain was there to build Iraqi military camps, all with U.S. money, and that's what he was going to do. The legality of his actions meant absolutely nothing to him. He was in Iraq not Des Moines, so what did he care. If I had a problem with it I could get out of his way, or get run over. David Murtagh just sat there because he, like all the civilians, was not about to go against a U.S. military officer. It didn't matter if I was there to do a job, that my client was the Iraqi Ministry of Defense, or that the captain was violating the property rights of Iraqi citizens. It was my problem and I could shove it.

During the initial phases of Operation Iraqi Freedom (OIF) the U.S. military (on behalf of the entire Coalition) took land anywhere it was needed for Forward Operating Bases, or FOBs. The U.S. Army Corps of Engineers Gulf Region District (GRD) made the effort to lease land or purchase it from its Iraqi owners. The Corps honored the private property rights of Iraqi citizens, and paid them just compensation for their land. After the main combat subsided the Coalition began the process of "transitioning" responsibility for security over to the Iraqis. This was the situation when I arrived.

The U.S. wanted the Iraqi Ministries of Defense and Interior to take on the responsibility for their country's security, and we would assist them by constructing their military bases, and police and border stations. There was no possible way they could have done this on their own. When "transition" kicked in under LTG Dempsey, J-7 had complete responsibility for building all of this. However, under J-7 all pretense of proper title and taking of land went out the window. LTG Dempsey knew this but did nothing. David Murtagh knew but didn't give a damn. The Corps of Engineers, being professionals in real estate and land issues, did it right during the opening stages of the war. But the U.S. Naval officers commanding J-7 didn't have a clue about land rights and clear title. If they did, they ignored it. Hell, it was Iraq. They didn't have to worry about title. By its actions J-7, and MNSTC-I, were telling Iraqi land owners to pound sand if they wanted to be paid rent for their property.

As time went by many of the old FOBs built during the initial phases of OIF were no longer needed by the Coalition, and it wanted them turned over to the Iraqi government. When I arrived in Iraq there was no system in place to accomplish this. I heard of FOBs being left vacant by Coalition units, with no prior coordination with the Ministry of Defense to have an Iraqi army unit move in and occupy it. How could this happen, especially when these FOBs cost the U.S. government tens of millions each to build? The reason was very simple, and it was the cause for 99% of the problems in Iraq—no one told the Iraqis what was going on, in this case that a FOB was going to be vacated and available for their new army to occupy. When the Coalition unit left, the local population living near the FOB moved in. They also gutted everything in sight, resulting in the losses of millions every time this occurred.

I contacted the basing and facilities staff from both MNF-I and MNC-I, the ones whose units occupied these FOBs, and asked them to let me know when they planned to vacate them. On only two occasions was I informed of a pending FOB transfer: for the transfers of FOB Sommerall and FOB Arlington. These were near the oil refinery at Baiji, which was captured by the Islamic State in 2014 to fund its terror operations. Baiji is north of Saddam's home town of Tikrit. I tried to coordinate their transfer from the Coalition to MOD with the U.S. advisors at JHQTT so an Iraqi army unit could occupy them, but this effort went nowhere. I'm not sure if an Iraqi army unit ever moved in, but I do know the Ministry of Defense's Director General for Infrastructure and the Director of the Real Estate Division never played a role in these two transfers, never knew what happened, never placed them in their inventory, and were ignored by both the Coalition as well as the Iraqi Joint Headquarters Staff. Other than these two locations, I was never informed of any FOB transfer to coordinate its turnover to the MOD, with the Real Estate Director and his staff assisting their military counterparts at the JHQ.

There were dozens of FOBs released and vacated by the Coalition, but the MOD staff section that existed to deal with these property turnovers was never involved. If a local Iraqi army unit was stationed nearby it could just move in if the commander had the backbone to do it. But if there wasn't an Iraqi military unit around, the FOB was left empty to be gutted by the locals. The Coalition's dysfunction made sure it turned out that way. Instead, all we heard General Dempsey talk about was transition, and General Casey telling everyone the Iraqis were ready to step up and take over any time. The Iraqis at MOD had no travel capability beyond their personal vehicles in Baghdad. Even if they knew that a FOB was going to be vacated, and they were going to be given it for free from the U.S. government, the Coalition refused to provide transportation for them to the location to inspect and accept it. The Iraqis insisted on conducting their own inspection of FOBs and everything the Coalition had built for them, and the Coalition knew this. Instead of cooperating, the Coalition wanted the Iraqis to accept and sign for any transferred FOBs without seeing them, which the Iraqis refused to do. Who could blame them?

It became clear that nothing was going to change the way the Coalition (i.e., the U.S. military) was going to conduct the business of land acquisition, basing of Iraqi military units, or the transfer of former Coalition FOBs to Iraqi control. I arrived in Iraq with over 20 years of experience in real estate at the time which included commercial real estate in both the Federal Government and in private industry. I had spent nearly 10 years working for the U.S. General Services Administration in Washington, DC, where I was a warranted Contracting Officer with no dollar limit to sign Federal contracts. I was also a licensed real estate agent in three states. I knew what I was talking about.

Around this time I started to realize the dilemma of being a contractor in Iraq. I was just a warm body who was a source of revenue for my company to collect fees off the U.S. government. That was it, and nothing more. No one cared if I accomplished a thing, or if I had years of experience to offer the Coalition and the Iraqis in my specific field. The U.S. military actually didn't want me to do anything if it was going to run counter to what they wanted to do, were planning to do, or were going to do, regardless of whether I was the real estate "subject matter expert" who they had hired through my firm. I later found out that my position was originally created by two officers who were on the J-7 staff before the arrival of the Navy Captain. They knew the importance of land ownership in Iraq, but they were both long gone. The navy captain wouldn't listen to a thing I had to say regarding a field he knew nothing about, but should have cared a lot about. The question for me became—why am I here?

The firm I worked for was started about 25 years ago by a group of retired U.S. Army lieutenant colonels who got Army contracts running rifle ranges. During the conflict in Bosnia the company started consulting and performing advisory work for DoD. A former U.S. Army Chief of Staff took over the reins of the firm about fifteen years ago, and his #2 man is another retired four-star general. The obvious reason for their presence is to rub shoulders with current Army brass to get contracts awarded to their company. If a retired four-star general walks into the office of an active duty 3- or four-star general, or senior civilian, and asks for business what are they going to say? Even in retirement a four-star general carries a huge amount of clout, and no one is going to make him wait outside their office.

My firm started to get these consulting contracts, but after 9/11 the barn doors flew open. From 2003 to 2007 the company made $1 billion in Afghanistan and Iraq. It's everywhere the U.S. military is. It even received a large contract to support the U.S. Centers for Disease Control in Atlanta, Georgia, assisting CDC in its preparation for the outbreak of the avian flu. Apparently it was able to sell its management expertise to the CDC Director. That's great for the firm, but it doesn't say much for the CDC's ability to manage an epidemic.

It would have been great if the company's management had allowed its staff to do what it was hired to do by the client paying the bill. I was hired by my firm, which was hired by the U.S. military, to advise the Iraqi Ministry of Defense on its real estate issues. This included getting its real estate staff up to a functional level. But when I saw J-7 doing something for MOD that was wrong, if I mentioned it to them I was ignored. The only other option I had left was to take it to my manager. Isn't that what you're supposed to do?

He was one of the most incompetent people I have ever met, and that's saying something. A retired U.S. Army lieutenant colonel, he was responsible for the contract I worked on. He never did anything except sit at his desk all day staring at his computer. If anyone had a question or a problem, he would start talking about anything that popped into his mind, like the two or three months he spent in Vietnam, or when he was with our firm in Afghanistan, or anything other than the issue you dropped by to discuss with him. (He arrived in Vietnam just as the war was winding down so he went around trying to find a "command." He commanded an Infantry company for about one month, but that's all he ever talked about. He had received his commission after graduating from the ROTC program at Niagara University.) If you really had a difficult situation, he was of no help at all. He simply refused to discuss it, and on occasion he threw people out of his office. The folks at our company headquarters knew all about it, but refused to fire him. People quit because of him, yet the firm did nothing. Needless to say, he was no help at all regarding my problems with J-7.

I went to this clown once with a leave request to go to Jordan for a few days. Our firm's leave policy for those of us in Iraq was pretty good. They didn't count days of travel to or from your destination. For example, if I wanted to fly back home to the States, I had two days of travel at either end of my trip that didn't count against my vacation, as long as I flew via Kuwait. If I flew via another route, such as Jordan, I got one free day of travel at either end of the trip. I wasn't aware of the one-day policy when I filled out my leave request, so it had two days at either end of the trip when I turned it in to my manager. He asked me what the request was for, when it was obvious it was for a vacation to Jordan. He suddenly went nuts and yelled at me to fill the request out again, but not because I had the travel days wrong. He was pissed off that I had the nerve to request a vacation to Jordan, and not to the United States! He said vacations were for going home to the States, which was complete bullshit. I told him he was wrong and that vacation time I had earned was mine to use any way I wanted. I also told him other people on his contract had travelled to Italy and Switzerland for vacations, a fact he was fully aware of. He went through the roof, telling me to return the next day with a revised leave request, and talking to me like I was one of his privates in the 82nd. I mentioned all this to a co-worker who had been there awhile, who said our manager had no idea what our firm's travel policy was.

I researched my company's leave policy and saw the distinction regarding travel days. I went back and gave my manager a revised request, this time bringing the company's policy as backup. My revised request was totally accurate, and I had accrued the days I wanted to use for my vacation. Then I handed him the company travel policy. He looked at it for about half a second and threw it on the floor. He started to berate me again, this time about my "attitude," to which I responded that must be the real reason he was putting me through this treatment. After this little exchange he kicked me out of his office. He wasn't upset about inaccuracies on the travel form, which he didn't know were inaccuracies in the first place. He wasn't really upset about my plans to travel to Jordan. He just didn't like my attitude, which was his way of saying he didn't like me.

If my manager thought I had a bad attitude, what sort of attitude was I supposed to have when he was denying my right to use accrued leave as I wanted? He knew leave could be used to travel anywhere on the globe, he just didn't want me to use it that way. When I stood up to him about the company's travel policy instead of crawling out of his office with my tail between my legs, he blew a gasket. Handing him the company's travel policy was the straw that broke the camel's back. He was the same manager who couldn't believe people would drink alcohol when they were precluded from doing so by General Order #1. He must have thought because he was the manager and I was one of his "charges," I would do whatever he said whether it made sense or not, just like in the army. The problem was we weren't in the army, he wasn't my commanding officer, and he didn't know the company policy, which was obvious when he threw it on the floor. He was totally incompetent, yet the company would do nothing about him. I never took the vacation because it wasn't worth the hassle. I began to see the writing on the wall.

It was sinking in that my place was not to advise the Iraqis as I had been hired to do. It was not to bring issues or problems to people's attention. It was not to get things done correctly. My job was to continue breathing and to keep my mouth shut so my company could continue to collect huge fees from my being over there, alive and in one piece and not in a pine box. If I was not there, then my position was not filled, and my company made no money. Not good for my company or its publically-traded parent. That was the real rub. I have an MBA in finance, so I have a little knowledge in this area. At companies like mine, a publically traded corporation, the only thing that matters to its management and the management of its subsidiaries, is shareholder value. It is certainly not the happiness or job satisfaction of its employees who are deployed to a combat zone. Who cares about them? Needless to say, I was not able to accomplish anything near what I could have for the Iraqi people and their Ministry of Defense. In order to do that I needed cooperation from the Coalition military staff who were constructing all the facilities for MOD, and that was certainly never going to happen as long as that Navy captain was around. I certainly wasn't going to get any help from my manager, who wasn't going to do a thing he thought might upset a U.S. military officer, even if that officer didn't know what he was doing.

What of the other MNSTC-I staff sections? On the Ministry of Interior side of MNSTC-I there was CPATT, for Coalition Police Assistance Training Team, and MOITT, for Ministry of Interior Transition Team. CPATT was led by a U.S. Army two-star general, while MOITT was led by a British Brigadier (one-star). When I first arrived in Iraq, CPATT was commanded by Major General Joseph Peterson, who was replaced about half way through my tour by Major General Kenneth Hunzeker, the guy who used to drink at the British Embassy. MOITT was led by British Brigadier Rob Weighill, who is mentioned in a later chapter.

MOITT was responsible for mentoring and advising the Iraqi Ministry of Interior, just as MODTT did for the Ministry of Defense. CPATT was separate from MOITT, but worked closely with the 'military' side of the Ministry of Interior—the National Police—which was organized and staffed like the Iraqi army. The National Police wore military uniforms like the army, only theirs were blue camouflage, whereas the army's was standard desert brown. I didn't work on the Ministry of Interior side of MNSTC-I, but I often spoke with my military and civilian colleagues who did. We all worked in the same building on Phoenix Base, the walled compound within the International Zone that was the headquarters of MNSTC-I. Many MOITT advisors also worked at the Ministry of Interior building on the other side of the Tigris River, in one of the worst sections of Baghdad. All of my MOITT colleagues preferred to work there because it was "away from the flag pole," meaning away from MNSTC-I headquarters at Phoenix Base and the accompanying bullshit. Many American military and civilian police advisors assigned to CPATT were killed or wounded while serving in Iraq. It was very much a combat assignment. These advisors worked with their Iraqi police counterparts every day in the middle of the cities and towns throughout the country. There was a hallway inside the building where we worked covered with pictures of those who had been killed-in-action as CPATT police advisors, the majority of them civilians, many of them retired police officers from the U.S.

On the Ministry of Defense side I had much more knowledge of the other sections besides the one I was assigned to. The JHQTT advised the military side of the Ministry of Defense, the Joint Headquarters Staff. The Iraqi Joint Headquarters Chief of Staff was General (four-star) Babakir, and the Deputy was General (also four-star) Abadi, whose son was a foreign exchange student at the U.S. Air Force Academy. General Abadi was an Iraqi Air Force officer, although the country's entire air force consisted of about a dozen helicopters and a few C-130 transport aircraft. The Iraqi Navy consisted of a half dozen Italian-made patrol boats in the mouth of the Tigris River where it dumps into the Persian Gulf (called the Gulf of Arabia by Iraqis), at the Al Faw Peninsula. The entire Iraqi coast is just a few miles long. The Iraqi army makes up about 98% of the country's entire military structure.

CAFTT, the Coalition Air Force Transition Team, was first commanded by Brigadier General Stephen Hoog, and later commanded by U.S. Air Force Brigadier General Robert Allardice. The mission of CAFTT was to transition the new Iraqi Air Force into an effective military unit. There was really no Iraqi "Air Force" per se. We had destroyed everything the Iraqis had that flew during both the Gulf War in 1991, and again during this conflict.

There was one incident I will never forget. One day I was sitting in a meeting with some MNSTC-I staff, mostly officers. General Allardice was the ranking officer at the meeting. He had the personality of a can opener. At one point he was in a discussion about manning strength of the Iraqi military with a U.S. Army full colonel. It got down to raw numbers, and how many Iraqi army personnel were needed versus air force personnel. General Allardice said to the colonel: "One Air Force person is worth at least 60 Army people." He was referring to the U.S. Air Force and the U.S. Army. The U.S. Army colonel just looked at him. I think the colonel thought he was joking. But it was obvious General Allardice was dead serious. You could tell he meant exactly what he said. To him a U.S. Army soldier wasn't worth a thing next to a U.S. Air Force airman. This clown just didn't get it. His Air Force supports the Army, not the other way around. He wouldn't know which end of a rifle was which, and he probably couldn't care less.

That's what a U.S. Air Force general thought of his sister service, and actually had the nerve to say to a U.S. Army full colonel, in public. He obviously looked down on the Army, the guys who have boots on the ground and take the bulk of the casualties. Brigadier General Allardice's comment brought disgrace to the U.S. Air Force. Of the U.S. military who died in Iraq since 2003, how many have been Army and how many Air Force? The ratio is about 20/1 Army/Air Force. But what did that matter to BG Allardice? What did matter was that a senior ranking U.S. military officer could say a thing like that, and get away with it. General Allardice was subsequently promoted to Lieutenant (three-star) General. The different branches of the service are all supposed to get along in the new "joint force" structure of today's modern U.S. military. That's a joke. And if he could treat an army full colonel without any respect, imagine how guys like him felt about contractors.

If General Allardice felt this way about our own army, how did he feel about the Iraqi's? What made his comment so ridiculous was the Iraqi army was probably 98% of its military strength. I don't know what General Allardice did while he was in Iraq, because there wasn't an Iraqi "Air Force" to advise. Did he think the Iraqi Air Force could defend the entire country with a half dozen C-130 transports, a dozen old Huey's, a few Bell Jet Rangers, and a handful of Mi-17 helicopters from Poland? General Allardice was one of the senior military advisors on MNSTC-I staff. If his opinion was given any merit, which it had to be based on his rank, Iraq would never be able to defend itself. BG Allardice was a geek with flight wings, but he was assigned to Iraq, so his next star was on its way.

The Ministry of Defense was supposed to be a balance between the military and the civilian sides, with the latter supporting the military in its mission of defending the country. It is led by 'civilians,' just like ours. But the reality of it is far different. All of the senior civilians at MOD were either retired generals, or active duty generals wearing suits. Because Iraq was run by a military dictator for so long, the military side runs the show. The Minister of Defense (while I was there the Minister was a former general) has a lot of power and runs the Ministry, but he can't do anything if the Joint Headquarters Staff doesn't go along. The Ministry of Defense was constantly in a state of flux, constantly changing. After I had been in Iraq about six months, we came into work one morning and the Minister of Defense, Abdul Qadir, had decided to completely reorganize the Ministry from top to bottom. So out of touch was LTG Dempsey, the senior U.S. military advisor to the Minister of Defense, and MNSTC-I commander, he didn't even know this was about to happen. Nor did David Murtagh, the senior civilian advisor to the Minister of Defense, and my MODTT boss. LTG Dempsey never included the Iraqis in on anything, so why should they let him in on what they were going to do? What goes around comes around. The entire Joint Headquarters Staff, as well as the civilian side of the Ministry of Defense, was reorganized, and no one at MNSTC-I knew it was going to happen until the day it was announced. The Ministry went through a reorganization that lasted nearly six months, and was still going through it when I left eight months after the reorganization was first announced. Of course, LTG Dempsey still got his 4th star.

There was another part of the MNSTC-I organization called CMATT, for Coalition Military Assistance Training Team. CMATT was led by a U.S. Army Brigadier General (BG) named Terry Wolff, a 1979 graduate of West Point who looked like he was 19-years-old. The first time I saw him I thought BG Wolff was a Specialist Fourth Class because his rank looked about the same from a distance. When he walked by I saw he was a one-star general and almost fell out of my chair. At first BG Wolff seemed to be a straight talker and a straight shooter. It was CMATT's job to train and equip Iraqi military units in the field, very similar to what CPATT did with the Iraqi National Police, only far safer. Instead of being embedded with Iraqi police forces in the middle of cities and towns like CPATT was with the National Police, CMATT advisors lived and worked in the middle of large Coalition camps, safe from harm's way. I never heard of a CMATT advisor being killed in Iraq, nor did it seem to get much accomplished. Its advisors were there to run training classes for the Iraq military forces. They would do this by getting in their armored vehicles and driving with armed convoy escorts down the road from the safety of the Coalition camp where they lived, which had amenities like Pizza Hut, Subway, Burger King and a Starbucks-like coffee emporium called Green Beans. They would drive from this to the squalor of the nearby Iraqi camp where the Iraqi troops they advised lived like animals.

CMATT was responsible for working with the Iraqi Joint Headquarters Staff, and so was JHQTT. This was one of the many examples of overlapping responsibilities throughout the MNSTC-I organization we had to work through and overcome. It caused nothing but problems. Each staff section at MNSTC-I did its own thing, and rarely communicated what it was doing with the others, even though their coordination would have helped the two Iraqi ministries that it was MNSTC-I's mission to advise. No one at MNSTC-I was held accountable for something if another part of the organization was also involved. It not only caused confusion, it was also a great way to deal with failure or inaction because no one was held accountable for anything. I think MNSTC-I was purposely designed that way. Of course everyone wanted to take credit when things went well, but that rarely happened. In a way MNSTC-I operated a lot like MOD itself—confusion, overlapping responsibilities, no accountability, and complete lack of coordination. It was a case of the blind leading the blind.

An example of the dysfunction of MNSTC-I was the construction of Iraqi army bases. The staff sections and transition teams involved in this one initiative were: J-5, J-7, JHQTT, CMATT, M-4-TT and MODTT. When I arrived in Iraq, I was told there was a strategic plan to have 85 permanent Iraqi garrisons (camps and installations) that would house and maintain all the forces of the Iraqi Army, Navy and Air Force for years into the future, a 'master plan' for Iraq's military installations. These garrisons were divided into groups arranged by size. The five largest were the Regional Support Units, or RSUs, and the smaller ones were the Garrison Support Units, or GSU's. The Garrison Support Units would each be capable of providing support for their own camp, to include low-level vehicle and weapons maintenance, feeding their soldiers, and storing bulk supplies. The Regional Support Units would be capable of doing what the Garrison Support Units could not do, such as higher levels of maintenance, more storage capacity, etc. On paper the layout and organization of the RSUs and the GSU's looked like an organizational chart. There were the five RSUs across the top of the chart, and the numerous GSU's underneath them, with the GSU's relying on the RSUs above them for their higher level logistical and other major support.

As time went by I heard more about the RSUs and GSU's, and what they were supposed to do. Because these bases would need land to be constructed on, the MOD Real Estate Branch was expected to be involved. The branch needed the experience of locating the best sites for these bases, so this would be great practice developing the skills of its staff. Instead, none of this happened, nor was it going to regardless of what we tried to do. I realized CMATT was selecting all the locations for these camps on its own, with minimal input from the Ministry of Defense. Neither the Iraqi Joint Headquarters Staff, nor the MOD Infrastructure Directorate (real estate, construction, and basing of all Iraqi military units) were involved. The only staff sections of the Ministry of Defense that had any role in these new camps were Base Management, under the command of Major General (two-star) Saad, and the M-4 staff, under the command of Major General Jawdat. Their involvement was minimal.

The military advisory teams within MNSTC-I completely ignored the civilian advisory teams. The Iraqis at MOD saw this. In a case of "monkey see, monkey do," the military side of MOD (the Joint Headquarters Staff), ignored the civilian side (the Directors General), because they saw MNSTC-I doing the same thing.

MNSTC-I was incapable of advising the Ministry of Defense. It was under the command of a United States Army three-star general who held a monthly meeting, the sole purpose of which was to discuss the status of "transition" from Coalition to Iraqi control of its military and national police. But LTG Dempsey never invited the Iraqis to the meeting! This was the single most important part of his job. Martin Dempsey is now a four-star general and Chairman of the Joint Chiefs of Staff, our country's senior ranking military officer.

LTG Dempsey let the Iraqi Ministry of Defense down by allowing this abysmal staff coordination within MNSTC-I to exist, and failed to do anything about it. Just as General Casey sat on his hands while the insurgency got out of control, General Dempsey sat on his while the Iraqi Ministry of Defense and Ministry of Interior spun around and got nothing done when they should have been moving forward. One general failed to use the forces under his command to defend Iraq, while the other failed to use the unit under his command to run a well-organized staff and get the two Iraqi security ministries on their feet. Looking at Iraq today, it is inconceivable how both General Casey and General Dempsey got promoted. Clearly, their performance had nothing to do with it.

I tried to make my presence known to CMATT because I wanted the MOD Real Estate Branch to play a role in the RSU/GSU initiative. CMATT worked just across the way in another building on Phoenix Base, but they ignored me because I was a civilian, and they didn't talk to civilians. On more than one occasion I was chewed out and treated like crap by one of their staff, a reserve lieutenant colonel who thought he was George Patton because he was wearing a uniform. His job in real life back in the States was with the Minnesota Highway Department. But he was wearing a uniform and I wasn't, and that's all that mattered.

I found out after being in Iraq for nearly 10 months that the Iraqi Joint Headquarters Staff had never agreed to the RSU/GSU concept. Even though CMATT had placed RSU and GSU staff at Coalition camps around the country, the Iraqis never formally accepted the plan. CMATT was doing this completely on its own, with no approval or buy-in from the Iraqis. RSUs and GSU's were just organizations on paper, without Iraqi concurrence to make them reality. The entire ten months I had been in Iraq up to this point, CMATT talked about the RSUs/

GSUs like they were the real thing, with U.S. Army lieutenant colonels working on them every day. What did they spend their time doing if the Iraqis never bought into the plan? It blew my mind that the Iraqi Joint Headquarters Staff hadn't formally approved this plan, especially after all the time CMATT had been working on it. And what was BG Wolff doing all that time? He left Iraq for the National Security Council in the White House, with the RSU/GSU plan approved and accepted by the Iraqis just days before he left. This was one of the primary missions of CMATT which was under his command. BG Wolff hardly accomplished a thing while he was in Iraq, but was rewarded with a huge job afterward. He most likely got a promotion as well.

I once found out through the grapevine (which was how I found out about most things) that there was a meeting planned concerning the RSUs and GSU's. This was before I discovered the Iraqis hadn't yet approved them. The meeting was going to be the next day, and would be chaired by BG Wolff's deputy, a Norwegian Navy Admiral! Why a Norwegian Admiral was the deputy of the group responsible for equipping and training the Iraqi military, 98% of which was its army, was anyone's guess. This was another example of the ridiculous staffing we saw every day under the Coalition concept. It was a mixing bowl of every nationality, title, rank and uniform one could imagine, like the bar scene in Star Wars. It was laughable. Because of Bush's "Coalition of the Willing," the U.S. was working with military from all over the world. This was good PR, except guys like the Norwegian admiral were placed in key positions on the MNSTC-I staff.

The meeting was held using interpreter headsets like those used at the United Nations. The Norwegian Admiral, who didn't know what was going on, started the meeting and immediately handed it over to Major General Saad, the Iraqi officer in charge of Base Management at MOD. General Saad was a very distinguished fellow. Like most Iraqi men, he always had his prayer beads in his hand and would constantly flip them one after another with his thumb. I always wondered what benefit Iraqis got out of doing this, but it did seem to calm them and help their concentration. He started to discuss the RSUs and GSU's, and eventually got to the point of saying that he didn't think there was a need for 85 of them. CMATT had been planning them for a year on its own. When the Iraqis were finally invited to discuss them, they had a completely different opinion about the entire concept. As the discussion went on the number was lowered to 80, with the same five Regional Support Units, and 75 Garrison Support Units. That was the last I heard of the RSU/GSU plan for several months. No one asked me if the MOD Real Estate Branch could assist, nor did I have any knowledge of more meetings on the subject.

About three months later I discovered the total number had changed again, from 80 to around 35! I had no idea of this change, but then again no one from CMATT would ever tell me anything, even though I constantly asked them to keep me informed. How could I advise the Ministry of Defense real estate staff, if I had no idea what MNSTC-I was doing that directly involved the Ministry of Defense's real estate staff? However, I was far from alone in this treatment. The MNSTC-I military advisers never told their civilian counterparts anything. Actually, the MNSTC-I military would have nothing to do with the MNSTC-I civilians. Most of them were reservists who had just put on their uniforms before arriving in Iraq, and as a result they assumed a superiority complex the likes of which I have rarely seen. The MNSTC-I military didn't want civilian contractors around, were jealous of the money we made, and in general had a pompous and arrogant attitude about everything. The civilian side was not kept informed nearly to the level it could have, and should have, by the military side. We were as bad, actually we were worse, than the Iraqi military who everyone complained about as being backward, arrogant and pompous. I never knew what the MNSTC-I military people involved in land and basing of Iraqi army units were doing. This specifically involved J-5, J-7 and JHQTT. I was always trying to find out what MNSTC-I was up to that affected Ministry of Defense land and basing. The best I could do was sit in on a meeting and take notes, or pipe in when I could, most of the time finding out about the meeting right before it started, usually by accident when I overheard someone talking about it. I was never kept in the loop.

I was hired to assist the Iraqi Ministry of Defense real estate staff, yet was only able to do a fraction of that because I had to fight for every bit of information from our own U.S. military staff at MNSTC-I. Just as the Iraqi military didn't keep their civilian counterparts informed because of their pro-military culture, the MNSTC-I military didn't keep their civilian counterparts informed either, and for the exact same reason. The U.S. military at MNSTC-I would work with the Iraqi military at MOD, and they would both exclude their civilian counterparts. Our problem was far worse because we had billions of U.S. dollars to spend. And we should have known better. I am convinced that this dysfunction, bad feeling, and poor communication within MNSTC-I was due to the vast majority of MNSTC-I military staff who were reservists, and civilians themselves. This led to two problems. Now that they were wearing uniforms, their power went to their heads and all civilians (which they were before being deployed to Iraq) were considered scum. In addition, because they weren't full-time career military, they didn't know how to work and interact with civilians who support the military, which occurs every day throughout the U.S. military around the world.

We at MNSTC-I were supposed to be rebuilding Iraq, so we should have been working together far better than we were. The MNSTC-I civilian contractors were hired by the MNSTC-I military, yet we were treated like dirt by the same people who hired us. Neither I, nor any of my civilian contractor friends, would have been in Iraq if we hadn't been hired by MNSTC-I and the U.S. Defense Department in order to support them.

Which led to the $64,000 question: why were we there? General Petraeus didn't want us there, nor did General Dubik, who took over MNSTC-I from General Dempsey. They both said they disliked contractors, specifically my firm, in front of people who passed it onto me. If they felt this way it is very likely their predecessors, Generals Casey and Dempsey, felt the same way and passed it on to their successors. If these generals didn't want our firm (or any of us) hanging around, how did it get these contracts? This is why two retired U.S. Army four-star generals ran our company. They could walk around the Department of Defense and schmooze their buddies to get these contracts, then people like me would go to Iraq and get treated like crap by the same military who didn't want us there. It was a Catch-22. The generals in the Pentagon didn't care what their commanders in Iraq felt about having my firm around. The commanders in the field didn't want us there, but their higher headquarters cut a deal with the two generals who ran my company, and we were hired and sent to Iraq. It's a different world between the Pentagon and Iraq. The two generals get the contracts and send guys like me to Iraq to be treated like unwanted guests by U.S. military personnel who had nothing to do with awarding the contract. But firms like mine and the stockholders of major corporations that own them make a ton of money. That's what it's all about. The revolving door keeps turning with DoD contractors (firms) hiring Pentagon generals after they retire—the same generals who awarded the contracts to the same firms when they were still in the Pentagon. Yet the American people are told this isn't a conflict of interest.

DoD contracts worth literally billions of dollars were awarded to American companies to send guys like me over to Iraq to do nothing. As I've stated, the U.S. military we were hired to support didn't want us there. We would complain about how narrow-focused and military-centric the Iraqis were yet the Coalition, especially MNSTC-I, was exactly the same. We would talk about this in our weekly MODTT "all hands" staff meetings with David Murtagh, and then with his successor John Cochrane, but they wouldn't pass any of this on to Generals Dempsey or Dubik for fear of upsetting them. And why should they say anything? They were both high ranking British civil servants who were there to punch their tickets, get a civilian medal from Dempsey or Dubik when they left, and then a promotion and a big fat job in the British Ministry of Defense when they got back to London. On the other hand, at least 80% of the MODTT staff were Americans like me, so why would Murtagh or Cochrane do squat for us? If I had a problem with the MNSTC-I military not listening to me, or not letting me in on what they were doing that affected the MOD real estate staff, I was on my own because David Murtagh was a Brit and didn't want to upset the same U.S. military people who were blowing me off. His successor, John Cochrane, wasn't much better.

When I left Iraq in September of 2007, the Iraqi Ministry of Defense, specifically the Joint Headquarters Staff, had finally approved the CMATT plan for the Regional and Garrison Support Unit locations, and the staffing of them. But not a thing had actually been done to implement the plan. I was there for 14 months, and from the time I arrived until the time I left not one single RSU or GSU facility had been built, not one RSU or GSU military unit had been staffed or manned, and not one RSU or GSU camp actually existed to support any Iraqi military units. This was after being in Iraq for 14 months, and the RSU/GSU plan existed long before I got there. This showed minimal accomplishment on the part of Brigadier General Wolff, and incompetence on the part of his Norwegian admiral deputy, and the admiral's successor, another Norwegian admiral. Both admirals had no business in that job. This also showed how the "Coalition of the Willing" was far more important for propaganda purposes than actually accomplishing anything or helping the Iraqis.

To say MNSTC-I was dysfunctional would be an understatement. By way of example, there were at least six different functional groups within MNSTC-I involved in the RSU/GSU plan: CMATT, JHQTT, J-7, M-4-TT, J-5 and MODTT. This was one initiative out of dozens, possibly hundreds, that MNSTC-I was planning for the Iraqi Ministry of Defense, not to mention the Ministry of Interior. Yet no one shared information with anyone else. Needless to say, no one let me in on anything they were planning that involved locating and basing Iraqi military camps and units, or the transfer to the Ministry of Defense of Forward Operating Bases that belonged to the Coalition. Yet I was the real estate advisor to the Ministry of Defense, the Iraqi ministry that MNSTC-I existed to support. If this was happening in the area of land and facilities, where else was it happening within MNSTC-I? It's safe to assume it was happening everywhere.

The decision to construct a camp for the Iraqi military was made by the MNSTC-I (Coalition) military, who included the Iraqi military after the plan was in the works. The MNSTC-I (Coalition) and MOD civilians had no idea what was happening. The camp was located without the MOD Real Estate Division having any idea what was going on. It was constructed by J-7 without the MOD Director General for Infrastructure having any involvement in the design or construction of the installation. The Iraqi army occupied it without any involvement of the civilian side of the Iraqi Ministry of Defense. The only part of MOD involved was the Joint Headquarters Staff, the military side of the Iraqi Ministry of Defense, and that was minimal. Our military only worked with the Iraqi military, barring all civilians, both Iraqi and Coalition, from playing any role. The Iraqi military was involved a fraction of what it should have been. In short, the U.S. military was doing everything for the Iraqis, even though General Casey had been blowing smoke up the President's backside for months that Iraq could take over any time and start doing everything itself. There were many parts of MNSTC-I and MOD with a legitimate role to play, but which didn't have any say in what was done. Whatever MNSTC-I did was copied at MOD. If the Coalition did it, why couldn't the Iraqis do it too? The Iraqis saw the dysfunction and confusion within MNSTC-I, yet we were supposed to set the example and show them how to do things right. Instead, we were showing them how to do things wrong. An Iraqi gentleman once asked me: "America put a man on the moon. Why can't MNSTC-I get this done?" It was hard to come up with an answer.

If the U.S. was trying to form an Iraqi Ministry of Defense similar to our DoD, the civilian leadership at MOD would have heavy sway in the running of their ministry, like our Under and Assistant Secretaries in the Pentagon. Such was not the case, as displayed by the crappy leadership at MNSTC-I. There was no senior U.S. civilian advisor to the Ministry of Defense—the counterpart to LTG Dempsey—who would have made sure the civilian leadership of MOD was doing its job. The closest we had was a Brit named David Murtagh who wouldn't say anything contrary to LTG Dempsey because he was intimidated by a U.S. general officer, and everyone knew it. To think a foreign national would say anything to an American three-star general that was at all controversial was barking at the moon. If there had been a strong American civilian advisor, who wasn't afraid of LTG Dempsey and his three stars, the entire situation at MNSTC-I would have been different. But when DoD won the food fight with State, the advisory role at MOD was completely taken over by the U.S. military, with no U.S. civilian oversight. If we had a senior American civilian advisor to the Minister of Defense most of these problems wouldn't have occurred. My colleagues and I would have had someone to go to who might have listened.

Another example of MNSTC-I's dysfunction was the "warehouse project." I had just returned to Iraq from vacation back to the States. It was December 2006. On my first day back at work my co-worker told me the Ministry of Defense was going to have warehouses built at bases around the country. For the first time I was being asked to assist in locating sites for Iraqi army installations. I couldn't believe I was getting something important to do! Major General Saad, head of Base Management for the Iraqi Army, and Major General Jawdat of its M-4 (supply) staff, wanted logistics locations around the country for storage and food preparation. (The two generals couldn't stand each other and refused to be in the same room.) There would be 23 warehouses at 22 locations (two would be at Taji, north of Baghdad) to provide support to the Iraqi Army, Navy and Air Force. The plan called for "life support" warehouses to store everything from uniforms to dry goods, with mess facilities and bakeries to feed Iraqi troops in the geographic areas served by these new facilities.

The job first began under the auspices of JHQTT, specifically M-4-TT, the MNSTC-I staff section that advised the Iraqi M-4 logistics staff. Right from the beginning there were problems. If our M-4-TT was assisting and advising the Iraqi Joint Headquarters M-4 staff, under the command of Major General Jawdat, and the Iraqi Base Management staff under Major General Saad, then what about the Coalition Military Assistance Training Team (CMATT), which was also advising the same MOD staff sections? CMATT was responsible for working with Major General Saad and Major General Jawdat in setting up the Regional and Garrison Support Units described above. These warehouses would be on the RSU and GSU complexes. Yet, when the warehouse project was first conceived (by the Iraqis themselves, not with MNSTC-I), it was given to M-4-TT to implement. CMATT wasn't involved.

My co-worker was an American woman who worked for four years in Iraq with the same company I did. She was a wonderful person, and extremely professional. She had been informed of the warehouse project by a U.S. Army major on the M-4-TT staff. The major deserves a brief description. He was born in Vietnam. When he was an infant his family left Vietnam on a boat and settled in Los Angeles. He was one of the famous "Vietnam boat people." Although he was a major in the United States Army Reserves, his English was so bad I couldn't understand a word he said. He had lived in the U.S. over 25 years.

The major came to see me after my co-worker told me of the project, and he handed me a list of the 22 bases where these warehouses were going to be located. It was going to be my job to coordinate the travel to these locations and find sites for them. I was all over it. This would involve bringing Iraqis from the MOD Infrastructure Directorate with me on every trip to find sites to locate the warehouses, each requiring a plot of land 400 x 400 meters in area. The major and I went over the list and began to prioritize the locations, starting with those in the Baghdad area, then going farther out. We decided to travel to Taji, about 20 miles north of Baghdad, for our first trip. We went on a U.S. Army UH-60 Blackhawk helicopter. Probably 90% of all air travel in Iraq is on these aircraft, which has a crew of four and can sit up to 12 passengers. We flew to Taji, conducted our site inspection, and returned the same day. At first I thought things were going smoothly. I soon realized I was very badly mistaken.

As time went by it became harder and harder to make these trips, not because of the distances involved, but because of the near impossibility of coordinating the U.S. military air transport. About the same time our trips began the insurgents started shooting down U.S. helicopters, which were doing most of their flying during the day because the air had been relatively safe. The month we started the warehouse project the first U.S. helicopter in a series of attacks was shot down, killing all 16 passengers and crew. One of them was my younger brother's West Point classmate. I don't recall the Army ever stating what caused the crash, but it didn't take a genius to figure out it was from enemy fire. Why the Army couldn't make an announcement on the cause of this crash was beyond reason. For the preceding four years the administration had been saying how great things were in Iraq, so it would make sense to keep this quiet. As the weeks went by more aircraft would get shot down, so daylight flights came to a swift halt.

One of the aircraft that went down around this time was an observation helicopter owned by a security firm. The company operated two or three McDonnell Douglass MD-500 helicopters that flew out of LZ (landing zone) Washington, across Haifa Street from the Republican Palace. This is the same model as the helicopter on the TV show Magnum PI. They're very fast and maneuverable aircraft, and we would watch them flying over Baghdad all the time. Their pilots would fly them so low and fast, I often wondered how they could observe anything. They would cut the sharpest banked turns I've ever seen helicopters do, almost like an aerobatic show. Two observers would be in the back with their legs dangling over the sides, carrying their weapons like they were riding shotgun on a stagecoach. I was at Phoenix Base one day when one of these helicopters flew right over my head toward downtown Baghdad. It was typical for them to fly the same route, often going right over Phoenix Base to the sector of Baghdad north of the IZ on the west side of the Tigris River. About two hours later we heard the helicopter had gone down. It had been hit by weapons fired from a building it flew past, ran into some power lines and then crashed on the street. Witnesses confirmed the pilot and three crew were still alive when insurgents ran out of the building and over to the aircraft, and shot each of the crew in the head.

From this point onward all flights would be made in the middle of the night. This caused tremendous hardship and loss of sleep, as we had to work all day prior to our departure and then fly at night. That's exactly what the insurgents wanted.

This made it practically impossible to fly into Anbar Province for our site inspection at Al Asad, which had been a major Iraqi Air Force base before the U.S. wiped out the Iraqi Air Force. The base was built by the Russians, with the airstrip on a plateau. The taxiway was a road winding downhill from the plateau, with spurs off the road leading into hangers built into the side of the hill. The roads continued to the flat lowland below, where the main part of Al Asad base was located along a waddi. I had been to Al Asad before on U.S. Army aircraft, but now the Marines wouldn't allow the Army to fly there. So much for inter-service cooperation. The MNF-I Commander, LTG Odierno, let the Marines get away with this nonsense. It took us 2-3 days just to get to Al Asad on Marine aircraft, and 2-3 days to get back, when the entire amount of time needed to get the inspection completed was about five hours. This would become the norm for anything involving Marine air support.

Thanks to the Marines, when we arrived at Al Asad we needed bunks because we had to stay for a couple of days. Our trip to Al Asad had been coordinated through the CMATT Garrison Support Unit chief there, a U.S. Army Reserve lieutenant colonel who was about as sharp as a door knob. He had two people working for him, a U.S. Air Force Captain and an Air Force sergeant. I have no idea what they did, because there was no "Garrison Support Unit" in existence at Al Asad, or anyplace else. The Iraqis hadn't approved the RSU/GSU plan yet. The lieutenant colonel and his staff referred to themselves as "the GSU," but in reality they were a team of CMATT guys hanging out at Al Asad, waiting for the RSU/GSU concept to be agreed to by the Iraqis. What these three did to kill time was beyond me, but what a great way to spend their tour in Iraq.

The most 'interesting' part of the trip to Al Asad was when we dropped by the Marine Base Commander's office. I had asked "the GSU" lieutenant colonel if we could visit the base commander as a courtesy and tell him about our mission. Al Asad is a huge base by Iraq standards, and we could have come and gone without him ever knowing we had been there, so I wanted to make sure he knew about our trip. We went to the base headquarters building and the lieutenant colonel walked inside. The rest of us waited outside for at least 20 minutes, then I went in to see what was going on. The lieutenant colonel was talking with a Marine full colonel in the main hallway. I walked up to them and said hello, and was introduced to the colonel who was the base commander. The two had been chatting the whole time, while the rest of us waiting outside in 110 degree heat. The colonel said he had to leave for a meeting, but would give us a few minutes of his time, most of which had been used up by the lieutenant colonel. We went into an office off the main hallway where there were several drafting tables and maps on the walls. This was a good place to have our short meeting, because we could use the maps to describe what our plans were for the warehouse. There were about 10 people standing around a drafting table, and another half dozen or so who worked in the room listening to us.

I was explaining to the base commander what the plan was for the warehouse when a Marine major turned to me and asked me question. I began to answer him when he started to say something else. He stopped himself and said he would ask me after the meeting. The meeting ended with the base commander saying he would help us any way he could, then he left. Most everyone was gone, leaving the Marine major, the lieutenant colonel and me standing at the drafting table with the people who worked in the office still there. The Marine major turned to me and the lieutenant colonel from CMATT and started yelling at us for not informing him of our presence on the base and our mission there. He screamed at me and the lieutenant colonel for not keeping him informed of plans we had for "my [his] base." Then he said if he had known we were on Al Asad and had plans to use part of the land there, "I [he] would kick you out the door."

I stood there and bit my lip as hard as I could. It was all I could do not to say "FUCK YOU" to this asshole. The army "GSU" lieutenant colonel looked like a punching bag. Finally, he mustered the courage to stand up to this insubordination from a junior officer. He told the Marine major he had called and spoken to him the previous day, and told him we were going to be there. The lieutenant colonel told the major to cool down, but the major didn't cool down at all. He was so belligerent toward me (a visitor) and the lieutenant colonel (a senior officer) I couldn't believe what I was hearing. I've always known the Marines as being pompous and arrogant, but this went way beyond anything I ever imagined. The lieutenant colonel should have locked his heels and ordered him to shut up, but he didn't. The lieutenant colonel was as shocked as me but afraid to stand up to this jerk, which he had every right to do, and should have done. The major was grossly disrespectfully toward a senior officer. It was the worst display of insubordination and disrespect I've ever witnessed—ever.

The craziest part was the comment about "my base" made by the Marine major. Al Asad was being used by the Marines as an air base to support their troops in Anbar Province. It wasn't a Forward Operating Base built by the U.S. Army Corps of Engineers (with legal title to the land) for the Marines to occupy. It was not "their base" or "his base." The Marines were using it with the permission of the Iraqis. But that was the problem. The Marines, the U.S. and the Coalition didn't really give a damn what belonged to the Iraqis, who we invaded but were supposed to be there to protect. If we needed it, we took it. If the Iraqis decided they wanted the base back the Marines would have been gone in a week (well, maybe). On the plus side, that would have been a land and base issue for me to coordinate with the Real Estate Branch at the Ministry of Defense—in my dreams, of course.

If this episode wasn't bad enough, the Iraqis were going to occupy a camp in a far corner of Al Asad anyway. It was going to be near the oasis where, according to legend, Abraham sojourned on his way across the desert. The warehouse was going to be located at this new camp, where the land stretched as far as the eye could see. The Marines were going to 'allow' the Iraqis to occupy a corner of their own base. How nice. The major was blasting us and making a fool of himself for no reason other than to show us (and the others in the room) that he was a Marine badass, and to inform us that nothing happened on his base without him knowing about it.

Al Asad was overrun by ISIS, the Islamic State of Iraq and Syria, in 2014. Sorry, but it's not the Marine officer's base anymore.

We were checking off more bases on our list, although getting to some of them was a huge effort. But when we tried to get north to "K-1," the base at Kirkuk, we hit a wall. We tried to fly there twice, both times getting as far as Balad, about 60 miles north of Baghdad. Getting to Kirkuk was just about impossible. We never made it there, but used up two or three days each time we tried.

After trying to get to the camps for about three months, we took a break after the second attempt to K-1. The Iraqis were getting tired of the wasted time and wanted to be with their families. With all the air resources the U.S. had in Iraq, it was like pulling teeth to get anywhere. I spent half a day on several occasions trying to get from Camp Victory at Baghdad International Airport to the International Zone, a distance of about five miles. Other than by helicopter, the only way to make the trip was by road convoy at around 3:00 in the morning in armored buses called "Rhinos." It could take 12 hours just to make this five mile trip, and that was just within Baghdad. That was how welcome Americans were in Iraq. Trying to get to a place like K-1 was impossible. One base was so hard to get to or leave from, people spent days waiting for the sound of in-coming helicopters (they always flew in pairs), like the credit scene from the TV show M*A*S*H. We decided to take a few weeks off. Around this time things got interesting with the warehouse project, but in a different way.

The U.S. Army major from Vietnam was rotating back to the States. He was nearing the end of his 6-month tour, which was short compared to other Army tours. He told me he couldn't take any more trips because he needed to get ready to go home, but he had a month and a half left in Iraq! He proceeded to dump the project onto another U.S. Army major, who was great to work with but about 100 pounds overweight. He was huge. I was gaining weight too because the food was so good, but the menu was for a 19-year-old. No sooner did we start working together than he informed me he would soon be leaving as well. His one-year tour in Iraq was ending. The person chosen to replace him was a young female U.S. Air Force first lieutenant.

The lieutenant was permanently assigned to an Air Force base in Germany, and was told she was going to Iraq with less than two weeks' notice. When she arrived she was assigned to the M-4-TT staff under a U.S. Marine full colonel, one of the nicest people I had the pleasure to work with the entire time I was in Iraq. Before the colonel left he asked me and the lieutenant to talk with him about keeping her busy. She had complained to him about not having anything to do. (I found out she sat at her desk all day playing on the internet and talking to her boyfriend in Germany. Her boyfriend, another U.S. Air Force officer, was on his way to Baghdad. The lieutenant would have plenty to keep her busy once he arrived.) I told the colonel I would try to keep the lieutenant occupied on the warehouse project, and the meeting ended.

The problem with this was the Air Force lieutenant didn't work for me. She worked for the Marine colonel. I wasn't her superior, but I was helping him by keeping her busy. It was his job to keep her occupied, not mine. Because the colonel was leaving in a matter of weeks, he had a lot going on and was looking for me to help, which I was happy to do. I needed assistance with the warehouse trips, and looked at this as a win-win situation. The warehouse project started with the Army major from Vietnam, who was on the colonel's staff. It belonged to the Marine colonel, not to me. And as a civilian, I had no official responsibility for anything, much less an Air Force lieutenant.

After getting involved in the warehouse project I eventually became the *de facto* guy in charge, even though I didn't belong to M-4-TT. I was asked by the Vietnamese major for help, so I wasn't going to say no. By the time the Air Force lieutenant showed up I was the only one still around who knew anything about the project. It was being handed over to me little by little as each military person rotated out, which was typical. The contractors stuck around, mostly because of the pay, but also because we were there for at least a year, but not the U.S. military. They left as fast as they could. The Air Force lieutenant was the third person from M-4-TT assigned to the project in a matter of months. By the time she got there the guy in charge of M-4-TT, the Marine colonel, didn't really care about the warehouse project, or anything else. The U.S. military were on 3 to 12 month tours of duty in Iraq, depending on which branch of the service they were in, yet all under the same command. There was inconsistent rotation of all forces within MNSTC-I, which left huge gaps in responsibilities. This project was just another example. The contractors were the only ones who were consistently around for any length of time. We were the only institutional knowledge MNSTC-I had, yet the military on its staff treated us like lepers. If the MNSTC-I military had treated us as members of their team, we could have accomplished a lot more. When the Marine colonel left he was replaced by a reserve U.S. Navy captain who was the biggest asshole in MNSTC-I. He was the latest arrival in what became a cabal of U.S. Navy captains who had nothing better to do than make life miserable for people trying to do their jobs.

The new Navy captain in charge of M-4-TT came by my office one day and asked me if I had a few minutes to discuss the warehouse project with him. I said yes and we went over to an empty cubicle to talk. Right away he asked why I had been to so few of the 22 locations on the list of bases that were going to have the warehouses located on them. Then he started in on me for a trip the Air Force lieutenant had made a few days before. She and I were going to one of the camps with a couple of the Iraqis from MOD who travelled with us to all the locations. At the last minute we lost one seat on the aircraft, so I let the lieutenant run the trip. She was new and I thought it would be a good experience for her. I was tasked with mentoring her, so I figured this was as good an opportunity as any for her to get her feet wet. But when she and the Iraqis got to the camp things didn't go well at all. The trip just didn't work out.

I sensed the confrontational tone in the captain's voice right away, and figured I was in for an interesting meeting. He and I had spoken on the phone once, and had never met face-to-face. I explained to him the difficulty we were having getting out to these locations, citing the number of times we had attempted to get to some of them, using K-1 as my best example, only to end up never making it there. I told him that of the seven camps we had been to up to that time, we had attempted to get out about 15 times altogether. He didn't seem to care a bit for my explanation. All he wanted to do was make me look bad, which became obvious as the conversation wore on. I explained to him the entire background of the project, which took some time. He then asked me why the Air Force lieutenant was involved in the project, clearly implying that she wasn't doing anything on it and that it was my fault. He was coming across as though I had gotten his staff involved, when his staff had gotten me involved. I told the captain that it was a former member of the M-4-TT staff, the Army major, who had originally started the project. It was clear he and the Marine colonel had not coordinated prior to the latter's departure for the States. Then again maybe they did, and the captain knew everything that had transpired, and wanted to pin the responsibility for the warehouse project on me. I was there to assist the Iraqis, but wanted to help the MNSTC-I staff whenever I could. Besides, the lieutenant didn't belong to me, she belonged to him. I honestly felt he got off the plane in Baghdad with a bone to pick with contractors, and I was the target of his insecure Napoleonic ego.

Then the captain said something I found to be very interesting. He said his office should never have been involved in the warehouse project in the first place, that it was a CMATT issue and not an M-4-TT issue. If that was the case, why was he coming down on me? If he was pulling his staff off the project, what difference did it make to him how it was going? I agreed and told him that's where the project belonged in the first place. CMATT was the MNSTC-I staff section responsible for assisting the Iraqi Joint Headquarters Staff in setting up the Regional and Garrison Support Unit camps, and the warehouses were an integral component of them. As far as I knew CMATT had never been involved in this project, which was clearly in its area of responsibility within MNSTC-I. The captain told me he was going to tell CMATT of his decision, that his staff was no longer going to be involved (even though it had been the lead on it from the beginning), and that the Air Force lieutenant was no longer going to be working on it with me. I said fine.

The next day the lieutenant dropped by my desk and told me she was no longer involved in the project. I told her I had spoken with the captain the day before and was aware of this. We chatted for a few more minutes and then she left. I decided to e-mail the captain to inform him of the conversation I just had with the lieutenant. I asked him if there was anything more we needed to discuss. I also wanted to make sure he had spoken to CMATT. It was a simple e-mail to close the loop on the issue after speaking with the lieutenant. The response I got from him blew me away. He said I didn't know my job and if I needed clarification on the warehouse project, or any other issues, I should speak to my co-worker. His response was totally out of line, insulting, inappropriate, and it was copied to a dozen other people. We had met face-to-face once.

If I had any doubt the captain had it in for me, I had no doubt now. There was a posse of reserve U.S. Navy captains at

MNSTC-I that he was the newest member of, among them the two successive Navy captains who ran J-7. I knew the J-7 ones wanted me gone. Now they could send their newest member to screw with me, like a frat initiation. Thus began my journey leading to the end of my tour in Iraq.

On August 6, 2007, an article by Glenn Kessler appeared in *The Washington Post* about nearly 200,000 AK-47 rifles and pistols that had disappeared in Iraq. The U.S. Army had purchased the weapons for issue to the Iraqi army and national police, part of $19.2 billion the United States had spent to train and equip the Iraqi security forces up to that time, but there was no record of where the weapons ended up or who had them. They were simply gone. The article went on to describe the background behind these weapons and came to the conclusion that no one knew where they were or in whose hands they ended up. The U.S. Government Accountability Office (GAO) had discovered this little mistake, and that's when it hit the papers.

> The United States has spent $19.2 billion trying to develop Iraqi security forces since 2003, the GAO said, including at least $2.8 billion to buy and deliver equipment. But the GAO said weapons distribution was haphazard and rushed and failed to follow established procedures, particularly from 2004 to 2005, when security training was led by Gen. David H. Petraeus, who now commands all U.S. forces in Iraq.

> ...the inability of the United States to track weapons with tools such as serial numbers makes it nearly impossible for the U.S. military to know whether it is battling an enemy equipped by American taxpayers.

> Iraqi security forces were virtually nonexistent in early 2004 [thanks to Paul Bremer], and in June of that year Petraeus was brought in to build them up. No central record of distributed equipment was kept for a year and a half, until December 2005...

> The GAO reached the estimate of 190,000 missing arms -- 110,000 AK-47s and 80,000 pistols -- by comparing the property records of the Multi-National

Security Transition Command for Iraq [MNSTCI] against records Petraeus maintained of the arms and equipment he had ordered.[63]

The GAO Report brought two issues to light. The first was the United States had no idea what it was doing when the insurgency began, and was totally ill-equipped to handle it. This was the direct result of having no post-invasion plan whatsoever, and not enough forces in the invasion to deal with the growing violence that was erupting. Based on the GAO's findings, it isn't hard to picture MNSTC-I practically throwing weapons and equipment at Iraqi forces because the insurgency got out of hand so quickly. This was because there weren't enough Coalition (i.e., US) forces to respond to the violence that resulted when Paul Bremer disbanded Iraq's security infrastructure.

And who were these Iraqi soldiers who were being issued these weapons in the first place? If there was no Iraqi army after it was disbanded by Paul Bremer, it's likely they were men that MNSTC-I was grabbing off the street and putting uniforms on, then handing them brand new weapons that didn't even have serial numbers on them. It would have been the easiest thing in the world for these Iraqi "soldiers" to walk away and never come back.

The second point in the GAO report was the total lack of command and control permeating the entire Iraqi theater of operations. The organization that purchased these weapons was none other than MNSTC-I, the unit I was assigned to. They disappeared in 2004-2005 when MNSTC-I was under the command of the newly promoted four-star general, and the new MNF-I commander, David Petraeus. It was when he was the first commander of MNSTC-I, and responsible for equipping and training the new Iraqi Army, that nearly 200,000 weapons disappeared. It would appear that once these weapons were issued to the Iraqi Army, David Petraeus just walked away. That these weapons could end up totally unaccounted for showed MNSTC-I's gross lack of oversight of the Iraqi Army and its supply system.

---

[63] "STABILIZING IRAQ: DOD Cannot Ensure That U.S.-Funded Equipment Has Reached Iraqi Security Forces," *Report to Congressional Committees*, United States General Accountability Office (GAO), July 2007.

However, this didn't stop David Petraeus from getting promoted from two-star, which he was at the time, to four-star general. (While a cadet at West Point, David Petraeus dated, and later married, the daughter of the Superintendent. They were still married when he was having his affair with Paula Broadwell.)

When I was attending Ranger School at Ft. Benning, Georgia, all of us had our personal weapon tied to our body with a long string or thin rope, so we wouldn't lose it. Losing one's weapon was at the top of the list of things that would get someone booted out of the Army. This was drilled into us from Day-1. David Petraeus went to West Point, and Ranger School. Yet, the unit he commanded lost 190,000 individual weapons due to his command's gross lack of accountability and logistical procedures.

How would the parent of a United States soldier or Marine feel if they knew their child was killed by an insurgent shooting one of these 190,000 weapons, and then watching David Petraeus getting his fourth star pinned on his collar? Why would a U.S. Army two-star general in Iraq order weapons without serial numbers? This had to be done purposely, with a reason. Weapons are not made without serial numbers unless they are specifically ordered that way. The reason for serial numbers is to control who owns a weapon, and where it is located. By ordering these weapons without serial numbers, was David Petraeus planning on there being no controls or accountability at the time they were ordered?

It's one thing to throw weapons at young Iraqi men and send them off to fight. It's another thing when they are handed weapons that can't be traced and could later be used to kill your own soldiers. Why these weapons were ordered without serial numbers raises questions just as important as where they ended up. This could have ended the career of any officer—except David Petraeus. All the American people got was a GAO report, while David Petraeus got two more stars. The only way to find out what really happened with these weapons would be a full-scale investigation by Congress. This has not been done. All we have is a GAO report that most people have no idea exists. What's the point of having a Government 'Accountability' Office if no one is held accountable for their gross negligence and waste of taxpayer funds?

General Casey blew his command of MNF-I and got promoted to U.S. Army Chief of Staff. Lieutenant General Conway was promoted to four-star general and Commandant of the Marine Corps after the Fallujah Brigade fiasco. General Petraeus got the same royal treatment. All three U.S. generals were derelict in their duties, and created circumstances that led to the deaths of hundreds of their own soldiers and Marines. But all three got huge promotions afterwards. It didn't matter how they performed their jobs before their promotions. They had been hand-picked for greater things, so they were going to get promoted anyway. Where's the "personal responsibility" Bush talked about during his 2000 campaign? It's at the same place it was after 9/11, when he allowed George Tenet to keep his job at the CIA—nowhere.

Iraq has been like a Greek tragedy. This isn't ancient Greece, but it's a tragedy just the same. Act I was Operation Desert Storm. Act II was about political, diplomatic and intelligence failure by Bush, Cheney, Rumsfeld, Tenet and Bremer; military failure by Franks, Sanchez and Casey; and transition failure by Petraeus and Dempsey. All because Bush had a score to settle with Saddam, and allowed himself to be led over a cliff by his close advisors.

Act III belongs to Barack Hussein Obama, a narcissist who would say anything to get elected, whether it made sense or not. The details can always be worked out later by his minions. Bush and Obama have both blown Iraq in a big way, but Obama still has time to do something about it. Unfortunately for everyone, however, Obama doesn't have the spine, the intelligence or the stomach to do what is needed. As much as the media plays up the killing of Osama bin Laden, all Obama did was say "OK," and bin Laden was toast. Where's the courage in that?

Barack Hussein Obama will go down in history as one of the nation's greatest teleprompter readers, and one of its worst leaders. Bush blew Iraq, but Obama had an opportunity to rectify Bush's mess, and failed. Instead, he made the quagmire worse and allowed the rise of the Islamic State and the fire of Islamic fundamentalism to spread across the region, destroying the lives of thousands in the Middle East and threatening the security of the United States, the country and the people he 'swore' to protect.

9—J-7

When I arrived in Baghdad the Ministry of Defense Real Estate Branch (later Division), consisted of about a dozen people whose chief was a former mail clerk, but whose brother was the head of the Infrastructure Directorate for the Ministry. The Real Estate Chief was out sick when I arrived, and his deputy was the acting chief. I never saw the full-time head of the office for nine months, when he decided it was time to come back to work. He continued to get paid, however, because of his brother's position.

It wasn't long before I realized MOD wasn't responsible for its own real estate and construction, MNSTC-I was. Even though MOD was supposed to be, and General Casey would have been the first to say so, nothing could have been further from the truth. MNSTC-I was responsible for the construction of all Iraqi military camps, all being built with U.S. tax dollars. With MNSTC-I responsible for the construction of all Iraqi military camps, bases, police stations, border stations, hospitals, schools, and everything else needed by the Iraqi security ministries (the Ministries of Defense and Interior), a huge weight had to be carried by its construction section, the J-7. Much has been discussed about J-7 already, but its role was so important to the reconstruction of Iraq, it deserves a separate chapter.

Because J-7 was responsible for all this work, it was also responsible for awarding the contracts to get it all done. One entity was responsible for the construction of every Iraqi military installation, every Iraqi police station, and every Iraqi border station, all in the midst of a war for the security of the country. J-7 had a daunting task, but wasn't up to it.

J-7 was not properly staffed with active duty officers and enlisted from the U.S. Army Corps of Engineers (USACE), adept at construction of land-based military installations and the facilities on them. Nor did it have civilians on its staff who knew construction and real estate acquisition, or who did this for a living. The two chiefs of this section when I was in Iraq were not USACE officers. They were U.S. Navy civil engineering officers who weren't equipped, trained or experienced to deal with a land warfare situation, or with expertise to construct facilities of the type needed to house police and army units. The J-7 staff should have been made up of U.S. Army engineers and civilians used to building such facilities. To make matters worse, nearly all the rest of the staff of the J-7 under these two chiefs were reserve officers who hadn't constructed a building in years, if ever. Just because someone was a reserve officer in civil engineering, that didn't mean he or she had the slightest clue how to do this type of work in real life, especially in a combat environment. This wasn't an island in the Pacific during World War II. The Seabees had no business building an Iraqi army camp in the middle of a desert country. This wasn't a naval war. It was a land warfare theater. It was an Army thing. Being reservists they trained one weekend a month and two weeks in the summer, not enough time to construct entire bases and all their facilities? They showed up for weekend "drill" at the local armory, usually staying at a nearby hotel and drinking in the bar all night. Most didn't construct buildings for a living, such as the deputy of J-7, the high school teacher from Mississippi. What practical experience did they have to construct military camps in the desert half way around the world in the middle of a war?

J-7 didn't actually build these Iraqi camps, but managed everything, including tracking the U.S. dollars spent. Regardless, its staff still required expertise in construction. Without this, it couldn't manage anything. The construction was actually done by four U.S. construction firms who have made a fortune doing this work in Iraq. They were hired by the U.S. Air Force Center for Environmental Excellence, or AFCEE, the politically correct name of the Air Force's equivalent of the U.S. Army Corps of Engineers. The entire infrastructure of Iraq's military forces, nearly all of which is the army, was being built by people who construct docks and aircraft hangers. They were all U.S. Air Force or Navy reservists. There wasn't a single officer from the U.S. Army Corps of Engineers on the staff of J-7.Contracting officers from AFCEE headquarters in San Antonio, Texas, executed all the construction contracts to these four companies on behalf of J-7. But these companies only acted as General Contractors, turning the projects over to local Iraqi companies with the labor to do the actual work. The money that was being spent on these projects was staggering.

It wasn't just camps and installations that were constructed by these American companies for J-7. In addition, hundreds of existing structures were renovated, and new construction from the ground up was done, both on military camps and off. J-7 was responsible for all construction for the Ministry of Interior as well. Because each building was considered its own project with its own tracking number and budget, the combined total number of individual construction projects being managed by J-7 was 2,500-3,000 projects, with hundreds more planned. These were being built with U.S. taxpayer money for the Iraqi Ministry of Defense and Ministry of Interior. The budget tracking for these projects was one of the most important financial exercises in Iraq. I was told by J-7 these projects had to be closed out. Even though these projects were being given to the Iraqi government as a gift, because they were being financed with U.S. Treasury money, their costs still had to be accounted for.

J-7 was attempting to get the Iraqis to accept each individual project, which numbered in the dozens at any one time. This required signing for each building constructed for the Iraqi government, and that was being conveyed as a gift from the American government. Signing for each project was a mandatory requirement by the U.S. government: it couldn't be waived. Even though all of these projects were being given to the Iraqi government at no cost, the United States Treasury still needed to account for the expenditure of the funds used to pay for the gift. When money leaves the U.S. Treasury, it has to be accounted for.

I was told the number of completed projects for the Ministry of Defense was several hundred, and over two thousand for the Ministry of Interior. The reason for the large number of MOI projects—individual buildings—was because this ministry had all of the police stations and frontier border stations throughout the country. I told a lieutenant colonel from J-7, who was a friend of mine, that I would try to get the buildings inspected and the documents signed for transfer to the Ministry of Defense. The MOD staff told me they would accept these facilities, but only after conducting a physical inspection first, which I passed onto J-7. I envisioned the Real Estate Branch, along with engineers from the Infrastructure Directorate of the Ministry, inspecting these facilities and signing the paperwork to close out J-7's construction files. Not a big deal. That was the job of the MOD Infrastructure Directorate staff, or it would be if J-7 let them do it. My vision couldn't have been farther off the mark. J-7 never accepted my offer to get the Ministry of Defense Real Estate Branch and Infrastructure Directorate involved. I found out after being in Iraq for a year that J-7 hadn't gotten the documents prepared for the Iraqis to sign. But J-7 was going on about how important all this was.

When I asked my lieutenant colonel friend why J-7 hadn't gotten these documents put together, he said they couldn't get the documents from the four U.S. contractors doing the work. Every contractor working for J-7 should have been called on the carpet for not getting that paperwork submitted. They were making huge amounts of money, yet they couldn't provide J-7 with the documentation needed for the Iraqis to sign. These contractors worked for my friend's boss, the Navy captain in charge of J-7. He could have gotten the paperwork if he had tried. The U.S. taxpayer was paying the freight on these projects without the documentation to account for the hundreds of millions spent on them.

Eventually the packages (folders) with the documents for each individual construction project finally started to trickle in for the Iraqis to sign. But many of the facilities had been built going back three or more years. J-7's failure to get the paperwork together for its projects, and then get the Iraqis to sign them, created a whole new problem. Now J-7 wanted the Iraqis to sign for buildings the Iraqi army had been occupying for up to three years. By this time the buildings had been completely trashed by the Iraqi army, whose concept of cleanliness and trash removal is non-existent.

As time went by and the Iraqis weren't signing for the facilities, the first J-7 Navy captain was replaced by the second, as I have mentioned. He quickly assumed the same personality and attitude as his predecessor. On the rare occasion J-7 talked to the Iraqis in the Real Estate Division at the Ministry of Defense, the captain would send his staff around me and my co-worker, whose job it was to advise the same Iraqis. My co-worker had served in Iraq as an activated National Guardsman in the Corps of Engineers for 15 months. Then she came back as a contractor for another three years. In all, she was in Iraq over four years by the time I left in September 2007. Both J-7 captains had no idea what they were doing, or the expertise they were blowing off. That was the culture of MNSTC-I and its military staff.

I asked the new head of J-7 if I could provide him with an overview of the Ministry of Defense's real estate and facilities program. We were in his office one afternoon, and I was drawing the MOD organization on a white board while his deputy, a U.S. Navy commander, listened off to the side. I thought this would help because he was new to the job and MOD was a very confusing place. About 10 minutes into the discussion the captain's phone rang and he took the call, leaving me to stand there for about 15 minutes until he finished. This was typical, and we had many other conversations like this. One that really stuck out was when we were talking about getting the Iraqis to sign for the hundreds of buildings J-7 had constructed for the Ministry of Defense, as I have described. I told the captain they would not accept these facilities without inspecting them first. He said it was their problem. I asked him if he would buy a house he had never seen, and of course he said no. I asked him if there was any way he could provide transportation for the Ministry's representatives to go to these locations and inspect the facilities, so they would sign for them. I'll never forget his response. He said he would not do that, and the Iraqis could travel to these locations themselves. This was impossible for them to do, and he knew it. They didn't have the resources to travel anywhere outside of Baghdad, which he was well aware of. I told him this would not work, and it was only after several weeks he agreed to try to transport the Iraqis to these bases. In the case of getting land title, I couldn't get any cooperation from the first Navy captain. In the case of facility inspections, I couldn't get any cooperation from the second one. In both cases I was trying to help them do their jobs.

This was another example of the many impasses I encountered dealing with our own U.S. military. Near the end of my time in Iraq, J-7 started making attempts to take over my function and that of my co-worker. Simply put, J-7 wanted us out of their way. The last thing J-7 wanted was me bringing up the fact that it had been constructing camps for the Iraqis on land it had taken without legal title in the U.S.'s name, or the Ministry of

Defense. Technically, J-7 was illegally constructing bases in Iraq with U.S. money. It was clear J-7 wanted me and my co-worker out of their way so they could continue to do this without the whistle being blown on them. It didn't want us holding them up on silly things like clear title. It also wanted to be the construction branch of the Ministry of Defense itself, regardless of whether the ministry had staff to do that. The Coalition was supposed to be transitioning control of Iraq's security over to MOD, not holding onto it. Back then, up to the present day, when I hear pundits say the Iraqis are going to take over and run their own show, I know it's nonsense because we never let them do anything while we were there. We have been saying for years that we're trying to get the Iraqis to take control of their own country, refusing to occupy it ourselves, yet we've never let them do anything on their own. They have the money, but we never let them spend it their way because we've insisted they follow our contracting procedures. This is impossible for Iraqis to do.

J-7 never involved the Iraqis in the design and construction of their own camps and facilities. They could have done this if we had given them the opportunity, whether it was done with their money or with ours. We could have supervised the expenditure of U.S. or Iraqi money, making sure they built quality facilities to house their armed forces and defend their country. This way the staff of the newly created Ministry of Defense could get hands-on experience doing the work themselves. What better way to ensure they could do it on their own after we left? Instead, we designed their facilities, built them with American contractors, let the Iraqis move in and trash them, and then expected the Iraqi Army to sign for the facilities three years later.

Near the end of my tour I was in a meeting with staff from J-7 and the new Director of Real Estate, who had replaced the former mail clerk. The J-7 staff wanted the new director, an Iraqi two-star general, to sign for hundreds of buildings he had never seen. The J-7 people said many of the buildings had already been occupied by the Iraqi army, so the general should sign for them. The general told the senior J-7 officer if he wanted MOD to sign for these buildings, then J-7 should have had the paperwork ready when the projects were completed, not years later. He said if the paperwork had been available when it was supposed to be, the

Ministry of Defense would have conducted its inspection and signed the forms at that time. The J-7 officer just sat there with his mouth open. There was nothing he could say. The Iraqi general was right. He wasn't going to be pushed around by some U.S. Army officer who just got off the plane, which the J-7 officer had just done a week before. As a side note, the Iraqi general had been sentenced to death by Saddam for insulting one of his sons. The sentence was reduced to life, and later commuted by Saddam with help from some of the general's friends.

The only time I thought this process might work was when J-7 finally arranged a trip to the Iraqi army camp called Q-West, near the town of Qayyarah West, about 20 miles south of Mosul. Several new buildings had been constructed at the order of J-7 by one of the American construction companies, which had been contracted to do the work by AFCEE. J-7 asked the construction company's security contractor, a firm called SafeNet, to fly a group of us to Q-West. We arrived and inspected 12 new buildings J-7 had constructed. After the inspection we gathered in the mess hall, ready for the Iraqis to sign the acceptance and transfer documents. The Iraqis wouldn't sign the paperwork because they didn't have the authority, but would make the recommendation to their superior, the two-star general, to sign them. This satisfied everyone, and we all thought we had broken new ground. But then the Project Manager from the American construction company, who knew we were coming a week earlier, didn't have the paperwork for us to take back to Baghdad! The Iraqis from MOD wouldn't have been able to sign anything, regardless of their authority. I couldn't believe the Project Manager didn't have this when we had gone through all the trouble to get up there. He assured us that the paperwork would be in Baghdad within two days for the Iraqis to sign, which would complete the transfer from Coalition to Iraqi ownership. A week went by and the paperwork didn't show up. Then one day I was told the paperwork had arrived, and everything had been signed. I asked who signed the documents, but I was never given a clear answer. I know it wasn't anyone at the Iraqi Ministry of Defense. I'm convinced the documents were signed by someone who did not have authority, so that J-7 could close the books on its projects without having to deal with MOD.

When the new head of J-7 said he wouldn't provide transportation for Iraqis from the Ministry of Defense to locations where he had constructed their facilities, I said travel for the Iraqis should be part of the construction budget for each project. He would hear none of this. But what was wrong with this suggestion? When I asked his predecessor for assistance helping the Iraqis travel to the Provincial Land Registration offices to determine ownership of land he planned to construct Iraqi military camps on, he blew me off as well. So did my own boss, David Murtagh.

When the Minister of Defense, Abdul Qadir, decided overnight to overhaul MOD (without General Dempsey even knowing about it), Iraqi Prime Minister Maliki created an initiative to add more units to the Iraqi armed forces. This was appropriately called the "Prime Minister's Initiative." It was a huge deal for everyone. This was going to add another army division to the ten already in existence, and at least another brigade to the three brigades already in each division, and in some cases two more. It also created the Samarra Brigade, an Iraqi army unit that would be spread along Route 1 between Baghdad and Samarra to protect travelers on their pilgrimage to the Al Askari Mosque. This was the "Golden Mosque" that was all but destroyed by Sunni rebels. The "PMI," as it became known, required more basing and facilities for the Iraqi army. One would have thought that J-7 could use all the help it could get. Not quite. J-7 ignored the MOD Real Estate Division, which was responsible for acquiring the land, with legal title, for these new facilities. Being what it was, J-7 was going to grab what it needed and start building to meet the requirements of the PMI. J-7 (and J-5, see below) started making its own trips, selecting locations for new camps without the input or participation of the people responsible for the real estate and installations of the Ministry of Defense—the Real Estate Division and the Infrastructure Directorate.

There was another MNSTC-I section called J-5 Plans. A lieutenant colonel on its staff took on the responsibility of determining where these new "Prime Minister's Initiative" camps would be located, to include the Samarra Brigade. I honestly believe he had nothing to do, so he decided to take this on. That was fine, but he didn't include anyone else who *did* have responsibility for this. Prior to the lieutenant colonel's arrival, a very junior U.S. Air Force captain was the real estate coordinator for the J-5 staff, which involved working with J-7 on Iraqi basing issues. The young captain was very sharp and knew what he was doing, but he was too junior in rank to have the amount of responsibility that had been placed on him. But it would make absolutely no sense for a lieutenant colonel (on the promotion list for full colonel—in the reserves) to assume the job previously held by a junior captain, unless he had nothing else to do.

I had no idea these new camps were required for the PMI because no one ever told me, yet I was advising the Ministry of Defense real estate staff. I was a contractor, so in the opinion of the MNSTC-I military staff why should I have a need to know anything. But MNSTC-I was not supposed to operate in a vacuum. Everything it did was supposed to be for the Iraqi Ministry of Defense and Ministry of Interior. MNSTC-I kept on doing everything on its own without involving MOD, which needed to learn how to function after we left Iraq. MNSTC-I, while saying it was there to help the Iraqis "transition" and be responsible for their own security, continued doing everything itself, sometimes taking a couple of Iraqis along for the ride because the colonel from J-5 had become friends with them. I asked him numerous times to include me and the real estate and infrastructure staff on his site selection trips. He did this twice, after being asked to by the Air Force captain whose job the colonel had taken, which confirmed that he knew we should be included. But on the rest of his trips he left us sitting in Baghdad with no idea what he was doing. As expected, after the J-5 colonel left for the States, most of the locations he selected for new "Prime Minister's Initiative" camps wouldn't work because of issues he had failed to consider. This was because he didn't have expertise in this area, whereas the real estate staff at the Ministry did, so it was no surprise. If he had included the Iraqi real estate and engineering staff on his trips, these problems would have been minimized, if not avoided completely.

After the invasion the U.S. Department of State occupied Saddam Hussein's former Republican Palace. The palace is located in the center of the International Zone, inside a bend on the west bank of the Tigris River in central Baghdad. It is a beautiful building, as many of the buildings in central Baghdad are (or were). The palace is long, with large wings at either end, two stories above ground, and has a huge rotunda in the center with a ceramic blue dome on top. The bright blue dome, typical of Iraqi architecture, can be seen for miles from the air, and is the landmark the helicopter pilots use in daylight to land at LZ (landing zone) Washington across the street.

After the Coalition Provisional Authority was shut down, the entity put in place by the State Department to staff up and advise the non-security ministries of the newly democratic Iraqi government was called IRMO, for Iraqi Reconstruction Management Office. The name changed just as I was departing Iraq for the States, but the mission remains very much the same. IRMO was the entity responsible for getting the non-security Iraqi ministries on their feet, which is another way of saying it had all the money. The amount of money IRMO had to dish out to the Iraqi government was staggering, and was very likely in the hundreds of millions, if not in the billions of U.S. dollars since the Iraqi conflict began in the spring of 2003.

When Paul Bremer disbanded the Iraqi Ministry of Defense and Ministry of Interior, leaving the country totally defenseless, he opened the door for every terrorist group to come in and set up shop, and he did all this with Bush's approval. He also took all the real property (e.g., land and buildings) owned by these ministries and turned it over to the newly created Iraqi Ministry of Finance. I was told he did this as a control measure, to gather all assets of financial value under one ministry. In theory this made a lot of sense. It was prudent to collect all Iraqi government-owned assets at the Ministry of Finance to determine their value for borrowing power on the world financial markets. Paul Bremer had to do this for another reason as well: he had disbanded the Ministry of Defense and the Ministry of Interior, so how could they hold onto land they once owned if they didn't exist anymore? He left this door open a crack for the

Ministry of Defense by enacting one of his many regulations, CPA Regulation Number 67.

CPA #67 stated that all former Ministry of Defense real property would revert over to the new Ministry of Defense assuming, of course, that Iraq would someday have one. I discovered this regulation shortly after arriving in Iraq. At first I thought this was the answer to the question of whether the Ministry of Defense still had claim to its former bases and camps. Back on my first day at the Ministry of Defense, I had asked the real estate staff to show me a list of all the properties it owned. I was told: "We don't own anything. Mr. Bremer gave it all to the Ministry of Finance." This wasn't entirely true. He did give it all to the Ministry of Finance, but CPA #67 gave it all back. It would be months before I got a solid legal opinion from anyone on this issue, specifically the validity of CPA #67. Only when the MODTT legal advisor arrived half way through my tour did I get this. He did the legal research and determined CPA #67 had the force and effect of law in Iraq, and all "old" Ministry of Defense land and real property did indeed belong to the "new" Ministry of Defense. Part of the problem regarding Ministry of Defense real property ownership finally got resolved, but it took far longer than it needed to.

What of privately owned land? As stated previously, J-7 was taking any land it needed, without permission of the owner, to construct military camps, and police and border stations. If the land had been a former Iraqi military camp, J-7 would go in and renovate the existing buildings, or construct new ones. Based on the authority granted by CPA #67, the land reverted over to the Ministry of Defense. Unbelievably, J-7 didn't know this until I brought it to their attention.

And what about land that wasn't previously used by the Ministry of Defense as a military camp, or land that hadn't been previously used as a police station? To the best of my knowledge there wasn't a similar CPA regulation pertaining to former Ministry of Interior real property like there was for former Ministry of Defense real property, as addressed in CPA #67. I only worked on the MOD side of the house. Therefore, I'm not sure if old Ministry of Interior police and border stations reverted over to the new Ministry of Interior. However, I do know that whenever J-7 constructed new military camps, police or border stations, in every case it was situated on land owned by a person or entity other than the two security ministries, who J-7 was building the installations for. J-7 was doing nothing to secure clear title, or acquire long-term leases, for the land needed to construct these facilities. The result was hundreds of land claims from people stating that a police station, border station, or military camp had been built on land that they owned. The IRMO advisor to the Iraqi Ministry of Justice told me that as of late-2006, there were 125,000 real estate claims in Iraq! This was a huge number, and was caused primarily by actions of the U.S. military, specifically J-7. But when I tried to bring this to the attention of the U.S. Navy captain running J-7, or his successor, or my British boss David Murtagh, I got absolutely nowhere.

Prior to the MODTT legal advisor's finding of the legal impact of CPA #67, I tried to come up with another solution to the issue of real property held by the Ministry of Finance (MOF). One day I looked up the name of the IRMO advisor to the Iraqi Ministry of Finance. I wanted to meet him to talk about the issue of real property in Iraq, specifically Paul Bremer's decision to transfer real property owned by the former Iraqi ministries over to the new Ministry of Finance. A meeting would be a chance to meet the guy who advised the Ministry of Finance, to talk about the overall strategic issue of real property ownership in Iraq, and a way to resolve land ownership issues for the Ministry of Defense. He refused to meet me. I e-mailed him half a dozen times and all I got were excuses why he couldn't meet, usually saying he was busy or travelling. Sometimes I got no response at all. The guy (another American) simply would not meet with me, when all I wanted was to discuss real estate and its implications for the Iraqi people, specifically as this related to the defense of their country. He wouldn't give me a minute of his time. I spent months working on land ownership and title issues, most of which could have been resolved in a matter of days if not hours if this jerk would have met with me.

I told David Murtagh about the difficulty I was having getting a meeting with this guy. Finally, David told me he would be in a conference with him the following day, and would specifically bring up my request for a meeting. The conference was going to be in General Dempsey's office, so it was a big deal. The following day I saw David and asked if he had any luck the fellow, specifically on the question of when I could meet with him. David looked at me, shook his head, and told me he couldn't repeat the guy's response. The real estate issues I was trying to resolve went on for months. So much for working as a team to help the Iraqi people.

The U.S. Embassy was temporarily located in the north wing of the Republican Palace, while the rest of the State Department operations were in the south wing. Being part of State, IRMO (now called ITAO) was in the south wing. One of my highest priorities was getting maps showing where former Iraqi Army camps and bases had been. With these, the Real Estate Division at MOD could at least start with an inventory of real property, and grow from there. But there were no maps to be found. Everyone I asked about old Iraqi maps said the same thing, that they had all been destroyed when the mapping and surveying facility on the outskirts of Baghdad was bombed by the U.S. during the opening days of the invasion.

After some digging I met an Iraqi expat (he had left after the first Gulf War and then returned to cash in as a contractor—there were many like him) working in one of the offices at IRMO. He said he knew of an Iraqi general with maps in his house that he had taken during the U.S. invasion in 2003. Then he said the officer would produce his maps if he could get a job. One day, before I had a chance to act on this information, an Iraqi brigadier general showed up at MOD as the new Deputy Director of the Real Estate Division, under the Iraqi two-star general I advised. He was a friend of the general, which is how he got his job. He was the same Iraqi general who had the maps. He had two huge folders with maps of the entire country, showing every former Iraqi army camp outlined in red grease pencil. I had hit the mother lode!

I heard that the U.S. National Geospatial-Intelligence Agency, or NGA, had an office in the Embassy. I contacting a couple of guys who worked there, who told me they could make all the maps I needed, even digitized! (NGA has changed its name so many times it's hard to know what it is called from one day to the next. It has also been called the Army Map Service, the Defense

Mapping Agency, and the National Imaging and Mapping Agency.) I took the map books brought in by the Iraqi general, and handed them over to the guys at NGA. After a long wait (actually, way too long) they scanned each map sheet, creating a digital copy of the general's maps showing where every former Iraqi army installation had been located. With this we could tell J-7 where old Iraqi camps were, and also load the information into the database of the Real Estate Division at MOD.

I couldn't help but think why, with all the resources at its disposal, J-7 wasn't able to come up with these maps on its own. The reason was simple—J-7 didn't have the close communication with the Iraqis that I did. But that was my job. If J-7 would use this information was another matter. At least once in a while something positive got done.

When Paul Bremer disbanded the Ministry of Defense, all of its camps and installations were taken as well. With a new Ministry of Defense, these could be returned and put back into MOD's inventory. I began working on this shortly after arriving in Iraq, but in spite of my efforts was getting nowhere. Then one day the Ministry of Defense real estate staff came up with their own solution. They listed all former MOD camps in a couple of memos which they sent to the Minister of Defense, Abdul Qadir. The memos requested his approval to place these locations back in MOD's name. The Minister signed two of these memos. There were only a few more for him to sign when the Iraqi Ministry of Finance (MOF) found out and stopped everything. The Ministry of Finance wouldn't allow anything without being in control, even if someone else came up with a system that worked.

Soon after this, MNSTC-I's J-5 and J-7 came up with their own joint memo, which was a "copycat" of the two memos that had been signed by the Minister of Defense. This was the only time the U.S. followed the Iraqi's lead on anything. The J-5/J-7 memo, which was signed by LTG Dempsey, was sent directly to the Minister of Defense, Abdul Qadir, for his approval. The memo listed dozens of new camps (not former MOD camps) that J-7 planned to construct for the Prime Minister's Initiative. The memo was using the same technique the MOD Real Estate Branch had used by asking for Abdul Qadir's approval to have title for the land automatically put in MOD's name. If J-5/J-7 had collaborated with the MOD Real Estate Branch, it could have gotten Abdul Qadir signature on their memo too. Even though J-5/J-7 never told me about the memo before sending it to Abdul Qadir, they wrote it identifying me as his primary point of contact! The memo was an admission by J-7 that land ownership and title had to be considered when it was planning to build camps for the Iraqi military. Up to that time J-7's chief acted as though land title didn't mean anything. This was shown by his reaction when I asked for transport of the MOD staff to the Land Registration Offices, which could have helped him do his job. Then the memo was written, indicating me as the point of contact, without the professional courtesy of telling me. Because J-7 and J-5 wrote the memo on their own, without going through the Ministry of Defense real estate staff, they were never able to track it down.

When the J-5/J-7 memo disappeared, the Navy captain and I were called to a meeting with Brigadier General Wolff, who wanted to know what had happened to it. But the real reason for the meeting was General Wolff's impending departure for the States. He needed to close the loop on the memo because his boss, LTG Dempsey, had signed it and it had never been found. I guess if he wasn't leaving so soon BG Wolff wouldn't have cared less about the memo. The meeting ended with no action or decision by General Wolff. He was leaving for a fat job back in Washington, so what did he care? He just needed something to say to get LTG Dempsey off his back.

A few weeks later I was called to the J-7 Navy captain's office. He was going over the memo (written by his own staff and J-5) line-by-line, and crapping in his pants. He had been ordered by LTG Dempsey to report on the status of the memo immediately. This meant he had to report to the MNSTC-I commander the status of land J-7 was illegally constructing MOD bases on. The captain discovered that half the locations listed in the memo had changed because J-7 was building camps somewhere else. He was just figuring out the bases listed in the memo didn't match what he was building for MOD. If he had looked at the memo when I handed it to him in General Wolff's office, he would have known what his staff was building for the Iraqis before being called into LTG Dempsey's office to explain it. It was bad enough that J-7 and the rest of MNSTC-I did everything on their own and never consulted with the Iraqis or anyone else. But the Navy captain didn't even know what his own staff was doing. If J-7 had included the MOD Real Estate Branch in what it was doing for the ministry, we could have worked together to come up with an accurate list of locations where J-7 needed to build Iraqi camps, and collaborated on getting clear title. J-7 could have found the best locations for new camps based the institutional knowledge of the MOD staff. J-7 created its own problems by doing everything on its own and not including the MOD Real Estate Branch on anything it did, or was planning to do, for the ministry. Yet, here was the J-7 Navy captain asking me which camps listed in his own memo were being built by him, and which camps weren't. But his staff wouldn't talk to me, so how would I know?

If there had been any sort of coordination, cooperation, and collaboration between J-7 and MODTT, this wouldn't have happened. The Navy captain was constructing camps for MOD, and didn't even look at the memo I gave him listing where these camps were going. His J-7 staff had written the memo prior to his arrival in Iraq. Simple common sense would have told him to read a memo his staff wrote prior to his arrival in Iraq, because he was now responsible for what it said. And it was signed by a three-star general! But because it was given to him by me, a contractor, he didn't give a damn what it said. That's why he never read it. The memo was now obsolete and full of errors, yet was still floating around MOD waiting for the Minister's signature. As I stood in front of his desk, the captain called in members of his staff to ask them about the locations listed in the memo—*his memo*. His deputy, the Navy commander, was there and said both he and the captain just received the memo, which the captain knew wasn't true. He hadn't looked at the memo until that day, and wouldn't acknowledge I had given him a copy of it at the meeting with BG Wolff, certainly not in front of his deputy. LTG Dempsey had no doubt just woken up to the fact that MOD camps were being built on land the ministry didn't own, which I had been telling anyone who would listen for a year. He was catching heat from our own Treasury Department over J-7's failure to get the transfer and acceptance documents signed by MOD. Without that, the books couldn't be closed on the U.S. money spent to build Iraq's army camps and facilities.

J-7 continued to build military installations for the Iraqi Ministry of Defense without any clear land title. Who knows how many individual projects have been signed for by MOD and MOI, of the thousands J-7 has constructed on their behalf over the past ten years? J-7 may have gotten the documents signed at some point, but about ten years late. Even if these documents have all been signed, what difference does it make if the projects never had clear title to the land they were built on? Everything J-7 did was a violation of Iraqi property law, and ran counter to the United States' intent of "transition" from the Coalition to Iraq's responsibility for its own destiny—under rules of law we were supposed to be following. It was also lousy accountability of U.S. Government funds on a grand scale.

About 10 months into my tour I was told by the first deputy chief of J-7, the Mississippi school teacher, that General Dempsey had received word of all the claims for land that had been illegally taken from its rightful owners, essentially by J-7. (There were 125,000 claims for the wrongful taking of privately owned land in Iraq.) According to the J-7 deputy, LTG Dempsey ordered a halt to all Ministry of Interior construction projects being done by J-7. When I heard this I was pleasantly surprised to hear that LTG Dempsey was finally taking action on this important issue. I assumed a similar order would be coming down from LTG Dempsey regarding Ministry of Defense construction projects too. But I never heard a thing about this. J-7 was doing the exact same thing regarding the illegal taking of land for both MOI and MOD projects, but a "cease work" order never came down regarding MOD. J-7 simply continued building camps for the Ministry of Defense like it always had. It was very likely a similar order would be coming down from LTG Dempsey regarding MOD, yet J-7 continued taking land from its rightful owners without any legal transfer or title documents. It was going to keep taking land illegally for the construction of MOD camps until it got caught and ordered to stop by LTG Dempsey.

A land war should be fought by a land force, to include all of its engineering and construction. U.S. Army engineers know how to do these things, Navy and Air Force engineers don't. Air Force engineers build hangers, and Navy engineers build docks, so why would you ask them to construct an army camp in a desert in the middle of a land war? But that's our new and improved "joint forces" way of doing things. The pathetic comment by U.S. Air Force General Allardice to the U.S. Army full colonel, or the Marines not allowing U.S. Army aircraft to fly into "its airspace" in Anbar Province, say all there is about how well the joint forces concept works. One of the U.S. Navy captains we worked with actually claimed to be equal to a U.S. Army one-star general. The military services got along better when they were separated. They knew where they stood with each other then, instead of the "one team" garbage being shoved down their throats now. But don't ask a senior ranking officer what he thinks about it. You know what his answer will be. I bet Major General Allardice would say it's a pleasure working with the U.S. Army. And the Marines would say they just love working with everyone.

By May 2007, the old J-7 staff started rotating out. It was being replaced by a new group, again all military reservists, again a new crop of people who didn't know facilities or real estate. Like their predecessors they all wore uniforms, so civilians didn't count, which soon became evident. They all acted as though the moment they put on their uniforms they knew all there was to know about everything.

Around this time I heard of a meeting with all the members of the J-7 staff, old and new, ten minutes before it was about to start. The meeting was to discuss the Iraqi's signing for hundreds of MOD projects, the same projects I had offered to help J-7 get Iraqi signatures for 10 months earlier. The outgoing J-7 staff was in a panic to get these packages signed because LTG Dempsey, who was leaving in two weeks, had ordered them to get this done. A lieutenant colonel from the old J-7 staff said that nothing had been done to get these packages signed and closed out. As he said this to the new staff he looked right at me, like he was baiting me. I spoke up and told the whole group that MOD's Real Estate Branch had been ready to help J-7 get this done for a year, and that the failure was not the fault of MOD staff. In other words, don't even think of pinning the blame for this screw up on me or my client. Getting these documents signed was entirely J-7's responsibility, not mine. I had offered to help, and was getting thrown under the bus by the same people who had dropped the ball. The outgoing J-7 staff was blaming me in front of their replacements because I was a contractor, and an easy target.

After the meeting I was in the hallway talking with a couple of the old J-7 officers when I heard for the first time that the acceptance packages were just being assembled by J-7's contractors for MOD signature. J-7 hadn't yet compiled the documents for the Iraqis to sign, in some cases for projects completed three years earlier, because it couldn't get its own contractors to provide the needed paperwork. J-7 was in a panic to close the books on hundreds of projects built for the Iraqi Ministry of Defense, as directed to by the United States Department of the Treasury. If an MOD representative was standing there with a pen in his hand, J-7 had nothing for him to sign! Yet J-7 had no problem trying to pin this fiasco on me.

In all the years I have been in commercial real estate and construction, I've never heard of a project where the General Contractor doesn't provide all the documents and plans to its client. This is always written into the contract. Yet this was how all of J-7's projects were being executed. There was no routine provision of paperwork given to J-7 by its contractors, American firms that had to know the requirements for submission of documents needed by their client. Maybe J-7 never asked for the documents, so its contractors never bothered to provide them. Now J-7 was asking its contractors to go back three years or more and produce the paperwork needed to close out projects it was managing on behalf of the U.S. Government—projects worth billions of dollars.

This was just one example of J-7's gross mismanagement of its projects, and its failure to properly account for the expenditure of U.S. Government funds. Among J-7's staff there were two lieutenant colonels and a major whose job it was to manage the closing out of these projects, yet the job couldn't get accomplished. When the initial group of J-7 staff was about to leave Iraq, I witnessed five of its officers get the Bronze Star. Two of them were responsible for closing out those MOD projects. Another one was the officer responsible for building all those bases and hundreds of individual facilities on land the Ministry of Defense didn't legally own.

For months I asked J-7 for plans and documents related to the camps it had built for the Ministry of Defense. As the ministry's real estate advisor, I wanted to get as much information from J-7 as possible for the ministry's real estate files and database. All I got were CAD (computer aided design) drawings for two camps on some 8½ x 11 sheets of paper. I was told by a reserve U.S. Army lieutenant colonel, one of the new J-7 staffers, that there were no such files in existence. This meant that J-7 had contracted out to several American construction companies to have hundreds of facilities and dozens of camps built for the Iraqi Ministry of Defense, over a period of at least three years, yet the contractors who performed the work never provided any drawings of their projects to their client, J-7. To the best of my knowledge, J-7 hadn't asked for them. I was blown away. If it wasn't a J-7 requirement for its contractors to provide drawings and other documents, it certainly should have been. Either way, not having this as a requirement in its construction contracts showed J-7's lack of knowledge and competence in the construction field. It was inexcusable.

When I left Iraq in September 2007, about 20 individual projects had been signed for by the Ministry of Defense, which showed some progress. These were 20 individual buildings, not 20 camps or military installations, out of roughly 300 that J-7 had built for MOD. It had built at least 2,000 for MOI. Many more could have been signed for and accepted by MOD if J-7 had been on top of its contractors for the required documentation, and if it had worked collaboratively with the Ministry of Defense real estate staff. Unfortunately, the first Navy captain in charge of J-7 would have nothing to do with the concept of cooperation, and he passed this attitude onto his successor. Getting to the 19 Land Registration Offices to determine land ownership was impossible. In the 14 months I spent was in Iraq, I never made it to a single one of these offices. J-7 could get to any one of them any time it wanted to. If J-7 was spending billions of U.S. dollars to construct these facilities, and it required the Iraqis to sign for them, why not pay a little money to get them there to inspect the facilities? But no, this was out of the question for J-7's two Navy captains who ran it while I was there. For some odd reason they blocked every attempt to get the Iraqis to these sites. All this was in addition to the transfer of old Coalition FOBs to Iraqi control, involving the real property staff of MNF-I and MNC-I, who I got no cooperation from either.

I felt as though I was the only one who cared about getting any of these tasks done, yet they were J-7's responsibility. The two Navy captains were incapable of doing their jobs using the most basic construction industry practices, not to mention any semblance of the rule of law. The awards given to these officers reflected the accomplishment of their mission, yet in a year they couldn't even get a stack of paperwork signed to close the books on the expenditure of billions of U.S. tax dollars. If they failed their primary mission, why did they get awarded medals for it?

The Iraqis told me they had no problem signing for the projects, but would not do so unless they saw them first. I passed this on to J-7, which didn't see it that way. At a meeting between a lieutenant colonel from J-7 and the Iraqi two-star general in charge of real estate for the Ministry of Defense, the colonel asked if Google satellite photographs would satisfy the Iraqis' requirement to inspect these facilities!

One of the main camps in Baghdad that had to be turned over and signed for by the Iraqi Ministry of Defense was FOB Honor. FOB Honor was on the grounds of one of Saddam's government complexes in the center of Baghdad and the International Zone (IZ). This was the same complex where the ziggurat-shaped (pyramid-shaped) Council of Ministers building was located, televised in flames the opening night of the war. FOB Honor was the home of the 5th Brigade of the 6th Division of the Iraqi army, whose mission was the defense of that sector of Baghdad. J-7 had constructed 19 new barracks and office buildings for the brigade. The Ministry of Defense building was located just across Haifa Street from FOB Honor. It was so overcrowded the Ministry decided to take several of the new buildings on FOB Honor away from the 5th Brigade and use them for its own needs. All 19 buildings on FOB Honor had to be signed for by MOD, just like the hundreds of others J-7 had constructed for the Ministry of Defense throughout Iraq. Again, I told J-7 that I would assist in getting MOD to sign for the buildings. I began to see a pattern now: every time I offered to help J-7 they would say OK, but when it came time to taking me up on it nothing ever happened.

MOD was always hiring more people, all with connections that got them a job. The hallways were constantly crowded with people doing nothing, hanging out and smoking cigarettes. But when an Iraqi general officer came walking down the hall the crowd would part like Moses and the Red Sea. Probably 85% of MOD staff didn't do a thing except collect a paycheck, but the 5th Brigade was still getting kicked out of buildings on FOB Honor to make room for them. When the Ministry of Defense decided to start moving people into the buildings on FOB Honor, J-7 suddenly insisted that the ministry sign for them before taking occupancy! FOB Honor was literally across the street from the MOD building, so J-7's request was easy. But if the facility or camp was outside the city limits of Baghdad, J-7 ignored the requirement.

I was coordinating the inspection of the 19 buildings with J-7. After a couple of missed attempts to get the inspections done, a "drop dead" date and time was agreed for the Iraqis from MOD to meet with the J-7 staff and the American contractor who had constructed the buildings. On the appointed day I assembled about six Iraqis, which was itself a monumental task, and was ready to bring them to FOB Honor. At the last minute we were informed that the MOD Secretary General, the second ranking person in the Ministry of Defense, had issued a memorandum directing that a "committee" be formed for the inspections!

After centuries of being governed in hierarchical and overly-bureaucratic ways, with the top-down nature of their society, and constantly being in fear of the reactions of their superiors, Iraqis can't do a thing without forming a committee first. This was one of the most frustrating things we had to deal with while working with them. Iraqis can't make a decision even if their lives depend on it. They practically need to form a committee to go to the bathroom.

As a result of the Secretary General's memo, the inspection was postponed until the following day. I e-mailed an Iraqi expatriate in the J-7 office, Mr. Saad, telling him of the change.

We both agreed the inspection would be the following morning at 10 a.m.

At 10 a.m. the next day I arrived with several Iraqis to conduct the inspection, but no one from J-7 was there. About 15 minutes later a vehicle finally showed up. A U.S. Air Force major from J-7, and another Iraqi expat from J-7 got out. The major said he didn't know anything about the inspection until 10 minutes earlier, and was told by someone on the J-7 staff to get over to FOB Honor right away. I found out later that the major was the Project Manager for all the 19 buildings. If he was the Project Manager, how could he not know about the inspection until 10 minutes before? I asked him if he knew where the General Contractor was, and he said he had no idea.

I had worked very hard to make this inspection happen for the sole purpose of helping J-7 and the Iraqis clear up the paperwork on the FOB Honor buildings. Obviously, J-7 didn't care. This was after J-7 suddenly began to make a big deal about the Iraqis signing for projects it had built for them, especially on FOB Honor. I asked where Mr. Saad was, and the major said he had been ordered by his boss, the Navy captain, to do something else. I couldn't believe Mr. Saad wasn't there. He was in charge of the turnover for all J-7 projects.

Realizing J-7 didn't care about the inspection, I told the J-7 major that I was going back to MOD. When I returned to my office I sent an e-mail to the Navy captain in charge of J-7. I explained what had happened at FOB Honor earlier that morning, and copied the MNSTC-I Chief of Staff, a U.S. Army full colonel who reported directly to the commander, a three-star general. I thought he should be aware of what was going on.

A few weeks after the FOB Honor fiasco, I was called into the office of the newly arrived Chief of Staff of MODTT, the organization I was in. The new chief was a female U.S. Army lieutenant colonel. She was replacing the current chief, who was leaving before completing his full one-year tour. The outgoing MODTT Chief of Staff had been in Iraq for about 10 months. When he first arrived we had a conversation during which he openly spoke about not wanting to be in Iraq. He went on to say he didn't agree with the Iraq war and only wanted to be with his family in New Jersey. I was shocked to hear him say all this, and couldn't believe he was sharing it with anyone, much less with me. This guy had no problem telling people he didn't want to be serving in Iraq, yet he was a career Army officer. At least he was speaking his mind, which was unique. While in Iraq he was selected for command of a "line" signal battalion in the States upon his return. Instead, he turned it down and requested command of a training battalion. If he commanded a "line" signal battalion, he might get sent back to Iraq. (A line unit is a maneuver or operational unit, not a training or support unit. Line units are the ones in actual combat.) The chief of staff was a lousy officer. He had no business telling a member of his staff his personal feelings on the war, or his desire to be at home with his family rather than serving his country in combat. If he didn't like the war or being away from his family, he should have shut up and resigned. But he was too lazy. The Army was too easy and the benefits were too good.

When I was in the Army the chance to command a line battalion was like striking gold. No one wanted to command a training battalion, with the responsibility of dealing with new recruits off the street. But this officer was not a leader in the "old school" sense. He was a modern day officer who wanted to cling to his wife's apron strings rather than command a line signal battalion. I was told he would get up in the middle of the night, waking his roommate, to talk to his wife for hours over his computer voice hookup. What did he care if he woke up his roommate? He had to talk to his wife.

When she called me into her office, the new MODTT Chief of Staff handed me a Letter of Reprimand written by her predecessor, described above. He had left Iraq two weeks earlier. The letter was given to me because I had "violated" its probationary period. The previous Chief of Staff never gave it to me. The letter was the result of several e-mails that had been sent to him from the J-7 staff relating to the inspection at FOB Honor J-7 had blown off. The letters also included everything else J-7 didn't like about me. The Navy captain in charge of J-7, as well as his deputy, must have gotten their staff together when I e-mailed the MNSTC-I Chief of Staff about the FOB Honor inspection. This is the only possible way all these letters had been written and sent to the MODTT Chief of Staff. These two senior officers must have ordered their people to write these e-mails to the MODTT Chief of Staff to discredit me to my chain of command. How else could a handful of e-mails, all from the J-7 staff, show up on the desk of the MODTT Chief of Staff at the same time? This was collusion by United States military officers to discredit a civilian contractor who was trying to do his job, a job created by J-7.

The Navy captain and his deputy were discrediting me in retaliation for emailing the MNSTC-I Chief of Staff about the poor way J-7, specifically the Navy captain in charge, was managing its construction projects for the Ministry of Defense. When I e-mailed the MNSTC-I Chief of Staff, the Navy captain in charge of J-7 must have felt the need to protect himself by ordering his staff to write their e-mails about me. I was simply doing the job I was hired to do, which wasn't what the captain wanted. But by doing my job, I highlighted flaws in the way J-7 was doing its job. My job was to advise the Iraqi Ministry of Defense on its real estate issues. These were being adversely affected by the sloppy way J-7 was executing its mission of constructing facilities for my client. When J-7 blew off the inspection at FOB Honor that was the last straw, which was why I sent the e-mail to the MNSTC-I Chief of Staff. I had an obligation to bring to his attention problems one of his staff sections (J-7) was creating for my client. Anything less and I wasn't doing my job.

The U.S. Air Force Center for Environmental Excellence, or AFCEE (which has been changed to the Air Force Center for Engineering and the Environment) was the politically correct name of the Air Force's equivalent of the U.S. Army Corps of Engineers. AFCEE was used exclusively by J-7 to provide contract management services for all its construction projects in Iraq. When it was decided to build a camp for the Iraqi military, it wasn't planned, designed or constructed by the Ministry of Defense's Director General (DG) for Infrastructure, the engineering and real estate staff of the Ministry. The DG wasn't involved at all. Instead, J-7 built the camp based on information it received from J-5 (Plans), which had decided where the camp was going, with minimal input from the Iraqi military. This entire process was contrary to the ideal of "transition" to the Iraqis any control of their own destiny and ability to defend their country. In reality, J-5 selected new locations for Iraqi military camps, the Joint Headquarters Transition Team (JHQTT) would determine what Iraqi units would be stationed there, and J-7 would build it. I tried to get J-5 and J-7 to involve the Iraqis more, but was ignored.

J-7 would turn to the AFCEE Contracting Officer, who sat in the same office as the J-7 staff, eliminating any pretense of separation of responsibilities. AFCEE would in turn go to one of the four designated American construction companies to get the work done. AFCEE was responsible for awarding the contracts to have all of the Ministry of Defense's camps built. But it was J-7 who ordered AFCEE to do it. By contrast, when Operation Iraqi Freedom began in the spring of 2003, the U.S. Army Corps of Engineers Gulf Region District (GRD) legally acquired the land from its owners that was needed for Forward Operating Bases (FOBs). The Corps of Engineers did the footwork and acquired title, or in most cases leased the land needed for these FOBs. By the time I arrived in Iraq GRD was gearing down, as all the FOBs needed for Coalition units had been built. It was now MNSTC-I's mission to reverse what Paul Bremer did when he disbanded the Iraqi military and national police, and get the new Ministries of Defense and Interior on their feet, with camps and buildings to operate from.

However, instead of doing what the Corps of Engineers did when it secured title or leasehold interest in the land, J-7 simply ignored this step entirely and started camps and facilities for the Iraqi Ministries of Defense and Interior. When it turned to AFCEE to issue its construction contracts, the same thing happened. Not only was J-7 failing to secure legal title for land, AFCEE failed to make sure its contracts didn't have a "cloud" over them, meaning a legal flaw that could open the contract to dispute later. Not having clear title to the land a project was built on greatly exposed the United States Government and the Iraqi Ministry of Defense to future lawsuit. But neither J-7, nor AFCEE, cared one bit. I don't think they understood the implications of what they were doing, or failing to do. Neither of them cared about Iraqi land ownership or property rights, but the U.S. Army Corps of Engineers certainly did. One of the U.S.

contractors in Iraq told me AFCEE was liked by him and the other contractors because it wasn't a "big bloated bureaucracy like the Corps of Engineers," and was "lean and got things done." It was "lean" all right, especially when it came to securing legal title.

If J-7 was building MOD's installations with U.S. money, it had the responsibility of making sure AFCEE's contracts were legally sufficient and adhered to the Federal Acquisition Regulations—the FAR. This meant ensuring that everything needed to construct an Iraqi military camp was in the Scope of Work (SOW), which was part of AFCEE's construction contracts. As the U.S. contracting entity, AFCEE had Contracting Officers who were warranted to sign U.S. Government contracts, which required adherence to the FAR. Because the contracts AFCEE awarded were being funded with U.S. Treasury money, they were U.S. Government contracts. It was J-7's responsibility to ensure that land ownership was the first thing it addressed when planning a new camp, before the first shovel was put in the ground. Failure to do this in the United States would cause the entire project to end up in court. J-7 made no attempt to do things correctly. Instead, it acted as if it was building a house in the United States but not securing title to the land first; and not caring at all what happened later. Even though this was Iraq, it didn't mean this step was not needed. But J-7 didn't look at it that way. Both Navy captains blew the whole thing off, rather than going out of their way to make sure these steps were followed, thereby demonstrating that the Iraqi rule of law actually meant something.

J-7's philosophy was, "show me where to build it and get out of my way." This was most apparent in the J-7 officer directly responsible for the construction of MOD projects. The officer, a U.S. Army reserve lieutenant colonel, wouldn't talk to me, even after I had asked to meet with him several times. All he did was sit at his computer and tell the AFCEE Contracting Officer what to do. (There was one AFCEE Contracting Officer for all the projects J-7 was building for MOD. That was way too much for one person if J-7 expected to get its projects done legally. When I worked at the General Services Administration (GSA), a typical Contracting Officer had a workload of 15 projects, no more than

20, at one time.) His carefree attitude towards the Iraqi rule of law and property ownership was evident. He made no effort to get the Iraqis to sign for new projects, showing that three years of this neglect by his predecessors was OK with him. He just continued doing what J-7 had been doing before he got there. The actual responsibility of getting the Iraqis to sign for the projects J-7 had built, and for new projects this lieutenant colonel was building, fell on two other lieutenant colonels and a major, all in J-7. But nothing was ever done in their area of responsibility. When they departed Iraq for the United States, all but one of these J-7 officers were awarded the Bronze Star, a medal for valor in combat. They didn't display valor in combat, and they didn't display "valor" in the management of their construction projects.

Because J-7 had no plans for the camps and facilities it had built for the Ministry of Defense, the ministry would need the capability to conduct surveys and produce plans and drawings on its own. This would apply to other real estate and installations that would someday come into its inventory. This is what J-7 should have been doing all along. Because J-7 hadn't done its job, the Iraqis would have to do it themselves, something like the "transition" General Dempsey talked about all the time but no one saw in action. I developed a Scope of Work (SOW) describing the tasks needed to accomplish this, which in turn would be the basis of a contract awarded by MOD. That was the plan, and everyone knows about plans. In an effort to keep everyone informed, I mentioned the SOW to two officers from J-7. They appeared to be interested in the idea and asked for the SOW to have an Independent Government Estimate (IGE) done. This would be used in negotiations with prospective contractors. These steps are basic U.S. Government contracting, the type of work that AFCEE's Contracting Officer would know inside and out, or so I thought. I gave them the draft SOW, thinking this would be a good project to work on together with J-7.

Two weeks later I was doing work at KMTB (Kirkuk Military Training Base), a camp about 25 miles from Iran. Because I had to return to Baghdad earlier than planned, I got a ride with the senior person from one of the construction companies used by J-7 and AFCEE. We were in a convoy of armored vehicles belonging to the security company hired by the U.S. firm that was doing work at KMTB. We were about half way back to Baghdad when the senior guy from the construction firm, who was sitting next to me, asked about the Request for Proposal (RFP) that had been put out by AFCEE to survey all of MOD's military installations. From his description, it sounded just like the Scope of Work (SOW) that I had given to the J-7 officers. They still hadn't gotten back to me with an Independent Government Estimate of the project's cost, based on my SOW.

I asked if he had a copy of the RFP. He said it was on his computer and showed it to me. The RFP was the same Scope of Work that I wrote, word for word. It requested proposals from the U.S. construction firms to do the work, including their proposed cost of the job. I told him the RFP was not out, that it had not been released yet, and that I would look into it when I got back to the IZ. After the trip, I went to one of the J-7 officers I had given the SOW to, and asked him what he had done with it. I told him the SOW was now an actual RFP that was on the street for bid. He said he knew nothing about the RFP, but had passed the SOW along to the AFCEE Contracting Officer.

I went to the Contracting Officer that same day and asked him what was going on. He told me he was asking the contractors he used for all the work in Iraq for their estimates of the cost of the project! I told him it was a violation of the FAR (the Federal Acquisition Regulation) to provide contactors he planned to bid the work out to with a copy of the SOW prior to an Independent Government Estimate (IGE) being performed. Without the IGE, he would have no idea if the bids he received from the contractors were fair and reasonable. He was asking them to come up with their own cost estimate of the job they were going to bid on, without the government having its own independent estimate to compare their bids to. That was the whole purpose of the Scope of Work that I had given to the J-7 officers. In effect, the contractors would be bidding against their own cost estimate of the job. This would nullify the competitive process and the U.S. Government's ability to get the best price for the Ministry of Defense.

I don't think the Contracting Officer knew what an Independent Government Estimate was. If he did, he was completely ignoring this most vital step in awarding a contract that was sponsored by the U.S. Government. He quickly got an attitude with me and started to make a joke of the whole thing. It was obvious he either knew nothing about the purpose of an IGE, or he didn't care. I told him I had been a warranted Contracting Officer at GSA, and what he was doing was grounds for an IG (Inspector General) complaint. When I said this he backed off and cancelled his RFP. Because of this I never went any further with the idea of the Ministry of Defense contracting with a firm to survey its installations, a task that was needed because J-7 (through AFCEE) hadn't done it. Even when I tried to help the Iraqis do something on their own, J-7 got involved and screwed the whole thing up. The AFCEE Contracting Officer was later shipped back to San Antonio where he was based.

I went back to the J-7 officers I had first given the SOW to and told them what had happened with the AFCEE Contracting Officer. The intent of the Scope of Work was for use by MOD in awarding its own contract, not J-7 awarding it for them. But these two officers said J-7 had to do the work for MOD, that the ministry couldn't award the contract on its own. This was nonsense. MOD did award contracts, but not many. Because J-7 hadn't done anything to produce plans or drawings of camps it constructed for MOD, the ministry had to do this on its own. But J-7 didn't want MOD to have the ability to do that. Two officers from J-7 were telling me MOD couldn't execute its own contract, which it needed because J-7 hadn't done its job. I'm convinced the two J-7 officers had no intention of helping me when they asked for the SOW I had drafted. They wanted it so J-7 could award the work, through AFCEE, to one of its preferred contractors.

I cannot close this discussion of MNSTC-I and its construction branch, J-7, without relating the story of the Iraqi army camp near the ancient city of Ur, the home of Abraham. Ur is about 20 miles above the northern tip of the Persian Gulf. At one point in time the Gulf went as far north as Ur itself. It has since receded 20 or so miles. The land between the Gulf and

Ur is lowlands of marsh and saw grass. We needed to locate a site at the camp for one of the supply warehouses mentioned previously.

We flew to Ur on a U.S. Army twin-engine fixed-wing aircraft called a "Sherpa." It looks like a flying boxcar, but is actually pretty comfortable inside. Like helicopters, Sherpa's were flown at treetop level in Iraq to avoid being seen and shot down. We flew to Ur at 250 miles per hour, 100 feet off the ground. When we landed we stayed at a Coalition camp 10 miles to the south, at Tallit. This was originally an Italian army camp, named after its commander. After several Italian soldiers were killed by a suicide bomber in November 2003, Italy began to withdraw from the "Coalition of the Willing." Of course, soldiers sometimes get killed. But when some actually were, the Italians pulled out. They wanted no more of Operation Iraqi Freedom. I suppose they thought none of their soldiers would die when they sent them there. Call it "Italian logic." Tallit had become an Australian Army camp, with CMATT advisors who convoyed twice a week to the camp at Ur to train Iraqi soldiers there.

We waited a day for the next convoy to take us to the camp, riding in Australian Army "Bushmaster" armored personnel carriers. This is an Australian home-grown and designed armored vehicle being adopted by the U.S. Army in Iraq because of its V-shaped hull. The hull deflects IED's (improvised explosive devices) and EFP's (explosively formed penetrators), preventing them from blasting through the undercarriage of the vehicle and killing the occupants. The driver sits on the right in British style, and the remote machine gunner sits on the left with pistol grips and a TV camera he uses to control the mini-gun mounted on the roof.

As an aside, the U.S. sent its initial forces to Iraq in the spring of 2003 without armor plating on their HUMVEE's, and not enough protective vests. In some cases soldiers were buying their own vests because they hadn't been issued one. Many American soldiers were killed as a direct result, yet Donald Rumsfeld refused to take any action to correct the problem until a soldier had the courage to confront him during his visit to U.S. troops in December 2004. A U.S. Army sergeant stood up and asked Rumsfeld why our HUMVEE's had been sent to Iraq without armor plating to protect our soldiers from enemy fire. He also asked why there weren't enough armored vests for soldiers who had been deployed. Rumsfeld blew the sergeant off, saying: "You go with the army you have, not the army you might want or wish to have at a later time." In other words, Rummy was telling the sergeant (and everyone else) to shut up and quit complaining. Rumsfeld's callous answer to this legitimate question was a slap in the face of every soldier who had died up to that point because he lacked adequate protection. It also highlighted the complete lack of planning and preparation for this war. In the case of body armor and HUMVEE armor, the person directly responsible for not protecting our soldiers' lives was Tommy Franks, the young sergeant's field commander. Franks spent more time pampering Rumsfeld than adequately preparing and equipping his forces for war.

We convoyed to the camp at Ur, going straight to the camp commander's office for chi (tea), which is Iraqi custom. Then we set out to inspect the camp for the warehouse site. Afterward we were asked if we wanted to see the rest of the camp. We said fine and started our "tour." That's when I saw something I will never forget. The camp had been built by J-7 for the Iraqi army, using one of the four U.S. construction companies as the General Contractor, with local labor. This was how J-7 constructed all camps for the Iraqi army. The buildings were all made with white sheet metal skin on the outside, like a "Butler Building" in the States. The interiors were concrete stucco and tile, very typical in Iraq. But what got my attention was the condition of the buildings. I have mentioned how Iraqis trash their buildings, but the camp at Ur took this to another level. Urine and feces were all over the latrine floors. Holes in the floors used for commodes didn't work because they were so clogged up. The plumbing didn't work, water was leaking everywhere, tiles were popping off the floors and walls, and windows were falling out of their frames onto the ground outside. The lack of trash cleanup was one thing, but the physical condition of the facilities was another. The buildings were so poorly constructed they were completely falling apart. Cleanliness would have helped, but superficially at best. The construction of the buildings at Ur was the worst I've ever seen in my life. The condition of this camp was so incredible I took pictures, and have included them in this story. The camp and its buildings were a year and a half old.

J-7 never included facility maintenance in its budget for these camps, nor did it include training of the Base Engineer to keep the facilities under his charge running efficiently for any length of time. J-7 just went in and built these camps on land the Ministry of Defense didn't own, then walked away. Not only did it fail to get the Iraqis to accept and sign for the work, it failed to get any useful life out of the facilities it built by providing a budget for training and follow-on maintenance. Anyone who knows anything about commercial facilities knows this. What of the cost for these facilities at Ur? Based on the amount of construction and the type, I thought the camp and its buildings might cost $5 to $10 million dollars. I asked the Project Manager from the U.S. construction company that did the work, and he gave me a very direct answer—$118 million! Not only was this an absurd amount, it also pointed to the very real possibility of fraud. It was difficult to come to any other conclusion.

My desire to get something done was in direct conflict with those at MNSTC-I, and the manager from my firm, who didn't want me to do anything that might expose what the U.S. military, specifically J-7, was doing wrong. If J-7 and I had worked together, which of course meant doing things legally and the way they are done in the commercial real estate and construction industry, things would have worked out better. Not that everything would have been perfect, but the things J-7 was doing that were screwed up, like those mentioned in this book, could have been addressed. I would ask myself if I was "out of my lane" trying to help J-7 in these areas—if I shouldn't even bother trying to fix what J-7 had screwed up that directly affected my client, the Ministry of Defense. But I wasn't the problem. I was merely bringing the problem to the attention of people who needed to know about it.

MNSTC-I didn't care about civilian contractors on its own staff, or the Iraqis it was there to support, and J-7 most certainly didn't. The amazing thing was that MNSTC-I's sole mission was to assist the Iraqi Ministry of Defense and Ministry of Interior to stand on their own. When I arrived in Iraq, General Dempsey's mantra was "transition!" We heard it every day. But as time went by and it became clear the Iraqis weren't getting anything done, he changed course and ordered his staff to do everything for the Iraqis—to get things finished and out of the way. General Dempsey may have been following orders of his superior, the Joint Forces Commander, General Casey. But he was still a very powerful three-star general, and had a lot of his own authority. General Dempsey was one of only two three-star generals in Iraq under General Casey. The other was General Odierno, the commander of MNC-I. General Dempsey could have done anything he wanted to. All he needed was to justify why. He commanded a three-star unit in combat, so if he couldn't make his own decisions, then what was he doing at that level? If General Dempsey wanted to, he could have let the Iraqis do it all themselves and watch, observe, advise, and correct where needed. But neither he, nor the entire U.S. effort in Iraqi, ever gave the Iraqis a chance to learn things for themselves. Whenever they tried the Coalition would talk about how stupid and backward they were, rather than helping them get on their feet. MNSTC-I did everything for the Iraqis, like building the camp at Ur. For what they got, the Iraqis would have been better off in tents.

It finally started to sink in what being a contractor in Iraq was really all about. I was just a warm body who was a source of revenue for my company to collect fees off the U.S. government. That was it, nothing more. No one cared if I accomplished a thing, or if I had years of experience to offer the Coalition and the Iraqis in my specific field. The U.S. military actually didn't want me to do anything if it was going to run counter to what they wanted to do, were planning to do, or were going to do, regardless of whether I was the real estate "subject matter expert" who they had hired through my firm. I later found out that my position was originally created by two officers who were on the J-7 staff before the arrival of the Navy captain. They knew the importance of land ownership in Iraq, but they were both long gone. The question for me became—why am I here?

We would always hear how inept Iraqis were. They would have to be because we never let them do anything themselves, in their own way, since we "liberated" them. They were forced by the Americans in control (but we're not "occupiers") to do everything our way, which they are culturally unable to do. We've never understood that, yet we were there to help them, to liberate them. What sort of help have we offered Iraq if the offer is extended on the condition it must do everything our way? That's not liberation, but that's exactly the way it's been since 2003. Iraq never needed our money. It has enough oil revenue to buy whatever it wants. But Iraq can't buy anything with its own money because we've forced it to contract for goods and services the American way, which they will never understand. And we call Iraqis inept.

The world can now see the effect of all this. The Iraqi military is no more able to defend the country today than it was in 2006-2007, because the Coalition never gave it the opportunity to do anything on its own. When MNSTC-I was under the command of David Petraeus and Martin Dempsey, the Coalition did everything for the Iraqis, who sat and watched. The only way they were going to learn was to do it themselves. Because of Paul Bremer's disastrous decisions, by 2006-2007 Iraq was sinking into a quagmire, so the Coalition completely took over. When the United States left Iraq in 2011, the country collapsed. When ISIS (the Islamic State of Iraq and Syria) forces attack Iraqi army units, the soldiers turn and run, led by their own commanders. We never took off their training wheels.

10—The Iraqi Ministry of Defense

For nearly three years, from 2003 to 2006, all the general public heard from the American media was how great the Iraqis were doing, all during the height of the insurgency. But in 2007 things started to change. By then the American people were getting tired of the same old story, and reality began to set in that the Iraqis may not be in such great shape after all. What people didn't know, and what the media never reported, was that the Iraqis were never going to be able to defend themselves with any degree of success after we destroyed their economy and removed their two security ministries. These institutions will take years, maybe decades, to rebuild. But it only took days for us to destroy them. How could anyone in their right mind think Iraq would be capable of defending itself when it had no economy and no security, when it was sandwiched between Shia (from Iran) to the east and Sunni (from Saudi Arabia and Syria) to the west, and everyone hates each other? Then there is the autonomous region of Kurdistan in the north of Iraq, whose people spread to Iran and Turkey. All three countries want Kurdistan's territory for its oil.

The United States took away Iraq's ability to defend itself when Paul Bremer disbanded its defense infrastructure—the Iraqi army and national police—firing every member of its armed forces and police down to the simple private and crossing guard. Then he fired everyone in Iraq who was a member of Saddam's Ba'ath Party, so there wasn't anyone around who knew how to do anything. They all left the country with the money they grabbed as the Americans were rolling up the road toward Baghdad. The ones who remained didn't have enough money to pay the $70,000 entry fee charged by Jordan to cross its border. They had nowhere left to go.

Although Saddam Hussein slaughtered many of his own people, that didn't mean every private in the Iraqi Army was also a mass murderer too. On the contrary, the typical Iraqi soldier just wanted a job, like our own soldiers. Within the ranks of the thousands of Iraqi soldiers and policemen who Bremer fired, with their AK-47 rifles and ammunition, there was an existing framework upon which the Coalition (the US) could have built a new army and national police force that was loyal to the new Iraqi Constitution. When Bremer disbanded everything, he also disbanded Iraq's ability to do even the most rudimentary things necessary to defend itself. Like the adult child still dependent on its parents, Iraq became a country that couldn't do anything for itself. It had to depend on the United States for everything, even its defense, when it had oil revenue in the billions. It had an army and national police that it could have equipped and trained, under our supervision. Until the U.S. pulled out, Iraq couldn't spend its own money as it wanted and on what it wanted. We wouldn't allow it to, due to our extremely complicated contracting and procurement methods that we have trouble following ourselves. We forced the Iraqi government to contract for goods and services the same way we do it here in the States. They couldn't do this because they didn't grasp the concept of open competition. I was there and saw it myself. The United States' policies in Iraq have not only dissolved its entire security infrastructure, it also built into the new Iraqi government obstacles that have made it impossible for the Iraqis to get anything done, including spending its own money to defend itself.

I was an advisor to the Iraqi Ministry of Defense for 14 months. The things I witnessed astounded me, not only those things related to the Iraqis I advised, but also the way the Coalition, the Americans, were doing things for the Iraqis. We modeled the new Iraqi Ministry of Defense like our own Department of Defense, with a military side and a civilian side. That was the beginning of the problem. We never stopped to look at the Iraqi culture, to observe how they do things in their own country. They are so different than we are, there is no possible way they can run a ministry like we run one of our cabinet departments. We would always complain about how backward the Iraqis were, yet we never realized their intelligence wasn't the issue, it was their culture.

Our complete failure to understand a society so different than our own ultimately led to the deaths of hundreds of thousands of people, and the international terrorist threat we see today. I witnessed one small part of the terrible dysfunction of America's intervention in Iraq, but this was enough to show why Iraq is now a basket case. It was also enough to understand why the Islamic State is now terrorizing Iraq's civil society and occupying increasing swathes of its territory.

Long before "Mission Accomplished" appeared behind President Bush on the deck of the *USS Abraham Lincoln*, the Coalition Provisional Authority, first under LTG Jay Garner and then Paul Bremer, began to set up the new Iraqi government. The CPA was needed to establish a caretaker government at the end of the initial round of fighting. But the way we (i.e., Paul Bremer) went about this became a huge issue. We took over the day-to-day operation of Iraq and then started to create a new government, placing Iraqis in key positions throughout, under the American model of our own Executive Branch. This might have been pulled off successfully. But when we started to put into place processes and methods of doing things, in this new government that mirrored our ways of doing things in the States, we lost them. Iraqis just don't do things the way we do them. In nearly every case, whatever we wanted them to do, they simply didn't see the need. On top of everything, we expected them to change the way they govern themselves in the middle of a war.

By modeling the new Iraqi government like our own, the new Ministry of Defense was likewise modeled like our own Department of Defense. The MOD's military side is called the "Joint Headquarters Staff," or JHQ. The civilian side is made up of branches, each lead by a "Director General," or DG, similar to our Under and Assistant Secretaries. These were simply referred to as the "DGs." There was the "DG for Personnel," the "DG for Armament and Supply," and the one that I advised, the "DG for Acquisition, Logistics and Infrastructure," or A,L&I. This DG would later be broken up into smaller parts. The DG for A,L&I was the civilian branch of the Ministry of Defense responsible for all purchases, acquisitions, supplies and infrastructure for the Iraqi armed forces. Like all the other DGs, it was headed up by a retired (sometimes active) Iraqi army general who was given the job by his old buddy, Minister of Defense Abdul Qadir, also a retired Iraqi army general. There were no qualified civilian executives to take these jobs. By 2006 they were all gone. They had been killed, fled the country, or they couldn't work because Paul Bremer banned them for being members of Saddam's Ba'ath Party. Every capable and educated man who could have taken one of these jobs had left the country after the Gulf War in the early 1990's, or certainly after our invasion of 2003. Needless to say, there were no women in the Iraqi Ministry of Defense above the level of secretary, translator, or the occasional soldier. I knew the senior ranking woman in the Iraqi army, a major who worked in the Surgeon General's office in the Ministry of Defense.

The DG for A,L&I had immense responsibility, yet never got anything done. None of the DGs in the Ministry got anything done. MNSTC-I staff would complain about how inept the Iraqis were, but never did anything to change the situation. This didn't stop General Casey from telling everyone how great the Iraqis were doing. One of the responsibilities of the DG for AL&I was contracting for supplies and services for the Iraqi army. When we created the new Ministry of Defense, based on the organizational model of our own DoD, we also established new ways for the Iraqis to contract for things. MNSTC-I forced the new Iraqi Ministry of Defense to use our contracting procedures when ordering supplies and services, including competition to get "the best quality at the best price," just like in the Good ol' USA. It didn't quite work in Iraq. As it's been done for a few thousand years, in Iraq you buy from your friend, your cousin, or whoever you want to buy from. Being a Director General in an Iraqi cabinet ministry only meant you had even more authority to buy from your friends, your relatives, and from whoever else you wanted to buy from. But the way the United States modeled the new Iraqi Ministry of Defense, with competition and everything else the Iraqis didn't understand, nothing got done. When MOD wanted to purchase something, it had to use a "Form 53," designed in true American bureaucratic fashion, requiring 19 signatures to complete. But I couldn't place all the blame on the U.S., the Iraqis shared it too. The form, requiring all these signatures, also brought into play another key aspect of the Iraqi culture—the sheer genius by which they avoid taking responsibility for anything.

Under the Saddam regime, in Middle Eastern feudal fashion, everything was done for the people by the government. This adhered to the Middle Eastern tribal tradition of having the leader run the show, while the rest followed. Saddam was that leader, and the Iraqis allowed themselves to be led. There is absolutely no initiative on the part of the individual. It is also the Middle Eastern way to let things go until another day, procrastination in its purest form. Why do anything today that can wait until tomorrow? In America, if it has to be done, it may as well be done now to get it out of the way. Add to this the possibility that something else could get in the way, so I better take care of it now. This makes sense to us, but not to an Iraqi. If it can be done later, what's the problem? "Form 53" was the answer.

Form 53 may not have required as many as 19 signatures when it was originally created, but by the time the Iraqis got through with it they needed everyone's signature except the dog catcher. By requiring so many signatures no single person could be blamed if anything went wrong. The whole group would have to take the hit, which would be too hard to prove and too difficult to punish. The Iraqis raised bureaucracy (i.e., inefficiency) to heights that a U.S. federal agency could only dream of.

By requiring so many signatures for its approval, not only did Form 53 take months to complete so supplies could be ordered and purchased, there was no way an individual could get blamed if something went wrong. But there was one slight problem with Form 53—nothing ever got ordered for the Iraqi Army. On the plus side, however, bureaucrats working in the Ministry of Defense slept soundly at night knowing they couldn't be personally blamed for something that didn't work out as planned. It was far better to get nothing done at all. Their job was to be present, at their desks, and collect a paycheck so they could feed their families. MNSTC-I (i.e., General Dempsey) enabled this inefficiency by doing everything for the Iraqis anyway, so why should they do anything on their own? It was just like welfare. The U.S. allowed all this to happen instead of training the Iraqis, including the senior managers at the Ministry, to get things done and take on more responsibility. We just let it go on, which meant getting nothing done, yet talked a lot about how well the transition was going. It was all "smoke and mirrors" on the part of the Coalition, especially LTG Dempsey.

When the media asks why the Iraqi Army runs away when under attack by the Islamic State, I know the answer. It is because it was never trained to stand on its own by MNSTC-I, under the successive commands of David Petraeus and Martin Dempsey, both of whom were promoted to four-star general in the United States Army. One of them, Martin Dempsey, became Chairman of the Joint Chiefs of Staff. The other, David Petraeus, was lifted up on a cloud of glory to Director of the Central Intelligence Agency, until he got caught with his pants down. It is *very likely* he's being blackmailed into silence over the Benghazi incident by Barack Hussein Obama.[64] It's an interesting world we live in.

The sheer inability to complete anything, repeat anything, by the Iraqis was astounding. We would often shake our heads at the ineptitude of the Iraqis, and to a large extent this was true. However, the title of this book tells the other side of the story. Where was America in this tale of woe? We were right down the street from the Iraqis we were supposed to be helping. MNSTC-I dumped billions into the Iraqi Ministry of Defense and Ministry of Interior, yet the rate of progress from these two agencies was abysmal, no matter what U.S. generals said at their press briefings. General Dempsey was paying the freight for everything at MOD and MOI, even though the Iraqi treasury was awash in oil revenue. Why couldn't we let the MOD order supplies for the army with its own money and in its own way? They haven't been able to do this, not because they are inept or have no money, but because the United States has forced Iraq to procure goods and services using our extremely complicated Federal Acquisition Regulations—Iraqi style.

America's problem is we have to control everything. We can't very well do that if we aren't occupying the country. We can't have it both ways: they run their own show, but do it our way. This is the primary reason Iraq has failed to get back to where it was 25 years ago, and why it can't defend itself against Iran, Syria, AQI and ISIS now.

---

[64] Eli Lake and Josh Rogin, "Why Is the FBI Still Targeting Petraeus?" *BloombergView*, December 1, 2014.

If the United States had allowed Iraq to spend its own oil revenue, and purchase things the way they do it, there would be no issue with the Iraqi armed forces manning and equipping themselves. Of course, this includes keeping the Iraqi Army intact and not disbanding it. With an existing army we could have taught them our military tactics and methods. The Iraqi Army would have been functional. Simply put, the Coalition (the U.S.) should have occupied Iraq after our invasion in March 2003. We should have done this to provide security only, and let Iraqis run their own country with their own money, with guidance and assistance from the United States. The effects of our failure can be seen today. It can be seen with Iraqi soldiers running away from ISIS forces, when the Iraqi Army outnumbers ISIS by a factor of 10 to 1.

Here is a list of some of our "accomplishments" in Iraq. The United States:

1) destroyed the infrastructure of Iraq with our bombing;

2) invaded with a fraction of the troops needed to fight an enemy we didn't know anything about;

3) fired everyone who knew how to do anything;

4) didn't have enough troops to secure the country when the main fighting ended;

5) disbanded Iraq's security infrastructure (army and national police) for no valid reason;

6) told Iraqi's to run their country "on their own," but using our systems and processes they will never understand, and finally;

7) kept General George Casey in his job far too long so he could tell everyone from the President on down that everything was just great, thereby preventing the truth from getting out.

Looking at Iraq today, would the Islamic State (IS) be doing the things it is if the list above hadn't happened? Not only is the answer "no," but IS wouldn't even exist.

Everything goes full circle back to the terrible planning for the war from the beginning. If Tommy Franks and Donald Rumsfeld had listened to Erik Shinseki, we would have gone in with enough troops to defeat any enemy, and therefore enough troops to occupy the country when the conflict was over. Then, if we had people during Iraq's reconstruction with an understanding of its culture, we could have allowed Iraq to spend its own money as it wanted, toward the development of a free, democratic society. If any of these things had been done, Iraq wouldn't have many of the problems it has today. Nothing is guaranteed, but there's no way any of this could happen the way we executed the invasion and followed up afterward. The study of warfare, and what happens when the fighting is over, proves this to be the case time and again. As the saying goes, "those who fail to study history are doomed to repeat it." Bush, Franks, Rumsfeld, Tenet, Bremer—they all fail the test of history, regardless of what their memoirs say.

When discussing the Iraqi Ministry of Defense one cannot leave out the Multi-National Security Transition Command-Iraq, or MNSTC-I. Because the information is not readily available to the public, it is difficult to determine the total amount of money MNSTC-I spent (or "wasted") trying to set up the new Iraqi Ministry of Defense (and the Ministry of Interior). It must have spent tens of billions of dollars. Looking at how the Iraqi Army operates now, one can definitely say MNSTC-I did a lousy job.

In terms of dollars alone MNSTC-I was responsible for at least $2 billion in construction projects per year, all executed by its J-7 construction branch. Many of its projects started in 2003, and were planned through at least 2010. Therefore, it follows that J-7 was responsible for at least $8-10 billion in construction projects during that time, but it couldn't complete the simple task of closing the books on the projects these funds paid for. This was just one of countless areas MNSTC-I was responsible for, with total U.S. funds likely reaching well into hundreds of billions of dollars. MNSTC-I failed in its mission to train the Iraqi Army as well. Unfortunately, the cost of that failure is in lives, not dollars.

When I arrived in Baghdad in July 2006, it was 120 degrees. My co-worker walked me over to the Ministry of Defense building next to Phoenix Base and introduced me to the Iraqis I would be working with for the next year. The building had been the former home of the Iraqi Parliament, and had been badly damaged by U.S. bombs the opening night of the invasion, as most of the government buildings had been. The United States spent $58 million dollars renovating this building. It was a dump. But the most noticeable thing was the lack of air conditioning. It felt like an oven inside the Ministry of Defense building that first day I went there.

Not long afterwards, I was walking down the hallway when one of the senior advisors employed by my company in Baghdad walked past me. He was the senior advisor to the DG for A,L&I. He had a very important job. As he walked by, alongside the DG and his entourage, he yelled at me, "Where's your tie!" It was an oven inside the building, yet he was yelling at me for not wearing a tie. We had to wear our 35 pound armor-plated vest and 10 pound Kevlar ballistic helmet everywhere we went. I had just taken these off when this guy made his comment to me, in a sneer as he passed me in the hallway. Whenever I took off my vest I would be soaking wet with sweat. It looked like I had just gotten out of the shower. I had been told to dress the same as the gentleman I advised, which I was doing, but this advisor just wasn't happy with that. He wanted me to wear a tie like him, so he took it out on me in front of the DG he advised, to put me in my place. It was just like being in the military again, only we weren't wearing uniforms. I went to my incompetent manager and asked him if our company had a dress code for Iraq, and he did what he always did, which was refer me to the company website. There I found the company dress code all right, for employees who work at the company headquarters in Alexandria, Virginia. I went back and told my manager this. As the Program Manager he was in charge of the firm's staff in Baghdad. He said he had no idea what the dress code was and then stared at me like I was from another planet. I asked him if he would enact a dress code. Like he always did he said he would "check with corporate" in Alexandria. I never heard another thing about a dress code in Iraq. I started to wear a tie.

As mentioned above, there was no air conditioning in the MOD building the day I arrived and was introduced to my new Iraqi friends, as they would soon become. The days went by, and then the weeks. In Iraq there are seasons just like in the States, only at much higher temperatures. The winter months coincide with ours, but the temperatures are in the 50s at night. In the summer things get dicey. On the hottest day it can get up to 130 degrees (F°). This is in July and August. It was at this time I arrived and found there was no air conditioning in a building the United States had spent $58 million dollars to renovate. One day I found out why. An Iraqi expatriate from New Zealand sat next to me in my MNSTC-I office. He was an electrical engineer, and told me there was a brand new 1.5 KVA Caterpillar generator behind the MOD building to power the air conditioning and the rest of the electricity for building. The building was on the Baghdad grid, which provided power about 3-4 hours a day, and the rest of the time the power was provided by a smaller generator that was crapping out, hence the brand new Caterpillar generator out back. All of Baghdad was powered the same way. Because the U.S. destroyed most of the power generating plants, the city had to ration power down to only a few hours during the daytime, while everyone had to provide their own power the rest of the day with small generators. The fuel for these generators was the key. It was almost impossible to get fuel most of the time. Only people who were connected got it. Without fuel people sweated all night long because they had no air conditioning, and in the morning no hot shower—if they had running water. Those who worked at MOD would then risk their lives coming to work.

I asked the Iraqi expat why there was no air conditioning with a brand new generator. That's when he told me about the power cable. When the Caterpillar vendor from Kuwait installed the generator, he placed it on a concrete slab that he poured behind the MOD headquarters building, in the best location he felt was available. But when the vendor went to connect the generator to the building the cable wasn't long enough. The generator came with a standard length cable, but it wasn't long enough to reach the building from the location out back where it had been placed. The contractor probably knew this all along, and wanted to make more money by selling MOD a longer cable, typical of any Middle Eastern businessman. Screw the client in order to make more money now. The Ministry of Defense, which had purchased the generator with much fanfare because it was actually able to get the contract awarded, refused to pay the vendor for a longer cable, saying it was the contractor's fault the cable wouldn't reach the building. The longer cable cost $48,000. The contractor said he would not pay for the longer cable because he had performed the contract to its specifications, which did not say anything about where to place the generator. (Needless to say, we made the Iraqis use our procurement procedures, but we never trained them how to write a valid legal contract, which would have prevented this oversight from occurring.) Of course, the contractor also took no responsibility for failing to check the length of the cable before laying the concrete slab and then dropping the generator on top of it, too far from the building for the cable to be connected. In addition, the contractor had not received his initial partial payment, which was due when the generator was first delivered. He said he would provide the longer cable when he received this payment. This went on for months. The MOD Inspector General (IG), the office responsible for investigating fraud, got involved and said that nothing could be done until an investigation was completed. The IG himself wanted the contract for the generator to go to his friend, and when it didn't he delayed the investigation for months.

The summer came and went, and then the winter. Most of the time half the lights in the MOD building were out, because the only power was either from the city or the smaller generator that was constantly breaking down. Finally, the contractor agreed to install the longer cable, still not having received any money from the Ministry of Defense a year after he had first delivered the generator. The new generator was finally connected to the building but only ran a short while. It failed to run due to the Iraqi concept of preventive maintenance, which isn't much to speak of. Even though half the men were engineers and would brag about this every time they opened their mouths, everything would break down. I don't know what kind of engineering degrees they get over there, but actually performing any kind of maintenance is 'beneath' them, so it never gets done. Even if they aren't running, generators require tremendous amounts of maintenance, especially in the dusty environment of Iraq. Without maintenance they go down all the time. The contractor refused to come and maintain the new generator, a requirement in his contract, because he still had not been paid a single dinar (Iraqi currency). But MOD wouldn't pay him unless he came out and provided maintenance on the generator. Another Catch-22.

The generator had been delivered and installed behind the MOD building prior to my arrival in July 2006, and was finally up and running when I left in September 2007, fourteen months later.

This story brings to light many things about the Iraqis and the Coalition. The United States spent $58 million dollars renovating the old Parliament building for use by the new Ministry of Defense, the same building we bombed during the opening stages of the invasion. If it spent this kind of money, why couldn't LTG Dempsey drop another $48,000 for the longer generator cable so we could all have air conditioning? I asked this question dozens of times while watching this fiasco transpire, and every time I walked into the oven that they called the MOD building. The answer was that General Dempsey, trying to play tough with the Iraqis, was forcing them to fix the problem themselves, and pay for it. Instead of paying for everything as before, one day General Dempsey stopped paying for anything. This forced the Iraqis to start paying for things they hadn't, which they could only do using our competitive contracting procedures which we forced them to use as well. In a word, this was impossible.

Did the Iraqis "learn their lesson" and straighten up? Of course not. They weren't going to snap to and change overnight because a U.S. general wanted them to. With the Iraqis responsible for buying what they needed, everything came to a halt and nothing was purchased at all, resulting in their refusal to pay the vendor for a generator that had already been delivered, and for a longer cable that cost $48,000. MNSTC-I probably dropped billions a year on MOD, but couldn't spend another

$48,000 to help us get through the 120 degree heat. And the jerk from my firm was yelling at me to wear a tie.

We all went to work every day at the MOD building in these conditions, while General Dempsey sat in his beautiful air conditioned office on Phoenix Base in the lap of luxury. So much for "leadership by example." He lived like royalty. Of course the Minister of Defense, Abdul Qadir, had separate air conditioning units for his office too. But their worker bees sucked it up, both American and Iraqi.

Winston Churchill once said, "Russia is a riddle wrapped in a mystery inside an enigma." Iraq has become the same thing because we have made it so. From 2003 to 2007, while Iraq fell apart because of what we had done, we refused to send over more forces other than the "surge." With much fanfare, the surge was touted as being the answer to everything, mostly because it was commanded by David Petraeus, touted by the media as our modern-day George Patton. The surge could have been very successful, but didn't achieve what it could have because it didn't have enough U.S. forces. By 2006 it was painfully obvious we had to do everything, or pull out completely and let the Iraqis do everything on their own. Instead, we tried to do both.

Much of the problem the U.S. created in Iraq can be traced to the lack of accountability of U.S. money. Construction projects run by J-7 are just one example of this. When supplies were procured for the Iraqi Army, the U.S. purchased everything but without any oversight as to where the products went. That's how 190,000 weapons purchased by General Petraeus' command managed to disappear in 2004-2005.

The U.S. utterly failed to account for the hatred between the Sunni and Shi'ite before our invasion of 2003. Iraq's army and national police were disbanded by Paul Bremer. Four years of U.S. inaction followed, capped with the surge, which wasn't anywhere near the size it should have been. Nouri al-Maliki's government never got off the ground. Al Qaeda in Iraq (AQI) and the Islamic State of Iraq and Syria (ISIS) threaten to overthrow the country, while Iraqi soldiers run away for fear of being executed if captured. The United States is responsible for the disasters that have befallen Iraq. There is open talk of splitting the country into three parts: Shia, Sunni and Kurd. Half its population is either dead, or has left.

The country we invaded in order to save is being destroyed—all under the pretense of creating a democracy modeled after our own.

11—Iraq

In grade school I remember hearing about the "Land Between the Tigris and the Euphrates Rivers," the "Fertile Crescent," and the "Cradle of Civilization." I never knew my teachers were talking about Iraq.

Iraq is about the size of Texas, or the Eastern Seaboard of the United States from Maine to South Carolina. It's approximately 650 miles north to south, and about 400 east to west. The western part of the country is desert, from the Persian Gulf (the Iraqis call it the Gulf of Arabia), along the border with Saudi Arabia, Jordan and Syria. To the east and north it's mountainous along the Iranian frontier, and up to the northern border with Turkey. In between the desert and the mountains is the "Fertile Crescent," where the land is suitable for agriculture.

Baghdad is the largest city in Iraq. The center of Baghdad is located on the Tigris River at a sharp bend. On the western edge of Baghdad is the Euphrates River, with the city's western half lying in between the two rivers. Just a few miles east and west of the rivers is desert, with no land available for farming without the extensive canal system emanating from the rivers in all directions. What trees exist are no more than 20 feet tall with few leaves to provide shade. Waddies—underground rivers—can be found in the middle of nowhere, and the oases are beautiful. There's hardly any grass in Iraq and, of course, date palms are everywhere.

The Iraqi people are very friendly. They're extremely religious by western standards, an estimated 95% of them being Muslim. Iraq was a sectarian country, not a "Muslim" country like Saudi Arabia, where Islam is the state religion. However, with the Islamic State and Iran making inroads Iraq won't be sectarian much longer.

Under Saddam a person could practice any religion, but by 2006-2007 this was falling by the wayside. When the subject of religion came up it was always in the context of Sunni versus Shi'ite, and the tension between these two sects of Islam. Once I was talking with the Iraqis that I worked with at MOD, and I happened to say I was a Catholic and believed Jesus to be the Son of God. Boy, did I get a reaction! Iraqis believe Jesus existed, but he's *not* the Son of God. I never brought the issue up again.

I was very surprised when I heard of the availability of alcohol. I had assumed alcohol was banned in Iraq, but not after I drove by a liquor store in the International Zone.

Iraqis love their families, and they love to eat. The former Prime Minister of Israel, Golda Meir, once said if a man wanted to eat like a king he should join the Iraqi army. Meals are considered very special to Iraqis, and they go to great lengths to set up a spread like I've never seen. I often visited Iraqi army camps to meet with the camp commander. We would be in the middle of a discussion about something very important, when one of the commander's soldiers would walk in and announce, in Arabic of course, that lunch (or dinner) was ready. That would end our meeting on the spot. We would leave for the dining room and sit down to a feast. Every time I made one of these visits the camp or unit commander would be in his very beautiful office, sitting at his ornate full-size desk, with flags of Iraq behind him and maps of the country on the wall, with couches and chairs all around the room. Officers on his staff would sit there and not say a word, listening to our conversation. The sign of importance would be the large TV in the office. If someone wanted to look important, they had a TV in their office that was on all the time. The rest of the camp wouldn't be fit for a dog, but not the camp commander's office. He was in charge, and that was that. He would always stop to talk on his cell phone whenever it rang, and I once saw an Iraqi army general talking on three cells phones at the same time. This was their only means of communication.

The conditions of Iraqi army camps were deplorable, but not the meals we ate. We would leave the commander's office and walk down hallways that had rooms on either side with soldiers sitting on cots and bunks that no American would go near, yet when we entered the commander's dining room everything changed. It was a festive atmosphere, with soldiers waiting on all of us, and the commander sitting at the head of a long table, always made up of smaller plastic tables pushed end-to-end. The food was always the same—the main course either chicken, or fish from the local lake, river or canal, with rice, bread and fresh vegetables. The Iraqis would reach for the chicken or fish, which was on platters in the center of the table, and pull it off the bone with their hands. Then they'd wrap it in bread with rice. I loved the bread, which was always baked in clay ovens right there on the camp.

I was amazed how the Iraqis would continue to have children in the midst of the war, but they didn't seem to care. It may have been out of fear of losing some of their children, so they wanted to ensure their legacy (like we used to do in the States a hundred years ago). Most of the single Iraqi men I worked with didn't want to get married because of the war. To them it wasn't worth the time, the effort, or the risk. Why bother while the war was going on? But what about the single Iraqi women?

My interpreter's name was Noor. She was a beautiful, single, 25 year old woman, which for marriage is old by Iraqi standards. Noor told me a few times that the only thing her mother ever talked to her about was getting married. Her mother was obsessed over it. To Iraqi women (like her mother) marriage is the single most important event of their lives. It means everything to them, other than having children, of course. It's as if marriage is their sole reason for living. At least it appeared that way. The only thought of an Iraqi mother is when her daughter will get married and start a family. Noor's mother was a basket case over it, but Noor herself didn't seem to be that upset.

The war and the unrest that followed have changed all this. With Iraqi men backing away from marriage, and for good reason, many Iraqi women will never marry during their child-bearing years, if ever. With so many people dead or gone, Iraq's population will continue to drop. The years of insurgency following our invasion of 2003, which continues to the present, will have negative long-term effects on Iraq's population.

When I first met Noor she wasn't an interpreter, but I started to use her as one because her English was so good. After a few months, I secured a job for her with an American firm called Titan, a division of L3 Corporation. This was a big deal, because Titan interpreters could get a tourist visa to the States after working for a year. There were thousands of Iraqis living inside the walls of the International Zone, and sometimes I would see small children. Once in a while I would see a baby and it would always get my attention, not only the novelty of it, but because of the life he or she would be living in the years to come. When I think back to my time in Iraq and seeing those babies, I have to force myself to realize they are now seven years old, or ten, or in their early teens. Those same children I used to see could be dead, permanently disabled, or even serving in the army by now. That's if they weren't fortunately enough to get out of Iraq entirely, but that takes money, connections, or both. We would always see young boys hawking for money and selling their 'original' Saddam-era Iraqi currency. I bought some for my nieces and nephews back in the States.

Iraqis are either orthodox or liberal in their Islamic beliefs. Likewise, they're either traditional or western in dress and custom. For women, it's pretty easy to tell the difference. A traditional Iraqi woman will always wear a scarf wrapped around her head, never letting a man outside of her immediate family see her hair. The only man who will ever see her hair, other than her family, is her husband. An Iraqi woman with more liberal western views will dress very similar to western women, with jeans and more revealing clothing. I didn't notice any animosity between traditional and western Iraqi women, but it would be hard for me to tell in any case. Westernized Iraqi women will date a man who is not Muslim or from Iraq, while a traditional Iraqi woman would never think of dating a westerner, or a non-Muslim, under any circumstance. It would bring shame upon her family, and she'd be considered a loose woman, the worst fate she could bring upon herself.

Iraqi men are harder to differentiate because they all dress the same, but one way to tell is during Ramadan, Islam's yearly month-long fast. The more westernized men will not fast, often having lunch in the middle of the day. The very traditional Iraqi men will never break their fast, under any circumstance. I worked with Iraqi men and women every day in the Ministry of Defense, and was initially surprised at the difference, thinking they were all going to be the same in this area. On the other hand, even a somewhat traditional Iraqi man will break his fast during Ramadan, even drinking alcohol out of sight of anyone other than his family and friends, and think nothing of it. I got the impression the more traditional women are far more serious about it than the men.

It is acceptable for Muslim men to marry outside his faith, but this is strictly forbidden for Muslim women. According to Islamic law, Mohammad declared it would be harder for a woman to be married outside the faith because of "all the problems" it would create if she did. But there is no mention of any problems if a man marries outside the Muslim faith, a clear example of religious discrimination between the sexes. Taking it a big step further, Islam allows a man to have as many as four wives at one time. All he has to do is divorce one and replace her with another, as long as the total never exceeds four. I was very surprised, almost amused, at the incredible double standards in Iraq, and Islamic society, between men and women. A man can pretty much do anything he wants, while a woman can't do a thing unless her parents, especially her father, approve. I was surprised at this, but impressed with it too. We hear of how terrible women are treated in Islamic (Arab) cultures, but like most things it's relative. They don't have the freedom to do things western women do, but that doesn't mean they are treated badly. On the contrary, women are cherished in Islamic culture, almost to the point of being treated like little girls well into adulthood.

My translator's mother, who just wanted her to get married, was constantly introducing her to young men who were friends of the family. Noor never liked any of the men her parents set her up with, and was facing singlehood as a result. In this regard she reminded me very much of a modern American woman, looking for "Mr. Perfect" but still in the search because she couldn't find him. I thought this showed a little snobbery, like many American women have who face being single because no man they ever meet is "good enough." I do think the war had a lot to do with her attitude. She wasn't going to marry the first guy who came along. Life was hard enough already. I'm sure that if she married the next guy to walk through the door she would have been unhappy, doing it only because of her mother, searching for a happiness that wasn't within herself. My interpreter was truly searching for something more than that.

The holy month of Ramadan is a grueling event for everyone who practices it. The beginning of Ramadan shifts each year. Every year it begins 10 days earlier than it did the year before. Because it calls for total abstinence from all food and water until sundown every day, the average person isn't worth much by midday. In the summer months this is almost torture, as the temperature in the southern part of the country gets up to 120 degrees or more by mid-afternoon. Imagine not being able to even drink water until around 6:00 in the evening every day for a month, especially in the summer, and in the midst of a war. Not a fun thing. However, I heard that Ramadan was an excuse to have some fun. Because it was so hard, Iraqis would "reward" themselves at the end of the day. I never got a clear interpretation of what this meant, but I got the impression it was sex, and maybe even some alcohol too, of course with a lot of food. When Ramadan was over there would be more celebrations, with another celebration called "Eid" at the end. Iraqis love to eat, and Muslims in general love to have religious holidays. They were taking days off for religious holidays all the time. It seemed every time I turned around they had some sort of religious holiday, so everything was shut down.

Then there is the difference between Sunni and Shi'ite. The Iraqis I worked with were Sunni because the Ministry of Defense was a "Sunni" ministry, while the Ministry of Interior was a "Shi'ite" ministry. This was partly because Saddam was a Sunni, therefore the MOD was a "Sunni" ministry. But this was also due to the way Paul Bremer set up the new Iraqi government. In his desire to balance the government after the fall of the Saddam regime, Bremer forced the Iraqis to practice their own form of segregation, whereby government ministries were staffed based on percentage of religious sects in the population. For example, if the country is 30% Sunni, then roughly 30% of the government must be staffed by Sunni people, and the balance by Shi'ite people. The problem with this, as well as everything else in Iraq, is that Sunnis and Shi'ites simply don't get along. One could go so far as to say they despise each other. The Sunnis I worked with at the Ministry of Defense thought the Shi'ites were ridiculous with their archaic practices, such as whipping themselves as they marched down the streets during some of their religious holidays.

Along with the terrible planning and execution of our invasion, and its disastrous aftermath, the United States Government made things worse by forcing the Iraqi government and people to live the way we think they should live, and do things the way we think they should do them. We have never, since the end of Operation Iraqi Freedom, allowed them to decide their own fate. On the surface it may have looked like they were, with the purple thumbs and all, but in reality they never had a chance. The hatred between Sunni and Shia illustrates the point. The only way they will ever coexist is if they work out their own problems by themselves. They will never be able to if the United States gives one ministry to the Sunni and one to the Shia, as we did. This created more problems than it solved because one sect was upset it didn't get a particular ministry, and the other sect was upset that it got what it did. Iraqis themselves needed to solve their own problems, not have someone else solve it for them. But how can the Iraqi people solve their own problems when they never had the opportunity to lead themselves for 25 years under the thumb of a dictator? They can't learn to do this within a few years, yet that's exactly what Bush wanted them to do. It's another Catch-22. Democracy isn't going to sprout up out of the ground in the middle of a civil war between Sunni and Shi'ite, fueled by a growing insurgency. Nouri al-Maliki's government can't defend the country while it's rebuilding the security ministries disbanded by Paul Bremer, and without American forces to secure the country in the meantime because of Rumsfeld's "Invasion Lite," and Obama washing his hands of the whole mess.

Sunnis and Shi'ites need to understand they are equal, hard as that may be. Their version of Islam is not the same, but it doesn't mean one is better than the other. But putting one ministry in the hands of one sect and another ministry in the hands of the other isn't going to solve the issue. This means Sunnis are responsible for the defense of the country (Ministry of Defense), while Shi'ites are responsible for the defense of the villages, towns, cities and provinces (Ministry of Interior). Separating responsibilities between national defense and domestic security does make sense. But it means the insurgency is high in Sunni areas because the National Police is pro-Shi'ite, so it will be more protective of Shi'ite areas. And it means the level of defense against forces from outside the country are directly related to whether an attack is coming from the Shi'ite east (Iran) or the Sunni west (Saudi Arabia and Syria), because the Ministry of

Defense is pro-Sunni. Could this cause the ministry to be weak against defending the western approaches to the country where their kindred Sunni brothers are from? It also means MOD is run a "Sunni" way, while MOI is run a "Shia" way. Neither ministry is run in the "Iraqi" way. By merging the two sects together at both ministries, each could look over the other's shoulder to avoid these scenarios, and learn to work together. But Bremer didn't want to do this because of the tensions he thought would result. Instead he took the easy route, leaving the mess we have now.

The Iraqi people have suffered incredible hardship and loss since the United States invaded in the spring of 2003. Of course they suffered long before that. But the theme of this book is America's failure in Iraq, not Saddam's failure in Iraq. The terrible things Saddam Hussein did during his reign of terror could fill volumes. We aren't Saddam. We're supposed to be better. How many Iraqis have died since the United States invaded in the spring of 2003? How many would be alive today if we had done things differently, such as plan the war with a shred of common sense? How many would be alive today if we hadn't invaded in the first place?

The Iraqi people are good, decent human beings. They believe in God, the Prophet Mohammed, they love their families, and they respect and treasure their women. They love to eat good food, and a lot of it, and they welcome visitors into their homes as if they were family. They practice a faith that most Americans don't understand, but we can understand their love for human life, which I saw every day. They hated Saddam, yet they were powerless to do anything short of a suicide attack to kill him, and even this they could not do because Saddam used look-alike doubles. He knew he was hated by most of his own people, so the only way he could rule the country was by sheer force to include torture, prison and murder. We know all of this. But under Saddam, if you didn't get into trouble or bring attention to yourself, you got by. If you didn't get in the way of Saddam or one of his associates, you lived a fairly comfortable life. I was told this many times by the Iraqis I worked with.

But after the UN sanctions during the 1990's, the invasion in 2003, the decade of misery that followed, and ISIS now threatening to overthrow the country, what does the average Iraqi have left? The Iraqi dinar, the staple of the currency, used to be about three to the dollar. When I was in Iraq it was around 1350 to the dollar! This is what the United States did to the Iraqi economy. Was Iraq better off under Saddam? A case could be made that it was. Before our invasion in 2003, a liter of gas was around 20 fils. A fil is 1/1000 of a dinar. This meant a liter of gas was 20/1000 of a dinar. If a dinar was three to the dollar, that meant a liter of gas was .67 cents, or 1/67 of a cent! It was basically free. Gas is impossible to get now. Iraq's economy is a black market. And because of inflation, the fil is no longer in circulation.

When I started working at MOD, I saw what the Iraqi people were going through as a result of the war. The hallway walls in the MOD building had photographs of MOD staff killed within the preceding weeks. There was once a picture of a very pretty young woman in her early 20's. I asked my translator about her. She said the girl had left the MOD building one afternoon at the end of the day, and walked down the street to the main gate for the IZ called "Assassins Gate." The girl went through the checkpoint and was standing on the sidewalk just outside. A shot was fired from a car driving by, and she was killed. There was no apparent reason for her killing. She wasn't involved with insurgents or other bad people. They probably just felt like killing someone leaving the IZ because they worked for the Coalition or the new Iraqi government. I wonder what the person who shot her was thinking. I doubt it was anything like, "Hey, she's pretty cute, I wonder if she's available for a date." Probably more like, "Kill the pig whore who works for the infidels." Nice guy.

One day my translator told me about her trip into work that morning. She and her father drove to the MOD together. They were turning a corner and there was a pile of dead bodies on the sidewalk. I asked how many there were and she said, "around 25 or 30." About a mile from the MOD building, just beyond the IZ wall, a house was discovered with 60 decapitated bodies. Yet the whole time he was MNF-I commander General Casey insisted everything was fine and the Iraqis could take over any time they wanted. General George Casey was incompetent. There's no other way to put it. All of this was happening right under his nose—for two and a half years.

The photograph on the cover of this book was taken the day after a suicide bomber drove a truck loaded with an estimated ton of explosives into the Sadriyah outdoor market, located in a predominantly Shi'ite area of Baghdad on Sunday, February 4, 2007. I was about a mile away from the explosion, walking down the sidewalk from the Ministry of Defense building back to Phoenix Base, inside the "T-wall" barricade that surrounded the International Zone. When the truck exploded the earth literally shook. I thought a mortar or rocket had landed just over the wall from me. It was a few hours later that we heard about the truck blowing up the market, and how far away from Phoenix Base the market was. All day long thick black smoke rose thousands of feet in the air while the market burned. I had already decided to write this book, so when the photograph appeared on the front page of Stars and Stripes the day after the explosion, I knew it would be on the cover. I purchased the rights to use it from Associated Press.

The bomb instantly killed 137 people while they shopped. The total injured was nearly 350. It was the deadliest suicide attack since the beginning of the U.S. invasion of Iraq in 2003. What got me was not just the photograph, but the accompanying story in *Stars and Stripes*:

> The explosion Saturday [February 4, 2007] was the fifth major bombing in less than a month targeting predominantly Shiite districts in Baghdad and the southern Shiite city of Hillah. It was also the worst in the capital since a series of car bombs and mortars killed at least 215 people in the Shiite district of Sadr City on November 23, 2006.
>
> "It is a tragedy. The terrorists want to punish the Iraqi people. There was no police or American presence in this market yesterday," said Adnan Lafta, a seller of gas cylinders.
>
> A day earlier, 16 American intelligence agencies made a National Intelligence Estimate that said conditions in Baghdad were perilous. "Unless efforts to reverse these conditions show measurable progress...in the

coming 12 to 18 months, we assess that the overall security situation will continue to deteriorate," a declassified synopsis of the report declared.[65]

Taken together with the Woodward series in the *The Washington Post*, this information made it abundantly clear that General Casey was asleep at the wheel. It was also clear that our intelligence community was screaming at the White House to do something. Steve Hadley and Meghan O'Sullivan of the National Security Council were the only ones listening.

I read a report a few days after the attack that stated a civilian Iraqi security guard had been posted at the entrance to the market. He had been ordered not to let any cars or trucks enter. When asked why he had allowed the truck to pass the checkpoint, he stated the driver of the truck insisted on making his delivery inside the market. The guard just let him pass through. Well, the driver wasn't lying. He certainly had a "delivery" to make.

The guard was just an Iraqi guy trying to make a living. No one can hold that against him. The problem was the complete lack of training, awareness, preparation and accountability this episode so clearly showed. The Sadriyah market bombing was just one attack. By 2006 attacks like this were happening constantly, and the count of Iraqis being blown up was growing exponentially. But General George Casey had no problem telling the President everything was just fine. And Donald Rumsfeld and Tommy Franks planned an invasion with a fraction of the soldiers and Marines needed for the initial assault, and afterwards. And Paul Bremer disbanded the entire security infrastructure of the country. Could there be any wonder why the guy who was 'guarding' the entrance to this market didn't have a clue what he was doing?

I was told by a very informed source who worked in the United States Senate during the planning for Operation Iraqi Freedom that 4,000 U.S. Army military policemen (MPs) were going to be sent to Iraq as part of a post-invasion plan. According to my source, Donald Rumsfeld flatly rejected the idea

---

[65] Sameer N. Yacoub, "Baghdad devastation reveals 'perilous' times," *Stars and Stripes*, February 5, 2007.

as being completely unnecessary. The invasion would be as he planned it to be, and talk of any post-invasion strategy was a waste of his time. When Paul Bremer decided, on his own, to dissolve the Iraqi Ministries of Defense and Interior, he proved that there was no post-invasion plan in place before we attacked Iraq. How could there be? A post-invasion plan would have addressed what to do with the Iraqi armed forces and national police after the fall of the Saddam regime. If Paul Bremer took the action to disband these entities on his own, their disposition was obviously not considered in any post-invasion plan developed in the Pentagon. Not only did Rumsfeld think no MPs were needed, he never considered the status of the Iraqi armed forces either, leaving Bremer to make his fateful decision. The results that followed speak for themselves.

This is all the direct result of the United States' failure to remove Saddam Hussein from power in 1991, and the decision to invade in 2003. We directed the United Nations to impose sanctions against the Iraqi people after the Gulf War, none of which affected Saddam, and we knew it. We disbanded the Iraqi military and national police. We didn't invade Iraq with enough forces to secure the Iraqi people so they would be safe enough to start new lives of their own choosing. This was all because George W. Bush wanted to kick Saddam's ass and finish what his father should have finished in 1991, and because those advising him didn't know what they were doing, but thought they did. Everyone is suffering now: Iraqis, Americans, and the entire Middle East. While all this has simmered the last 10-plus years, al Qaeda and its new affiliates (ISIS, IS, ISIL, etc.) have been licking their chops waiting for their next opportunity.

Their wait is over.

People walk past destroyed buildings in the Sadriyah outdoor market, located in a predominantly Shi'ite area of Baghdad on Sunday, February 4, 2007. The day before, a suicide bomber driving a truck loaded with a ton of explosives obliterated the market, instantly killing at least 135 people while they shopped. The total injured was nearly 350. It was one of the deadliest suicide bombing attacks since the beginning of the U.S. invasion of Iraq in 2003. The following day I saw this picture on the cover of Star and Stripes, the newspaper for U.S. military personnel. I decided then it would be on the cover of this book.

(AP Photo (with permission)/Khalid Mohammed)

The Iraqi army aid station at KMTB (Kirkush Military Training Base). The LZ where we landed was across the street from the aid station, which had just received about 20 soldiers from a truck accident. One was dead, and the rest seriously injured.

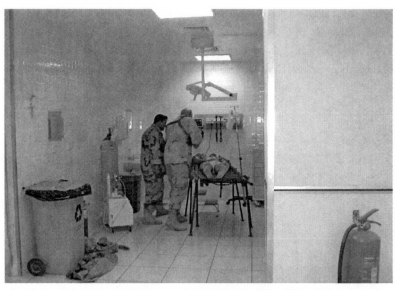

Iraqi Army doctors working on an injured Iraqi soldier. The clinic where the picture was taken was relatively new, but had no medicine. The doctors could only provide bandages for these soldiers, many of whom were in very bad shape. All they could do was wait for the U.S. Army medevac helicopters to take them to Baghdad for treatment by U.S. doctors.

My roommate helps carry one of the injured Iraqis to the U.S. Army medevac
helicopter for the flight to the U.S. Army hospital in Baghdad. Without that
hospital, thousands of Iraqis soldiers would have died. Once the U.S. leaves
Iraq they will.

Two U.S. Army medevac helicopters on the LZ at KMTB.

New Iraqi army recruits learning how to march. Not quite like my first day at West Point.

Lunch at KMTB.

Preparing to depart Baghdad International Airport on SafeNet's twin engine plane to inspect the facilities J-7 had built at Q-West, near Mosul.

Ready to fly to Q-West. This was the only time J-7 provided transportation for Ministry of Defense representatives to a camp it had built for the Ministry. The trip lasted five hours and went like clockwork until we realized J-7's contractor didn't have the paperwork for the Iraqis to sign. We flew there on a plane owned by SafeNet, a private security contractor in Iraq who provided escort security for the trip.

Q-West. J-7 constructed buildings inside old ammunition storage bunkers.
Great if they got bombed from the air.

Ammunition waiting to be destroyed.

An old factory built by the British at FOB Arlington, down the road from FOB Sommerall. Many Iraqi bases were originally built by the British, including this one.

An ammunition storage bunker, built by the French, at FOB Sommerall.

The 'kitchen' for the Iraqi workers at FOB Sommerall.

Major General Saad, Base Management Commander for the Iraqi Armed
Forces, speaking to the Iraqi workers at FOB Arlington.

Trying to make bread without catching on fire.

At the former Ministry of Defense headquarters across the Tigris River in
Baghdad, north of the IZ.

Me and my closest Iraqi co-worker at the
Ministry of Defense Real Estate Branch.

The U.S. Army air base at Taji, about 20 miles north of Baghdad,
the largest former Iraqi army and air force base in the country.
The Coalition (US) took over many of these bases for its own use,
but the Iraqis would occupy sections of them at the far end of the base.
The U.S. bases would be clean and well laid out, with Subway and
Burger King, while the Iraqi camps down the road were dumps.

The former Iraqi army depot on the north side of Taji.

Scrap at Taji. The amount of scrap metal throughout the country was immense. Near the end of my tour General Petraeus commissioned a study group just for this. An American contractor from Alexandria, Virginia, who had the scrap metal contract for Taji several years earlier, had been murdered.

More scrap at Taji.

Scrap parts from destroyed Iraqi aircraft.

More scrap at Taji.

A renovated building at Taji. This was a typical construction project of J-7's that didn't involve building something new on raw land the Ministry of Defense didn't have clear title to. The building shown here would have been one of hundreds (over 2,000 in the case of the Ministry of Interior) that J-7 had spent U.S. dollars on and had never gotten the Iraqis to sign for to close out the books for the U.S. Government.

The gate at the new Iraqi Air Force Headquarters at Taji. General Casey said the Iraqis were ready to take over the defense of their country any time they wanted to.

The Iraqi Air Force Headquarters building.

Preparing for a road convoy out of the IZ. These guys were from a reserve Infantry unit in the States who did nothing but road convoys. These were handled like a combat patrol with a full five-paragraph (situation, mission, execution, command and signal, service and support) field order briefing before each convoy departed. The unit did an excellent job. Contractors would ride in "up-armored" Chevrolet Suburbans, which had armor plating and bullet-proof windows. I took many of these convoys.

One of the convoy vehicles. The sign was not a joke. Warning shots would be fired over the heads of Iraqi drivers all the time if they got too close.

Passing underneath Assassins Gate leaving the IZ for "No Man's Land"—
Baghdad. The blue tinge is from the bullet-proof glass.

Bridges and underpasses were the most dangerous place along any convoy
route. Bombs, RPG's and machine gun fire could be brought down from all
directions onto the vehicles in the convoy below, leaving no place for them to
escape.

Convoy through Baghdad.

The old Iraqi army officers club pool at Zayuna.

US Army Apaches in their "pens" at Balad. The concrete barricades in between the aircraft provide protection from shrapnel when mortar rounds hit.

A U.S. drone in its hanger at Balad.

Helicopters arriving at Habbaniyah to take us back to Baghdad. The first two are Blackhawks, and the last two are Apaches providing escort for the others.

US Army Apache gunship in a hover before landing.

The bakery at the Iraqi army camp at Habbaniyah. This was the typical condition of any former Iraqi army building. They were essentially unusable.

The U.S. Army "Sherpa." We flew one of these to Irbil, in Kurdistan, and also to Ur, both times at 100 feet above the ground and 250 knots.

Inside the "Sherpa."

Two of my closest friends at the Ministry of Defense about to travel with me.

The ziggurat at Ur during a dust storm. It is 5,000 years old.

After the dust storm.

Australian "Bushmaster" armored personnel carriers. These have V-shaped hulls to deflect IED's and EFP's. The U.S. Army had plans to purchase about 1,500 of them for Iraq and Afghanistan. This was at Camp Tallil, near Ur.

The remotely controlled automatic machine gun on top of the Bushmaster.

Convoying from Tallil to Ur.

The Ur camp commander. Iraqis love to have their picture taken.

The Ur camp commander preparing to eat lunch—and have his picture taken.

A latrine in one of the barracks at Ur. These buildings were a year and a half old when the pictures were taken. They were built by MNSTC-I J-7 for $118 million dollars.

Typical ceiling in one of the barracks at Ur.

Typical latrine in one of the barracks at Ur.

Notice the water-stained walls. This wasn't due to lack of cleaning, but to poor construction. The U.S. paid an American construction company $118 million for this.

Typical shower stall at Ur. The walls were covered with mold, the floor of the shower was rusting, and the floors were filthy. There was no maintenance of the facilities at all. This facility was 18 months old.

Year and a half old J-7 construction. Notice the 'drainage' for the rain water. Storm water management wasn't included in the design of the camp's construction.

Inside the ablution building.

The doors to the stalls were so cheap they just hung there. There was no bracing, or any other type of support, to keep the entire row of doors from falling over. This building was constructed by J-7 after the others. It was six months old at the time these pictures were taken.

Six month old construction.

Newer, six month old construction at Ur. Notice the water damage in the beam above, and more going down the wall.

After coming inside the building where I worked at Phoenix Base. I had just removed my vest. I gained about 35 pounds in Iraq. There was simply too much food in the DFAC and eating was one of the few pleasures we had. The weight is gone now.

With my closest friend and co-worker from the Real Estate Division at the Ministry of Defense. We were on the road from Irbil to Diyanah in Kurdistan. This was one of only two trips the colonel from MNSTC-I J-5 included us on to locate sites for new units under the Prime Minister's Initiative. My friend was the acting chief of the Real Estate Branch, later made a Division. The permanent chief had left the job due to "health" reasons. He was gone the first nine months I was in Iraq, but continued to get paid because his brother was the Infrastructure Division Director.

PART III: THE BUSH DOCTRINE

12—The Bush Doctrine

During his 2008 presidential campaign, Barack Hussein Obama changed his official website from saying the surge of 2007 was a failure, to the surge was a success. But his staff made it clear he wasn't "flip-flopping," he was just clarifying his website to make it more accurate with the times…how convenient!

By that point in the campaign no one cared if Obama was flip-flopping. He had the election wrapped up, in very large part because the racially charged videos of Obama's preacher, Jeremiah Wright, were kept from the American people until he had enough delegates to secure the Democrat nomination. Wright was shown repeatedly screaming "God-damn America" for its unjust war on terror, and claiming Jesus was a black man living in a rich white society. Obama attended Wright's 'church' for 20years, but claims he never heard any of this.

I was in a pizza shop on MacArthur Boulevard in Washington, DC the night of September 5th, 2008. "Larry King Live" was on TV. Larry was interviewing Michael Moore, and was asking him about the upcoming presidential election. The topic turned to the Iraq war and the "surge." Moore said something that really caught my attention. He likened the Iraq war to a kid in the kitchen who is playing around and spills a glass of milk; but then wants all the credit for cleaning it up. But the milk wouldn't have spilled if he hadn't been screwing around in the first place. Moore said the "surge" was the same thing. We screwed up the war, conducted the "surge," and then wanted all the credit for being so great. Moore said one more thing—that the surge wouldn't bring back the dead American soldiers or the "100,000" dead Iraqis that had been killed in war. His estimate was low.[66]

Moore's comment was a metaphor of the pro-Iraq War folks who think our invasion in March 2003 was good, moral, and justified. This is due to their neo-conservative view of American foreign policy. Although I'm a very strong conservative, I don't think the war was moral, justified or good. Moore's comment highlights the reverse logic of justifying our invasion in 2003

---

[66] "Larry King Live," Michael Moore interview, *CNN*, September 5th, 2008.

because the surge of 2007 was successful, which clearly makes no sense. The surge was executed because the previous four years were a disaster, so how can the entire operation be a success? It doesn't make rational sense, but neither did the invasion. To screw something up like Operation Iraqi Freedom, fail to do anything for nearly 4 years while Iraq went down the drain, and then say the entire thing was justified because of the actions we took after the fact is irrational. Yet, that's what we've been getting from many on the ultra-conservative side. Although I personally agree with most of what they say, I strongly disagree on this.

Michael Moore also told Larry King that he doesn't think there is any threat to the United States from Islamic terrorism. Really? I would recommend he watch the DVD, *Obsession*.[67] In Moore's limited opinion the threat exists in the imagination of conservatives. I'd like to know if Moore has an opinion on the way Bill Clinton and Madeleine Albright handled the situation when Osama bin Laden was offered to the U.S. on a silver platter by Sudan. Or the fact that while Clinton was president 59 Americans died at the hand of Osama bin Laden, but he and Albright did absolutely nothing about it. How does Moore feel about Clinton having sex with women he wasn't married to, while Albright spent all her time travelling the world with an entourage the size of a small army, buying her broaches and stupid hats?

What would be Michael Moore's opinion of ISIS today, of their beheadings, and the threat to our national security by Obama opening our border with Mexico? Because Obama is president, Moore would be fine with all of this. From 2004 through the end of his presidency, George W. Bush attacked anyone who disagreed with the war by claiming they weren't "supporting the troops." The stories of what soldiers went through upon their return from Vietnam were on the minds of those old enough to remember. What those brave young men went through at the hands of the anti-war crowd was terrible. The Vietnam War wasn't their fault—it was the fault of those at the highest levels in Washington who were running it from their desks. The American people weren't going to let that happen again. Unfortunately, George W. Bush was using the treatment

---

[67] *Obsession*, The Clarion Fund, 2005.

our soldiers got when they returned from Vietnam and applying it to this war. That's a cheap shot.

Soldiers returning from Iraq and Afghanistan have been welcomed as heroes, which they are. (No one mentions contractors.) But for Bush to say that people against the Iraq War weren't supporting our troops was below the belt. Nothing could have been further from the truth for the majority of Americans. Unfortunately, this line was picked up and repeated by the conservative media. To tell me I didn't support our soldiers and Marines if I was against the invasion of Iraq was not only a stretch, it was an insult to my patriotism and intelligence. I wrote this book because I love my country, not because I don't support my country. What I don't support is my country doing really stupid things. There's a big difference.

On May 31, 2008, *The Washington Post* reported on a study conducted by eight Iraqi physicians, which estimated the total death toll from the war to be 655,000.[68] Almost nothing was reported about the study in the U.S. Although the "main stream" media was biased against the war, it's amazing this information was hardly mentioned. If this estimate was made in 2008, what would it be if done in 2015? At the time of this writing, Iraqi deaths are at the same levels they were in 2006-2007, the height of the insurgency. In May of 2014, over 4,000 Iraqis were killed. This monthly rate equates to nearly 60,000 for the year. As much bad press as George W. Bush received in the years since his invasion, he has been given remarkably light treatment on this. We will never know the total death count from this war. One reason is because it keeps increasing. But we know it is very high. Regardless how many have died—American, Iraqi, Coalition and contractor—none of them would be dead if we had not invaded Iraq in 2003.

If the United States had entered into this conflict with a legitimate reason for doing so, a clearly defined objective, the resources to achieve it and an exit strategy, these deaths would not have been in vain. And if we had executed this conflict properly, the number of deaths would have been significantly lower as well. Even a timeline for withdrawal wouldn't have been

---

[68] David Brown, "Study Claims Iraq's 'Excess' Death Toll Has Reached 650,000," *The Washington Post,* October 11, 2006.

so ridiculous, as long as we knew why we were there and what our objectives were. We had none of these things.

What of our real enemy, the radical Islamic fanatic who wants to kill every non-believer in the world? What are we doing about him? What has our involvement in Iraq done to address this killer, to wipe him out before he destroys the world as we know it? The battle is not in Iraq, it is world-wide. It is right here in America. Some say we took the fight to Iraq in order to take it away from here in America. That's plausible, but a pipe dream when looked at in relation to the magnitude of the actual problem. Islamic terrorism is everywhere. There are millions of young men willing to die for what they believe, even if what they believe is nonsense. But it isn't nonsense to them, and that's all that matters.

As discussed previously, President Bush should have re-instituted the draft after 9/11. It would have been a reasonable response in light of what happened, but he was afraid to do it. We will need hundreds of thousands of men and women to take on new enemies like the Islamic State, with a pipeline of fresh recruits coming in to take the load off the ones who have been fighting. Regardless of what Barack Hussein Obama thinks, we can't do it with technology alone, or with air power alone, or with ships alone. It will take everything our country has, to include all of these resources. It will take hundreds of thousands soldiers to combat this new enemy, fighting on the ground in very harsh conditions.

We don't have this capability now, and if we don't do something about it soon we won't have it when we need it. If Obama thinks he can destroy the Islamic State with drones alone, he's dreaming.

Obama has illegally opened the southern border of the United States to create a new democrat voting bloc, and is reducing the size of the country's military forces. He is opening the southern border to make it easier for terrorists to get in, and at the same time reducing America's ability to fight the growing threat of Islamic terrorism abroad, and right in America's back yard. Barack Hussein Obama swore an oath to protect and defend the United States from all enemies foreign and domestic, leaving a reasonable person wondering who our domestic enemy really is.

In December of 2014, WikiLeaks released a secret report by the CIA's Directorate of Intelligence which found that drone strikes and other "targeted killings" of terrorist and insurgent leaders could strengthen extremist groups and be counterproductive. According to the leaked document, "high value targeting" (HVT) involving air strikes and special forces operations against insurgent leaders could be effective, but could also have negative effects including increasing violence and greater popular support for extremist groups.

Taking this report at face value, our options lead right back to the original premise of this book: either completely withdraw from Iraq, or go back in with overwhelming force and totally destroy the enemy, not just its leaders. Destroy the leader only, and someone else is right there to take his place. Half-measures never work in war. Our previous wars have taught this, but our so-called "leaders" always think they know better.

My firm's deputy contract manager spent 35 years in the U.S. Army Special Forces (Green Berets). He once told me the only way to win in Iraq was with small Special Forces teams in the villages and towns throughout the country. Our soldiers would be living among the people, in their homes and side-by-side with them in their fight for freedom. Instead, we continued to fight this war with the same conventional tactics we used coming up the road from Kuwait in its opening phases. That makes sense against a conventional enemy, but it's worthless against the new enemy we are going to face in the years to come. The United States has done nothing in Iraq to show that it's aware of this new enemy, or has the will to fight it. Instead of base camps (FOBs) all over the Iraqi countryside, with Subway, Pizza Hut and Burger King, we should have hundreds of thousands of special operators and elite soldiers in civilian clothes, just like their enemy, living and working with the Iraqi people to help them start a new life in freedom. If we can do this in Iraq, we can do it other places too. We're not even close. We care more for the creature comforts of our soldiers and generals than preparing for the real battle we will face—which has essentially already started.

I have attempted to describe—and compare—life of the typical Iraqi before and after our invasion. I conclude they would have been better off if we never invaded Iraq in 2003. Although

I'm a big fan of hers, I'm amazed pundits like Laura Ingraham have just come to that conclusion. I reached it 10 years ago. Then again, Ms. Ingraham didn't spend 14 months in Iraq like I did. She's a die-hard Bush supporter, which I used to be. After all the time I spent in Iraq, seeing what he created there, I'm not a fan of George W. Bush anymore. Why would I be?[69]

What could I say when the Iraqis I worked with asked me why we were conducting the war on terrorism in their country instead of someplace else? No one disputes Saddam Hussein was a monster. But I knew Iraqis who never had a problem with him or his thugs—as long as they kept their noses clean. Of course we would say this was a lousy way to live, but is dying better? To the Founding Fathers of our country, like Patrick Henry who said, "Give me liberty or give me death," it was. But our Founders were fighting for their own freedom, not someone else's. The Iraqi people are dying to fulfill our version of freedom for them, in their own country. Let them decide if they want to be free in their own country, like our Founding Fathers did so many years ago here. No Iraqi ever took out Saddam Hussein, although many wanted to. Unfortunately, if they really wanted Saddam Hussein gone, it would have taken the ultimate sacrifice to do it. The average Iraqi was content to live under Saddam, no matter how bad he was. If no Iraqis were willing to risk their lives for the price of freedom, wasn't that their choice? Instead, we made that choice for them, without any provocation from Saddam Hussein before we did.

One Baghdad local summed up the way it was under Saddam, versus the way it is today. He was with a reporter as they drove past the stump of the bronze statue of Saddam Hussein that was famously toppled over and shown around the world. The dictator's right foot remained, prompting the man to observe: "Everyone talks of how safe it was, if not good under Saddam – you were safe if you didn't discuss politics."[70] Everyone in Iraq talks politics now, but no one feels any safer than before.

---

[69] "Laura Ingraham: 'Iraq Is Worse Off' Now Than Under Saddam," *The Daily Caller* (August 10, 2014).

[70] McGeough, Paul, "Welcome to Baghdad, city of burnt trees and bravado," *The Sydney Morning Herald*, October 17, 2014.

Wednesday night is called "quiet night," indicating the fear of retaliation when openly discussing politics and the political situation. That's some democracy they've got in Iraq now.

The United States has laws that prohibit assassination of foreign government officials. We don't want to get into the business of assassination, primarily because we wouldn't want someone to try it here. If Saddam Hussein had to go, as President Bush decided, were as many as a million people worth the price? The only reasons to invade another country are to conquer it, or stop its assault against another. If Iraq wasn't invading a neighbor, and we had no intention of taking over the country ourselves, what was the point? If it was to get rid of Saddam, then all those people died to get rid of one man. One bullet would have been a lot cheaper, and a lot more effective.

If the people of Iraq wanted our help, we would have been there. No one ever asked us to come except a few opportunists who wanted to run the country after we took out Saddam. This is why the United States is disliked so much. We stick our nose under way too many tents. If people don't ask for our help, we should stay out of their business. Why do we have to decide what is right for them? If we espouse freedom, doesn't that imply leaving other nations alone, leaving them "free" to make their own decisions on how they want to live? If the reason for invading Iraq was Saddam's WMD (that we never found), what about all the countries in the world we know have WMD but we do nothing?

This war was a pipe dream, plain and simple. The only plausible reasons why we entered this war were:

1) Bush's issue over Saddam's threat against his father;

2) Bush wanted to show the world and his father that he was a real leader and not a lousy businessman;

3) Bush wanted to prove he could do something on his own and without his dad's help;

4) Bush was duped into the invasion by a small group of neocons on his staff who had their own agendas.

It's difficult to come to any other reasons for our invasion in light of no WMD ever being found.

I have often wondered what George W. Bush's legacy would be if he never invaded Iraq, focused on the Taliban and Al-Qaeda, and didn't stop until Osama bin Laden's head was stuck on top of a pole. Instead, George W. Bush pissed away the best opportunity a president in modern history has had to seize the moment and do what was needed to prepare our country for a new enemy and a new battle. Being weak like his father, George W. Bush was easily swayed in the other direction by neoconservatives like Douglas Feith, James Wolfowitz, Donald Rumsfeld and Dick Cheney, and dupes like Colin Powell who played along so he could remain on the world stage. Of course, George Tenet was throwing in his two cents, which was far more than what his advice was worth.

If Saddam posed such a serious threat, why couldn't we park a fleet of the U.S. Navy in the Persian Gulf while we waited for him to do something? Saddam wouldn't have done a thing. He wouldn't have had the nerve. Despots like Saddam Hussein are easy to deal with. All it takes is force. Just rap them on the head a few times and they back right down. They know force when they see it. They use it on their own people, so when someone uses it on them they have great respect for its value. But the United States is worried about "waterboarding" and panties wrapped around the heads of killers at Abu Ghraib prison. We will spin our wheels until the shit hits the fan, and then we won't know what to do or how to deal with it. The enemy is just waiting and watching, in disbelief at our stupidity.

I am amazed at the lack of will on the part of our presidents to use the forces we have, and that our taxes have paid for. One would think they are afraid to use it for fear of being looked upon as "bullies" by the likes of the UN. (Colin Powell felt this way at the end of Desert Storm, and passed his fear on to President Bush.) They're afraid the world will think we don't pick fair fights. But no fight should be fair against the United States. It's the president's job to make sure they're not "fair," and to make absolutely certain our soldiers are sent into battle with everything in their favor, with everything they need to win!

Instead, our leaders seem to go out of their way to make us an easy target. They are failures at protecting our nation's image and reputation in the world, which puts us right in the enemy's crosshairs.

Two examples highlight this: 1) Clinton's response to the attack on the USS Cole, and; 2) Carter's response to the hostage crisis in Iran.

Because of our power, we have the obligation to use our force wisely, yet decisively. This doesn't mean we fight with one arm tied behind our back to make it "fair" for our enemies. With the results we've gotten from our recent military operations, we've gone in blindfolded as well. In war "fair" is for losers.

There is *ex post facto* speculation the United States purposely invaded Iraq with a low number of soldiers, then kept it low, so as our casualties grew we could draw Al-Qaeda into a fight there, rather than here. Supporters of the war believe we purposely did so in order to bring the fight to the enemy who attacked us on 9/11, rather than having another attack on our soil—to "protect our freedom." While it may sound plausible, it's just another example of reverse logic (e.g., "The war isn't going well, so we must have planned it that way."). Does anyone really think the Bush administration was sophisticated enough to come up with such an intriguing strategy? The political risks of intentionally creating another Vietnam, splitting our country down the middle because it was such a disaster, would have been too great. Besides, whoever came up with the idea would have bragged about it to get all the credit. In the end we got a lousy plan that no one wanted to take credit for, and a scenario that has done to our country and our society just what Vietnam did.

If our invasion was intentionally planned to turn out the way it did, then 5,000 U.S. soldiers and Marines, and at least 500,000 Iraqis, died to execute it. If that is indeed the case, our military paid the price they volunteered for. But who will thank all of those dead Iraqis and their families for the sacrifices *they* made for *our* freedom? Whenever I hear a pundit refer to Operation Iraqi Freedom as a success, I want to ask them for an example to prove it.

There's another *ex post facto* explanation for our invasion, which was to "export democracy" to Iraq, then watch it spread throughout the Middle East. OK, but why wasn't this given to the American people as one of the reasons for the invasion beforehand? If it had been, the reaction of the American people would have been overwhelming not to invade. I have no doubt our country would have said that idea was crazy, and that the style of government in Iraq was none of our business. Bush would never have been able to pull it off. Instead, we were told Saddam had WMD to generate fear in the American people, and get the votes from the U.S. Senate to authorize the invasion. The "exporting democracy" theory is just that, a theory. It's another example of the reverse logic from the pro-war neocons.

On the other hand if the United States had a valid reason for invading Iraq in 2003 (like it did for invading Afghanistan), and in the process instilled democracy there, who would have had a problem with that? It is for this reason the first Gulf War was such a wasted opportunity. We had the justification for being there, the forces in place, and every reason in the world to get rid of Saddam Hussein. All President George H.W. Bush needed was some backbone to see the job through. But to invade a country which was no threat to us, for the purpose of exporting democracy there, makes absolutely no sense. If we actually invaded Iraq for this reason we caused the deaths of thousands of Iraqis, all so they would have a government like ours. One is reminded of the American officer in Vietnam who was quoted while a village burned to the ground: "We had to destroy it in order to save it." We didn't save the village in Vietnam, and we haven't saved Iraq either.

Our nation's leaders (i.e., our presidents) are pathetically weak and naive. Why possess all our military strength if we don't even use it to rattle our sword to deter rogues like Saddam Hussein? Instead, we plead with the United Nations to send inspectors. When that fails we over-react and invade the place, doing it with a fraction of the forces needed to properly execute the mission. George W. Bush could have shown that we possessed overwhelming force, and the will to use it, and kept an eye on Saddam. If we had the need to attack, we could have done so. Then we could have left or occupied Iraq depending on how the situation developed. But all this would have taken cool heads, good planning, the will to use all the forces we had, the determination to get the job done right and in a timely manner, and the flexibility to adapt to conditions in the combat theater. It can be said of Operation Iraqi Freedom that none of this was done.

"The Bush Doctrine" of preemptive strike proved to be a dismal failure. I don't think for a moment the liberal left in American would have liked George Bush if he hadn't invaded Iraq in the spring of 2003. But it's safe to say they wouldn't hate him as much. Liberals will never like a Republican president, no matter how good a job he does. It's another thing entirely when liberals are right about something, even if it's for the wrong reason. If George W. Bush had not invaded Iraq, all other things remaining the same, he might have been a very popular president. He prevented another terrorist attack on our soil, which is monumental.

The day after 9/11 George W. Bush was given a mandate few presidents ever get. He could have led the country on a legitimate path toward the defeat of Al-Qaeda and the Taliban, and the destruction of Osama bin Laden, without invading Iraq unless he was given provocation to do so, which he wasn't. He could have made an inroad into the destruction of radical Islamic fanaticism by increasing the size of our active duty military, especially the U.S. Army and Marines, and preparing our country for a new enemy and a new type of warfare. If he had done this he would have been going after the real enemy, and building up the force strength we will need in the future. Unfortunately, Bush never increased the size of our active duty military at all. Even during the war Rumsfeld was 'reinventing' the U.S. Army, as if we were in the doldrums of peace time, when the Army was up to its ass in two wars half way around the world. Bush completely blew his opportunity to build what our country needs, and thousands of American forces, Coalition forces, and Iraqis have died as a result of his incompetence.

Bush invaded Iraq in 2003 against an unknown enemy, which in modern warfare is inexcusable. No one in his administration had a clue. In fact, Bush and his team had as much knowledge of the enemy we would be fighting in Iraq, as they did Saddam's possession of WMD. Needless to say, they had no knowledge at all. They were operating on assumptions. Referring to the now infamous quote of George Tenet, they all thought the invasion would be "a slam dunk." When we arrived in Iraq the enemy we faced turned out to be the tip of the iceberg compared to what we will face in the future, and what we're starting to face today with groups like the Islamic State.

Barack Hussein Obama is considering the possibility of going back to Iraq. If our military is smaller today that it was in 2003, what does he plan to go back there with—drones? If Obama thinks he can go back without a significant number of ground combat forces, he's setting our country up for failure in Iraq all over again.

Iraq cannot be looked at today without looking back to the Gulf War of 1991, because it was the pathetic manner in which that war ended that contributed to this one. But the main cause of the current conflict in Iraq was George W. Bush. His father screwed up the previous conflict (Phase I) with the help of Colin Powell, Norman Schwarzkopf and Dick Cheney, who served both Bush presidents. But that didn't mean the son had to repeat the father's mistake. There is really no excuse for it. As the saying goes, "the acorn doesn't fall far from the tree." My last assignment in the Army was in San Antonio, Texas. There are acorn trees all over the place down there.

13—Toy Soldiers

Napoleon once said:

> *Conscription forms armies of citizens, voluntary enlistment forms armies of vagabonds and criminals.*[71]

His comment is as true today as when he said it 200 years ago.

When George W. Bush declared the global war on terror he didn't reinstitute the draft, but instead asked for volunteers to fight it. Rather than a draft to beef up our regular forces, we called up the Reserves and National Guard, who only want extra cash and have no desire to get "activated" and deployed. If they wanted to get deployed they would have joined the active component in the first place. Now we send these forces right into the thick of things because our full-time military is spread too thin. It's spread too thin because our country won't reinstitute the draft. And our country won't reinstitute the draft because of what happened during the Vietnam War, when campus protesters turned our nation's leaders into jellyfish.

On top of all this the military can't afford the salaries of a larger full-time active force because our country is going bankrupt, yet we still declare "global" wars. Our Government is dependent on the Reserves and the National Guard like a Federal agency depends on contractors, part-time employees. The company they work for makes money as long as they are employed at an agency, which has the option of not renewing the contract when it ends. The Reserves and National Guard are essentially the same thing. We send them in to fight our wars, then send them back to the grocery store where they came from when they're no longer needed. They get full pay only when they're activated. It's a stretch, but there isn't much difference between a mercenary and a member of the Reserves or the National Guard. We pay them when we need them, and send them away when we don't.

---

[71] Esdaile, Charles, *Napoleon's Wars: An International History (VIKING, 2007)*, p. 131.

The United States gets around this little obstacle by blurring the lines between the Reserves and National Guard, and the active duty military. The National Guard belongs to the individual states, yet the uniforms of the Army National Guard say "U.S. Army" on them. This is technically incorrect. The Army National Guard only becomes part of the U.S. Army when the President federalizes it and incorporates it into the ranks of the active duty military forces. The President rarely calls up the National Guard, so what's the point of having "U.S. Army" on the uniform? The state's name should be on the uniform, and switched to "U.S. Army" when the President activates the state's militia and makes it a temporary component of the U.S. Army. That's why God invented Velcro.

(During the Hurricane Katrina disaster, Louisiana Governor Kathleen Blanco pleaded with President Bush to send in the Louisiana National Guard. Bush told her the Louisiana National Guard belonged to her. She was the "Commander-in-Chief" of her state's National Guard, and she didn't even know it. She was later defeated and kicked out of office. Now there's a leader for you! On February 12, 2014, former mayor of New Orleans, the "Honorable" Ray Nagin, was convicted of corruption and later sentenced to 10 years in prison.)

When I was in Iraq, it was crawling with reservists and National Guardsmen who didn't do that work for a living. So what purpose were they serving? Their best use would have been back-filling the full-time components of our national defense structure. If the 24th Infantry Division was sent to Iraq (or Afghanistan), and had to leave its permanent location at Fort Riley, Kansas, a reserve unit could come in to run the installation while the 24th was deployed. Reserve and guard units should be used to do all the "back office" staffing of the full-time components of our military, not go right into combat on the front lines like they have been doing since Desert Storm. The only time this should ever happen is as a last resort, when we need every fighting unit we have, like we did in World War II. Isn't that what "reserve" means? In that conflict we had millions of men in uniform, so sending a reserve or guard unit into front line combat made sense.

Reserve and guard members are not full-time soldiers and therefore don't have the level of training, unit discipline, equipment, and commitment to fight our wars that full-timers do. If someone is a full-time soldier, he will have the commitment to stay as long as he is needed (and if he knows he's getting a reenlistment bonus to buy a new car). But our leadership didn't make the full-time soldiers stay in Iraq longer than one year at a time, spreading our forces thinner still. Even with the high number of reservists and guardsmen that were sent over to augment the active-duty forces, the total force strength figures never amounted to enough force to do the job, which was never clearly defined anyway. Our military is so small by comparison to when I was on active duty it boggles my mind. When I was in the U.S. Army there were 16 active duty divisions. Today there are 10. One more point: in my example above I should have used a different unit than the 24th Infantry Division. It's been deactivated and no longer exists.

To add insult to injury the tours of duty in Iraq were a joke. Each component of the U.S. military had different lengths to their tours of duty, yet they were all working side by side in the same office or at the same camp and for the same commander. The Air Force was the biggest offender. This is typical of the Air Force, which has a reputation among the services as being a county club. (There is a joke about the new Air Force base. The first thing that is built is the Officers Club, then the golf course, then the Enlisted Men's Club, then the PX (Post Exchange), and then the commissary. The Air Force runs out of money and has to go back to Congress to ask for more to build the runway.)

There were two young U.S. Air Force officers, a captain and a major, who showed up at Phoenix Base to work at CAFTT, advising the new Iraqi Air Force. Their job was to come up with locations and facilities for the new air force and its fleet of aircraft. Of course, the Iraqi Air Force consisted of a half dozen C-130 transports and about the same number of Bell Jet Ranger helicopters. Iraq had just purchased a number of Polish Mi-17 "Hip" helicopters, which were pretty sharp when painted with the Iraqi colors. One day I saw the major walking along with some party-like things sticking out of his plastic shopping bag. When people left Iraq their co-workers would throw a going away party for them, getting gifts at the PX or the local "Haji Shop." I asked the major who was leaving, and he said "Captain So-And-So," the other officer. I got concerned because the captain had just arrived in Iraq, so I asked the major if everything was OK with him. The major said the captain was fine and that his tour was over. The captain had been in Iraq three months! The major smiled like it was a big joke. The captain was an U.S. Air Force Academy graduate. Our country didn't get much for all the money it cost to send him there. I hope he didn't break a nail packing his duffel bags. And General Allardice thought one "airman" was worth 60 army soldiers.

What made this ridiculous was that we all had to work together. Imagine the effect on morale when one person leaves after three months, but the guy next to him has to stay for a year? There was no consistency in Iraq because there was no consistency in the length of military tours. The contractors were the only ones who gave stability to the place because of their institutional knowledge, which only comes with time. Yet the military at MNSTC-I thought they were the only ones getting anything done. We contractors didn't wear uniforms so we didn't count, and we made a lot of money so the military were envious of us.

The amount of money spent to send someone to Iraq was staggering. When you considered the training before they went, the cost of replacing them at their old job, the transportation costs involved, and of course the hardship, it was tremendous. But to go through all that and only send someone there for three months was pathetic. How serious could our efforts in Iraq be if we allowed people to serve there for such short periods of time? These absurdly short tours had a direct impact on our overall force strength in Iraq. If people were rotated out every three or six months, then we needed two to four times the number of people to get a full year of service out of them, a full "man-year." For example, if one person went to Iraq for a year, that was the same as four going for three months each, one after the other. That assumed one always arrived as the one before them left. With such huge turnover the chances of a gap between tours of duty was much greater, resulting in periods when no one was serving in a particular position at all. One year tours would have drastically reduced the potential for gaps because the turnover rate was that much lower, not to mention the increased effectiveness of our forces due to staff cohesiveness and institutional knowledge. It took a month just to figure out where the laundry was, and the Air Force captain was leaving after three!

We had a huge problem with force numbers in Iraq, which was our own doing because the Secretary of Defense and the President allowed services like the Air Force to get away with three and six month tours. Were they afraid the Air Force would throw a tantrum? If we were using the "combined force" structure in Iraq, whereby all four services were working side by side, they should have required all those in the combined force served the same length of time. But that would have taken leadership, so it never happened. The Secretary of Defense could have directed the Secretary of the Air Force to make all tours one year. That would have been the end of it. The Air Force would have bitched for a few days and then moved on.

Before anyone went to Iraq, military or civilian, they were sent to a CRC, or CONUS Replacement Center (CONUS stands for Continental United States). There were several of these, but the one I went to was at Fort Bliss, Texas. We spent a week there getting trained and issued our equipment, which included our ballistic vest, Kevlar helmet, and protective (gas) mask. The cost of this training, and the time and effort to send us to Iraq, was huge. This was all the more reason to make tours for the military at least one year in order to achieve cost effectiveness and maximize the benefit of our training. We attended one lecture after the next during this week. One was all about what life was like in Iraq. It was taught by a female contractor who had never been there. But the one subject we were given more lectures on than any other, before being sent to Iraq and into a combat zone, was sexual harassment. We were given more lectures on sexual harassment than on IED's, nerve agents, heat exhaustion, or anything else. This is where our nation's priority is.

One item I was not issued was a weapon. After I arrived in Iraq I realized what a major issue this was. As it turned out, even though we were serving in a combat zone, LTG Dempsey wouldn't allow us to carry side arms. We were told by our lapdog manager that in the event we came under fire, we'd be protected by the military serving side-by-side with us. Following that logic, I was safe as long as I was near a soldier with a rifle or pistol. What was this mystery soldier going to do, shield me with his/her body and hold off a hoard of insurgents at risk to his/her life? What about when I wasn't near a soldier? LTG Dempsey didn't have a solution for that scenario, which meant I wasn't safe when caught in that situation—but I still wasn't going to be issued a side arm. The real reason we weren't issued weapons was because LTG Dempsey didn't want to bother his staff with the extra paperwork. I was told this by a senior member of the MNSTC-I staff. So if we found ourselves in need of self-defense we were screwed, all because LTG Dempsey didn't want the administrative hassle. In the weeks leading up to my departure for Iraq, several contractors were beheaded after being captured by insurgents. Many contractors wanted a side arm to avoid being captured alive, and who could blame them. LTG Dempsey had about 20 security guards protecting him, so what did he care if one of us got captured? He didn't want us there anyway. Based on the experience of the contractors in Iraq, nearly all of whom were former military, most of them were far more familiar with weapons than the military were. We would have been protecting the soldiers, not the other way around.

Everything in Iraq was dysfunctional, from top to bottom, Iraq and Coalition (U.S.). The only thing that kept the wheels from falling off completely were contractors, who were there because our military wasn't big enough to do all the things it needed to do on its own. But within MNSTC-I we were treated worse than insurgents. Contractors were there primarily to make money, which kept them from leaving the day their tour was over like the U.S. military did. The U.S. military were jealous of the money contractors made, but did they ever stop to think who would bother going to Iraq if they were making the same money as they were in the States? American contractors were the only continuity in Iraq. The U.S. military left as fast as it could get on the plane, greeted like conquering heroes upon their return, but bitching and moaning the entire time they were there and complaining about the money contractors were making. If it wasn't for the contractors there would have been nothing in Iraq to keep the place together.

The contractors were the only institutional knowledge in Iraq. They cooked the food for the U.S. military because there weren't military cooks any more. Back in the States no one ever heard about the contractors in Iraq except when the media blasted Dick Cheney and Halliburton. Without firms like Halliburton, Iraq would have been in worse shape than it was. A woman employed by KBR, a former subsidiary of Halliburton, was killed one day by a mortar round that landed behind the U.S. Embassy in the IZ. Halliburton's employees, and those of every firm in Iraq, were in danger every day. The contractors were the ones who drove the truck convoys hundreds of miles to feed the soldiers and fuel their vehicles, because the U.S. military didn't have enough trucks and drivers to do it. The contractors ran the precious PX, but when one of them got killed no one except their family even knew about it.

There were primarily two types of contractors in Iraq: security contractors and everyone else. By 2010 it was estimated security contractors had billed the United States Government as much as $5 billion dollars since the beginning of the war. The last week of June 2006, the week before I started my job, I saw the documentary film *Shadow Company* by Nick Bicanic and Jason Bourque.[72] The film was about security contractors in Iraq. I saw the same contractors (not the same individuals) when I arrived there. The theme of the film was: were these contractors actually mercenaries? After spending 14 months in Iraq, I had absolutely no doubt they were.

The best example of this was the security contractors who protected Unites States military flag officers—generals and admirals. Every day I saw civilian security contractors guarding U.S. general officers. They were driven around in black up-armored Chevy Suburbans, with an entourage of plain clothes "security contractors" wherever they went, sunglasses and all. I think it made the officers feel like rock stars. There was no legitimate explanation for it. (Whenever a general in Iraq or Afghanistan was photographed he always had his helmet off so his face could be seen by the cameras. He was out of uniform, but a good photograph was more important. So much for setting

---

[72] *Shadow Company*, by Nick Bicanic and Jason Bourque (A Purpose Built Film, 2006).

the example to his troops by wearing his helmet.) If the governor of a state goes someplace he or she is protected by plain clothes state police. The President and Vice President are protected by the U.S. Secret Service. They aren't protected by civilian contractors. But U.S. general officers in Iraq were. This was absurd. If security contractors were doing this, which was clearly the job of a soldier, then they were doing what soldiers do, which means they were mercenaries. Today the U.S. employs mercenaries around the world.

The way our Government got around this was with semantics. Security contractors in Iraq were called PSDs, for Personal Security Detail. In the case of general officers, contractors were providing "personal security" protection for them. "Security contractor" made it sound like security guards protecting an office building so the American people wouldn't know what they really did for a living. PSDs like Blackwater, Triple Canopy and others, were fully equipped combat forces capable of engaging with any enemy in Iraq. The truck driver hauling fuel was there because the U.S. Army no longer has enough drivers. PSDs were protecting high-ranking officers because we didn't have enough soldiers to do it, which was their job. Only in rare cases did I see U.S. soldiers providing security for general officers, like they did for LTG Hunzeker.

We allowed PSDs in Iraq for two reasons: 1) our military is no longer big enough to do its job, and; 2) we continue to feed the military-industrial complex that President Eisenhower warned us about all those years ago. Well, here we are. If we didn't have PSDs, maybe we would have to increase the size of our military. But the private security companies wouldn't be making all that money. One would think they are indirectly responsible for limiting the size of our armed forces. We are hiring PSDs to cut corners and "privatize" how we fight our wars, just like a Federal agency hires private contractors to augment its lack of full-time employees. When you privatize warfare, you've got a mercenary force for hire. What is there not to understand?

The most widely known security contractor in Iraq was Blackwater, the largest and most profitable firm providing these services in the world. Blackwater was founded by a former U.S. Navy SEAL, who touted his firm's expertise by claiming all his employees were ex-SEALs, Rangers or Delta Force. Based on my observations while in Iraq for 14 months, as well as personally knowing a few security contractors, I am convinced this was nonsense. Anyone who wanted to go to Iraq and be a badass could get a job with one of these firms. If you really wanted to experience the "thrill" of killing someone, without any consequences, there was no better job than as a security contractor in Iraq. They were as well armed, or better armed, as any soldier because they could "pack" whatever weapon they felt like, whereas soldiers can only carry what they are issued. They had carte blanche to shoot at anyone or anything they wanted to, for whatever reason, and get away with it. There were no "Rules of Engagement" for security contractors in Iraq. For them it was the Wild West. Too bad Iraqi civilians who got in their way didn't know that.

Just about every PSD in Iraq looked exactly the same, as if they had come out of a "PSD factory." Every one of them had long sideburns and a goatee, and wore a tan baseball cap with the beak in a tight curl, sunglasses (which we all needed), tan slacks with cargo pouches, a black golf shirt, and tattoos—lots and lots of tattoos. They had more body art than I had ever seen. One moron actually had Roman armored 'shields' tattooed all over his body! They thought they were total studs, while the rest of us thought they were clowns. They did nothing but hang out at the gym, and it was obvious most of them were steroid freaks. I knew one who said the drug problem inside the PSD compound was out of control. There was no way they would have been able to get away with their behavior if they were soldiers, at least not to the extent they were. And if they looked like jerks, they acted that way too.

On September 16, 2007, several Blackwater employees murdered 17 Iraqi civilians at Nisour Square in Baghdad, which was nothing more than a legally sanctioned massacre. The U.S. State Department's Diplomatic Security Division, which oversaw all security contractors in Iraq, gave the massacre's perpetrators immunity if they gave statements describing what occurred, thereby eliminating any possibility they would be prosecuted. If a U.S. soldier had done such a thing he would have been court marshaled and thrown in jail for the rest of his life. But the

Blackwater contractors walked away. On Christmas Eve of 2006, one of them got drunk at the tiki bar behind the U.S. Embassy and killed an Iraqi. He was sent home and went on his merry way. To the best of my knowledge no charges were ever filed against him because it happened overseas in a combat zone, and because he was a "security contractor." Blackwater agreed to pay the dead man's family a chunk of money, and that was it. I later heard the man's family had to hire an American lawyer to sue the Blackwater employee. Blackwater never paid the dead man's family what it had promised. Not only was the dead Iraqi's life not worth anything, the promise to pay off his family wasn't either.

Blackwater doesn't take criticism very lightly. On June 30, 2014, a Fox News story shed more light on the firm:

> A manager with the security contractor formerly known as Blackwater Worldwide reportedly threatened to kill a State Department investigator in 2007 — shortly before the investigator was pressured to abandon his probe despite finding serious problems with Blackwater's work.
>
> *The New York Times* reported Sunday that Jean C. Richter wrote in an Aug. 31, 2007 memo to State Department officials that Blackwater contractors "saw themselves as above the law" and described a situation in Baghdad where "the contractors, instead of Department officials, are in command and control."[73]

There was no U.S. government oversight of Blackwater other than the management of its contract. When, on the rare occasion the government tried to exercise its legal authority, the federal employee involved was threatened with his life. How have Blackwater and other firms been able to get into these roles, with no oversight and no accountability? The main reason is that we don't have enough soldiers to do the job that soldiers are supposed to do, because political correctness prevents our

---

[73] "Blackwater manager reportedly threatened to kill State Department investigator," *Fox News*, June 30, 2014.

leadership from reinstituting the draft. The other reason is because the American people don't care if someone gets killed who isn't wearing a uniform. This way our weak presidents can order military operations someplace and tell the American people we don't have "soldiers" there. Only the loss of uniformed soldiers gets reported and gets any attention. Civilian contractors who get killed are truly expendable. If they are doing the work of soldiers, but their deaths aren't given the time of day, what else do you call it? The only time these guys get the attention of the American people is when they murder 17 innocent civilians.

> The investigator reportedly warned his superiors that lax oversight of the firm had created "an environment of liability and negligence," just weeks before a group of guards allegedly opened fire on Iraqi civilians at a Baghdad traffic circle in 2007.

> The Times report claims that Richter's inquiry, though, was abandoned after Blackwater's project manager in Iraq, Daniel Carroll, warned Richter that "he could kill me … and no one could or would do anything about it as we were in Iraq," according to a memo sent by Richter to senior State Department officials. According to the Times, the American Embassy sided with Blackwater and ordered the investigators out of the country.[74]

In other words, Blackwater was calling the shots, not the State Department's own investigators. This can only be due to Blackwater having senior State Department official in its back pocket. How else could such gross negligence on the part of senior State Department officials be allowed to happen?

> Before the investigation was halted, the paper reports, Richter found evidence that Blackwater was overcharging the State Department for its work by falsifying staff data, understaffing security details, allowing contractors to carry weapons that they were

---

[74] Ibid.

not authorized to use, and housing non-American workers in squalid conditions.[75]

Blackwater was out of control, and this investigator knew it. But when he tried to do his job he was threatened with murder by the Blackwater manager, and then ordered out of Iraq by his State Department superiors. And Blackwater was able to stick around! If this isn't an example of corruption within the State Department, what is? It's also an example of the military-industrial complex, where contractors hired by the government tell the government what to do. It's the tail wagging the dog.

> Sixteen days after the date of Richter's report, Blackwater guards allegedly opened fire in Baghdad's Nisoor [*sic*] Square. Seventeen Iraqi civilians died in the violence, including women and children. The shooting inflamed anti-American sentiment in Iraq in the midst of growing insurgent violence[.] Blackwater's license to operate in Iraq was revoked by the Baghdad government the following day.
>
> Four Blackwater guards are facing trial on manslaughter charges in connection with the Nisoor [*sic*] Square shooting, which prosecutors argue was unprovoked. Attorneys for the men say they had come under attack by insurgents.[76]

The Backwater employees were eventually charged for the Nisour Square murders, which is a good turn of events. Prior to being charged, however, their immunity was the same as me killing someone and later walking out of the police station for telling the cops I did it!

> In 2009, Blackwater changed its name to Xe Services after founder Erik Prince resigned as CEO. The

---

[75] Ibid.

[76] Ibid.

following year, a group of investors purchased the company and renamed it again, to Academi.[77]

Will the United States build up its active duty forces to fight the war on terrorism by reinstituting the draft? Or will we remain increasingly dependent on reservists and guardsmen who do it part-time, contractors who do it for profit, and drones flown by someone at a control console half-way around the world? The draft is the sane response to the threat, but politically incorrect. Therefore, political correctness in the face of the growing dangers from radical Islamic terrorism, such as the Islamic State, is insane.

The other reason why we don't have the draft is because we can hire contractors and pay them to do anything we want them to. People will do anything for money, and our country is taking this to its logical conclusion. Congress debates how many troops to send into a conflict, yet no one blinks an eye when we send tens of thousands of contractors to the same theater of operations, in many cases into the same level of danger. But they don't wear uniforms, and they get paid well, so who cares? Our country avoids the issue of a draft because we can augment our forces with contractors. By the same token, using contractors makes going to war a lot easier. We literally don't have any "skin in the game." Did we have contractors during the Second World War like we do today? We had the draft and everyone wanted to volunteer. Logic then follows that employing contractors is the reverse of having a draft and taking in volunteers. It's also very convenient when we're fighting an unpopular war like Vietnam or Iraq. By using contractors we don't have soldiers in uniform, we have civilians with goatees.

During the Second World War everyone wore a uniform, no matter what their job was. They were all the same. Only their rank separated them. We had to mobilize millions of soldiers to go to war then, which meant we had to have a clear objective to satisfy the American people that we were doing the right thing. Today we can send a token force of soldiers from the few we have available, and make up the difference with contractors. Because we are sending a relatively few number of soldiers into

[77] Ibid.

combat compared to the number that should be going, the American public isn't as alarmed. Our nation then sends thousands of contractors over along with the soldiers in uniform, and no one is the wiser. With contractors our nation can avoid resorting to the draft, and at the same time going to war is much easier to pull off. It's a "win-win" situation, depending on your perspective. But this means going to war isn't as deliberate as it used to be, resulting in fuzzy goals and objectives, or none at all. The reasons for going don't have to be as solid as they used to be, and the public is more easily kept in the dark. The problem with fighting wars this way is the results turn out to be disastrous because we don't send enough soldiers.

At the beginning of this book I made reference to the "military-industrial complex" that President Eisenhower spoke of shortly before he left the White House in 1961. He could see the problem in its infancy, and it bothered him enough to tell the American people they needed to be aware of it. It would be difficult to prove that we went to war just to satisfy the companies that employ contractors in Iraq and Afghanistan. But a case could be made that having these companies, and the staff they employ, makes going to war much easier for the United States. We don't have to be as committed to the conflict as we used to be, such as during the Second World War. We can go for flimsy reasons, and be there as long as we want. The contractors certainly won't complain. They're making the best money of their lives. The longer the conflict lasts the better. And many of these companies are led by retired four-star generals, or have them on their Boards of Directors. Our active duty generals are more like contract administrators then leaders of military units. By the time they retire they should know how to run these companies as well as anyone.

Contractors are certainly not to blame for everything. The real blame lies in the weak leadership our country has been saddled with. Weak leadership leads to lack of commitment, no clear goals or objectives, too much debate and hand wringing and, of course, the need to get the UN's permission to do anything. Strong leadership, which we don't have, would mean the development of clear goals and objectives, the mobilization of more than enough military force to accomplish the mission, and directly telling the American people what is going to be done and why. Of course, this also implies the leader (i.e., the President) knows what he's doing and is telling the American people the truth. When is the last time we had anything close to this?

This begs the question—who will fight global Islamic terrorism? It won't be contractors. The only way to fight this new enemy is with two types of military forces working closely together:

1) Small units of special operators and Special Forces who understand the culture of the local population where the enemy is based, and;

2) Large elite units of Army Rangers and Infantry, and Marines if they can learn to play well with others.

The small units would be among the population, living side-by-side with them and undergoing the same hardships. There wouldn't be any Burger Kings and Pizza Huts. They would gather the intelligence and take out small pockets of the enemy. They would alert the larger units, which would take out the bigger enemy forces and their encampments.

It will take tens of thousands, more likely hundreds of thousands, of highly trained soldiers to conduct this fight. We don't have this capability now, and we can't do it with contractors, unless we just accept the fact that our country employs mercenaries. The United States is getting complacent using so many contractors, and will pay the price for not looking the situation in the eye and growing our active duty forces to the numbers we will need in the future. We reduced the size of the U.S. Army when the Berlin Wall came down. Now it's time to get it back up to where it needs to be with the draft and volunteers.

14—Warm Bodies

I decided to leave Iraq at the end of my one-year obligation. My firm sent resumes of candidates to take my place, and I was asked to review them. One of the candidates had absolutely no experience at all in real estate. He had worked as a dispatcher for a trucking company and as a clerk in a hotel, but because his resume said he was a graduate of the U.S. Army Command and General Staff College at Fort Leavenworth, he was recommended for the job. His resume didn't even say he had been in the Army. But the senior advisor in my group, also employed by my firm, recommended this guy for my job. This was an insult to my experience, and proof once again that we were just there to collect fees for our employer. This was the same as saying anyone could get a job in Iraq regardless of their qualifications. You might not end up doing what you were hired to do once you got there, so what difference did it make what your qualifications were? This was a blow to my already bruised ego. I actually thought, for a very short time, that I got the job because I was the best candidate.

My co-worker and I formally disagreed with the senior advisor in our group, so they decided not to make an offer to the guy. As a result I decided to stay, which I did partly for the money. I also did it because my firm couldn't find someone to take my place that was qualified to do my job, or should I say what was on the job description. Call it professional pride, but I didn't want to leave Iraq knowing they hired a moron who didn't know squat about my field. And I didn't want everything I had done at the Ministry of Defense ruined. In the end, however, my decision to stay beyond one year turned out to be a very big mistake. This will be described below.

That my firm would consider a dispatcher/front desk clerk to replace me showed that many contractors, but certainly not all, had no experience or qualifications for the jobs they were hired to do. When I was introduced to a couple of officers in J-7, one of them told me I was the first contactor he met in Iraq who actually did the same type of work in the States. That wasn't a good sign. Many contractors and advisors at MOD had years of experience, some of it directly related to what they were doing in Iraq, and some not so directly related. The one thing most of us brought with us was our age, and with that our overall experience in matters that could help the situation in Iraq. I honestly believed most of us really wanted to get something done and to earn our pay. In my case, I was bringing experience directly related to the subject I was to advise, which made me all the more upset when I was ignored and brushed aside. If I hadn't been experienced, being blown off wouldn't have bothered me as much. I would have probably just walked away hoping not to be found out for a fraud. Maybe that's why my manager wanted all of us to keep our mouths shut. He didn't want anyone being discovered for the sham "subject matter expert" they were. He had to keep those contract dollars coming in.

Near the end of my time I was told about the guy who had been offered my job before they gave it to me. He had been given a formal job offer, and was soon contacted by my future co-worker in Iraq. In no time this clown started calling her and others before he departed the States, telling them he planned to fly his private plane to Iraq to survey the land needed for Iraqi bases. He also told everyone he was going to bring his personal weapons over with him. Around this time my company received my resume and immediately rescinded their offer to him.

Anyone could get a job in Iraq regardless of their qualifications, or if they had none at all. It didn't matter to my firm if a candidate had nothing to qualify them for a position, much less anything to offer the Ministry of Defense. If our senior advisor thought a dispatcher at a trucking company and the front desk manager at a hotel was qualified to advise the Iraqi Ministry of Defense, then anyone could get a job there. The guy who was offered the job before me would have gotten himself killed. That wouldn't have been so bad, but he would have gotten someone else killed along with him. All because my firm had no legitimate candidate screening process beyond making sure the person was breathing.

(My co-worker told me before I left the States that my job required travel throughout the country to conduct land surveys, etc. After I arrived, I found out it took an act of Congress to travel five miles, and if there was a single cloud in the sky the

Marines would ground their aircraft due to weather. Of course, J-7 made anything I tried to do impossible. It was all bait and switch on the part of my firm to get people like me to go over there thinking we'd be getting something done. Getting work done wasn't important. It was all about collecting fees.)

The "warm body" syndrome was alive and well in Iraq. It still is, only to a lesser extent after Obama's troop withdrawal. Some of the guys left at the end of their year commitment, only to return after a few months. Either they were desperate for the money, which most folks who went to Iraq were, or they were running away from something or someone. One guy I worked with, who went back after six months, was on his fourth marriage. To guys like him marriage is just an extended date. If you have nothing going on in the States, and you can go over to Iraq and make $200,000 or more a year, doing nothing if you don't feel like it, why not go? Especially if you're running away from a wife breaking your balls because of your drinking and drugging, or you're broke. My roommate was an active duty the full colonel who left the Army on a month's notice to come to Iraq for the money, nothing more. His first wife built up so much debt, he was still paying it off six years later. She had 38 credit cards when they split up, every one maxed out. When he used his own credit card to buy a gift for his girlfriend, his wife nailed him to the wall for adultery. Years later he was still paying off the money she got out of him for his little slip. In the five years he had been married to his second wife, they had been together under the same roof for about 7 months. The rest of the time he had been deployed to the Middle East—in uniform during the first part of OIF, and now as a contractor, all the while making great money. I knew another guy who was there simply to support his wife's spending habit. She wanted him to go to Iraq because of the money, nothing more. They had small kids. He was in Kuwait before coming to Iraq and had nearly been killed when he was hit by a truck. He had undergone half a dozen operations on his shoulder, and went back to Iraq because the money was simply too good to pass up, and because his wife made him. When he was on the phone with his wife all they talked about was money. She was spending them into the poorhouse, and he was making $200,000 a year.

One particular case of the "warm body" syndrome could have easily turned out to be the "cold body" syndrome. Early into my tour, I was called into my manager's office and his deputy asked if I was willing to escort someone from Baghdad back to Kuwait. I said sure, and he proceeded to explain the reason for the trip. It turned out my firm hired a guy who had just arrived in Baghdad the day before, but needed to return to the States immediately. The man was 67 years old, and in such poor health he couldn't even wear his helmet, must less his 35 pound vest. Someone had removed the SAPI plates (SAPI—Small Arms Protective Insert) from his vest because he couldn't wear it with them still inside.

(The vests had ballistic ceramic plates in them which gave them their weight. The plates could stop a 7.62mm AK-47 round, and could be removed by sliding them out of their pouches in the vest. Most of the civilian women in Iraq didn't have the plates in their vests because of the weight, and they didn't look nice with the plates inside. Comfort and fashion were far more important than protection from an AK-47 round. Most of them simply refused to wear their helmets because it messed up their hair. They carried them instead, which provided absolutely no protection for their head from a bullet or shrapnel. One female nurse was killed by shrapnel from an exploding mortar round that landed a block down Haifa Street from the U.S. hospital. I don't know if she had her SAPI plates in her vest or not, but the civilian women started wearing all their protective gear after that.)

When the older gentleman arrived at Ali Al Saleem Air Base in Kuwait everyone noticed him. He was in terrible shape. He had a heart condition, and by the time he got to Baghdad he couldn't make it up a flight of stairs. He should never have been allowed to leave the States, but the Army doctors who screened him at Fort Bliss weren't allowed to give him a physical. No one was given a physical before they left for Iraq. I honestly think it was because DoD knew half of them wouldn't pass it. (Many of the contractors who went to Iraq wouldn't have made it past a drug screening. The guy who had been married four times was a walking pharmacy. He had something for anything that ailed you. He had been a Medical Services officer in the Navy and was a prescription drug addict.) The doctors at Fort Bliss had to go by the medical report from the guy's doctor in his home town in upstate New York, which wasn't worth the paper it was written on. My company never met the man in person (they rarely did when they hired someone—it's too expensive to fly them to the corporate office), so how could they know his condition? Everyone was so concerned with people's privacy, they couldn't make the determination that someone was physically incapable of the rigors of Iraq. In short, there was no screening process whatsoever before you went to Iraq, professionally or otherwise. I had to stay with the man until he walked down the jet-way at Kuwait International Airport, to make sure he didn't die while under my care. I had to carry his empty vest and Kevlar helmet for him. He didn't have the strength to carry them himself.

There was one case that stood out from all the others. One of our firm's employees was an outright fraud. I met him the day I arrived in Baghdad in July 2007. He was one of the few contractors who had his own up-armored Chevy Suburban, and had been pressed into service to drive some of the new arrivals from the airport into the IZ. I didn't go in his vehicle that day, but would get the ride of my life a few months later.

He was a PhD in "Arab-Israeli Conflict" from the University of Maryland who had taught at the University of Japan. He had been in the Special Forces. A couple of months before I left Iraq his story started to unravel.

In July 2007 he was arrested by the IZ police (U.S. security) with a half-naked Iraqi girl in the front seat of his Suburban near the Crossed Swords at Saddam's parade field. He had his subordinate, a female U.S. Air Force major, come to the police station to bail him out. He was released from custody and turned over to her, with both of them claiming she was his superior. This was outright fraud by the two of them, and she was a commissioned officer. He told the MODTT Chief of Staff, the Signal Corps lieutenant colonel, that he had been arrested because he had unauthorized weapons with him (several AK-47's, MP-5's, .45's, 9mm's, etc.). Our crack Chief of Staff let him get away with it.

More came out on him as the months went by. It was discovered that he had been arrested in September 1988 for larceny, forgery and filing a false official statement while a captain in the U.S. Army. In December of 1988 he was dismissed from the Army with an Other-Than-Honorable discharge, not an easy thing to pull off for an officer. He even had an FBI arrest number. Needless to say he didn't have a PhD, although his business cards and his signature on all of his documents said "Dr." (I refer to him here as "Dr. X.") Of course, he wasn't a colonel in the Army reserves either. He had forged several letters to convince a young female Iraqi woman she had received a Fulbright Scholarship, the U.S. Government-funded exchange program run by the State Department. He even forged the signatures of high ranking U.S. Government officials in Washington, DC to substantiate the story. Apparently, he did this so the young lady would be 'grateful' to him. She was the same half-naked girl arrested with him in July 2007 near the Crossed Swords. Dr. X deceived her into believing he had submitted her application and had obtained the Fulbright Scholarship for her. But he hadn't done a thing. The letter from the Fulbright program was fake, but she thought she had been accepted. He put his own name in the letter of acceptance as her "point of contact," in case she had any questions. He must have been explaining the Fulbright Scholarship program to her that night in his Suburban.

A good friend, who stayed in Iraq for a year after I left, told me the final straw for Dr. X came in October 2007. Dr. X lied to the FBI, saying he had gone into the Red Zone (Baghdad outside the IZ wall) and "placed eyes" on an Iraqi captain who was a fugitive wanted for murder. He convinced the FBI, who in turn gave the information to the CIA's Office of Regional Affairs (ORA) to raid the house where he said the fugitive was located. The ORA raided the place (the FBI did not participate—they rarely left the IZ) on October 12, 2007. During the raid a young Iraqi man was shot and maimed for life. He had been sleeping on the roof of the raided house. Dr. X suddenly left the country on vacation a few days later.

The FBI and CIA neglected to follow their own protocol and verify the original "source" of information about the raid's target beforehand. Instead, they relied solely on the third-party information provided by Dr. X. My friend spoke to the "source," who claimed he told Dr. X the fugitive was not at the home, but had moved to Egypt two years earlier. The corruption of the

Iraqi government was bad enough, but according to my associate, "the cover-up by our own gov't [government] agencies is disturbing and another form of corruption! The DR ['Dr. X"] case could be a book alone as he was a dangerous person who lied about virtually everything and committed numerous crimes and eventually his lies almost cost an innocent young man his life. For our gov't to then refuse to accept responsibility for their negligence is compounding matters."

My friend spent more than a year fighting with the FBI and CIA to get compensation for the young man who was shot during the botched raid. Three different CIA Station Chiefs came and went, and each one blew him off. The third went to the intelligence staff at MNSTC-I to exert pressure on my friend to drop the case. To quote my friend: "...this was a serious case that deserved attention and compensation...but when it came to us practicing what we preached we chose to stonewall, deny, lie and avoid responsibility. MNSTC-I had a COL [colonel] who was not my supervisor speak with me and he said: 'You need to remember who pays your salary, whose side you're on and that you're an American, drop the case!'"

In the colonel's distorted mind, because we're Americans whatever we do is OK and those who rock the boat, like my friend, aren't playing on the same team. One has to wonder what team the colonel was on. The colonel was a Marine, by the way.

When all of this information about Dr. X was revealed, he was reluctantly fired by our company. They didn't want to take any action against him, even though he knowingly provided false information that resulted in the CIA conducting a raid in an extremely dangerous neighborhood of Baghdad, placing its "Tier I" operators' lives in danger. (Prior to the raid a VTC (video teleconference) was held with Dr. X, my associate, and the operatives who were going to conduct it. Dr. X sat there knowing the raid was based on his lies, and the operatives could get killed for nothing.) He was criminally dangerous, a narcissist, a habitual liar, and an unstable sociopath—and he successfully snowed our employer for 18 months. But our firm's management didn't care. Not only should he have been fired, he should have had criminal charges filed against him. Instead, our firm wanted to hold onto him after everything he had done. The MNSTC-I chain of command finally told our firm to fire Dr. X for the incident with the young Iraqi girl. This was another violation of General Order #1, in addition to the prohibition of alcohol.

On February 8, 2008, CNN World News reported that: "As many as 133 women were killed in Basra last year—79 for violation of "Islamic teachings" and 47 for so-called honor killings."[78] The 47 were beheaded for not wearing their hijab, or head scarf. If the Iraqi police had found Dr. X and the girl in the Suburban instead of the U.S. police, there is a good chance she would have been executed for violating Islamic law. After all, she had half her clothes off and was in a vehicle with a man who wasn't her husband.

When he returned to the States from Iraq my former colleague contacted the CIA to follow up on the issue of the Iraqi who had been shot and permanently injured during the raid. He wasn't trying to get anyone in trouble, just trying to get compensation for the young man. Finally, when CIA management refused to do anything and referred my friend to their General Counsel, he knew nothing was going to be done. He was right. The CIA claimed the young man was not innocent of wrong-doing himself. In effect, the CIA was taking the position the young man had gotten what he deserved. But the raid wouldn't have happened at all if the CIA and FBI had checked with the "source" of the intelligence on the fugitive Iraqi captain. If they had, they would have known he wasn't there before they conducted the raid, and the young man wouldn't have been shot. But that didn't mean a thing to the CIA. They went out of their way to whitewash the entire affair, and a young man asleep on a rooftop will never be the same again. At least some money would have helped him out. But that might have been taken as an admission of guilt on the part of the CIA, so it wasn't going to happen.

My employer never checked Dr. X's academic credentials, his criminal record, or even his DD Form 214 (his record of military service). My colleague told me he checked all of this in a short time and with minimum effort, so our firm could have done it as well. He even found out that Dr. X had lied on his application to

---

[78] Arwa Damon, "Violations of 'Islamic teaching' take deadly toll on Iraqi women," *CNN World News,* February 8, 2008.

have his Embassy security pass renewed, stating on this official U.S. Government document that he had never been arrested. My colleague knows he was arrested at least twice. One of those arrests was six weeks before he lied on the application, when he was arrested by the IZ police with the half-naked Iraqi girl. He even lied when he didn't have to. One day he said two bullets had gone through his windshield and had just missed his head. He went to the maintenance shop and they replaced the windshield while he waited. Later, my friend was borrowing Dr. X's Chevy Suburban. He decided to check Dr. X's claim about the windshield, and it turned out the windshield had never been replaced the entire time the Suburban had been in Iraq. Dr. X just wanted people to think he was James Bond and had just missed getting killed on his way into the office. "Just another day on the job old boy. Shaken, not stirred."

The Dr. X story was an example, albeit an extreme one, of how characters, cowboys, frauds and liars could get work in Iraq because it meant about $200,000-$400,000 for our firm just by filling their position. It was a glaring example of the type of people who could obtain work in Iraq without the most rudimentary background checks. Dr. X was able to work there for a year and a half in spite of his serious personal and professional flaws. Although the vast majority of the contractors really were "Subject Matter Experts," some were just plain con artists. But it's one thing to be a fake. It's another thing entirely when the company who employs you knows it and allows you to get away with it—without any repercussions—because they like you. Was our purpose in Iraq to show the Iraqi people how things were done right, and hiring people of integrity to do it? Or was it just about money, some adventure, and screw the Iraqis? Was it about achieving peace, or getting promoted?

There's one final story about Dr. X. When I escorted the geriatric back to Kuwait, our PhD in Arab-Israeli Conflict gave us a ride to Baghdad International Airport. Because he was such a badass, Dr. X always packed several weapons in his personal Chevy Suburban. He had a 9mm on his belt, and an AK-47 and MP-5 shoved next to his seat. He also had a young PSD (Personal Security Detail—see below) riding shotgun with him, completely against regulations. The PSD was a kid, about 21 years old, and was having a ball.

Dr. X picked us up at FOB Blackhawk, and then got on the main road leading from the IZ to the airport called "Route Irish," and away we went. About five miles long, Route Irish was the most dangerous road in all Iraq, with more deaths from insurgent fire and IED's than any other stretch of road in the country. Individual vehicles drove very fast down Route Irish to make themselves harder targets, but Dr. X must have had a busy day ahead. As soon as he got on Route Irish, which was a 6-lane divided highway, he hit the gas. It was the second fastest I've ever gone in my life (the fastest was in high school in my friend Danny Davis' Dodge Challenger RT going to Ocean City, Maryland—147 mph!). At one point I looked at the speedometer and we were going 125 miles an hour, weaving and dodging cars the whole way. The entire trip I kept trying to fasten my seat belt, but couldn't because the armor plating inside the vehicle was blocking the strap. Forget being blown up by an IED, the shrapnel wouldn't have been flying fast enough to hit us. Because Iraqis are lousy drivers, if one of them had pulled in front of us we were all dead. Dr. X was a cowboy trying to show off, and risking our lives in the process. I told our deputy manager about the ride from hell when I got back from Kuwait and he just laughed. Dr. X was a rock star as far as my company was concerned. It was only after MNSTC-I ordered my firm to fire Dr. X that it did what it should have months earlier.

My associate told me a similar story:

> In June 07, Dr. ["Dr. X"] was driving the armored SUV and I was in the front seat and we had two local men in the back.........and he was driving on the opposite side of Route Irish outbound in the inbound lane. He was doing about 100 mph and a young local lady dressed in an all black abayah with a young girl about 6 or 7 holding her hand was crossing the street. They never looked to their right because the traffic was only coming from the left, but the DR was driving the wrong way at 100mph! Note that there was very little traffic so there was no need to be in the opposite lane. Well, he continued driving, never slowed and

never even blew the horn and the lady and little girl continued to walk into his path and he missed them by about 5' at the most!

It was bizarre and he showed no concern whatsoever about almost turning two innocent civilians into pink mist. I had an argument about this and he acted like I was the strange person to be concerned about his dangerous conduct. If he had hit that lady and child I am certain he never even would have slowed down!

Many of the contractors in Iraq were on their third, fourth and even fifth year there. I ran into a construction contractor who had been there for over four years. He had a family in the States, and a six year old daughter who he hardly knew. To most of them the money was just too good. It was an addiction. Many people made the decision to place money over everything else. There was a culture of pure love for money, and nothing more, in Iraq. I realized after being there a while it was simply the money that mattered to most contractors there, but the military were not exempt. They were making the best money of their lives, all tax free up to the level of pay of a Sergeant Major. I knew an Army major who was making over $100,000—tax free.

Sure, the money was great. I never made that kind of money in my life. But I really wanted to do something, to do the job I was hired for. Why go there if not to get something done? The place was a mess, so why not try to fix it. I honestly wasn't thinking of just myself when I went to Iraq, especially after I had been there just a short time and had worked with the Iraqis at MOD, who just wanted to live their lives. I didn't want to go there for the money alone.

Being employed in Iraq by a U.S. company, the first $82,400 I earned was tax free. The only requirement was that I had to be outside the United States for 330 days out of 365. I made $210,000 and got a $10,000 bonus, for a total of $220,000. If the taxes on $82,400 was $20,000, which I didn't have to pay, this meant I was making the equivalent of $220,000 + $20,000, or $240,000 a year before taxes.

That's quite a sum considering no one wanted to hear anything I had to say about legal title to the land MOD camps were being built on by J-7; no one wanted to hear what I had to say about the way MNSTC-I constructed military installations for the Iraqi army; that U.S. taxpayer money was being spent with minimal accountability (or none at all) by the U.S. military responsible for managing it; and no one would let me assist in the transfer of FOB's from the Coalition to the Ministry of Defense. That was pretty good money for a contractor who no one wanted there, and who was treated like dirt by the company he worked for and the military he was hired to support.

I wanted to do something in Iraq, to get something done and serve a useful purpose. I went to Iraq for the adventure, but also to add more experience and accomplishment to my life. I wanted to make good money, who doesn't? But I really wanted to earn it. That was my first mistake. And I wanted to be treated with respect, which was my second. I was barking up the wrong tree from the day I got off the plane at Baghdad International Airport. The lowest private was a field marshal compared to the most experienced civilian contractor in Iraq. Because he was wearing a uniform, the private had more power than the highest paid contractor. At the PX (Post Exchange) in the IZ there were two lines at the checkout counter, one for soldiers and one for everyone else. There would be a couple of soldiers in their line, and 50 people in the other one. Whenever a register opened up, they would call for the next soldier to come up, while we stood there and watched. Our line moved only when the soldiers' line was empty, or when one of the people at the register felt sorry for us. We'd wait for 30 minutes while a soldier wouldn't wait at all, he'd just sail right through.

All the stuff we hear about the military "volunteering" to go to places like Iraq and Afghanistan is mostly nonsense. They might volunteer to join the military, but most of them have no desire whatsoever to go to Iraq. This is especially true of the Reserves and the National Guard. They volunteered, but this wasn't supposed to happen. They were just supposed to do a weekend a month and two weeks in the summertime, and get their monthly pay check. They weren't supposed to actually get deployed!

Contractors made good money in Iraq but didn't wear uniforms. That's all that mattered, but the psychology of it made sense. Because most of the military didn't want to be there, especially reservists, and because contractors got paid more than they did, they could use their uniforms to screw with us. It was their way of coping. We were their scapegoats. It was nothing more than petty jealously and an outlet for their anger.

No one ever talked about the danger contractors were in along with the military, the fact that contractors were getting killed too, and the fact that contractors didn't have to be there but had volunteered. No one back home ever heard about the number of civilian contractors who got killed all the time. In the first six months of 2007, nearly 60 contractors were killed in the IZ alone. That didn't count the rest of Iraq. The Republican Palace served as the U.S. Embassy and the MWR (morale, welfare and recreation) facility. Behind the palace were trailers where hundreds of military and contractors lived, along with a huge swimming pool from Saddam days, and the dry cleaners. There was also a trailer for the KBR (Kellogg Brown & Root) staff who handled the housing, assigning trailers to people when they arrived. I probably walked past this trailer 10 times a week. One day a woman who worked in the trailer went outside for five minutes to take a break, and never made it back inside. A mortar round landed right next to her, killing her and an Army sergeant, and wounding a third person. She had been in Iraq for three years and was leaving in two days. She was going home to see her brand new grand-daughter.

The U.S. military didn't want anyone back in the States to know how many civilians were getting killed in Iraq, which would have had a major impact back home. Of course the civilians were there because we didn't have enough military to do the jobs they used to do. Because our military is too small, we have to augment it with civilians. But when the civilians get killed the American people are kept in the dark. What's it going to be? Either increase the size of our military so we don't need civilians, or treat the civilians with the same respect as a military person. Well, almost. Instead, our country does neither. The military doesn't want to report the high number of civilian deaths in places like Iraq, but it hires civilians because it can't handle the job on its own, and treats them like crap.

The only time I heard of anything being written about the number of contractor deaths in Iraq was a *New York Times* story on May 19, 2007. The article referred to these deaths as the "hidden casualties of the war."[79] At the time the article was written 917 contractors had been killed and over 12,000 had been wounded since the beginning of the war in the spring of 2003. In the first three months of 2007, right in the middle of my tour, 146 were killed. This was the highest number for any 3-month period of the war, and the closest ever to the number of military deaths (244) during any other 3-month period of the conflict. The article was no surprise to me. I was there when mortar rounds and rockets were coming into the IZ every day. One day in particular, 22 rounds landed in succession in an area about a half mile wide. The closest rounds were landing about 200 yards away from where I sat at my desk—wearing my helmet and vest.

One day a U.S. Army brigadier general made an astonishing statement to the world on cable news. He said the U.S. would not send "counter-battery" fire to locations where enemy mortar rounds and rockets were being fired from. The U.S. has the technology to fire off a round within seconds of an enemy round being fired at us, thereby destroying the location the insurgents fired their round from. We can do this fast enough to kill them before they can pack up and take off to fire at us another day. But the general said we didn't want to inflict "collateral damage," i.e., kill innocent civilians. Of course we don't, but we were at war. When we invaded did we think there wouldn't be any civilian casualties? How many Iraqi civilians died up to that time because we invaded, yet this general was telling everyone we wouldn't defend ourselves if it meant one civilian might become a casualty? In effect, the general was telling the insurgents they could fire at us all day long and we wouldn't fire back. That's all they needed to hear. We were declared open season by one of our own general officers. If we fired back and wiped them out, maybe they'd get the message and stop. But that would make too much sense. I wonder how much money was spent developing our "counter-battery" technology. Too bad we couldn't use it.

---

[79] John Broder and James Risen, "Iraq's hidden casualties: 13,000 working for contractors," *The New York Times*, May 19, 2007.

All anyone heard about since the start of OIF were military deaths. I'm as American as any U.S. soldier, but if I was killed they would have put me in a pine box and shipped me home, and that would have been it. But when a soldier was killed, as sad as it was, they treated it like the Chief of Staff of the Army had become a casualty. There was a major disconnect in Iraq over the way civilians were treated, both alive and in death. One wore a uniform and his death was treated like a state funeral, while one didn't and his death was equivalent to a pauper's burial. Very often civilian contractors were in as much danger, and sometimes more, than military personnel were. This was especially true for the civilian advisors to the Ministry of Interior, who worked side-by-side with the Iraqi National Police in the villages and towns throughout the country, and of course Baghdad itself. The casualty list of civilians who did this work was extensive, yet no one ever heard about it back home, except the beheadings. We always heard "Support the Troops," which was great, but what about supporting the contractors? They were ignored at home as much as they were in Iraq.

There were inequities across the board. A U.S. Navy commander in the branch that awarded contracts for MNSTC-I was killed by an IED. He worked in a building called "The Barn," about 150 feet from the building I worked in. The memorial service held for him was really something. It was held in our DFAC (dining facility, i.e., mess hall), and was attended by General Petraeus and half a dozen other flag (general and admiral) officers. The place was packed. As I walked from the DFAC back to my office a thought came to me, "Why don't they have services like that for everyone killed over here?" Because the ceremony was so elaborate I knew this wasn't possible, but why did they do it for this officer? What was so special about the Navy commander? This may seem callous, but anyone at that memorial service who saw what things were like in Iraq might have thought the same thing. Why have such an incredible service for just one person and not everyone who served under the same conditions, or much worse, as the Navy commander? Then it hit me: the commander was not a combat soldier, but in the Navy and in contracting. Being both in the Navy and in contracting, he wasn't a "combat type" by a long stretch. The reason for the ceremony was most likely to make the death of a non-combat officer appear like every other front line soldier or Marine. His death was an anomaly due to his military branch and his job. The vast majority of the U.S. military deaths in Iraq were Army and Marine combat soldiers (Infantry, armor and aviation). They didn't get memorial services like the Commander's. General Petraeus didn't attend all of their memorial services. I tend to think this memorial service was to show all the military at MNSTC-I they were held in as much regard as the soldiers and Marines who were outside the "safety" of the IZ. (I wasn't going to waste my time on a civilian contractor getting a service like that.) But the IZ wasn't safe at all because we—military and civilian alike—were easy targets for mortar and rocket fire from 360 degrees within a couple of miles radius. We were sitting ducks. There should have been equal treatment across the board, in life and in death, combat military and non-combat military, and civilian. We were all deployed into a combat environment in Iraq, so what made one person's death more important than another's?

The U.S. military also didn't want anyone back home to know about the high number of accidental shootings. One of the biggest causes was the clearing of pistols outside all the mess halls (DFAC's) in Iraq. Because all the U.S. military carried a side arm, a 9mm semi-automatic pistol, they had to "clear" them before entering mess halls to avoid the accidental discharge of a round while inside. The first time I watched someone "clear" his 9mm pistol, I couldn't help notice how improperly he did it. As time went by, however, I saw everyone doing it the same (wrong) way. When I served in the Army in the late 1970's and early 1980's, we were taught the right way to clear our .45 caliber pistols, which is very similar to the M-9 (9mm), only far more lethal.

We would take the .45 out of the holster, point it into the clearing barrel full of sand, push the button on the side of the weapon to let the magazine drop out of the pistol grip (even if there wasn't a magazine in the weapon), pull the slide back to eject a round if one was still in the chamber, look to make sure no round was still inside, release the slide forward, and pull the trigger. If by some fluke there was still a round in the chamber of the weapon after all these steps, it would be fired safely into the clearing barrel and no one would get hurt. This was always done deliberately, and we took our time because we were dealing with a potentially loaded weapon. It made sense then, and it still makes today.

But not in Iraq. Everyone would take their M-9 out of its holster, and with their index finger on or near the trigger pull the slide back as they pointed the weapon in the general direction of the clearing barrel, pulling the trigger at the same time. This was done as a single motion, with no attempt to take time and deliberately ensure each step was done correctly. Not once did I ever see anyone check to see if they still had a magazine in their weapon or a round in the chamber. They didn't because they assumed one wasn't there. They also didn't check because that's the way they had been trained to clear their weapon.

One day I was at my desk and heard a round go off very nearby. We all ran outside and saw a crowd standing around a soldier in front of the DFAC, about 100 feet away. The soldier was covered in blood that was pumping out of his leg. It turned out he was a lieutenant colonel on MNSTC-I staff who I saw every day. The report we got later said he shot himself as he was entering the mess hall. Witnesses said before he entered the DFAC he walked up to the clearing barrel, pulled the slide back on his M-9, released the slide and holstered the weapon—just as the round went off. No one saw him check to see if there was a magazine in the weapon. He had been walking around Phoenix Base all morning with a loaded weapon. This wasn't necessarily wrong, but it almost turned out to be deadly because he never bothered to unload the magazine when he cleared his weapon. As a result, instead of ejecting a round that might have been in the chamber, he did just the opposite and chambered a round from the top of the loaded magazine still in his weapon. Like everyone else he did this in one sweeping motion, so when he slipped the M-9 back into his holster he pulled the trigger at the same time, shooting a 9mm round into his leg. The round entered his thigh above the knee, and traveled down the length of his leg to his ankle, a very severe wound. We heard afterward that he might lose his leg. Later we heard that he was probably going to be discharged with a negative efficiency report because of his negligence and the danger he posed while carrying around a loaded weapon all day. It was harsh punishment, but he could have killed someone, or himself.

The officer was a reservist in Special Forces (Green Berets) who had no clue how to properly clear his weapon. But he was doing it the exact same way everyone else was. I found the whole thing a gross safety violation, yet it seemed to be condoned by the ranking officers. I had to assume this was the new method of clearing one's weapon being taught back in the States, but that didn't make it right. After this incident I heard this was happening all over Iraq, with hundreds of these cases being reported. Why wasn't the U.S. chain of command doing anything about this? It's ironic, but if the lieutenant colonel had been carrying a .45, he most certainly would have lost his leg. It would have turned into meat. Was the sloppy method of clearing weapons in Iraq because the 9mm was less dangerous than the .45 if a round accidentally went off? Was that why we took so much care to clear our .45's when I was in the Army? Maybe it's better our soldiers were carrying M-9's in Iraq. Because it's not as lethal as a .45 they won't kill themselves.

A little history on the U.S. Army .45 caliber M-1911 pistol will help. One shot from a .45 will drop anyone, usually killing them. That's why it was developed by the U.S. Army for the Philippine Campaign from 1899-1902. The U.S. Army was fighting Moro guerillas, who used drugs to eliminate the sensation of pain, thus allowing them to continue attacking after being shot multiple times by the standard weapons of the day. The .45 semi-automatic pistol was introduced for its one unique characteristic —stopping power. One shot from a 9mm will slow down the average size person, but it will often take more than one shot to drop him. Getting off more shots takes more time, which a person being attacked doesn't have. You may only have time for one. A visual comparison of the two rounds tells the story: the .45 round is about twice the size of the 9mm. Its mass is huge by comparison. Add velocity to its mass and the results speak for themselves. (The U.S. Army announced in July 2014 it would be phasing out the standard 9mm for a higher caliber pistol, either a .357, .40 or .45 caliber, for the same reason it developed the .45 back in the Philippines—stopping power.)[80]

The overall handling of weapons in Iraq left much to be desired. Once I was in the back seat of an up-armored Chevy Suburban on the way to a safe house rented by one of J-7's construction companies. I was sitting next to the new AFCEE Contracting Officer who worked with J-7. She was from San Antonio, where AFCEE is located, having been sent to Iraq to replace the previous Contracting Officer who had messed up the Independent Government Estimate described above. Because she was a U.S. Government employee she had been issued a 9mm pistol. There was a guy in the back seat sitting on the other side of her, and he whispered something in her ear. The next thing I knew she was pulling her pistol out of its holster and removing the loaded magazine! We weren't going on a combat patrol, just riding to a safe house in the IZ. There was no need to have a loaded magazine in her weapon, especially since we were in close quarters in a vehicle. She didn't know how to remove the magazine and was trying to extract it from the grip of her weapon, the entire time waving the pistol around and pointing it right at me while we bounced down the road. Clearly, the concept of safely pointing her weapon up toward the roof of the vehicle or down toward the floor was unknown to her, most likely because she hadn't been trained how to properly handle it. She obviously had no idea what she was doing, her training with the weapon likely consisting of a few shots at a range before getting on the plane to Iraq. While she tried to figure out how to disengage the magazine from the weapon, the muzzle (the end of the weapon the bullet comes out of) was pointing right at my face about 10 inches away. For all I knew she had a round loaded in the chamber, like the lieutenant colonel described above. If her finger had touched the trigger, and if the safety switch was off, I could have been sitting there without a face.

Just as I saw what the woman was doing, the guy on the other side of her saw it too. The weapon wasn't pointing at him, so he could move without fear of spooking her and getting shot in the face too. He reached across her and took the weapon out of her

---

[80] Matthew Cox, "Army Wants a Harder-Hitting Pistol," *Military.com*, July 3, 2014.

hands. Then he removed the magazine and cleared the weapon because she had no idea how to. The look on the woman's face was not one of horror at the tragedy she nearly caused. It was a look of great relief that she didn't have to mess with that oily gun any more. Of course, there was no apology from her for pointing a loaded weapon in my face. That was my problem. However, when I got back to my office I emailed the Captain in charge of J-7 telling him what had happened, and informing him the Contracting Officer didn't have the slightest clue how to handle her assigned weapon. I received a reply from his deputy, the U.S. Navy Commander, informing me the Contracting Officer would be given remedial training on how to handle her weapon. Somehow that didn't make me feel any safer. When I was in the Army, if anyone had done what she did they would have been seriously reprimanded for committing a gross safety violation. Whenever I saw the Contracting Officer after that she would sneer at me because I sent the email to her boss.

What bothered me more than anything else was how civilian contractors were completely ignored, when many of us had tremendous experience and so much to offer the U.S. military. The military didn't give a damn, except a small handful who appreciated us being there and what we had to offer, not the least of which was helping them do their jobs. What made it worse was the company I worked for couldn't have cared less about us either. It hired us to travel half-way around the world to take a job in a combat zone, where we had to wear a 35-pound ballistic vest and 10-pound Kevlar helmet just like the military, and put up with the same living conditions they did, and sometimes worse. Why did it bother if we were ignored by everyone when we got there? Obviously, it was just for the money.

I shared a 9x12 foot (108 square feet) room with a guy from Texas (was he a piece of work!). Our room was on one side of a pre-fab trailer that had another 9x12 room, with a bathroom/shower in between. This gave each man 54 square feet of space, all four of us sharing one bathroom that always ran out of hot water. Most lieutenant colonels, and all full colonels, had their own room with a private bath depending on the design of the trailer. This was huge in Iraq. Most contractors were retired military, many of them retired lieutenant and full colonels. Now they were contractors, so they could stick it. My manager kicked one of his own people out of a room he had to himself, and moved him to a room with someone else so that he (my manager) could have his own room. The guy he booted was a retired Command Sergeant Major, a great guy. He was so pissed off at our manager that he went home.

My job wasn't advertised as needing a security clearance, but MNSTC-I classified everything short of the menu at the DFAC. I had a Top Secret/Sensitive Compartmented Information (TS/SCI) clearance in the White House while working for Tom Ridge, but it was no longer valid. I went to my deputy manager and asked what I could do to get a clearance. (The deputy had been Special Forces his entire Army career, and was very down to earth. While I was on vacation in December of 2006, he had a massive heart attack and was sent back to the States. He survived only because he was about 100 feet from a defibrillator at the Embassy. I was told he had turned blue, and was as close to buying the farm as anyone can get. He was replaced by another good guy, a retired Warrant Officer.) The deputy told me to go online and fill out a clearance form on the Government's website, eQip. I filled out the Standard Form 86, submitting it on-line to the Office of Personnel Management (OPM), the federal agency that processes security applications.

Sometime later our Cracker Jack manager poked his head into my office and said something about my "interim clearance" being denied, then he left. He said it so fast I didn't understand him, so I followed him down the hall to his office and asked what he had said. He told me the Security Officer at our company had denied my interim clearance because of my answer to one of the questions on the eQip application. I asked him what an interim clearance was, because I had never heard of it before. He said it was a temporary clearance the company could issue, while the full background check was completed. He told me I could e-mail the women at our firm who handled clearances, and gave me her name and e-mail address.

I e-mailed the woman, asking her what the problem was with my application. She emailed back saying I had answered a question about having seen a "mental health professional" in a way that led "the adjudicator" to think I was a "violent" person. I couldn't believe what I was hearing, and asked her who "the adjudicator" was, but she wouldn't answer me. It had to be her, but she refused to tell me who "the adjudicator" was. I asked her why "the adjudicator" had come to this conclusion, and she referred me to question #21 on the SF-86, the security clearance application.

Question #21 asks whether a person has ever seen a mental health professional. The question has two parts. The first asks about ever seeing a mental health professional, requiring a yes or no answer. The second part says: "If you answered "Yes," provide an entry for each treatment to report, unless the consultation(s) involved only marital, family, or grief counseling, not related to violence by you." I have seen a therapist, so I answered yes to the first part of the question. I hadn't seen a therapist because of marital, family or grief counseling, or any violence by me, so that meant I should put down the counselor's name and the dates of treatment. It didn't make sense, but that's the way the question was written, and that's what I understood it to mean. I was reading it literally. That was my mistake. Well, the woman (or should I say, "the adjudicator") had other ideas. She told me because I had put the name of the therapist and the dates of treatment, it meant the treatment was because of violence by me! I tried to explain why I answered the question as I had, but this woman would not listen to a word I said. The decision had been made by "the adjudicator," and that was that. There was nothing I could do. She said I could send a registered letter to a federal agency in Columbus, Ohio explaining my answer, and that I would hear back from them in ten days. I did, and I never heard a thing. (I have answered the same question the same way before, and never had a problem. I had a TS/SCI clearance in the White House. But what did "the adjudicator" care? The question was so poorly worded, it could have been written by a fourth grader. I understand this question has been re-worded to eliminate the ambiguity.)

The day I started with my firm I reported to its corporate headquarters in Alexandria, Virginia. Four other guys showed up the same day, all of us heading for Iraq. We were going to be briefed into the firm and put through the new employee paperwork drill. Before we got started, a guy walked into the room and introduced himself. He was the Senior Vice President for Personnel. He came into the conference room, walked around and shook everyone's hand, handing out his business card as he made the rounds. He introduced himself, making a big point of telling us he had been a brigade commander in the 82nd Airborne Division. That way we'd be duly impressed. Then he said if we ever needed anything, anything at all, we should contact him. "Anything I can do for you guys, you just let me know, blah, blah, blah." After getting screwed by the woman in charge of security clearances ("the adjudicator"), I decided to take Mr. Senior VP up on his offer. I sent him an e-mail describing the problem I was having, specifically about the woman not letting me explain why I answered the question on the SF 86 as I did. I never heard back from Mr. Senior VP, the former brigade commander in the 82nd Airborne Division, who told us to contact him "any time" we needed his help.

To add to this circus the lady ("the adjudicator") told me she was putting my application into the system for normal processing, so I'd get my clearance when that was completed. If she could say that, why couldn't she ("the adjudicator") give me the interim clearance? I had to wait for the clearance process to run its full course, which takes about a year, all because of my answer to one stupid question she ("the adjudicator") didn't like.

Around February 2007, I decided to check on my security clearance application to see how things were moving along. After all, the lady ("the adjudicator") said I would get the clearance. I sent her an e-mail, but instead got a reply from the guy at our firm who handled all of us in Iraq. He told me the lady had been fired, and wanted to know what I needed. I told him I wanted to check on the status of my security clearance application, and he said he would get back to me. The next day he e-mailed and simply asked me to re-submit my application! What about the application I had submitted five months before? I asked him why I had to re-submit my application. He said my fingerprint cards, which I had originally submitted with my application, had never been turned in. They had been thrown out by the woman ("the adjudicator"), meaning my application process had never been started. I was never in the system at all. It takes about 12-18 months to get a security clearance from the Federal Government.

I had just lost five, and had a black mark on my record for having had an interim clearance denied. All of this could have all been avoided if Mr. Senior VP had answered my e-mail asking for his help. She ("the adjudicator") worked for him. But I didn't count except as a warm body to collect fees for my company. He just hired warm bodies. He didn't care beyond that.

I told the guy who handled the employees in Iraq what the VP said when he introduced himself to us that first day. I described my email asking for the VP's help, but never receiving a reply. The guy said the VP was "very important" and had "other things to worry about." My personal needs didn't mean anything to the company, the U.S. military, the VP, or anyone else. I was on the other side of the world, in a combat zone, and on my own. It wasn't a good feeling.

15—Transition

One day a co-worker from my company, who was soon leaving for the States, came up to me with a printed copy of an e-mail sent to him that morning. He handed it to me and said I could keep it. The e-mail was written by Brigadier Weighill, mentioned above. The e-mail was sent to the MNSTC-I Chief of Staff and copied several other senior MNSTC-I officers. It said:

> Now that I have surfaced from my trip to the UK I have picked up the traffic on the [he wrote the name of my firm here, which I have deleted] moratorium. [MNSTC-I had implemented a hiring freeze on my firm due to serious questions about our value.] Emphatically I agree with you that we must not pay contractors (and their companies [i.e., my firm]) huge sums of money for the benefit of their 'advise' [*sic*] only. Where possible we should ensure that each and every contractor has the capacity to determine specific outputs over a period of time and create the ability to monitor and assess the fruits of their labour. The TRA helps here (although it remains crude – I think the CMM will help) but it will remain a challenge to determine an objective assessment model and define a means of remediation.

After all this wordy nonsense, Brigadier Weighill proceeded to contradict himself by recommending that the legal advisor remain on his staff. The legal advisor was the same guy who had given me the e-mail. He was also employed by my company, the same company Brigadier Weighill blasted in his message. The legal advisor was leaving in disgust over the whole situation at MNSTC-I.

British Brigadier Weighill was accusing contractors like me and my colleagues of not doing anything. But in the hallway outside his office were pictures of dozens of contractors who had been killed in Iraq. Brigadier Weighill sat behind his desk on Phoenix Base in the IZ, living in the lap of luxury at the British Embassy that was on par with a resort hotel compared to what everyone else lived in. Yet he had the nerve to complain about U.S. civilian contractors, all of whom were volunteers who weren't ordered there, some of them working for British civilians and officers whose country didn't even pay for their services. The saddest part of all was that we were treated this same way by our own employer and our own military. The only "positive" to come of all this is the money being made by the owners of U.S. contracting firms, the promotions being handed out to military officers, and the adventure for State Department employees.

Brigadier Weighill, a British officer, was openly declaring that my employer and its people in Iraq were making way too much money, and he couldn't see what the Coalition was getting for it in return. Yet his country wasn't paying the tab, so it wasn't his problem! He just wanted to stick his nose in it.

If Brigadier Weighill's message wasn't a public announcement that my company was on thin ice, I don't know what was. It upset me because I wanted to do something in Iraq, wasn't being listened to at all, and this guy was saying to very senior officers at MNSTC-I that people like me, employed by companies like mine, were all lard asses and didn't do anything but collect money. Some were indeed there to collect money and nothing more, but not everyone. I certainly wasn't there just for the money. Me, and many of my colleagues, were there to make a positive impact. In our case, Brigadier Weighill's comments were below the belt.

His e-mail was an indication that a very senior Coalition officer had no concept of the role of my company, and its staff at MNSTC-I, were there to do. He was not alone in his sheer ignorance of what we had to offer, that we were hired for our "advice" in the first place. As a group, we had years of experience, and the majority of us were "subject matter experts" in our respective fields. The U.S. Government was paying top dollar for us, and why the hell not. I knew more about real estate, land title, construction and facilities than any other person at MNSTC-I, especially the Coalition military who were in Iraq to do these tasks.

If Brigadier Weighill wanted to bitch about people getting paid a lot of money for doing nothing, he should have started with people in uniform doing jobs they had no clue how to do, such as the officers and staff of J-7. He should have asked why the deputy in charge of J-7, a high school teacher from Mississippi, was the second ranking person in the entire country responsible for the construction of every single building, camp, police station and frontier border station for the Iraqi Ministry of Defense and Ministry of Interior. Why didn't Brigadier Weighill question how the deputy J-7 got his job and what experience he had in that line of work before pointing a finger at my firm and its staff? But we didn't wear uniforms and guys like the J-7 deputy did, so he was totally off limits. And let's not even talk about the fact that we volunteered, that we committed to stay for a full year, and that U.S. Air Force personnel had tours as short as three months. Was MNSTC-I getting its money's worth out of them? But in Brigadier Weighill's opinion, because guys like me didn't wear a uniform, we were dead weight and collecting fees for sitting on our butts. Brigadier Weighill's e-mail was all I needed to see about how my firm, its staff, and guys like me were viewed by the military officers at MNSTC-I we were hired to support.

But the more I thought about it, the more I realized Brig. Weighill had a point. Because contractors working for MNSTC-I weren't treated with any respect by the military, and were in most cases marginalized, our value was minimal. It stood to reason that if we weren't allowed to add value, then we had no value to add. My case is as good an example as I can come up with. If I was hired for my experience and knowledge, yet was unable to voice my opinion or have any input into how things were conducted, then in a perverse way Brigadier Weighill's comments were true. If you don't treat subject matter experts as they deserve to be treated, beginning with courtesy and respect as volunteers, and then moving up to what they have to offer professionally, then you are left with a pool of folks making a lot of money and not contributing to the effort. It becomes a self-fulfilling prophecy, and you end up with e-mails like Brigadier Weighill's. But no one in uniform, to include the good general, bothered to ask a simple question: why weren't these contractors contributing more if we asked for them and paid their way here?

I wasn't just upset at the implications made by Brigadier Weighill, a British subject whose country didn't even pay for my company's services. At an MODTT staff meeting weeks earlier

John Cochrane, the Brit who had replaced David Murtagh as head of MODTT, made a rather surprising comment to his entire staff. He said General Dubik, the new MNSTC-I commander, did not like my firm. (I bet the guys at the Pentagon weren't saying that to the two retired four-stars who ran my company back in Alexandria, Virginia.) Nothing prompted Mr. Cochrane to say this. It appeared he just had the need to get it out. It's interesting that at least 80% of Mr. Cochrane's staff were employees of my firm. He was telling us that the commanding general, who we all worked for, really didn't care for us or for our employer. I told this to a military friend of mine who worked at the U.S. Embassy, and he said General Petraeus did not like my firm either.

By this point I had already experienced being treated like a second class citizen by MNSTC-I military staff. I had been experiencing the things I have described here for the previous 11 months. Therefore, I didn't appreciate a British brigadier making derogatory comments about employees of my firm, which included me, all of whom had volunteered to come to Iraq. I went to Iraq to try and make a difference and have a positive impact. I was having a difficult enough time doing this without bogus comments like these from a British general whose country didn't even pay for my services. I decided to do something about it.

I scanned the general's e-mail (which was not classified) and e-mailed it to the colleagues from my firm. I wanted to let them know our company was not particularly liked by MNSTC-I senior staff. I also did this to make my firm's management aware there was a big problem with its MNSTC-I contract, as if they didn't already know. What would the shareholders of our parent corporation do if they found out our client (DoD) was openly showing dissatisfaction with our firm, yet our local management in Iraq had failed to do anything about it? If my firm lost its MNSTC-I contract, and its managers failed to act beforehand, heads would roll. Not that this would be a bad thing. The brigadier's e-mail, and the other negative comments being made about my firm, were all that my company's management needed to see. I was doing my fellow employees, and the company, a favor by sending the brigadier's e-mail to them. But my manager in Baghdad didn't give a damn about Brigadier Weighill's e-mail. All he cared about was that I had sent his email out, and the MNSTC-I Chief of Staff had gotten wind of it and was pissed off. My manager couldn't have cared less about what the e-mail said, or how his employees were viewed by the MNSTC-I senior staff, or that we were all miserable at the way we were being treated.

The following day I was called into the office of the MODTT Chief of Staff and handed the letter of reprimand written by her predecessor two weeks before, but which I had never seen or even knew existed until she handed it to me. This was the same letter that had been written concerning the events at FOB Honor. She was giving me a letter of reprimand written by someone else, and was applying its probationary period to my sending out the British brigadier's e-mail, which I did before I was given the letter. So how could I know I was under probation? I told her she could not do this, but she handed it to me anyway. The following day my manager called me into his office and told me the MODTT Chief of Staff, John Cochrane and the MNSTC-I Chief of Staff, "want you out of here." He told me I could resign or be terminated. After some discussion I decided to resign.

I was being terminated (but offered to resign instead), because everyone was pissed off at me for sending out the British general's message. The official basis of my termination was that I "violated" the probationary period in the Letter of Reprimand written by the previous MODTT Chief of Staff. But I didn't know the letter—or the probationary period in it—existed at the time I sent out the brigadier's e-mail. The previous MODTT Chief of Staff wrote the Letter of Reprimand, tucked it away in his desk drawer, and then told his successor to save it for a rainy day. The rainy day had arrived.

If this wasn't bad enough, the new MODTT Chief of Staff lied. My manager asked me why I had sent the brigadier's message out, when I had been placed on probation by the previous MODTT Chief of Staff's Letter of Reprimand dated two weeks before. I told him that I didn't know the Letter of Reprimand existed until after I sent out the brigadier's e-mail message. He said he had met with the new MODTT Chief of Staff the previous day, and she had given him a copy of the letter of reprimand and said I had violated its probation. I asked my manager if he realized that I had no idea the Letter of Reprimand existed until just the day before, when the new MODTT Chief of Staff handed it to me. He refused to answer me. I asked him again if she told him I didn't know about the Letter of Reprimand until she handed it to me the day before, which meant I wasn't aware it existed when I sent out the British brigadier's e-mail, and therefore the letter of reprimand could not be applied to that action. Finally, he admitted the MODTT Chief of Staff had not told him she had just given me the letter the previous day, clearly misleading him into thinking I had been given the letter on the date it was written two weeks earlier.

The new MODTT Chief of Staff committed a gross act of unprofessionalism and dishonesty. She purposely led my manager to believe I had already received the letter of reprimand before I sent out the British brigadier's message. This gave him the false impression I had knowingly violated the letter of reprimand's probationary period. After pressure from me, my manager finally realized what was going on with the MODTT Chief of Staff's disingenuous act (he probably knew already but didn't want to say so), and reversed himself on the statement he had made about me being terminated. He said he would look into the timing of when I was given the Letter of Reprimand. He told me not to resign but to wait for him to get back to me.

Around this same time I was asked by my co-worker for information on the warehouse project mentioned above. I asked what she wanted it for because she wasn't involved in the project. She grinned and said the Navy captain who had taken over M-4-TT from the Marine colonel had asked her for it. I told her this was all very interesting because the captain had pulled himself and his staff off the project weeks before, and now he wanted information on it, but he wasn't coming to me for it. I figured he must have been directed to stay involved in the project by someone of higher rank. Then my co-worker asked me to come over to her computer. She showed me an e-mail recently sent out by the captain to several people. The e-mail was all about me, accusing me of not doing my job, and said I had completely messed up the warehouse project. The captain and I hadn't spoken to each other, or had any dealings with each other, since his last email weeks before.

The Navy captain's message was entirely false. He said I had no files or information from the trips I had made with the MOD real estate staff to the locations we had visited, and that I had no information on the sites for the warehouse locations. This was an outright and boldfaced lie. I had everything he was accusing me of not having in his e-mail. He had never asked me for this information, and would therefore have no idea whether I had it or not. He was simply making up bogus accusations and spreading them around behind my back. My colleague asked me for the same information (which the captain said I didn't have), because he asked her to. In other words, he was stating in his e-mail that I didn't have this information, yet at the same time asking her to get it from me because he probably figured I would have it. He was right, I did. I gave it all to her within an hour.

About two days later I was at my desk when this same Navy captain came into the area where I worked and walked over to the desk of another U.S. Navy captain (that makes four!). This other captain had been placed in charge of me and my two associates at MODTT, and didn't know squat about real estate, facilities or construction. These two naval officers constantly hung out together, with the one coming over to our building to stand by the other's desk and watch him type on his computer. When the captain in charge of M-4-TT came into our office this particular day I was very busy at my computer. I was working on something that was taking all of my attention, and I was talking in a low voice to myself. This was helping me keep my concentration. Suddenly I heard the M-4-TT captain say to the other captain, in a loud and very sarcastic voice, "Listen, he's talking to himself." He had a big shit-eating grin on his face, thinking himself to be rather funny. I stopped what I was doing and asked him if he ever talked to himself, and he said no. At this the captain sitting at his desk joked and said he talks to himself all the time. I then said to the captain from M-4-TT that if he wanted to insult me and tell lies about me, he should do so to my face instead of doing it behind my back in his e-mails. At this he snapped and started yelling at me. I asked him why he had taken it upon himself to discredit me, which only made him yell at me even louder. The other captain just sat there and did nothing, when he could have defused the whole matter instantly. He was probably enjoying it. The MODTT Chief of Staff, whose office was around the corner, heard this and came out to the area where the captain and I were. She told me to come into her office. I told her I would only if the Navy captain joined us. I told her, in front of the captain, that he had provoked the entire incident. She was not about to deal with him, her superior officer, so she walked away. A minute later I followed her into her office. I tried to explain to her what I had gone through with the Navy captain, specifically his treatment of me since he had arrived in Iraq. I asked her if she was going to make an issue of what had just happened with the captain, and she said she would not.

The following day my manager called me into his office and said I was going to be terminated. This was after he had instructed me to wait until he got to the bottom of the issue with the MODTT Chief of Staff and the Letter of Reprimand. I had not heard a thing from him since then, which by this time was about three days prior. His statement that he would get back to me when he figured out what had happened with the Letter of Reprimand, specifically the timing of when the MODTT Chief of Staff gave it to me, and that I should not resign until he got to the bottom of it, was all out the window. He said the MODTT Chief of Staff had directed that I was not allowed to return to my office at Phoenix Base. I was not allowed to go to work from that day until the day I left Baghdad, which was nine days later. I had to get up in the middle of the night and walk into my office at 2:00 a.m., when no one was there, to logon to my computer and get my e-mails.

I had been in Iraq for almost 14 months and was being treated this way by military people who had just arrived in country weeks before. I was given a Letter of Reprimand by someone other than the person who wrote it, because the one who wrote it didn't have the balls to hand it to me himself, and he wrote it two weeks before he left Iraq. He left that job for his female replacement to do, if and when I did anything they didn't like. When his replacement gave it to me she applied it retroactively to something I did that people didn't like, because it exposed huge problems within MNSTC-I between its senior officers and the civilians on its staff who were there to support them. On top of all that, she lied to my manager concerning the timing of its delivery to me. I was being harassed by a U.S. Navy captain who hardly knew me, but who had taken it upon himself to go out of his way to lie about me in his e-mails to others, and to discredit me for work I had done on a project that began with his staff before he got there, that he knew nothing about until a few weeks before, and that I had been involved in for six months.

The treatment I received as a result of trying to do my job and help the Iraqi people and the Ministry of Defense was absurd. What is more, the waste of U.S. taxpayer money due to the inept mismanagement by J-7 of U.S. funded contracts, executed for the benefit of the Iraqi Ministry of Defense, constituted gross negligence and mismanagement, at a minimum. Senior U.S. military officers on MNSTC-I staff lied, acted unprofessionally, and failed in their duty as commissioned officers to behave with integrity. And a U.S. Government Contracting Officer with AFCEE did much of the same.

The day I arrived in Baghdad, July 19, 2006, my manager told me and the others who arrived the same day that we may be doing what we had been hired to do, but we may not. He told us things change a lot in Baghdad, and we may end up doing something entirely different than what we had been hired to do by our firm. In other words, our employer was sending us half way around the world into a combat zone simply to collect fees by our presence, and whatever we ended up doing was immaterial. This was an open, yet indirect, admission by our manager in Baghdad that our main function was not to do the job we had been hired to do as "Subject Matter Experts," but to collect fees for our company by simply being present—and staying alive. His comment was the first thing that came to my mind when I read Brigadier Weighill's e-mail. With attitudes like my manager's, I could almost see how military officers like Brigadier Weighill could feel as they did toward us. The problem stemmed from the fact that the U.S. military hired us, but then didn't use us. So it would be easy for MNSTC-I officers to think we didn't do anything. And with managers like mine, who failed to do his job of making sure we were put to work in the areas we were hired for and treated with the respect we were legitimately due, the problem just got worse.

If my employer's contract was terminated, what would the shareholders think when they found out nothing had been done by our management to prevent it? It looked like this could happen with the attitude shown by Brigadier Weighill, that he shared with a dozen senior military staff at MNSTC-I. Instead, my firm's management, especially my manager in Baghdad, allowed its staff in Iraq to be treated like dirt by the MNSTC-I military, doing nothing on our behalf that would upset anyone in the MNSTC-I command structure. In effect, anyone could do anything they wanted to us, and say anything about us they wanted to say, and our own management had no problem with it. When my crack manager saw the e-mail from Brigadier Weighill that I sent out, rather than going into panic mode that our contract was in jeopardy, all he cared about was going after me because the MNSTC-I Chief of Staff wanted my hide. If we didn't like the treatment we were getting from the MNSTC-I military staff, we could go screw ourselves. We could pack up and go home, and that was OK with our management. They would replace us with the next round of suckers and the situation in Iraq would go on. All that mattered to our management was keeping its positions in Iraq filled, so the money would continue coming into our firm.

All U.S. Government contracts in Iraq were under the overall control of the Joint Contracting Command-Iraq, or the JCCI, commanded by a U.S. Air Force major general. I never met the JCCI Contracting Officer responsible for the contract that I was on. We never spoke about my situation. He didn't know that my manager told me sending out the British brigadier's e-mail was grounds for termination. The Contracting Officer didn't know my manager had backed off when he realized the MODTT Chief of Staff had lied to him about when I had been given the Letter of Reprimand. He didn't know about the U.S. Navy captain's harassment of me, or that I had been told by my manager that the MNSTC-I Chief of Staff, and the MODTT Chief of Staff, "want you out of here."

My employer was ordered by the MNSTC-I Chief of Staff, a U.S. Army full colonel, to terminate me. But the only person who could do that was the Contracting Officer. The Contracting Officer couldn't be commanded by a senior officer to do anything. This is against U.S. Government contract law. But that is exactly what happened to me. Only the Contracting Officer can decide if someone on a contract he manages can be terminated, and he must have a valid reason for doing so. The Contracting Officer is supposed to reach his own conclusion as to what should be done with anyone on his contract. Instead, the MNSTC-I chain of command had complete say over which contractors were allowed to stay and who they wanted gone, and they simply ordered the Contracting Officer to make it happen. The managers of the companies that employed these contractors, like my manager, did as they were told. Instead of asking what had happened and trying to sort things out, in other words coming to my aid, my manager rolled over like a lap dog and did whatever the military at MNSTC-I told him to do with me. The Contracting Officer was never involved. This was a clear violation of U.S. Government contract laws and regulations. I know because I used to be a Level III warranted Contracting Officer myself.

The way my company managed its contract with MNSTC-I, and that our services in Iraq weren't wanted by the military we supported, led to the reasonable conclusion that people like me were nothing more than sources of revenue for our firm. We weren't wanted for anything other than revenue for our company, based on contracts awarded to it under the crony system at the Pentagon. This was a gross waste of U.S. taxpayer money, and put the lives of unwanted contractors in needless jeopardy. The only winners were the stockholders of firms like mine, and its senior managers in their corporate offices far out of harm's way hauling in huge salaries. This could be applied to every contracting firm in Iraq, and no doubt Afghanistan too.

The amount of money spent by J-7 was probably known, but what it was spent on was a complete mystery. When I asked a lieutenant colonel from J-7 for plans of the buildings and camps J-7 had constructed for MOD, he replied there were none. That told me J-7 had no idea what it had spent billions of U.S. taxpayer dollars on, just for the Iraqi Ministry of Defense alone.

It can only be assumed the same was true for the Ministry of Interior projects J-7 had built, which numbered over 2,000.

This complete lack of financial accountability started in 2004, because that's when MNSTC-I was created under the initial command of General David Petraeus, the same officer under whose command 190,000 weapons were lost. General Petraeus was the commander, and as such he was responsible for everything that occurred during, under, and within his command. Yet he was never held accountable for this little 'mistake.' If the loss of 190,000 weapons could be brushed aside and not impede his promotion to four-star general, what else has been brushed aside in Iraq that we don't know about? The things I experienced firsthand happened under the command of LTG Martin Dempsey. And like General Petraeus, he got his fourth star, and was eventually promoted to Chairman of the Joint Chiefs of Staff, the senior officer in the United States military.

Every month LTG Dempsey held a Transition Readiness Assessment (TRA) run by MNSTC-I, which he personally chaired. The TRA was "Death by PowerPoint." The PowerPoint slides would go on and on, in graphic splendor, and everyone's eyes would glaze over. The print was so small you couldn't read it, and it covered the entire page of every slide, the worst use of this otherwise effective presentation tool. The purpose of the TRA was to track every aspect related to the "transition" from Coalition to Iraqi control at the Ministries of Defense and Interior—yet the Iraqis were not invited to the TRA by LTG Dempsey. I attended many of these TRA's during the 14 months I spent in Iraq, and never saw an Iraqi officer or senior MOD civilian there. I was in Iraq for eight months of LTG Dempsey's tour of command. Colleagues of mine who had been in Iraq the entire time LTG Dempsey was in command of MNSTC-I told me they had never seen any Iraqis at the TRA. The absence of Iraqis at the TRA was obvious enough to me and my colleagues that we talked about it frequently. How could the Iraqis play a role in their own transition if they weren't at the TRA to see what the Coalition was doing for them, was planning for them, and what was about to be transitioned to them that they would soon be responsible for themselves? How could the TRA be held if the client wasn't there to provide input? For that matter, how could General Casey continue telling President Bush the Iraqis were doing great and could take over any time they wanted, when they weren't even invited to the TRA to discuss the transfer of responsibility from the Coalition over to them? In reality, nothing was being transitioned over to the Iraqi Ministry of Defense and Ministry of Interior, so maybe that's why LTG Dempsey didn't feel the need to invite them. That's the way everything was done at MNSTC-I.

The TRA was the "capstone" of everything MNSTC-I was there to do—to stand up these two Iraqi security ministries. Every senior staff officer and advisor was present, to include the heads of all the "J" staffs and the Transition Teams. They were all assembled at one location at the same time to discuss the transition of the Iraqi Ministry of Defense (General Dempsey chaired a separate TRA for the Ministry of Interior). What better opportunity to directly tell the Iraqis what was going on and where the problems were, and then work together to figure out solutions. General Dempsey chaired it. He could have invited Abdul Qadir, the Iraqi Minister of Defense, as well as the senior military and civilian staff from MOD to go over the things that were slowing the transition down. With the joint influence of the Minister of Defense and the commander of MNSTC-I, chairing the meeting together, the message would have gotten across to everyone present. Instead, all we did was crap our collective trousers the week leading up to the TRA to make sure the green bar at the bottom of the PowerPoint slide was moving to the right, to show General Dempsey what progress was being made in our respective areas. The Ministry of Defense only executed one contract for goods and services in a six month period, but damn if we weren't going to find some way to move the bar to the right to show progress for the Directorate of Acquisition, Logistics and Infrastructure at MOD. And that was just one component of the ministry. The rest of them went through the same thing. The TRA could have been used to get things done, but in the end it was just another "dog and pony show."

To the best of my knowledge General Dempsey didn't invite the Iraqis to the TRA the entire time he was the MNSTC-I commander until the month he left, most likely because he didn't want it to get out they had "never" attended a single one. Well, at least General Dempsey could say the Iraqis did attend the TRA —once. The gross lack of cooperation, and collaboration, between the Coalition and the Iraqis we were all there to support, and also within MNSTC-I itself, started at the top with LTG Dempsey and trickled down to my level and below. Because MNSTC-I was a small place, this could be seen by everyone. Chairing the TRA's without the Iraqis was one of the most inept failures committed by LTG Dempsey, who later got his fourth star.

In the spring of 2007 the U.S. House of Representatives Committee on Armed Services issued its report entitled *Continuing Challenge of Building the Iraqi Security Forces*,[81] which described in detail the complete chaos at MNSTC-I, specifically its total lack of accountability. The report concluded with the very strongly worded "recommendation" that MNSTC-I report its activities to Congress on a regular basis. This was a huge red flag that MNSTC-I was completely out of control, and that it was not doing its job, yet Lieutenant General Dempsey was still getting promoted to full four-star general, the same rank as General George Casey and General David Petraeus.

About a month before I left Iraq, I decided to make a formal complaint concerning many of the things I have written about in this book to the MNF-I Inspector General (IG) at Camp Victory, the lakeside resort home of General Casey, General Petraeus, and later General Odierno. The IG was a U.S. Army full colonel who I had never met. As we introduced ourselves he saw my West Point class ring and asked me when I had graduated. I said 1977, to which he replied he had once been a classmate of mine. I didn't remember him. It turned out he had indeed been a classmate, for about three years. He told me he was one of the 150 of our class who were kicked out of West Point in the electrical engineering cheating scandal in the spring of 1976. The Secretary of the Army, Clifford Alexander, allowed anyone who had been kicked out because of the scandal to return to West Point and re-enter the academy into the Class of 1978, which the colonel had done. Allowing cadets to return to West Point after

---

[81] Lorry M. Fenner, "Continuing Challenge of Building the Iraqi Security Forces," U.S. House of Representatives, Committee on Armed Services, Subcommittee on Oversight & Investigations, January 6, 2007.

having been kicked out for an honor violation had never been done before. Now here he was a full colonel and the Inspector General for the entire Multi-National Forces-Iraq, commanded by a four-star general. And what was the IG's job? He investigated, among other things, lying and cheating.

I was sitting in the IG's office and his deputy, a Marine lieutenant colonel, was sitting nearby at his own desk. I began to tell my story to the full colonel when the Marine walked over and sat near me. He kept interrupting when I started to say something, arguing with me on every point I tried to make. The IG is a place where people go to file complaints, which are then investigated. It is also supposed to be completely impartial. It's not a place where you're interrogated while you file your complaint. The Marine colonel was as far from impartial as he could be, and committing an IG violation every time he opened his mouth. I wasn't even speaking to the Marine but to the Army full colonel I had made the appointment with. I had to look directly at the IG while I spoke, with the Marine off to the side harassing me at the same time. I kept trying to tell my story, but the Marine wouldn't stop. Finally I had it with the Marine, and told him if he said one more thing to me I would get up and walk out. The Army colonel just rolled his eyes and let me continue. Needless to say, I never heard another thing from the MNF-I Inspector General's office.

How has the transition from U.S. to Iraqi control gone? One "concrete" example of how we have performed in Iraq is the new U.S. Embassy in Baghdad. The "embassy" is actually 21 reinforced buildings on a 104-acre site along the Tigris River. It was obviously designed this way to prevent extensive damage and loss of life if and when the mortar rounds start coming in. If the embassy was one huge building and a mortar or rocket hit, an entire wing of the building would be wiped out, resulting in years of reconstruction.

But if everything is supposed to be going great in Iraq, as we've been told, why be worried about a mortar round dropping on top of the U.S. embassy? Of course, it was a mortar round that killed the lady who worked at the KBR housing office, which happened to be located behind the former embassy building, the Republican Palace. Needless to say, the design of the new embassy complex refutes the veracity of statements we've been getting from our national leadership about the conditions in Iraq. Things have not been "great" there since the day we invaded, and they're getting a lot worse now. At the rate things are going, our new embassy complex is going to become a military command and control center, not a diplomatic mission. Ironically, its design should work quite well.

Reports of the embassy's cost range from $600-$750 million dollars, with an annual maintenance budget of $1.2 billion. It's by far the largest and most expensive embassy in the U.S. inventory. The embassy was designed to house 16,000 staff, of which only 2,000 would be diplomatic corps. The rest (about 14,000) would be contractors, all housed on U.S. Government property. No doubt the vast majority of these would be "security contractors" (i.e., mercenaries), because we don't have any military forces there anymore.[82]

The Embassy was a nightmare construction project for none other than my former boss, General Charles Williams. The project was completely infiltrated with corruption on the part of the Kuwaiti general contractor and sub-contractors because, well, that's the way they do business over there. If it was built with U.S. dollars, why did we use a foreign contractor?

All U.S. embassies and consulates used to be built by American contractors and with American labor. Every person on the project had to get a security clearance before they went over to start working on it. Our embassies and consulates were built right—the first time. In the 1970's Jimmy Carter started to screw the whole thing up. Sound familiar? He ordered that the U.S. Embassy in Moscow be built by Russian workers. When it was finished the place was so full of electronic "bugs" it could have flown away. It had to be re-built, almost from the ground up. On the wall outside General Williams' office at OBO there was a large chunk of marble that had been taken out of the U.S. Embassy in Moscow. You could see the tiny microphone the Russians had planted in it when they constructed the building. The chunk of marble was on a wall at the same Federal agency responsible for building all U.S. embassies around the world, to

---

[82] William Langewiesche, "The Mega-Bunker of Baghdad," *Vanity Fair*, November 2007.

include the one in Baghdad. Carter preferred Russians over his own U.S. government agency to build the embassy in Moscow. He is either the most naïve person ever to walk the earth, or he is un-American and had no problem with Russian spies building our Embassy in the capital of the Soviet Union.

If one needs an example of the abysmal leadership our country has been stuck with the last few decades, they need look no further than Jimmy Carter to see why we're in such a lousy state of affairs. But we can't dismiss the fact that Jimmy Carter got the Nobel Peace Prize. Let's see, did he get it for brokering the deal with North Korea allowing it to continue its nuclear weapons program? Or was it giving away the Panama Canal, the primary strategic transit for our naval forces between the Atlantic and Pacific Oceans, and the main link for commercial shipping in the northern hemisphere? (The Panama Canal is now run by China.) Or maybe it was when he allowed revolutionary students to get away with taking 53 Americans hostage during the U.S. Embassy crisis in Tehran in 1979? (He did nothing when they were taken, and then executed one of the biggest military flops in our nation's history five months later trying unsuccessfully to get them back. They remained in captivity for 444 days while he lectured our country about its "malaise.") Or, it might have been when he showed the Soviets how tough he was when they invaded Afghanistan by boycotting the Olympics, thereby shafting thousands of American athletes who had been training for most of their lives. There are so many examples of Jimmy Carter's brilliant leadership and diplomacy, it's hard to keep track of them all.

The Embassy in Baghdad was delayed when it was discovered the Kuwaiti general contractor had not installed the fire suppression (sprinkler) system in accordance with State Department specifications. (There were other major problems with the project as well, but this was by far the worst.) OBO brought in a firm to inspect the sprinkler system and found it to be unsatisfactory. The Kuwaiti general contractor hired another firm to conduct an inspection, which found it to be satisfactory. What a surprise! In the end the sprinkler system failed to meet U.S. State Department construction guidelines, but General Williams signed off on the sprinkler system as being compliant with State Department construction standards—on his last day at OBO.

Billions of Iraqi dinars are held in U.S. banks for the Iraqi government to spend through a U.S. Government program called Foreign Military Sales, or FMS. The program enabled Iraq to order American and foreign military equipment, paying for it with funds the country had in American banks, collecting interest while held in deposit. The Iraqi government could go through the FMS procurement system, managed by the U.S. government, and order what it needed. It all sounds good in theory, but in reality it's a disaster.

We were trying to order furniture for the buildings at FOB Honor that the Ministry was taking away from the 5th Brigade. Because the Ministry of Defense's procurement system was so broken, they wanted to use FMS to buy desks, when it's supposed to buy things like tanks. Mid-way through my tour I heard that 600 HUMVEE's had been purchased by the Iraqi army through the FMS system and shipped from the United States to Iraq, but no one knew where they were. A fully "up-armored" HUMVEE cost about $500,000 at the time. If FMS was such a great system, why did half a year go by with only one contract being awarded for the entire Ministry of Defense? In the first half of 2007, the MOD awarded one contract! One contract in a six month period for the entire Iraqi military that was started from scratch after Paul Bremer disbanded it. A year prior to that same six month period, General George Casey was saying Iraq was just around the corner from being able to completely take over and run its own show. How was Iraq going to do that if it couldn't even order clothes for its soldier or pay for a generator cable that costs $48,000, or when it lost 600 HUMVEES it had ordered from the States, or when nearly 200,000 weapons bought for them were lost by General Petraeus' command? One contract in six months to feed, cloth, equip, train and arm the entire Iraqi army, and that was after we had been there for four years.

The situation in Iraq is a mess, and has been since 2004 when David Petraeus was the first commander of MNSTC-I. The violence went down for a few years only because of the surge, which was a purely U.S. military operation. Now Iraq is completely under siege. By mid-2014 the Islamic State had overthrown the northern Iraqi city of Mosul, captured the oil fields in the town of Beiji near Kurdistan, and was threatening Baghdad itself. The Iraqi military has been against the wall for more than 10 years, and the former government of Prime Minister Nouri al-Maliki spent its entire administration in near-collapse.

The futility of America's involvement in Iraq and the region was highlighted by news about the exodus of U.S. contractors from Iraq, the futility of the Foreign Military Sales system, and the influx of Russian personnel and equipment:

> ...U.S. contractors, U.S. Embassy personnel and most of the U.S. service members from the embassy's Office of Security Cooperation have abandoned the threatened capital. The exodus has coincided with Russian contractors and support personnel pouring into BIAP [Baghdad International Airport] to help launch the 25 Russian SU-25 warplanes that Moscow is rushing to Iraq in its hour of need.

> The retreat of U.S. contractor and embassy personnel, and failure to follow through in a timely fashion on U.S. promises of military equipment for Iraq, is feeding a widespread narrative of declining American influence and commitment to the Middle East. The perceived power vacuum as the U.S. military presence wanes has been noted by adversaries and allies alike.

> The perception of a U.S. retreat from the region was reinforced by the Obama administration's failure to follow through on promised military strikes against Bashar Assad's regime in Syria after it used chemical weapons last year[83]

The U.S. Foreign Military Sales system is a story of complete bureaucratic dysfunction, especially during combat operations when time is of the essence. For example, not one of the 34 F-16

---

[83] James Kitfield, "How Putin outmaneuvered the US in resupplying the Iraqi military," *Yahoo News*, July 9, 2014.

fighters Iraq ordered in 2010, not one of the 24 Apache helicopter gunships held up by the U.S. Senate until January 2014, and not one of the 24 Beechcraft AT-6 Texan II armed turboprop planes the State Department approved for sale to Iraq in May 2014 have been delivered.

Regarding the U.S. Foreign Military Sales program:

> Requests must be approved by both the secretaries of state and defense, and then sent to the Congressional armed services, foreign affairs and appropriations committees, which carefully review the projects. The relevant U.S. ambassador and U.S. military commander for that region must also personally sign off on any proposed sale. Approved recipients of U.S. military equipment under the FMS program must then complete a training course on human rights and humanitarian law, which includes seminars on respect for human rights and civilian authority, rules against torture and gender violence, and laws pertaining to international armed conflict and internal armed conflict.[84]

The Congressional Research Service (CRS) states that under ideal circumstances the process results in Department of Defense target delivery times of 18 months, and six months when the equipment is needed to meet "surge" requirements in a crisis. "There have been multiple causes for delays, not all of which can be remedied," according to the CRS. "Delivering defense articles and services to U.S. representatives in multiple partner nations, with national customs and import processes, presents unique challenges."[85] I would say so.

Iraq is now poised to go down the drain for the following reasons:

---

[84] Ibid.

[85] Ibid.

1) Barack Hussein Obama has withdrawn all U.S. forces.

2) Iraq's ability to defend itself was taken away by Paul Bremer.

3) MNSTC-I failed to rebuild the Iraqi Army to a level where it can defend the country, and deal with these new crises on its own.

We know the damage Paul Bremer did. But LTG Dempsey did nothing to make effective use of his time as commander of MNSTC-I to get the Iraqi security forces to the level needed to defend their country. LTG Dempsey was handed so many problems created by his predecessor, David Petraeus, it wouldn't be surprising if he spent half his time just clearing these up.

The following example, that I personally witnessed, showed the state of the Iraqi Army:

By 2006 the Iraqi Army had to recruit enough soldiers for units to be operational with one third of their men absent. When I heard of this while visiting one of their camps north of Baghdad, I asked the obvious question: why? Iraqi soldiers didn't have bank accounts, so when they got paid they took off to give the money to their families. They would be gone up to three weeks. Every unit had one third of its soldiers on leave all the time just to bring their pay home. Iraqi Army units had fleets of buses just for this purpose. The U.S. probably supplied the buses, but never instituted direct deposit of soldiers pay into bank accounts so they could remain at their duty station. Anyone who has been in Iraq knows something like direct deposit is laughable. But if we couldn't institute something as basic as this, when its effects on the defense of Iraq were so drastic, how could we say its army had "transitioned" into something resembling a modern military force? Iraq's military is still in the Stone Age by comparison to most other countries in that part of the world. As backward as Middle Eastern armies are, Iraq's is worse, especially after what we've done to it.

The example of soldiers' pay, with a third of them gone just to carry their money home, shows the abysmal shape the Iraqi

Army is in. If one of Iraq's neighbors possessed a slight technological advantage, and had a professional officer and non-commissioned officer corps, Iraq would be toast if that country attacked it. Paul Bremer destroyed the security infrastructure Iraq already had, marginal as it was. But LTG Dempsey was unsuccessful with all the time and money he spent trying to reverse what Bremer did. He talked about "transition" all the time but never made it a reality. Now Iraqi soldiers run in the face of the enemy because they can't fight, while the country's only salvation is sending several hundred thousand U.S. soldiers back there to finish the job—again.

During my last week in Iraq I went to the office of the Special Inspector General for Iraq Reconstruction, SIGIR, in the Republican Palace in the IZ. SIGIR was created to investigate corruption, waste, fraud, abuse, and mismanagement related to the U.S. involvement in Iraq. I met with one of the senior staff there, who gave me some information on how to file a complaint about some of the things I have described in this story. He said he would send my information to his superiors in the SIGIR office back in Washington (Crystal City in Arlington, Virginia). I followed up with a formal complaint to SIGIR when I returned home. I never received any word back from SIGIR other than an e-mail saying I was free to forward my complaints to the Department of Defense "Hotline."

PART IV: AMERICA'S LEADERSHIP VOID

16—America's Leadership Void

Why has America continually failed in its foreign policy efforts over the past several decades? Many would say the wars we have been involved in were mistakes, but at least in World War I and World War II we didn't start either conflict. Beginning with Vietnam, however, we began to get ourselves involved in conflicts we could have avoided, but we went into them stating it was for our "self-defense" and to "save democracy."

If we had avoided getting sucked into Vietnam, what would have happened? This is hindsight, but people are paid a lot of money for their knowledge of questions just like this one. How many PhD's in political science, history, economics and international affairs crowd any presidential administration? What was the threat to our national security if we didn't go to Vietnam in the early 1960's? The country is on the other side of the world, so any threat of Vietnam invading our soil was nil. What other threat could it have posed? The only other argument was the spread of communism. If the United States didn't go there, and Vietnam eventually went communist, what would have been the threat to the security of the United States? Half the world was under communist rule, so what difference did it make if this tiny country went communist as well? But Cuba, 90 miles off the coast of Florida, did go communist and JFK did nothing to stop it from going down the rat hole. Which one was a bigger threat to our national security: Cuba or Vietnam? By the time JFK achieved martyrdom by being assassinated, he had already started sending troops to Vietnam, including my father, who was an advisor to the South Vietnamese Army in 1961. LBJ followed JFK's lead to siphon off some of JFK's immense popularity. He began by lying to the American people about the Gulf of Tonkin incident, using it as an excuse to get us involved in Vietnam, just like FDR lied to us about the "surprise" attack on Pearl Harbor. (Anyone who still thinks he and General George Marshal didn't know the attack was coming must still believe in Santa Clause.)

The best example of a country that posed a serious threat to our national security and was being taken over by communism was Cuba. We had a country only 90 miles away, and led by a communist dictator who hates America, yet we did nothing. But we went to Vietnam, half a world away, and wasted 58,000 Americans lives for nothing. This shows how abysmal our leadership has been since the 1960's. We let Cuba go down the drain, but we took up the fight in Vietnam! What were the "best and brightest" of the Kennedy and Johnson administrations thinking? At least losing 58,000 American soldiers in Cuba would have made more sense than losing them in Vietnam. In the end, Cuba went communist and we almost ended human civilization with the Cuban Missile Crisis. But half a world away Vietnam went communist, and nobody cared. It doesn't matter that Vietnam went communist in 1975 any more than it does now.

But it's these "best and brightest" who are supposed to know these things, who are supposed to study these historical events, and who are supposed to make sound recommendations to the Presidents they serve based on all they know. Who's kidding who? In reality they get their jobs because they know the new President and worked on his campaign. They get their jobs because they know someone who knows someone who knows someone in the White House. Or, worse yet, they are from academia and think they know everything yet haven't got a clue what's going on in the real world. They have no practical experience in what they profess to know everything about, then turn around and start making policy. (What better example than Paul Wolfowitz, a university professor turned Deputy Secretary of Defense, who was the single biggest proponent of our invasion of Iraq in 2003.) They talk a good line and get high level positions in the White House leading our country into these disasters. Where were these men coming from when they recommended we go into Iraq in 2003, when many of them were either serving in the administrations during Cuba and Vietnam, actually served in the military during these periods, or spent decades in academia studying and teaching about it?

Look at Vietnam and the damage it has caused our country. Why did we get involved in Iraq, especially when the leaders of our country were all alive when Vietnam was being fought? How is it that men with high levels of education, men of vast experience in the government of our nation, and men from the professional military who fought in that conflict, could turn right around and repeat the mistakes of Vietnam almost as if it was scripted? There is no possible way that Vietnam and Operation Iraqi Freedom cannot be compared. The more I study the two, the more I read about them, the more strikingly similar they become.

As I've said, McNamara and Rumsfeld even look like each other, which to me is some kind of weird paradox. It stands to reason if one doesn't study history they will repeat it, but why "doomed" to repeat it? When history is repeated, and the lessons from the past are not taken into consideration, the result is always negative. It never turns out well. When an event in history such as war is not studied and analyzed, and is executed in the same manner as one fought before, the results are always bad. In the case of Vietnam, the United States fought a war that lasted from 1960 to 1975. Actually, we were indirectly involved in the early 1950's when the French got slaughtered at Dien Bien Phu. The Vietnam War was a disaster. It split our country in two. It energized the liberal (i.e., socialist) movement, and it was lived through and experienced by all the so-called leaders of our country today—draft dodger, military officer, political wonk and academic. Then we got ourselves involved in Iraq, whose threat to our national security was as questionable as Vietnam's, and it produced all of the same negative effects on our society Vietnam did. In the case of Iraq, however, we made things worse than they ever were before we showed up.

Why does our nation do this? Why do our leaders keep making these huge mistakes? It is because we don't have real leaders any more, either politically or in our military. It is because we don't have leaders who possess common sense, and are not afraid to speak their minds and take action when it is needed, regardless of what the media thinks.

When it comes to our military, officers shooting for general will not say anything contrary to what they believe their boss wants to hear for fear of hurting, or ending, their careers. Speaking of courage under fire, senior military officers may have courage on the battlefield, but they can turn into cowards in a heartbeat. Give a military man a mission and he will accomplish it (most of the time), but ask him for his honest opinion on something that goes against the party line, and good luck. You will not get it. What you will get is what he thinks his boss wants to hear. It is only when the military officer feels comfortable enough to speak his mind you will get the truth, but that is usually when he has already submitted his retirement papers. That's why U.S. Army Major General John Batiste resigned midway through our current involvement in Iraq. He was so disgusted at what was going on he left, even after he was offered promotion to three-star general. The promotion was most likely meant to muzzle him into silence so he wouldn't voice his opinion on the war. (He wasn't the only general officer who resigned.) In our politically correct world, senior ranking generals are more afraid of a sexual harassment complaint then they are a terrorist with a bomb. They're more afraid of a geek political appointee who doesn't have a clue what he/she is talking about, than an insurgent pointing an AK-47 at them. I don't say this lightly. I truly believe it.

In his book *Fiasco*, Thomas Ricks described the complete lack of leadership exhibited by both U.S. Air Force General Richard Myers, the Chairman of the Joint Chiefs of Staff, and Marine General Peter Pace, the Vice Chairman (later Chairman). Both were in their respective jobs during the period leading up to Operation Iraqi Freedom, and both went out of their way to avoid confrontation with Donald Rumsfeld. This is another way of saying they never spoke up or objected to anything their boss ever said or did. How do two men of this rank and position avoid confrontation with their boss when the job of all three is the execution of our nation's warfare? Myers was a complete lapdog, and Pace most likely got where he was because he cut a dashing figure in his fancy Marine uniform and never said a word contrary to what his boss wanted to hear. But when it came to actual leadership, they were completely lacking. Pace was personally involved in the lousy planning of the Iraq invasion, to the point of insisting the number of invading troops remain absurdly low, as Rummy wanted, which led to the later disaster. And Myers would have done anything short of getting Rumsfeld's coffee and taking out his dry cleaning. These guys may have been brave on the battlefield or in the cockpit of a jet, but in the halls of the Pentagon they ran away from their duty.

When Tommy Franks called the Joint Chiefs of Staff "Title Ten motherfuckers," I wonder who he was referring to.

General Pace had two defining moments near the end of his career, both when he was the Chairman of the Joint Chiefs of Staff. The first was when he was so overcome with emotion he started to cry in front of a Senate committee when asked what it was like growing up the son of Italian-American immigrants. As Pace dabbed at his tears, Senator Lindsey Graham of South Carolina made the moving comment, "It takes a strong Marine to cry." Talk about getting in touch with his feminine side. Could there be a more pathetic display from the nation's senior military officer. His parents came from Italy, so what. My grandmother came from Ireland. What has our country come to? Was General Pace able to look at himself in the mirror the next day? Sadly, he probably had no trouble at all. A real tough Marine, General Pace. I'm sure the rest of the Marine Corps just loved that little chapter in their history.

(The country's reaction the day after Senator Edmund Muskie appeared to cry during the 1972 presidential primaries, was devastating. When responding to a story about his wife, Senator Muskie appeared to be crying, although he insisted it was snowflakes on his cheeks. No matter, his presidential aspirations ended that day. The country wasn't about to go for a man who "cried." Times have changed since then. Men who cry, to include the highest ranking officer of our nation's military, get accolades from the likes of Lindsey Graham.)

General Pace's other defining moment came when he was denied another term as Chairman of the Joint Chiefs of Staff, which he had taken over after General Myers retired. Pace's job as Chairman had been questioned for some time, but the real reason he lost it was his comments about homosexuality several months earlier. He said homosexuality was "immoral," but then said he supported the country's "don't ask-don't tell" policy of allowing gays in the military. General Pace was talking out of both sides of his mouth, typical of officers in high positions (and most politicians). If he supported the "don't ask-don't tell" policy, why on earth give his personal opinion on homosexuality, which is the complete opposite? If he really thought homosexuality was immoral, he had no problem keeping his mouth shut about gays in the military in order to get to the top of his profession. This is another example of senior military officers thinking and feeling one way, but then going along with policies they detest. Getting to the top is more important than their core beliefs and values. They are incapable of being true to themselves and to their country. As a result, we get lackluster military leadership because these officers don't really know what they believe. Or, if they do believe in something but it happens to go against the politically correct line, they are completely afraid to act or speak for fear of jeopardizing their precious careers. In the end all we get are yes men who do and say whatever their civilian leaders want them to do and say, regardless of whether they believe in it or not. They won't stand up and say what's really on their mind and speak from experience because they're intimidated by their civilian boss who has no idea what's going on—and soldiers die as a result, and tens of thousands of innocent civilians die as a result too. The only member of the Joint Chiefs who said what he believed, and knew to be true based on his experience, was General Eric Shinseki of the Army. We know where he ended up.

Officers who do say what's on their mind don't make it to the top. They can't. To say what's on their mind could call into question what their civilian boss wants to do. If you have a boss like Donald Rumsfeld—an egomaniac who didn't have a clue what he was doing—to open your mouth meant your job. Either you say what's really going on and likely get fired, or you don't open your mouth and contribute to the needless death of thousands of soldiers and, in this case, Iraqi civilians. Or you resign. It's sad, but today there's really no other way to get to the top in the U.S. military—and keep your job. The system's broken. The only way it can work is when the Secretary of Defense knows what he's doing (i.e., knows about warfare and the deliberate use of force), and the Joint Chiefs of Staff work well with him. When's the last time we had that combination? What is such a waste is all the military education and training senior officers get during their careers, yet if they work for guys like Rumsfeld or McNamara they never get a chance to use it. What's the point of being a general and having attended the U.S. Army

War College, when your boss is a civilian who tells you it's going to be his way or the highway? Maybe he ran a Fortune 100 company and contributed to the President's campaign, so surely he knows how to invade a country! You can have stars on your shoulders and know global military strategy all day long, but if you work for men like Rumsfeld or McNamara all you need proficiency in is nodding your head up and down. They run everything else. It's ironic that the higher an officer gets in the military, the less direct authority and control he has over situations he has trained to deal with for 30 years or more. A platoon leader has more real power and authority than a four-star general.

The Joint Chiefs of Staff during the Vietnam War were seriously considering mass resignation, so much was their disgust at the way the war was being managed. In the end they decided not to. Regardless of General Wheeler's heart attack, I would venture to say they changed their minds out of fear, plain old cowardice. Imagine what would have happened if the rest of the Joint Chiefs had gone ahead with their plan? The country would have known it wasn't the military who was botching the war, but their civilian leaders. The country would have been very proud of those officers for resigning if they believed the war was a disaster. Hell, everyone else did. If they really felt that way about the war, to the point of contemplating resignation, how could they in good conscience stay in their jobs and continue to prosecute the war effort after they changed their minds? But they stayed and the war went on, and look at the needless deaths that occurred after they wimped out?

Most people don't know that the Uniform Code of Military Justice (UCMJ), the legal code of the U.S. armed forces, allows a soldier or officer to refuse an unlawful or immoral order from his superior, whether civilian or military. After the Second World War the Germans tried to use the excuse that they were just following orders. But the Nuremburg trials clearly showed this doesn't work. No U.S. soldier is obligated to follow an order he feels (and knows) to be illegal or immoral. This is tough stuff, but look at what happened in Vietnam. Look at what happened in Iraq. Did our senior generals have reason for not following orders in these conflicts? A case could be made they did. To say otherwise implies that no order is ever illegal or immoral, which is impossible.

And then there's Robert McNamara, who wrote in his memoirs decades later he thought the Vietnam War was really a mistake—while he was running it—but he couldn't tell the President. After all, he had a "duty" to continue working for his boss. The lives of 58,000 Americans was just the price he had to pay for doing what his boss wanted him to do. Life sure is hard at the top, isn't it Bob. Apparently, after writing his book McNamara felt pretty darn good about himself, like he had undergone some cleansing of his soul. I saw a political cartoon after McNamara's book came out. It showed him standing in front of the Vietnam Memorial looking at the names of all the fallen with his book under his arm. The caption was him thinking to himself something like, "I feel pretty good about myself now guys, how about you?" How could McNamara sleep at night after what he did? For that matter, how can Paul Bremer? McNamara was a corporate executive who thought he could win the war using statistical models. He couldn't, and his generals knew it, but they didn't have the courage to do anything about it.

Vietnam. Iraq. Is there much difference between the two? There is one. Our political and military leaders had nothing before Vietnam to learn from in order to avoid the mistakes they made. But in Iraq they had Vietnam staring them in the face as a history lesson, and they allowed it to be repeated all over again. The two wars are exactly the same, but they didn't have to be.

Civilians in our national leadership, as opposed to military officers, are generally clueless when it comes to waging war, and from what this country has seen since Vietnam they're clueless in most other areas too. They don't spend their careers studying war. That's why they need to depend on the military for its advice in waging it. But the military has to have someone willing to listen, and of course they have to say what they believe is the right course of action. In the case of Iraq the military utterly failed to advise their civilian superiors, except for General Shinseki, the Chief of Staff of the Army during the initial planning of Operation Iraqi Freedom. But their civilian bosses weren't about to listen to anyone, so it hardly mattered. Not knowing anything about warfare is to be expected of our civilian leadership, save for rare occasions. Rumsfeld and McNamara both served in the military, Rumsfeld as a pilot and McNamara as a statistician (i.e., number cruncher). It's fair to say neither of them learned much beyond their specific tasks and failed to grasp what strategic military force is and how to use it. The problem is people like them get into positions where they can make these terrible decisions, usually thought up over drinks in a DC bar. They have such power and influence over the President that their dreams (or should I say daydreams) often become reality. The ones called upon to implement these dreams, and the decision of the President to execute them, are the soldiers of our military.

Does it ever occur to the geniuses running our country that people are going to get killed when their plans get executed? It's safe to say it never does. This is all the more reason to wage war for reasons that make sense. To involve our nation in a war without legal and moral justification borders on the criminal, but our presidents get away with this through loopholes. Iraq and Afghanistan are offspring of the way the United States has been fighting wars since Vietnam, because that war was so devastating. Rather than commit "overwhelming force," we send a token number of military to fight what we now call "police actions." In these two conflicts we've taken it a step further by sending mercenaries. Sure, we send soldiers in the initial stages, but then contractors take over, led by Regional Security Officers from the State Department to give the mercenaries their legitimacy and legal cover.

The Unites States likes to waste money, and lots of it. We waste too many lives as well. Our political leaders make these crazy plans, send our soldiers half way around the world to risk their lives for a cause that doesn't make any sense to anyone except the clown who came up with the idea, and the President gives him the permission to do it. Iraq was Paul Wolfowitz's baby. He sold it to Dick Cheney. Cheney sold it to George W. Bush, who saw it as a way to vindicate his father's mess of 12 years before, and as a way to spin his spurs and show the world he was from Texas and liked to kick some ass, just like Johnson tried to do in Vietnam. The same cockiness and ego of two different men from Texas got us involved in two wars that were disasters, and both places are about as far from the United States, and from being threats to our security, as they can get. In the case of Vietnam, nothing was accomplished other than the kick start of our country's downfall. In the case of Iraq, nothing has been accomplished other than giving us Barack Hussein Obama—and having the hatred of the world heaped on us.

I am not a four-star general, but I know that you never, ever, invade a country unless you use overwhelming force to do it, and are prepared to occupy it afterwards. If you bring too many forces, just send home what you don't need. But if you don't bring enough forces, you're up the creek. One other ingredient is absolutely required: the will and resolve to fight the conflict to a clear, decisive and complete victory.

Since World War II we've never pulled this off, even though our nation had an impeccable war record up to that time. It's as though we were great students who suddenly started screwing up, and now we don't give a damn about school anymore. In Vietnam we had the force to do the job, and essentially occupied the country, but we lacked the resolve to execute the mission and bring the conflict to a decisive and meaningful conclusion. Even a stalemate would have been better. Instead we walked out. We left the field. We didn't have the will to finish the game we got ourselves into. In effect, we forfeited. McNamara was a clueless egomaniac, a corporate executive who thought he knew more than his generals, all of whom were weak officers and went right along with him, except for General Greene of the Marine Corps. He was the predecessor of General Shinseki 40 years later. The Joint Chiefs tried to win the war in Vietnam by asking for more troops after we got involved, but McNamara would never let them fight it, and Johnson sat on the sidelines wringing his hands with his head in the clouds. The result was the disaster we call "Vietnam."

Look at Grenada and Panama. True, they were small countries and small military operations, but look at the results they achieved. After President Reagan was briefed on the invasion of Granada he asked the commanding general if he had everything he needed to complete the mission as planned. The general said that he did. Reagan then told him to double the number of soldiers for the operation. He knew whatever the plan was, the unexpected had to be accounted for, so he sent in far more than what the general thought was needed. The result was a swift and overwhelming victory and the operation ended. That was it. Although we are discussing Iraq here, the principles are the same. They are always the same. There is no need to change them because the size of the country is greater. As a matter of fact, the principles hold even more based on the larger size of the country. The fewer soldiers we have to do the job, the worse the situation will become because the large geographic area will be impossible to fight across and manage effectively during combat operations, and after the initial fighting is over. This is exactly what happened in Iraq.

I started this book with a discussion of the Gulf War of 1991. If the principles I have discussed were followed then, we wouldn't have found ourselves in the situation we eventually did in Iraq. What makes the Gulf War of 1991 so depressing is that we had so much going into it. We had the overwhelming force and strength to do the job. We had half a million soldiers in the theater of operations, which included Saudi Arabia, Kuwait and Iraq. We had the political cover from the UN, and world opinion was behind us. Because of this overwhelming force we had Saddam and his tinker toy army on the run back to Baghdad, which we could have captured and occupied when we got there. This isn't crackpot theory. Is there any way the Iraqi army could have stopped us as we kicked them up the road to Baghdad? Is there any way they would have been able to turn us around and force us back to Kuwait? We had Saddam and his entire military and government on the ropes—and we let him go. With half a million allied forces on the ground and total air superiority, who would have been able to fill the "vacuum" created with Saddam's departure? This was the single worst political-military decision the first President Bush could have made.

However, the worst performance of a U.S. President's handling of an armed conflict was Lyndon Johnson's handling of the Vietnam War. I say this based on the body count of U.S. soldiers balanced against the results achieved. 58,000 dead in Vietnam is a lot higher than 4,500 dead in Operation Iraqi Freedom. (Richard Nixon almost won the war with Operation Linebacker, the strategic bombing campaign over North Vietnam. But he stopped it because of the war protests, allowing the North to continue aggressive actions until the war finally ended in 1975.) When looked upon in terms of the disastrous effects both wars have had on the social fabric of our country, Vietnam and the current conflict are extremely close. Iraq didn't have to be so. It is, however, because of the terrible way it was planned and executed. The lessons from the previous conflicts were right in front of the planners of this conflict to see—if they had bothered to look. Vietnam led to the beginning of the radical anti-American movement, which for years had been waiting for an opportunity to come out of its cave. This conflict has placed extreme liberalism (i.e., socialism) in the White House. And it's all because of lousy leadership at the very top.

During the Gulf War of 1991 we had overwhelming force, and it appeared we also had the will and the resolve to use it toward the swift termination of the conflict. We were winning! We haven't done that in a while. We lost around 300 soldiers, mostly from car accidents with lousy Saudi Arabian drivers. The 82nd Airborne Division went into combat riding in buses. You can bet they all got their CIB's (Combat Infantryman's Badge). Then Colin Powell and the President got together and ended the whole thing on a dime. A West Point classmate of mine was the pilot of the helicopter that carried Norman Schwarzkopf to the treaty signing at the conclusion of the Gulf War. He told me that Schwarzkopf was furious we were ending the war and letting the Iraqis off the hook. He had his chance to tell the President how he felt and he blew it, so it was too late. He had no business being pissed off now. When the aircraft landed and the Iraqi generals came out of the tent where the treaty was going to be signed, they all had shit-eating grins on their faces because they knew they had gotten away with the whole thing. They invaded Kuwait, were kicked out, but never had to suffer any consequences for what they did. Saddam never paid for the little stunt he pulled. The only ones who suffered were the Iraqi and Kuwaiti people. If Saddam could gas his own countrymen, what did he care about the effects of the economic sanctions on them? We had the overwhelming force, but we didn't have the resolve and the will to use it and see the conflict through. That's because of one man—President George H.W. Bush. He obviously didn't have the desire to occupy the country if he didn't have the will to finish off Saddam. It is one of the saddest moments in our history that President Bush ended the Gulf War as he did. We now have a debacle on our hands because his son couldn't leave Saddam alone. It's a whole new enemy now: militant Islamic extremism that uses suicide bombers and mass murder as its weapons of choice. The less resolve we have to fight this conflict to a conclusive end, the more enemies there will be who want to take a shot at us. The documentary *Obsession* is a clear depiction of the true enemy of western civilization. Have we made a dent in that enemy by going into Iraq?

With the Gulf War ending as it did, George W. Bush decided to go back and finish the job. We are told this was prompted by the attacks of 9/11, but we will never know if there was a plan to invade Iraq beforehand. Maybe there was, but it doesn't really matter now. The American people were told that because of the 9/11 attacks we were going into Afghanistan. Then we were told we had to expand the fight to Iraq, which doesn't even border Afghanistan. We seemed to be doing well in Afghanistan, having taken out the Taliban regime. But then we took forces away from an already good operation and sent them to Iraq, totaling our forces to about 125,000. If we had 500,000 soldiers in Vietnam and couldn't get the job done, how were we going to get it done in Iraq with only 125,000? If we had Saddam and his army on the run in 1991 with half a million soldiers, how could we think only 125,000 would do the same job? What had changed?

But we had 'leaders' who thought everything had changed in just a dozen years—in the same location and with the same dictator. At first Donald Rumsfeld wanted to invade Iraq, destroy its entire military and take down its government, with 35,000 soldiers! As mentioned above, it's safe to say roughly 20,000 of these would have been actual combat soldiers, who were the only real fighting force. The rest would be support. Where did Rumsfeld come up with this number? I speculate he pulled it out of thin air. He just wanted to go to Iraq and kick Saddam's ass, and thought we could pull it off with an initial number of around 35,000. At least Tommy Franks got that number raised, but that's about all Franks did that made any sense. The number eventually got up to around 100,000 U.S. forces, but nowhere near what would constitute an overwhelming force. How could it be close, with Iraq being a country 650 x 400 miles in area, with an army estimated to be as large as a million men, albeit not worth a damn? That's still a lot of firepower. All you have to do is tell them where to point their weapons.

The cover story of *Time* magazine on March 31, 2003 begins with these words spoken by President George W. Bush, "Fuck Saddam. We're taking him out."[86] He said this in the hallway outside Condoleezza Rice's West Wing office while she was meeting with three U.S. Senators. This was the attitude Bush had going into the war. I don't disagree with his attitude toward Saddam Hussein. But taking that same attitude and applying it to estimates of the number of soldiers needed to execute the war was another matter. Obviously, all objectivity in the planning of this conflict went out the window. And who paid the price for these lousy decisions, the people in their cozy offices and high salaries and future jobs as lobbyists after they leave the administration? No, it's the soldier on the ground who pays—and their families.

After two and a half years running the show in Iraq, General George Casey was promoted to Chief of Staff of the United States Army. During the time he was the Commander of the Multi-National Forces-Iraq (MNF-I) he did nothing and sat on his hands while the situation in Iraq went down the drain. If Bremer did his part to destroy the country by disbanding its military and national police, Casey did his by doing nothing to stop the civil war right in front of his nose. If he had done something it may not have gotten as bad as it did. Because George Casey didn't do his job (i.e., engage with and destroy the enemy), things escalated to the point where hundreds of Iraqis were being slaughtered weekly, sometimes daily.

On September 30, 2005, *The Washington Post* reported on the "progress" of the new Iraqi army, stating the number of Iraqi army battalions capable of fighting the insurgents without U.S. and Coalition support had dropped from three to one—battalions! U.S. generals reported to Congress the security situation in Iraq was too uncertain to predict when any large-scale

---

[86] Michael Elliott and James Carney, "First Stop, Iraq," *Time*, March 31, 2003.

American troop withdrawals would be taking place. Of course, that was in 2005. Obama hadn't yet arrived on the scene.

However, what stood out in the story was the comment made by General Casey. He said there were fewer Iraqi Army battalions at "Level 1" readiness than there had been a few months previously. He then claimed that the number of troops and overall readiness of Iraqi security forces had steadily increased in recent months, and that there had not been a "step backwards." The story commented that both Republican and Democratic senators had expressed deep concern that the U.S. was not making enough progress against a resilient insurgency.[87]

In one statement General Casey said the number of Iraqi army battalions that could fight the enemy on their own was down from 3 to 1, but then he said they were not taking a "step backward" but were making progress. What planet was General Casey on at the time he said this? What's even more painful about this story is that it refers to Iraqi army "battalions," not brigades or divisions. There are three battalions in a brigade, and three brigades in a division. When I was in Iraq, less than one year after this story was written, there were 10 divisions in the Iraq army. Doing the math, there were 90 battalions in the Iraqi Army at the time General Casey made this statement (10 divisions x 3 brigades x 3 battalions = 90), with plans to add more per the Prime Minister's Initiative. Taking General Casey's statement at face value, the number of battalions in the Iraqi army capable of fighting the insurgency *on their own* had been three, and was now down to one, out of a total of 90 battalions! And this man was telling the President of the United States the Iraqis could take over any time they wanted!

What happened to General Casey after his tour in Iraq? Instead of being sacked, he was promoted to the highest ranking officer in the U.S. Army. The United States Senate didn't want to approve the nomination because of the lousy job he did in Iraq but, holding their noses, went along with it because they were saving themselves for bigger fights down the road.

Which begs the question: why would President Bush nominate General Casey for U.S. Army Chief of Staff when the results of

---

[87] Josh White and Bradley Graham, "Decline in Iraqi Troops' Readiness Cited," *The Washington Post*, September 30, 2005.

his performance in Iraq were so poor? Obviously, if General Casey were fired that would be an indication to the American people—and the all-important media—that things weren't going so well in Iraq. Needless to say the President didn't want the American people to be told the truth about the war, so General Casey got promoted following two and a half years of telling the President time and again things were just fine in Iraq. Based on the Woodward piece in *The Washington Post*, George W. Bush promoted the guy who was selling him a bill of goods. Not only did President Bush never hold anyone accountable for their screw ups, he actually promoted the guy who was blowing smoke in his face, and he knew Casey was doing it! Anyone with a shred of leadership would have ushered Casey out the back door, not caring whether it hit him in the ass.

In the magical mystery tour that is Washington, if Casey got his promotion then he must have done a great job, right? Not quite. No sooner did Casey get his promotion then General Abizaid, Casey's commander and the CENTCOM chief, got sacked. If Casey got promoted for doing a good job in Iraq, why did Abizaid get sacked for doing a lousy job as Casey's boss, and in over-all charge of operations in the Middle East? There's a big disconnect somewhere. It doesn't make any sense, but then again it doesn't have to. It was just another example of the "things are just fine" nonsense we got from the Bush White House from the outset of the war, and during its execution.

The last point about George Casey getting promoted to Chief of Staff of the Army is the issue of "personal responsibility" that we heard so much about from George W. Bush during his presidential campaign in the summer of 2000. We heard time and again how individuals should be responsible for themselves and accountable for their actions. Bush was going to hold people accountable, turn mediocrity and laziness around, and surrounded himself with people who would get the job done, and done right! Well, just like he said we were invading Iraq to find weapons of mass destruction, and never found any, we also got the shaft from Bush on people being held accountable for the crappy job they did during his watch as Commander-in-Chief. What happened to the top level people in the administration after

9/11? The same thing that happened to the top people in the administration after we invaded Iraq—nothing.

If President Bush was a man of his word, and of basic principle:

1) Casey would have been forced to retire from the Army after doing nothing in Iraq while thousands were being slaughtered

2) Bremer would have been sacked

3) Rumsfeld would have gotten the same

4) Wolfowitz the same

5) Franks the same

6) George "Slam Dunk" Tenet would have been booted out of town with his tail between his legs the afternoon of 9/11/01, and

7) General Petraeus would have been relieved as the first commander of MNSTC-I and sent into retirement after losing 190,000 weapons

Instead:

1) Bremer, Franks and Tenet got the Medal of Freedom presented to them by President Bush

2) Wolfowitz was made head of the World Bank, where he was embroiled in an ethics controversy over the employment of his girlfriend, with critics claiming he left the World Bank after displaying the same qualities that created the wreckage of the Iraq War: grandiosity, cronyism, self-dealing and lying

3) Tenet wrote a book about why nothing was his fault, but everyone else's

4) Franks wrote a book at the same time he was commanding two major wars telling everyone about his poor country

roots, what a great general he was, and what he thought about his superiors, the Joint Chiefs of Staff

5) Franks got away with allowing his wife to sit in on classified briefings that would get anyone else thrown in jail

6) Casey got the top job in the U.S. Army after doing nothing in Iraq for two and a half years except tell Congress and the President how great things were going, and

7) General Petraeus kept going up the ladder from two- to four-star general and commander of all U.S. military operations in the Middle East, and was allowed to hand-pick his favorite colonels for promotion (see below).

It's all a bad dream come true, especially after the lessons we *should* have learned from Vietnam.

In 2007 General David Petraeus was selected as the new commander in Iraq. As mentioned previously, he was the original commander of MNSTC-I, the organization that lost the 190,000 weapons. This was the same organization whose very existence was to reverse what Paul Bremer did when he disbanded the Iraqi military and national police. It was the same organization I was assigned to. General Petraeus said he would take the job (like he was really going to turn it down) only if the President allowed him to do what he felt was necessary in Iraq. Apparently, the President said OK. What was Bush going to say, "No, I want you to go over there and sit on your ass like George Casey has done for two and a half years." I doubt that's how the conversation went. Of course it meant a fourth star for Petraeus, who was on top of the world. Not only was he getting away with losing nearly 200,000 weapons that were likely being used to kill his own soldiers, he was getting the coveted fourth star of a full general. What could be better?

At the same time George W. Bush was promoting Casey to Army Chief of Staff for the great job he did in Iraq, he was making predictions of what would happen if the United States withdrew from Iraq too soon. On July 12, 2007, Bush was interviewed on *The Kelly File*, hosted by Megyn Kelly, and he listed several things he thought would occur if we pulled out of Iraq before the country was ready to stand on its own.

On September 11, 2014, a Fox News article titled, "Bush in 2007 delivered eerily accurate warning about Iraq unrest," described the *The Kelly File* interview:

> "To begin withdrawing before our commanders tell us we are ready would be dangerous for Iraq, for the region and for the United States," Bush cautioned.

> He then ticked off a string of predictions about what would happen if the U.S. left too early.

> "It would mean surrendering the future of Iraq to Al Qaeda.

> "It would mean that we'd be risking mass killings on a horrific scale.

> "It would mean we allow the terrorists to establish a safe haven in Iraq to replace the one they lost in Afghanistan.

> "It would mean we'd be increasing the probability that American troops would have to return at some later date to confront an enemy that is even more dangerous."

> Bush speechwriter Marc Thiessen says all these predictions have come true.

> "Every single thing that President Bush said there in that statement is happening today," he told Fox News.

Then the Fox News article dropped a bombshell:

> Bush, before he left office, signed an agreement setting the stage for U.S. troops to withdraw by December 2011.[88]

---

[88] "Bush in 2007 delivered eerily accurate warning about Iraq unrest," *Fox News*, September 11, 2014.

President Bush was telling us in July 2007 that we shouldn't withdraw from Iraq "before our commanders tell us we are ready." Then, right before he left office six months later, he set the stage to begin withdrawal in 2011. Who was telling Bush we would be ready to withdraw by 2011, and how would they know what conditions in Iraq would be four years down the road? Even if senior military officers were telling Bush things would be great by 2011, why would he sign an order predicated on conditions four years into the future—during wartime? The president was making plans to do something four years down the road, as if he had the power to stop the war on the day of his choosing.

One possible reason why Bush felt confident Iraq would be rosy by 2011 was the presence of David Petraeus, who had been commander in Iraq for a year by the time Bush signed the order to start withdrawing our forces in 2011. So much glory was heaped on Petraeus, it was taken as fact things would be great once he had a chance to turn them around. He was being compared to George S. Patton, and touted as the greatest military officer in a generation or more. He was Colin Powell with different skin tone. But anyone who took over from General George Casey would have looked good, so lousy was his 'leadership.' Casey himself was the reason for the "surge" that Petraeus was given the mission to lead.

I was in Iraq when President Bush was making his predictions to Megyn Kelly. Although I wasn't aware he was making them at the time, I would have been in full agreement. I was back in the States by the time he signed the order to start withdrawal in 2011. Unlike his predictions, I would have felt Bush was out of his mind to consider withdrawing four years down the road, or even 10. I had just returned from Iraq, and the place was a disaster. Signing a military order to do something four years into the future is crazy. But to do that with respect to Iraq was completely insane. The false confidence the Pollyanna's in Washington had in David Petraeus and his bogus "counter-insurgency" doctrine (or should it be called the "Bible"), had everyone believing he would turn things around in Iraq with a wave of his hand.

After I had been in Baghdad for about two months, a U.S. Army full colonel I knew walked up to me in the chow line. He was one of the "good guys." Whenever we talked about the war he would do a 360 degree scan to make sure no one could overhear us, because we were about to talk about reality. With his voice lowered so no one would hear him, he asked what I thought of the war. I said, in a normal tone of voice, that I thought it was a "cluster fuck." He nodded his head in agreement. Then he asked me if I had been in the Infantry when I was in the Army. The question was important because it implied that by being in the Infantry, the U.S. Army's primary combat branch, as opposed to one of its support branches, I would have a clue as to what was going on. I said I had been. Then he asked me an interesting question: "What would you do?" Without hesitation I said I'd take two U.S. Army Infantry divisions, drop them in the middle of Baghdad, and clean the town up. I said Baghdad is Iraq, and if you secure Baghdad you secure Iraq. He just nodded his head in agreement again. I tell this story exactly as it happened. I was asked these questions by the colonel just the way I have written them here, and I answered them just as I have described. What I said made sense then, and did for several years afterward. My only mistake was that I underestimated the number of soldiers needed to clean the mess up. I said two divisions. I should have said at least five.

This conversation took place about four months before the announcement that David Petraeus was going to take command of Iraq after George Casey, and that he was going to institute the "surge." What was the surge? It was the exact same thing I told my friend, the U.S. Army full colonel, when he asked me what I would do while we stood in the chow line. I understand General Petraeus has a PhD, and when he arrived in Iraq surrounded himself with an entourage of U.S. Army full colonels, all rising stars destined for promotion themselves, many with PhD's as well. It was also known, for what was likely the first time in the history of the U.S. Army, General Petraeus was asked to participate in the promotion board to offer 'suggestions' on the suitability of colonels being considered for brigadier general, rather than this important decision being made by a secret board of un-biased officers based on the records of those being considered. General Petraeus was executing the war in Iraq while at the same time hand-picking his own people to run the U.S. Army for years into the future.

Politics always plays a role in promotions, but this was a hand dealt to General Petraeus to play any way he wanted. It meant one man was running the U.S. Army. He wasn't even the Chief of Staff, and was making personal selections for promotion. This had never been done before, and it made the entire promotion process an open admission of who you know in order to make the grade. It meant promotion to brigadier general in the U.S. Army depended on whether you were one of David Petraeus' people or not.

I never attended the U.S. Army Command and General Staff College at Fort Leavenworth, Kansas, or the U.S. Army War College in Carlisle, Pennsylvania. But I graduated from West Point and served in the Infantry for five years. With that experience alone I knew standing in a chow line what needed to be done in Iraq after being there only four months. It's not rocket science. You don't need a PhD in this stuff. Put 25,000 U.S. Army Infantry soldiers in one spot and tell them to start kicking some butt! That's what the surge was. It was 25,000 U.S. Army Infantry soldiers—about two divisions, what a coincidence—put into the worst parts of Baghdad and told to start kicking some insurgent ass. What happened? The insurgency and bombings dropped like a rock in those areas, and the Iraqis who lived there felt safer walking down the street then they had in the previous four years. Thank you General Casey for doing such a great job before getting moved up to Chief of Staff. We had an expression when I was in the Army—"Fuck up and move up!"

By 2007-2008, David Petraeus had reached the pinnacle of success. He followed his military career with appointment as the Director of Central Intelligence, the CIA. But as the saying goes: the higher they fly, the farther they fall. On November 9, 2012, he crashed and burned following revelations of his affair with a West Point graduate of a different stripe, the 'alpha female' Paula Broadwell. An FBI investigation discovered that Broadwell was stalking a Tampa socialite who was close friends with Petraeus and Marine Corps General John Allan, the commander of all forces in Afghanistan at the time. (The scandal prematurely ended Gen. Allen's career. He was slated to become NATO commander, but his nomination was pulled.)

Since then Petraeus has been under investigation for possible violation of the Uniform Code of Military Justice (UCMJ), which forbids adultery. If it is proven he was having an affair with Paula Broadwell while still on active duty, he could face a court-martial and reduction in rank. He is also being investigated by the Obama/Holder Justice Department (FBI) for possible security violations pertaining to classified documents he gave to Ms. Broadwell.

On September 11, 2012, two months before David Petraeus' sex scandal became national news, the CIA compound in Benghazi was attacked, resulting in the deaths of four Americans, including Ambassador Chris Stevens. David Petraeus became Director of the CIA on September 6, 2011, one year before the attack. Therefore, he knows everything that occurred that night. Yet, no testimony has been forthcoming from the former U.S. Army four-star general and CIA Director, who swore to uphold and defend the Constitution of the United States.

On September 5, 2014, three CIA operatives who were members of the quick response team one mile from the Benghazi compound went public with their story of what happened the night of September 11, 2012. They claim that the senior CIA officer in Benghazi ordered them to "stand down" three times during the siege of the compound, delaying their response by a half hour. If they could have responded sooner, they might have been able to save the ambassador and the others.

The day their claim became public, Representative Louie Gohmert was interviewed on by Martha MacCallum of *Fox News'* *America's Newsroom*. Rep. Gohmert described the Obama administration's efforts to silence anyone with knowledge of the Benghazi attack. Then, without any prompting from Ms. MacCallum, he mentioned David Petraeus:

> Ms. MacCallum: "Why would all these people be told not to talk?"

> Rep. Gohmert: "Obviously somebody had a vested interest in keeping them quiet. Well, look at Petraeus. We find out that the administration knew about his

affair for nearly a year. Why did they sit on it until Petraeus knew that the Susan Rice talking points were a lie, and then they run him out so he can't be out there blasting that. I mean, these people are very insidious in what they have done to some of the true patriots out there on the field, and it really needs to be exposed."[89]

A United States Congressman asserts the Obama administration knew about David Petraeus' affair "for nearly a year" before the 9/11/12 attack. He states that after Susan Rice made her White House-scripted claim that the Benghazi attacks were the result of a YouTube video, David Petraeus was silenced so he wouldn't have a chance to refute her. If Obama knew about Petraeus' affair for a year before the Benghazi attack, why didn't he do something about it sooner? Maybe Obama didn't care about the affair. Then again, maybe Obama saw it as something to use later on, to save for a rainy day. If Petraeus was hooking up with Paula Broadwell while still on active duty, or gave her classified documents he wasn't supposed to, then Obama really had something on him he could use whenever the need arose. Silence about what happened that night in Benghazi was that need.

David Petraeus knows everything that went on that night in Benghazi, but he hasn't opened his mouth for two full years. Some critics have suggested he is being blackmailed by Obama to keep his mouth shut about Benghazi, in exchange for avoiding a court-martial, keeping his four-star retirement, and not being charged with a security violation by the Obama/Holder Justice Department.

---

[89] "Rep. Gohmert reacts to Benghazi attack discrepancies," *Fox News: America's Newsroom*, September 5, 2014.

17—America's Failure in Iraq

The story of Iraq is the story of the United States' destruction of its critical infrastructure (its electrical power plants, grids, dams, etc.); the firing of everyone who had knowledge of how to run things; the firing of every soldier and policeman, many of whom became recruits for the insurgency; and the loss of weapons we purchased that likely went to the insurgency, and were very likely used to kill American soldiers. Now we've left Iraq in the lurch to defend for itself, and provide the most basic services to its people, all because we invaded the place. It's a mess, almost to the point of being laughable. But it's not funny.

For the United States, Iraq represents many things:

1) Mismanagement of United States Government contracts;

2) Private companies who send people to Iraq without regard for what they do, and then turn their backs on their employees;

3) Murder by private security contractors paid by the U.S. government;

4) Waste, fraud and abuse of U.S. taxpayer dollars;

5) Gross dereliction of duty by senior military officers and senior State Department employees;

6) Gross inequalities in the tours of duty of the different U.S. military services;

7) Waste of time and effort to maintain a coalition of countries in a strictly American operation for political reasons only, and;

8) Allowing citizens from those countries to be placed in leadership positions over U.S. military and civilian personnel.

How many Iraqis have died because we didn't finish the job we should have in 1991? How many Iraqis have died because we invaded in the spring of 2003? How many Iraqis and American soldiers have died because we're more concerned with political correctness and the "sensitivities" of others than killing insurgents who murder innocent people by the thousands? How many have died because of gross incompetence on the part of the Bush administration? How many have died because of senior U.S. military officers who cared more for their own careers then the Iraqi people they were sent to "free?" How many U.S. soldiers have died due to inept planning and pathetic execution by those same senior military officers? How badly has the reputation of the United States suffered as a result?

In a February 24, 2005 article, Hearst White House correspondent Helen Thomas wrote that approximately $9 billion dollars was missing in Iraq. She claimed that, "Profiteering from the Iraq war is not a surprise, especially in light of the Bush administration's pandering to the military-industrial complex." Stating the $9 billion was missing from the sale of Iraqi oil, which was to have been used for humanitarian aid and reconstruction for Iraq, and that the war was, "costing the United States more than $50 billion a year." The missing funds had been reported by Stuart W. Bowen, the Special Inspector General for Iraq Reconstruction (SIGIR), On January 30, 2005.

SIGIR found that no banking system had been implemented in Iraq, even though "a lot of dinars and American dollars" were in circulation. The money had been "stashed" in the basement of CPA headquarters (the Republican Palace), and released from time to time to contractors, who were making a killing. The Inspector General found "insufficient managerial, financial, salary and contract controls." For example, in one Iraqi ministry 8,026 guards were officially on the payroll, but the presence of only 602 guards could be validated. Of course, Paul Bremer had to defend his former organization, the Coalition Provisional Authority (CPA), after being obviously stung by Bowen's scathing report.

> It [the report] "does not meet the standards Americans have come to expect of the inspector

general," he said, claiming it had many "factual errors."

Both Bremer and the Defense Department -- which controlled the CPA -- complained that the report did not acknowledge that the Western-style budgeting could not be immediately implemented in a wartime atmosphere.[90]

The same could be said of the inability to implement "Western-style" democracy in Iraq. I didn't know Paul Bremer was an accountant.

One of my closest friends in Iraq was a retired U.S. Secret Service agent named Tom Cruise (no relation to the actor). Tom spent 30 months in Iraq. He was responsible for investigating human rights violations of detainees held by the Iraqi Ministry of Defense. According to Tom: "Torture is a part of that culture and is tolerated or accepted...we really did not make much of an impact in spite of our efforts! I had some amazing issues with the MNSTC-I command where they refused to act upon torture cases I revealed like murder, torture, beatings, castration and execution of civilians that I worked. In fact the FBI was corrupt in a case and I revealed it all."

Tom Cruise created a sensation when he was interviewed by the British newspaper *The Times*, where he described his investigation of torture and murder at the Ministry of Defense prison in the Abu Ghraib area west of Baghdad, the same prison where in 2012 Islamic militants broke free hundreds of terrorist suspects being held by the Iraqi government. He labeled the torture and murder of a detainee, the Iraqi refusal to prosecute, and the Investigative Judge's lying about the incident as yet more examples of Iraqi government corruption, where no one was ever held accountable for human rights violations. He also described how two lead Iraqi investigators were arrested for accepting approximately $800,000 in bribes and payoffs to release detainees.

---

[90] Helen Thomas, "$9B Goes Missing In Iraq-Huge Sum Disappears Without A Trace," *WCVB TV News, Boston*, February 24, 2005.

The following excerpts are from Tom Cruise's interview with *The Times of London*, where he describes the fate of an Iraqi named Adnan Awad Mohammed Thaib al Jumaili to Ann Clwyd, MP, Gordon Brown's human rights envoy to Iraq:

> In the worst case encountered by the former adviser, Mr al-Jumaili was arrested in a raid in May 2007 in Abu Ghraib, an area west of Baghdad that shares its name with the notorious prison where a group of U.S. soldiers abused Iraqi detainees in the aftermath of the invasion.
>
> Mr al-Jumaili, suspected of terrorist activity but detained illegally because there was no arrest warrant for him, was taken to an Iraqi army holding centre for questioning. The detainee was moved to an American medical facility but no serious health problems were diagnosed so he was returned to the Iraqi base.
>
> The next morning Mr al-Jumaili was dead. An Iraqi post-mortem examination concluded that he died of internal bleeding caused by physical trauma.[91]

Pressured by Tom Cruise, the Iraqi Ministry of Defense began an investigation into the suspected torture and murder, but Mr. Cruise said the case was hampered by a "general lack of will" on the part of the Iraqis. It took six months to get permission to examine the room where Mr. al-Jumaili was interrogated. Tom Cruise said, "We found implements of torture, including wooden clubs and a black electrical cattle prod. We also found blood splattering on the walls from three different males. This shows that the torture of Adnan wasn't an isolated incident."

An Iraqi government spokesman said that torture was vastly improved from Saddam Hussein's era: "We have formed a committee that looks into any alleged violation." Great, more committees.

---

[91] Deborah Haynes, "Iraqi Government hit with claims that man died in detention after torture," *The Times (UK)*, August 4, 2009.

Tom Cruise's story was critical because it highlighted the culture of the Iraqi people and the Middle Eastern way of dealing with one's captured prisoners. It also highlighted the "blind eye" the Coalition (i.e., the United States) turned toward it. If we go back to the reasons for invading Iraq that we were given by President Bush, one of them was to instill democracy—to change Iraq from the days of Saddam into a place more like the United States. What was the point of invading Iraq for this purpose, when we did nothing in the face of overwhelming evidence the Iraqi government was torturing its detained prisoners to include maiming, causing permanent physical injury, or death—just like the old days when Saddam was in charge? (The debate over the United States' use of waterboarding will go on forever. But waterboarding doesn't ruin people for life, like what goes on in Iraqi prisons. It saves lives. There's a big difference.)

It's not just the Iraqis, however. What's the point of DoD hiring companies who send employees like Dr. X to Iraq, and do nothing after he is found to be a complete fraud? What's the point when this same company wanted to retain him after he needlessly caused the permanent injury of a young man, could have gotten CIA operatives killed due to his lies, and could have gotten an Iraqi woman beheaded if she had been caught by Iraqi security forces? What's the point when two of our own agencies fail to follow procedure and blow a raid leading to the young man's injuries, and then blame it on him?

I heard from my female colleague that the U.S. Navy captain who was busting my ass continued with the same behavior toward her after I left. He repeatedly lied and made false accusations against her as well. He would completely blow his stack and throw tantrums in front of U.S. general officers, even in front of Iraqi generals, insisting that she and officers on his own staff were incompetent. Imagine what the Iraqis thought of all this? He was a paranoid nut job. My colleague presented evidence against his accusations in order to prove to everyone what he was up to, and he was formally reprimanded. But he was still allowed to extend his tour so he could continue making the big money in Iraq, which was probably way more than he made in his civilian job back in the States, if he had one. He should not have been wearing the uniform of a United Stated commissioned officer, reserve or active duty. He was a total disgrace to himself, the U.S. Navy, our country, and our efforts in Iraq. If contractors and military officers with no integrity could be sent to Iraq, and be allowed to extend their tours, then it really is just about money and a little adventure.

At the time of this writing Barack Hussein Obama has been "President" of the United States for six years. He never definitively proved he was born in the United States, which throws his legitimacy to hold the office of President into question. Article. II., Section. 1. of the Constitution states:

> No Person except a natural born Citizen, or a Citizen of the United States, at the time of the Adoption of this Constitution, shall be eligible to the Office of President;....

Only after the real estate mogul Donald Trump resurrected the issue of Obama's birth in 2012 did Obama produce, for the first time, "evidence" of his birth. But what he produced was a document that only made the issue more contentious. For example, the hospital on the document didn't exist when he was born in 1961. A hospital was there, but it went by a different name, not the name it uses today. The people who fabricated the document assumed it went by the same name. But Obama's biggest omission is the original birth certificate itself. It exists, but no one has ever seen it. I say this from my own personal experience.

The *original birth certificate* of every person born in the United States is in the custody of the "Secretary of State" of the state where the person was born. I am a citizen of both the United States and Ireland. I was able to apply for my Irish citizenship because my father's mother was born there, which meant that my father was an Irish citizen at birth. Therefore, being the child of an Irish citizen, I was eligible to apply for Irish citizenship. When I produced all the documents at the Irish embassy in Washington, DC, I was told everything was there, with one exception—my birth certificate. I showed them the "birth certificate" I had brought with me, but was told it was only a document attesting to the fact that my birth certificate was on record. The form was on blue-pink colored paper, with the information typed on it, and a notary seal. I was told the form didn't satisfy the requirement that I produce a copy of my *original birth certificate*. I followed the instructions of the embassy staff and contacting the Secretary of State of New York, where I was born. In less than a week I received a copy of my *original birth certificate*, which was identical to the original on file in Albany, the state capital. The document was on faded yellow paper, and was obviously a copy of a birth certificate from 1954, the year I was born. It had the signature of the doctor who delivered me, and was notarized. When I brought this to the Irish embassy it was accepted, and the process to get my Irish citizenship began.

Barack Hussein Obama has never produced such a document, a copy of his *original birth certificate* kept by the Secretary of State for Hawaii. It would be as simple as paying a minor fee and completing a form. Hell, I'll lend him the money. Obama could have done this any time, but he never did. Why not? If it exists, just produce it and put the issue to rest. Obama has refused to produce the single document that would end the entire debate over his birth. He hasn't produced it for one of only two possible reasons: 1) it doesn't exist, or; 2) there is something on it he doesn't want the American people to see. Either way, until this document is produced the question of Obama's his legal status to hold the office of President of the United States will be in doubt.

If we don't adhere to our own laws, such as enforcing the qualifications to be president, why bother adhering to laws in Iraq? Barack Hussein Obama violates the United States Constitution every day, but the Republican majority in the House of Representatives does nothing to stop him because they're physical cowards like Clinton, Bush and Cheney—and because no one wants to get stuck with Joe Biden if Obama is impeached. (Obama's choice of Biden was brilliant. It made him impeachment-proof!) Obama has cut our military to the bone. U.S. Immigration & Customs Enforcement (ICE) releases convicted illegal aliens by the tens of thousands because the Obama administration is flipping the bird at our border enforcement laws already on the books—all for the Hispanic vote. At the time of this writing, tens of thousands of illegal alien children (and adults) are pouring across our southern border, supposedly having trekked over 1,000 miles to get here, completely on their own, which defies credulity. You need a driver's license to open a bank account, but democrats want to allow everyone to vote without an ID in order to continue their campaign of vote fraud. The fate of our national defense and homeland security hang in the balance. The welfare state is here, and a socialist oligarchy is just around the corner.

The first President Bush gave us Bill Clinton. The second President Bush gave us Barack Hussein Obama. Thanks guys. If you're looking for real leadership going back to FDR, you're not going to find it—with one exception (see below). What you will find is weakness, lack of direction, and senior advisors surrounding their presidents with their own agenda—but not the agenda of the American people, or the Iraqi people for that matter.

The only exception to the above would be Ronald Reagan. He was a leader, and believed in people. He made his mistakes, but he ended the Cold War. Franklin Delano Roosevelt, on the other hand, rolled over for "Uncle Joe" Stalin and gave him Eastern Europe on a silver platter, thereby creating the same Cold War that Reagan ended. Those who worship FDR need to ask the people of Poland, Rumania, Czechoslovakia, Hungary, East Germany, Yugoslavia and all the former vassal states of what was once the Soviet Union how they feel about FDR. Without our weapons, ammunition, tanks and airplanes Joe Stalin would have gotten crushed by the Third Reich. He stayed alive because of the United States. Roosevelt didn't owe Stalin a thing, but handed him half of Europe because "Uncle Joe" was a nice guy, and FDR had become feeble. Obama has been compared to FDR, which is appropriate because they're both socialists.

Barack Hussein Obama pledged during his victorious presidential campaign that he would pull all U.S. forces out of Iraq within a year to 18 months. Then he said he would leave around 50,000 there. I submit the reason for this about-face was a combination of two things:

1) He was saying whatever it took to win the election without having a clue of the actual situation in Iraq, and;

2) When he got into the Oval Office, he realized we couldn't pull out without Iraq completely falling apart.

If everything was going great in Iraq, as General Casey had been saying for years, what was the problem? All Obama had to do was quote General Casey, and he could claim that withdrawing from Iraq was the prudent thing to do. The reality was entirely different from what General Casey was saying, for as soon as Obama started talking about withdrawal, senior officers in our military said it would be a huge mistake. So how could Casey say Iraq was fine, while the generals in the Pentagon were saying just the opposite? We keep getting smoke blown in our face.

Because of what we have done in Iraq, much of the world hates the United States. Although I had such high hopes for George W. Bush when he was elected, thinking he might be another Ronald Reagan, I was soon proven very wrong. He did succeed in the single most important job of the president—he defended our country. However, just about everything else he did was a disaster: from introducing immigration reform (amnesty); to the nomination of Harriet Myers; to the mismanagement of the Katrina disaster; to the bailout of Wall Street orchestrated by his Treasury Secretary, Henry Paulson, which was the first step toward the nationalization of our economy. Barack Hussein Obama can blame the bailouts on Bush. After all, Bush started it.

The disaster in Iraq would not have happened if George W. Bush had just stayed in Afghanistan. Instead, he created a reason for invading Iraq in the spring of 2003 rather than sticking with the problem in front of him. If he had stayed focused on Al Qaeda, the Taliban, Afghanistan, and the real threats to our nation's security from radical Islamic fanaticism, as he said we were facing, the world wouldn't hate our country as much as it does now.

I have mentioned the wise saying: "Those who do not study history are doomed to repeat it." It is very evident the United States repeated the same mistakes made by previous administrations when it invaded Iraq in 2003. Anyone who disagrees with this is entitled to their opinion, but as far as I'm concerned the facts are undeniable. I have also said that I hope our country never repeats the mistakes we've made in Iraq, going back to 1991. There's no need for these mistakes. Too many innocent people have died because we haven't learned our lesson.

In November 2008, a former co-worker from Iraq e-mailed to say he was back in the States. He wanted to tell me our employer in Iraq had lost its contract and had been replaced by another company. My translator e-mailed me a few weeks later and told me the new company sent a woman to be the real estate advisor to the Ministry of Defense. She was an accountant and had no experience in real estate or construction. She left Iraq after a couple of months. Her replacement was a guy who didn't know anything about real estate either. But who cares, he's breathing. The company can continue to bill the government.

18—"Commander-of-Chief"

During his 2008 campaign Barack Hussein Obama said he wanted to be the "Commander-of-Chief." It's "Commander-in-Chief." He didn't even know the correct title of the job he was campaigning for. The media intentionally corrected what he said so the American people wouldn't know, yet we're supposed to believe they're not biased.

On August 2, 2010, Obama gave a speech to disabled veterans. He proudly declared that he was keeping the promise he made on February 27, 2009, to withdraw all "combat" forces from Iraq by August 31, 2010. He also said that 50,000 U.S. troops would remain in Iraq until the end of 2011. These troops, called "advise and assist brigades," would focus on supporting and training Iraqi security forces, protecting American personnel and facilities, and conducting counterterrorism operations.

> Mr. Obama hailed the improved security in Iraq without mentioning that he had opposed the 2007 troop buildup ordered by Mr. Bush, which along with a strategy change, is credited by many with turning the war around. Mr. Obama has now assigned the architect of that plan, Gen. David H. Petraeus, to do the same in Afghanistan.[92]

How's that "improved security in Iraq" looking now, Barack?

After Obama's announcement, his semantics became a topic of discussion in an interview with Secretary of Defense Robert Gates:

> "All of the combat units will be out of Iraq by the end of August [2010] and those that are left will have a combat capability. There will be, as the president said, targeted counterterrorism operations. There will be continued embeds with some of the Iraqi forces in a training capacity and so on.

---

[92] Peter Baker, "In Speech on Iraq, Obama Reaffirms Drawdown," *The New York Times*, August 2, 2010.

"So there will be the capability, but the units will be gone, and, more importantly, the mission will have changed. And so the notion of being engaged in combat in the way we have been up until now will be completely different."[93]

If a U.S. army unit is conducting "counterterrorism operations," then it is conducting combat operations. What's a "counterterrorism operation" if it isn't a combat operation? *Washington Post* Pentagon reporter Thomas Ricks was quoted as saying, "There is no such thing as non-combat troops."[94]

Then on August 18, 2010, just two weeks later, Obama announced he was planning to have thousands of State Department contractors in Iraq indefinitely, instead of U.S. soldiers wearing uniforms. He would fill the void left by the removal of American soldiers with civilian contractors. *The New York Times* described Obama's use of mercenaries as a "remarkable civilian effort." To rags like *The Times* there isn't anything Obama can do wrong. Instead, everything he does is "historic" and "remarkable."

> As the United States military prepares to leave Iraq by the end of 2011, the Obama administration is planning a remarkable civilian effort, buttressed by a *small army of contractors*, to fill the void. [Italics mine.]

> By October 2011, the State Department will assume responsibility for training the Iraqi police, a task that will largely be carried out by contractors. With no American soldiers to defuse sectarian tensions in northern Iraq, it will be up to American diplomats in two new $100 million outposts to head off potential confrontations between the Iraqi Army and Kurdish peshmerga forces.

> "We need strategic patience here," Ryan C. Crocker, who served as ambassador in Iraq from 2007 until early 2009,

---

[93] Brian Montopoli, "Iraq Withdrawal: What Are Non-Combat Troops?" *CBS News*, August 2, 2010.

[94] Ibid.

said in an interview. "Our timetables are getting out ahead of Iraqi reality."[95]

In 2014, Ambassador Crocker's assessment could not be more on target.

To travel around Iraq without U.S. soldiers, the State Department plans to purchase 60 mine-resistant, ambush-protected vehicles, called MRAPs, from the Pentagon. It also planned to expand its inventory of armored cars to 1,320, and create a "mini-air fleet" by buying three planes to add to its lone aircraft. Its helicopter fleet, piloted by contractors, would grow to 29 choppers from 17. The State Department's plan to employ 6,000 to 7,000 security contractors, who are also expected to form "quick reaction forces" to rescue civilians in trouble, is a sensitive issue.[96] This would be due to Iraqi anger about shootings of civilians by American private guards in recent years (i.e., the Nisour Square massacre by Blackwater).

The U.S. State Department is becoming a branch of the U.S. military.

Clearly, the Obama administration picked up where previous administrations left off. Contractors make going to war easier for America now. If anyone says we are not "at war" because there are no soldiers wearing uniforms in Iraq after 2011, then the "military-industrial complex" will have reached the point President Eisenhower warned us of. Administrations will continue to avoid the tough decision to send our military to fight in a conflict no one wants, and will also avoid having to sell the mission to the American people. "Security contractors" and other companies that provide services in places like Iraq and Afghanistan, will continue raking in the cash for their shareholders. Contractors are in the catbird seat now. The tail is wagging the dog.

---

[95] Michael R. Gordon, "Civilians to Take U.S. Lead as Military Leaves Iraq," *The New York Times*, August 19, 2010.

[96] Ibid.

Because our national 'leadership' is weak, we don't declare war any more. This is just what these contractors want. Our country will continue to send a fraction of the soldiers needed to do the job right, thereby prolonging the mission, and will throw in 100,000 contractors. The contractors won't mind because they're making all the money, and the American people will continue to live their lives as if nothing's happening. Just give them their big screen TV's.

According to the article above, one State Department Regional Security Officer (RSO) will be on each mission with these security contractors. Instead of U.S. Army soldiers lead by officers and a non-commissioned officers (i.e., sergeants), the U.S. Department of State will be conducting military operations with a bunch of contractors lead by a single embassy security officer. Will these contractors and the RSO train as a cohesive military unit before they are sent to Iraq, like conducting a raid or repelling an ambush? Will they be able to conduct a mission like a U.S. Army Infantry or Ranger unit? Of course they won't. They'll just get on a plane in the States, show up in Iraq, and start running combat missions. Because they won't be trained as a cohesive combat unit, they'll end up getting themselves killed at a far higher rate than U.S. Army soldiers or Marines. But they won't be wearing uniforms, so who cares?

The American people don't really care when a civilian contractor comes home in a pine box, only when a soldier comes home in a casket draped with a U.S. flag. The thousands of civilian "security contractors" that will remain in Iraq are mercenaries, plain and simple. If it walks like a duck and quacks like a duck, it's a duck. They will be under contract to the U.S. Department of State, will be paid with U.S. dollars, will be in combat on a U.S. government operation in a foreign country, but they won't be wearing uniforms. They are mercenaries any way you look at it. Obama can say he met his timelines as promised, but his timelines are meaningless. Wars don't end on a pre-set date. The war in Iraq will be over when the Iraqi people are safe. They haven't been safe since the day we invaded in March 2003. They weren't safe for years under the watchful eye of General George Casey, and they aren't safe today because the country is under siege by al Qaeda, ISIS, Syria and Iran.

After returning from Iraq I was talking with a professor at the School of International Service at American University (AU) in Washington, DC. This is one of the country's preeminent academic institutions, teaching students the intricacies of Foreign Service, international affairs, diplomacy and foreign relations. During our conversation the professor revealed something quite incredible. She said Paul Bremer had been offered a professorship at AU, and was going to start teaching at the school beginning the fall 2010 semester. (This decision was later changed. See below.) The professor said many meetings were held over a period of weeks with faculty and staff at AU to discuss Bremer's job offer. But, according to the professor, in the end the decision to hire Bremer was made by a select group of a few individuals. One would have to be brain dead not to realize the decision to hire Bremer had already been made. The meetings were merely window dressing.

Who were those few select people at AU? It is very likely they served with him in the Foreign Service, and they wanted to bring him to AU so they could hang out together as they went into retirement. Maybe he just needed a job. At least that would make sense. It would stand to reason Paul Bremer would have difficulty finding work after his performance in Iraq in 2003-2004.

In all honesty, how can American University have a school devoted to "international service," when the guy it hired is the most glaring example of what "international service" is not supposed to be? Paul Bremer is the poster child of poor international service. Wasn't it Paul Bremer who disbanded the Iraqi Ministry of Defense and Ministry of Interior, dismembering the security infrastructure of the country and leaving it defenseless against a growing insurgency—that he created? Didn't Paul Bremer feed that same insurgency with fresh recruits, the policemen and soldiers he fired? And wasn't it Paul Bremer who fired everyone in the Iraqi government and Iraqi society who belonged to the Ba'ath Party, thereby firing everyone who had a clue how to run the government's institutions and bureaucracy? It was Paul Bremer who did all these things, but he was offered a position at American University to pass along all that knowledge and experience to our kids?

One could almost feel sorry for Paul Bremer. He screwed up at a level few can match. But that doesn't mean AU should hire the guy responsible for the deaths of thousands of people simply because he's got a recognizable name. Did AU also hire George W. Bush, Donald Rumsfeld and Tommy Franks? I don't think so. They weren't in the Foreign Service like Paul Bremer. And they're neocons, so that's out. The decision to hire Paul Bremer makes no sense, but who says it has to? As is often the case, Bremer probably got his job because he was connected. In Washington, DC more than any other city in the country, that's what counts.

How does Paul Bremer fit into the mission of American University's School of International Service if that mission is to offer students instruction from the best and most experienced professionals in the field—unless he teaches a course in what *not* to do. Maybe he could teach a course titled: "How to Create an Insurgency and Destroy a Country's Ability to Defend Itself." It would be standing room only.

Like many of the three and four-star generals mentioned in this book, Paul Bremer is set for life by having been selected for the job as head of the Coalition Provisional Authority. It doesn't matter how poorly he performed in that position. For the generals in Iraq, and for Paul Bremer, their assignments were nothing more than place holders, fillers of time while they waited for their next promotion to come along. America is not a performance-based country anymore. It's a popularity-based, media run carnival.

When will America learn from its mistakes? Obviously, if Bremer was hired to teach at AU, it hasn't learned anything. While the Chief of the Iraqi armed forces, General Zerbari Babakir, proclaimed his country was a decade away from being able to defend itself, the person responsible was being made a professor at AU's School of International Service (see below). Because AU is a liberal school I can imagine the idiots who hired Bremer were the most vocal in their opposition to the invasion of Iraq in 2003, to George W. Bush, and to Donald Rumsfeld. If that were true, how could the same people hire the person responsible for the worst aspect of our Iraq policy? The biggest mistake America made in Iraq wasn't executed by Bush or Rumsfeld, it was executed by Paul Bremer, the expert in international affairs and foreign policy. Even with the low numbers of soldiers in the invasion, the insurgency wouldn't have grown to the levels it has if Bremer hadn't disbanded Iraq's army and national police. It might not have happened at all. Paul Bremer definitely has blood on his hands.

The primary reason Iraq still can't defend itself more than a decade after we invaded is Paul Bremer. Bremer might have had years in the field of foreign service, but when it came to the actual execution of foreign affairs and foreign policy he was an abject failure. But that's not going to stop him from imparting his 'knowledge' and poisoning the soft brains of young students entering the field. Those at American University who teach about the mistakes the United States has made in its foreign affairs have more to learn if they've made the mistake of hiring Paul Bremer.

Paul Bremer reportedly did not start teaching at American University in the fall 2010 semester. He still holds a faculty position, however. The reaction to his being hired was probably more than the school bargained for. The decision to add a diverse and controversial individual to the AU faculty was likely overshadowed by the reality of what Paul Bremer did. Maybe someone came to the realization that Paul Bremer's job performance was more important than "academic freedom," and he didn't deserve a seat at the table of academia.

On August 17, 2010 Afghanistan's President, Hamid Karzai, declared that all private security contractors had four months to leave the country. The next day Secretary of Defense Robert Gates announced he would be leaving his job some time in 2011. Hamid Karzai probably saw what was going with these private security firms, both in Iraq and Afghanistan, and wanted no part of them. He likely knew they would be there forever, and would create more problems than they would solve, so he decided they had to go. It almost appeared that he has a better grasp of the implications of the "military-industrial complex" then anyone here in America. He wanted his country protected by soldiers, not contractors.

What has all this meant for the war in Afghanistan? What has it all meant for the United States' efforts there, and for a peaceful resolution to that country's problems? Conditions in both Iraq and Afghanistan have begun to look more and more like

Vietnam: go in, mismanage everything, get slapped around, get thousands of innocent civilians and American soldiers killed, and then leave the place to the enemy we went there to destroy. The only twist now is that we leave thousands of "security contractors" behind to rake in money for the firms that employ them, but the mission is never accomplished. We don't need them there, but their employers sucker DoD and State into believing that we do, and away they go making $200,000-$400,000 a year. That's why those same firms need retired four-star generals like Carl Vuono and Jack Keane to walk the halls of the Pentagon to close the deal. Again, the contractors aren't soldiers in uniform, so who cares?

I am not the same person that I was before going to Iraq in the summer of 2006. Before then, I had my opinion of the Gulf War and its key participants, the futility of the UN and its sanctions, and my disappointment in the performance of George W. Bush. But in Iraq I saw the effects of all this with my own eyes. Our country is not led by men of integrity or courage anymore. It hasn't been for a long time. It is led by men who are connected to very wealthy people who provide the needed financial support to get them elected. In return, these people of wealth get laws passed that advance their own agenda. It takes a lot of hard work to become the President of the United States, but that doesn't mean the person who gets elected is right for the job. That's the problem.

Our military leadership is lacking as well. Although money is not as critical to becoming a four-star general as it is in politics, getting along is. Instead of needing money, those who succeed in the military have the innate ability to be at the right place at the right time, and never saying a word contrary to what their superiors want to hear. Another asset is being the son of a general officer, as Stan McChrystal was, or marrying the daughter of one, as David Petraeus did. Anyone who thinks these two officers were not guaranteed making general the day they graduated from West Point is kidding themselves. They got the best assignments, and never had to worry about their evaluation reports. None of their superiors would dare give them a sub-standard report for fear of upsetting their father, or father-in-law, and jeopardizing their own career in the process.

As is so often the case, rules that apply to the rest of us don't apply to the select few who are at the top tier of the Washington elite. Stanley McChrystal committed gross insubordination when he allowed a *Rolling Stone* reporter to hang around his staff for a month and take notes of everything McChrystal and his staff said about anybody, to include McChrystal's boss.[97] What resulted from this ridiculous mistake was the famous article that ended his career. Though not a fan of Obama, I agreed with him firing McChrystal. He had no choice. But then Obama turned around and allowed Stan McChrystal to retire at full four-star rank, even though he hadn't held it for the mandatory three years. McChrystal got what he deserved when Obama fired him, but he didn't get what he deserved when allowed to retire as a four-star general. But if you're famous, which by that time Stan McChrystal was, the rules are ignored. He is now teaching "leadership" at Yale University, a joke in itself, and earns around $60,000 per speech. He wouldn't have either of these perks if he hadn't retired as a four-star. The "military-industrial complex" just keeps rolling along.

(On June 18, 2013 Michael Hastings, the author of the *Rolling Stone* story on Stan McChrytsal, was killed in a car accident in Los Angeles.)

There will always be a need for political and military compromise, and for political and military objectives to work well together. Unfortunately, this was not the case with the invasion of Iraq. The only side that had any say was the political (Rumsfeld, Feith, Wolfowitz, Cheney, etc.), while the military bent over backwards and did exactly what their civilian bosses told them to do (Franks, Myers, Pace, Casey, etc.). Those who didn't know what they were doing were in charge, while those who did know were afraid to open their mouths and say the invasion plan was nonsense. The results speak for themselves.

Obama's troop withdrawal speech mentioned above was delivered on August 2, 2010. Ten days later, the Chief of the Iraqi Joint Headquarters Staff, General Zerbari Babakir, said that Iraq's armed forces: "...will not be able to secure the country until 2020 and that the U.S. should delay its planned withdrawal." On

[97] Michael Hastings, "The Runaway General," *Rolling Stone,* June 22, 2010.

August 12, 2010, Al Jazeera English published a statement by General Babakir who said his forces, particularly the air force, were not ready to take over. He said the planned withdrawal will create a "problem" and increase instability in Iraq.

On August 12, 2010 General Babakir declared: "At this point, the withdrawal is going well, because they [the US] are still here. But the problem will start after 2011—the politicians must find other ways to fill the void after 2011. If I were asked about the withdrawal, I would say to politicians: the U.S. army must stay until the Iraqi army is fully ready in 2020."[98]

It's clear the highest ranking officer of the Iraqi armed forces wasn't asked for his opinion about the U.S. withdrawal. Maybe the reason he wasn't asked was because no one wanted to hear his answer to the question. The senior military officer of the Iraqi armed forces openly stated that he doesn't want the U.S. to leave—for another ten years! This astounding revelation was in complete contrast to Obama's troop withdrawal announcement, and his proclamations that everything was OK in Iraq. Was Obama saying things were great because we had hit the date he said the war would be over? Did the Obama administration ask General Babakir for his opinion, or just go ahead with the troop drawdown because we had hit Obama's deadline? How could Obama announce the withdrawal of U.S. forces without consulting with the Chief of the Iraqi Joint Staff? But it appears that's exactly what happened. To look like a leader, Obama drew down our forces according to his timetable, consequences be damned. The only deadline in warfare is when on the offensive, such as the day and hour of attack, but not the date of withdrawal. This is like saying we will surrender on a certain date. How great is that for our opponents? All they have to do is wait until we leave, and then move in. But how would Obama know any of this? His senior military officers knew it, but they would never say it to his face. Keeping their jobs is more important.

Clearly, the White House was ignoring Iraq's commanding general and moving ahead with it's ill-conceived, and totally political, plan for withdrawal.

---

[98] "Iraq army 'not ready' until 2020," *Al Jazeera English,* August 12, 2010.

General Babakir's prediction that the U.S. Army would need to stay in Iraq until 2020 has turned out to be as accurate as George W. Bush's on *The Kelly File*. Today (2014), we hear almost daily of Iraqi soldiers running away from ISIS forces, while at the same time we're told Obama was under the impression Iraq's army was up to the task of defending its country. Where did Obama get that idea, or is this another lie from his administration? Because Obama had his own agenda to pull the U.S. out of Iraq, come hell or high water, and because he didn't listen to General Babakir there and his own generals here, Iraq's slide continues. To Obama it's all about politics and his image, even if his image is in the mirror. It's not about life and death.

Obviously, General Babakir knew what he was talking about in August 2010. He was there, on the ground in Iraq. He knew what was coming, yet his warning was ignored. Not only did we walk away from our ally, we didn't bother to listen to its highest ranking general. But what can you expect when we don't even listen to our own.

General Babakir said the main weakness of the Iraqi armed forces was its air force. The reader will recall the head of the Coalition Air Force Training Team (CAFTT) was U.S. Air Force Brigadier General Robert Allardice. What was BG Allardice doing in Iraq if the Chief of the Iraqi General Staff said its air force was his biggest concern? BG Allardice was the chief of CAFTT when I left Iraq in 2007. He was a one-star general then. He is now a three-star general. He got promoted twice for doing such a great job getting Iraq's air force up to speed. Like I've said, once you're selected for promotion and sent to Iraq for a year, it doesn't matter how bad you perform your job, that next star is on its way. Generals like Allardice, Petraeus, Conway, Dempsey, Casey and Wolff were all going to get their next star no matter what they did in Iraq, or how poorly they performed their jobs. Their assignment to Iraq was nothing more than a rubber stamp on their resume to support their next promotion.

While these officers have moved up the ladder as a result of their tours in Iraq, General Babakir's cautioning against a hasty U.S. withdrawal from Iraq has become prophetic.

Since 2010 al Qaeda has grown into multiple splinter groups called the Islamic State of Iraq and Syria (ISIS), the Islamic State of Iraq and the Levant (ISIL), the Islamic State of al-Sham (ISIS), and simply the Islamic State. They all contain the word "Islamic" for a reason—it's all about Islam and establishing a caliphate over the Middle East and the world. George W. Bush created a nightmare in 2003, and Barack Hussein Obama has allowed the nightmare to grow into a monster. We are sending soldiers back to Iraq by the hundreds every week, but still call them "advisers." The United States just can't accept the reality of the situation in Iraq. Or rather, the president of the United States can't. But millions of ordinary citizens can.

A good example of our "Commander-of-Chief's" grasp of the crisis in Iraq was his interview with *The New Yorker* in January of 2014:

> *New Yorker* editor David Remnick pointed out to the president that the Al Qaeda flag is now seen flying in Falluja in Iraq and in certain locations in Syria, and thus the terrorist group has not been "decimated" as Obama had said during his 2012 reelection campaign.
>
> "The analogy we use around here sometimes, and I think is accurate, is if a jayvee team puts on Lakers uniforms that doesn't make them Kobe Bryant," Obama told Remnick. "I think there is a distinction between the capacity and reach of a bin Laden and a network that is actively planning major terrorist plots against the homeland versus jihadists who are engaged in various local power struggles and disputes, often sectarian."
>
> Remnick characterized Obama's analogy as "uncharacteristically flip."[99]

Barack Hussein Obama is the most arrogant and egotistical snob to ever occupy the White House. For him to compare Islamic fanatic scum to the "JV" of a basketball team is beyond pathetic. It's disgusting. While Americans are beheaded, he's off to another fundraiser or round of golf. Everyone knew what

---

[99] David Remnick, "Going The Distance," *The New Yorker*, January 27, 2014.

Obama was about by the time the 2012 election came along, yet he got reelected anyway. America is definitely getting what it asked for, and therefore what it deserves—screwed.

The day Obama equated the new al Qaeda to the "JV" squad of the LA Lakers, those same neophytes blew up 28 people in Baghdad. The "jayvee" might be going for first string. *Fox News* reported on January 20, 2014:

> A series of bombings in central Iraq killed 28 people on Monday, as a government official claimed that al Qaeda-linked fighters have dug in to a city they seized last month and possess enough heavy weapons to storm into the country's capital.
>
> Since late December, members of Iraq's al Qaeda branch — known as the Islamic State of Iraq and the Levant — have taken over parts of Ramadi, the capital of the largely Sunni western province of Anbar. They also control the center of the nearby city of Fallujah, along with other non-al Qaeda groups that also oppose the Shiite-led government.
>
> "The weapons that were brought inside Fallujah are huge and advanced and frankly enough to occupy Baghdad," Deputy Interior Minister Adnan al-Asadi said in a speech, adding that Iraqi forces are still fighting "fierce battles" there and in Ramadi. He did not elaborate on the type or quantity of the weapons.[100]

How do we fight this new enemy? How do we help the Iraqi people being massacred by the Islamic State of Iraq and the Levant? U.S. Army Special Forces (Green Berets), Delta Forces, and U.S. Army Rangers are the only ground forces capable of this mission. Conventional U.S. Army forces should be used for major attacks, and to support these smaller forces. We don't need SEALs. They can stay home. Iraq is a land war, which means it is fought by the U.S. Army, not the U.S. Navy, which owns the

---

[100] "At least 28 dead in Iraq bombings as al Qaeda closes in on Baghdad," *Fox News*, January 20, 2014.

SEALs. Admiral Mike "Milktoast" Mullen is no longer Chairman of the Joint Chiefs of Staff, so we don't need to find something for the Navy to do. The story continued:

> Tuesday's attacks bring the death toll for this month to at least 387, according to an Associated Press count. Many attacks may go unreported.[101]

While Obama was saying al Qaeda was no big deal, it occupied Fallujah. al Qaeda and its spin-offs are a very big deal, and will overrun Baghdad if the U.S. doesn't step in. But Obama thinks they're just the "jayvee".

On August 11, 2014, the internet posted a video of then-U.S. Senator Barack Hussein Obama "promising not to take vacations if he were elected president."

> The future president was talking about how those running for president need to be prepared to "give their life to it."

> "The bargain that any president strikes with is, you give me this office and in turn my, fears, doubts, insecurities, foibles, need for sleep, family life, vacations, leisure is gone," Obama said. "I am giving myself to you."

> …"the American people should have no patience for what's going on in your head because you've got a job to do" and that people should only run for president if they're willing to make that sacrifice.

> When asked by the host if he could imagine himself making that kind of commitment, he said, "Sure."[102]

As of August 8, 2014, Obama had taken 19 vacations totaling 125 days. As of August 11, 2014, he had hit the golf course 186 times. (George W. Bush took 65 trips to his Texas ranch and his

---

[101] Ibid.

[102] "FLASHBACK: Obama Promises No Vacations For Himself As President," *The Daily Caller*, (*Weasel Zippers* archive video posted on *The Daily Caller*), August 11, 2014.

parents' home in Kennebunkport, Maine, totaling 407 days at the same point in his presidency. That's quite a lot, but I don't recall Bush saying he would never take time off if elected.)[103]

On November 13, 2014, the Associated Press wrote about the merging of al Qaeda and the Islamic State (IS).[104] The terrorist groups decided to stop fighting each other, and join forces to murder as many others as possible. Someone among them probably got his MBA from Harvard before going back home to become a terrorist. The Islamic State and al Qaeda have now formed a "joint venture" ("JV") by merging to become more effective and efficient terrorists. Never having a real job in his life, and therefore not having a clue about business, Obama was more accurate than he could have known when he called the Islamic State the "JV.".

[103] Jacobson, Louis, "Who took more vacation -- George W. Bush or Barack Obama?", *Tampa Bay Times*, August 23, 2014.

[104] Deb Riechmann, "IS, Al-Qaeda Reach Accord in Syria," *Associated Press*, November 13, 2014.

19—A Desire for War

The theme of this book is the failure of America's intervention in Iraq from 1991 to the present. I have shown that we had no valid reason to invade in 2003. I have demonstrated that our invasion and post-invasion were pathetically planned and executed. I have laid the blame on the individuals responsible, which is my right to do as an American, and as one who served in Iraq for 14 months and witnessed firsthand the tragedy we created in Iraq.

The United States invaded Iraq in March 2003 on the *assumption* that Saddam Hussein possessed weapons of mass destruction—WMD—and was ready to use these against us, and others. This deserves to be repeated:

The United States invaded Iraq in March 2003 based on the assumption—actually based on the hope—that Saddam Hussein possessed weapons of mass destruction, when in fact we had no solid evidence to support this at the time, and twisted what little information we had to justify the pre-determined decision to invade.

The threat that Saddam possessed, and was ready to use, WMD has been proven to be a fabrication by the President of the United States, who was driving a bandwagon his subordinates jumped on. As far back as 1997 it was known by the experts that Saddam did not possess WMD, nor had the capability to produce them in any usable amount: "There are no indications that there remains in Iraq any physical capability for the production of amounts of weapon-usable nuclear material of any practical significance."[105] The lack of any proof supporting the WMD claim existed before we invaded Iraq. Hindsight has only served to confirm this, as this chapter will explain. The point needs to be made again: if there was no solid, verifiable proof that Saddam Hussein possessed WMD, that means the United States made up

---

[105] Seymour Hersh, "The Stovepipe: How Conflicts between the Bush Administration and the Intelligence Community Marred the Reporting on Iraq's Weapons," *The New Yorker,* October 27, 2003.

the 'evidence,' and sold it to the American people and the world, with the help of demigods like Colin Powell.

Saddam Hussein used to be an ally of the United States. Throughout the 1980's and 1990's we supported Iraq's war against Iran, but never trusted Saddam's intentions. Claims by Iraq of sovereignty over Kuwait territory had been brewing for some time, culminating in Saddam's invasion of Kuwait on August 2, 1990. The United States knew he was going to invade, but stepped aside and watched while he slipped his head through the noose. President George H.W. Bush crushed Saddam's forces during Operation Desert Storm, also known as the First Gulf War. The conflict ended when he stopped our advance up the road toward Baghdad, based on the recommendation of General Colin Powell, Chairman of the Joint Chiefs of Staff.

There is speculation that President George W. Bush invaded Iraq in 2003 because of his anger at Saddam for planning to assassinate Bush's father. There is also speculation that Bush wanted to prove to his father that he was a man worthy of the office of president, the same office his father held. He even said: "Dad made a mistake not going into Iraq when he had an approval rating in the nineties. If I'm ever in that situation, I'll use it—I'll spend my political capital."[106] It has recently come out that Bush invaded Iraq because he wanted "someone's ass to kick."[107] Well, he certainly kicked Saddam Hussein's ass. Now Iraq is kicking ours.

Bush's desire to take out Saddam Hussein may have started before he even became president. But after 9/11 all the stops were pulled out. As early as December 2001 the Bush administration was investigating the possibilities of installing a new democratic government and ally in Iraq.

> If the United States overthrew Saddam Hussein next, it could create a reliable American ally in the potential superpower of the Arab world....It was to provide a

---

[106] Robert Draper, *Dead Certain: The Presidency of George W. Bush*, (New York: Free Press, 2007), p. 173.

[107] "We Went Into Iraq Because 'We Were Looking For Somebody's Ass To Kick'," *The Huffington Post*, October 20, 2013.

justification for a war....An American-led overthrow of Saddam Hussein [replaced] with a new government more closely aligned with the United States—would put America more wholly in charge of the region than any power since the Ottomans, or maybe the Romans....Bush needed something to assert, something that made clear that September 11 and Saddam Hussein were linked after all and that for the safety of the world, Saddam Hussein must be defeated rather than deterred.[108]

The United States could be as powerful in the region as the Ottomans, or even the Romans. Interesting.

But there was no link between Saddam and 9/11. And there was no evidence Saddam possessed WMD. The only other reasons Bush had to invade Iraq in March 2003 were: 1) he wanted to take out the guy who planned to assassinate his father; 2) he wanted to show the world (and his father) he was a badass, and; 3) he wanted the legacy for all time as the guy who brought democracy to Iraq and the Middle East. There has never been a bigger waste of time, money, reputation, and human life—for the sake of a pipedream—than George W. Bush's invasion of Iraq in March 2003.

In the fall-winter of 2002-2003, President George W. Bush presented justification to invade Iraq upon information that Saddam Hussein possessed of weapons of mass destruction, or WMD. Shortly after the initial invasion the White House Communications Director had this to say: "The President of the United States is not a fact checker."[109] That same President of the United States invaded a sovereign country, but couldn't bother checking the facts. This illustrates the problem with our decision to invade Iraq in 2003: facts didn't matter, weren't important, weren't needed, and weren't relevant to George W. Bush.

The debate in Washington over this issue culminated with Colin Powell's speech to the United Nations Security Council on

---

[108] David Frum, *The Right Man*, (Westminster, MD: Random House Adult Trade Publishing Group, 2003), pp. 196, 224, 233.

[109] Jacob Weisberg, *The Bush Tragedy* (New York: Random House, 2008), p. 196.

February 5, 2003. Powell's presentation and evidence was bogus. It didn't prove anything. However, because it came from the mouth of Colin Powell, it was taken as gospel. Colin Powell's appearance at the UN was one of the primary justifications used to support our invasion of Iraq. In fact, it could be said it was the single thing that tipped the scales and cleared any hurdles that remained. It certainly gave the UN the cover it needed to approve of George W. Bush's intention of getting Saddam Hussein by invading a country that posed no threat to the United States, or to anyone else.

Powell's February 5, 2003 speech at the UN falsely showed that he was the diplomat of the ages. But Powell's glory was based on the whimsical hope that Saddam Hussein actually possessed WMD. If he did, all would be well. But if the gamble went bust, and Saddam didn't have WMD, Powell and everyone else involved in our invasion would have to answer for it. With such drastic alternatives facing them, it is inconceivable that grown men and women at the highest levels of our government treated the decision to invade a sovereign country, without provocation, like throwing a pair of dice.

Powell's glory didn't last very long. After the invasion and the ensuing debacle, Colin Powell lost any credibility he had left. During the first Gulf War he was a general but wanted to be a diplomat. He convinced the first President Bush to cease hostile action against Saddam's Republican Guard, placing world opinion ahead of the destruction of America's enemy, and allowing them to fight another day. In 2003, because he wanted to remain a player on the world stage after being shoved to the sidelines by Donald Rumsfeld, Powell felt the need to prove he was still the greatest statesman alive, and critical to George W. Bush's team of senior advisors. Powell's ego sent him to the UN, where he made a fool of himself. This would have been fine, except it turned out to be a primary reason for our invasion of Iraq. As a result of Powell's arrogance, hundreds of thousands of people are dead. How ironic that Powell got permission to invade a sovereign country, without provocation, from the organization created and dedicated to the preservation of world peace.

The same month the U.S. invaded Iraq (March 2003), a former senior official at the White House and State Department, Randy

Beers, had an interesting take on the Bush administration's march toward war:

> They still don't get it. Insteada goin' all out against al Qaeda and eliminating our vulnerabilities at home, they wanna fuckin' invade Iraq again. We have a token U.S. military force in Afghanistan, the Taliban are regrouping, we haven't caught bin Laden, or his deputy, or the head of the Taliban. And they aren't going to send more troops to Afghanistan to catch them or to help the government in Kabul secure the country. No, they're holding back, waiting to invade Iraq. Do you know how much it will strengthen al Qaeda and groups like that if we occupy Iraq? There's no threat to us now from Iraq, but 70 percent of the American people think Iraq attacked the Pentagon and the World Trade Center. You wanna know why? Because that's what the Administration wants them to think![110]

In his excellent book, On the Brink, former senior intelligence officer Tyler Drumheller described the situation at the CIA during the run-up to the invasion. His story of the machinations inside the Central Intelligence Agency during this time is fascinating. His information on Curveball, however, is evidence of how the Bush administration twisted the truth, and fabricated unsubstantiated intelligence to make the case for invading Iraq. (Curveball was the codename of an Iraqi 'defector' held by German intelligence.)

> In January the issue resurfaced when a draft of a speech appeared in our division. By then we knew that the speech was to be delivered by Powell to the United Nations in an attempt to stiffen the international community's spine for an attack on Iraq. Ava [a pseudonym for one of Tyler Drumheller's colleagues] and my executive officer told me about the language

---

[110] Richard A. Clarke, op. cit, p. 241.

that was included from Curveball and we highlighted it for removal.

...I said to a colleague at the counterproliferation division that WINPAC [the center for Weapons Intelligence, Nonproliferation, and Arms Control] must have something else apart from Curveball to back up their case for war. "No," he said. "This is it. This is the smoking gun."

On January 24 we intervened again, after hearing the president himself was planning to include Curveball's intelligence in a speech.

On January 28, 2003, Bush delivered his State of the Union address, and included the following words, built on Curveball's claim he had been involved in creating a mobile biological weapons capability:

"From three Iraqi defectors we know that Iraq, in the late 1990s, had several mobile biological weapons labs. These are designed to produce germ warfare agents, and can be moved from place to place to evade inspectors. Saddam Hussein has not disclosed these facilities. He's given no evidence that he has destroyed them."[111]

WINPAC was created during the George W. Bush administration, "in an effort to bring together experts on foreign weapons into one center." Alan Foley, WINPAC's first director, addressed his subordinates in December 2002 telling them, "If the president wants to go to war, our job is to find the intelligence to allow him to do so."[112]

Tyler Drumheller describes how the other informants referred to by the president had either grossly misrepresented their claims, or had been proven to be fabricators before the speech. He continues:

---

[111] Tyler Drumheller, *On the Brink* (Carroll & Graf Publishers, 2006), pp. 83–85.

[112] Peter Eisner and Knut Royce, *The Italian Letter* (Rodale Books, 2007).

The message was that the leadership wanted to avoid "unwelcome surprises" including Curveball making public statements, press accounts of his credibility, or journalists tracking him down. The assistant asked for the view of our Berlin office on what would happen in the German media after the speech.

Looking back, this e-mail makes clear that there was in fact a genuine concern about Curveball's reliability. I didn't see it at the time that the political atmosphere was driving our every decision, and that these concerns would be swept aside.[113]

In his book, Drumheller claims Colin Powell was diligently scrutinizing his UN speech before he flew to New York on February 5, 2003. I don't see it that way. Why would Powell need to scrutinize a source that his president had already referred to in a speech a week before, on January 28, 2003? Why would Powell second-guess his boss, the President of the United States? If Bush used Curveball as a source, why was Powell re-examining the same source, being used for the same purpose, a week later? This leads to the conclusion that Powell (and most likely others in the administration) knew Curveball's intelligence was not credible, regardless of whether Bush had used it in his speech or not. Powell was trying to come up with anything he felt reliable enough to tell the UN. But nothing had come up in the preceding week that made Curveball's information reliable. This information was just as unreliable when Powell gave his speech as it was a week earlier when the president gave his.

Incredibly, while all this was going on George Tenet, Director of Central Intelligence, made no attempt to get permission from German intelligence for his own people to question Curveball in person prior to our invasion. It wasn't until March 2004 that the CIA obtained permission to conduct a personal interview with Curveball, but the Germans made every effort to prevent it. Only after George Tenet called the head of the German intelligence service did they relent.

---

[113] Tyler Drumheller, pp. 85–86.

Why did he take so long to make a phone call? One would think heads of allied intelligence agencies call each other every day. Or maybe George Tenet didn't want to make the call because he didn't want to find out Curveball's intelligence was bogus, which he would then have to tell the president. This would have taken courage which neither Tenant, nor Powell, possessed. The Germans are one of our staunchest allies, but George Tenet couldn't call them to ask if his people could meet Curveball in person. Anyone who thinks George Tenet did the best job he could needs to think again. Drumheller wrote:

> As an institution, we were ill-prepared to deal with the consequences of being dragged into the Bush administration's rush to war, and its subsequent fight to justify the invasion. The White House took our work and twisted it for its own ends, and Tenet set the tone whereby people knew what he and the White House wanted to hear. We all felt under pressure. The mere fact that our boss was discussing Iraq every day with Bush and his colleagues at the agency made war seem inevitable. *The bureaucratic imperative was to prove one's worth by supporting the presidents' case for war.* [Emphasis mine.] That is why WINPAC was so passionate in its support for Curveball.[114]

In addition to Curveball, the Bush administration came up with another excuse for invasion, that Saddam Hussein was purchasing weapons-grade uranium from Niger. This led to the Valarie Plame scandal, which in turn led to the conviction of Dick Cheney's Chief of Staff, Scooter Libby. It later led to the admission by Richard Armitage, the Deputy Secretary of State under Colin Powell, that he was the person who leaked Ms. Plame's covert CIA status. Richard Armitage never stepped forward to clear Scooter Libby's name while he sat in prison. Like they say, if you're looking for a friend in Washington, get a dog.

According to Drumheller, Tenet "fell on his sword" for Bush in the summer of 2003, saying that it was his fault Bush had stood up before the nation in the State of the Union address in

---

[114] Ibid, p. 87.

January and accused Iraq of trying to buy uranium from Africa. By that time the CIA was also being blamed for the failure to find WMD, and for the growing insurgency in Iraq that started May of that year. That was right around the time Bush declared that the war was over. Drumheller says of those days: "It was like watching a car wreck."

> I was not involved directly in the story behind those famous "sixteen words" that were spoken by the president but that marked the beginning of the end of Tenet's career at the CIA: "The British government has learned that Saddam Hussein recently sought significant quantities of uranium from Africa." The speech had not been sent to our division for review...
>
> It all revolved around an Italian journalist who had passed on a package of forged documents backing up the supposed uranium procurement attempt to an American embassy official in October 2002, a month after the British government issued its white paper making the claim that ended up in the president's speech. The documents consisted of faked messages and contracts "showing" that Iraq had agreed to buy five hundred tons of yellowcake uranium, a material that could be used to make a nuclear bomb, from Niger.[115]

The invasion of Iraq came down to politics, specifically the political decision to invade because President Bush wanted to. However, he couldn't have done it without help, and that help had to come from within his administration. A president appoints people to the highest positions in his administration because he wants to have the confidence they will do what he tells them. A president who has self-confidence also wants people to tell him the truth. George W. Bush didn't want the truth. He wanted to be surrounded by "yes men." He got what he asked for. Drumheller wrote:

---

[115] Ibid, pp. 119–120.

I believe he [Tenet] was politically seduced in the rush to war that he failed to create the necessary professional distance between himself as an intelligence expert and the White House and its desire to begin the invasion. He became part of the policy-making apparatus as a result of being dragged into the inner workings of a White House that behaved as if it was on a constant war footing. In the process he sacrificed the objectivity any intelligence chief must have if he or she is to deliver unwelcome information to the policy makers….

That's not to say that he lied about his belief that Saddam had weapons of mass destruction. He appeared to believe that whole-heartedly, despite the warnings he received from me and the concerns being raised within the organization he ran. Perhaps, like the administration's leadership, he too was gambling that the weapons would be found. The atmosphere at the time was that as long as we remained certain of our convictions, everything would work out. That approach trickled down from the president.[116]

The evening of February 4, 2003, Tyler Drumheller was called at his home by George Tenet.

I had no idea how important this phone call would become. I'm not sure who was there with Tenet, but there was almost an air of comic hysteria in the voices I heard…But I was curious about all the horseplay I could hear in the background, so I asked: "How are you doing? It sounds like you're having a party!"

He said, "We've been up seventy-two hours and we're a little goofy."

Then I decided to speak about Curveball. Despite all my reports and flag-raising to others, it couldn't hurt to mention it to Tenet himself, even if I knew in my

---

[116] Ibid, p. 121.

heart it was probably a waste of time. After all, Powell was due to speak at 10:30 the following morning [in New York].

"Look," I said, "as long as I've got you, and I'm sorry to sort of spring this on you, but make sure you look at the final version of the speech because, you know, there are some problems with the German reporting [i.e., with Curveball].

He was distracted and answered with, "Yeah, yeah, yeah, don't worry about it. We are exhausted. I have to go."[117]

The following day, February 5, 2003, Powell delivered his famous speech to the United Nations.

The Silberman-Robb Commission (the "Commission on the Intelligence Capabilities of the United States Regarding Weapons of Mass Destruction") was created by Executive Order in February 2003. During its deliberations it interviewed many sources, to include George Tenet and Tyler Drumheller, who refers to the commission's report throughout his book.

I doubt I will ever receive a complete explanation for why he [Tenet] stuck to his story about the telephone conversation we had that night before Powell's speech at the United Nations. Perhaps he thought I would be willing to perjure myself by not mentioning it to the Silberman-Robb Commission, and felt that I had betrayed him. I suspect there was some reason why it was important for him to say we spoke at 7 P.M. rather than 11 P.M. I do not know why.

Mostly I felt that we were two good friends and colleagues who accomplished a lot together, until we were set at odds by the manipulations of an administration acting ideologically instead of intellectually.[118]

---

[117] Ibid, p. 100.

[118] Ibid, pp. 121–122.

Tyler Drumheller's reference to "perjury" is monumental. Either he lied to the Silberman-Robb Commission about Curveball being discussed during the phone call with Tenet the night before Powell's UN appearance, or Tenet did. If Tyler Drumheller went to the lengths he did to explain his side of the story about the phone conversation, I know which one of these two men I believe.

Not only did Tenet deny to the commission that the phone call with Drumheller discussed Curveball, he also said it took place much earlier in the evening, not at midnight. Drumheller questions why he would do this, but the answer is obvious. It wouldn't look good if Tenet told the Silberman-Robb Commission that he and his staff were up for 72 straight hours, until midnight the night before he and the Secretary of State flew to New York. The Commission's immediate question would be "why," and Tenet didn't want to get into that. The reason can only be that Tenet, Powell, and the Bush administration were grabbing at straws to come up with something to say at the UN, and they were up for 72 straight hours, until midnight the night before, trying to pull a rabbit out of a hat. It would have been embarrassing for Tenet to say this to the Commission, so he didn't. Nor did he say the phone call with Tyler Drumheller included talk about Curveball. That way he, the Director of the CIA, could play dumb and act as if he didn't know anything about the single primary source we used to justify our invasion of Iraq. It doesn't get more cowardly than that.

Tyler Drumheller's reference to "perjury" makes more sense by going back to the beginning of his book. In the Prologue he describes a phone call he received in April of 2005 from a *Los Angeles Times* reporter named Greg Miller. The call began with Miller asking Tyler Drumheller if he was the un-named person mentioned in the Silverman-Robb Commission report.

> The report revealed details of a telephone conversation I had had with George Tenet the night before Secretary of State Colin Powell's speech before the United Nations that justified the plan to invade Iraq. Without mentioning my name, the report delved into the other details of the debacle over "Curveball,"

the main Iraqi source for the claim that Saddam had weapons of mass destruction.

But then the reporter hooked me. "Just let me tell you what Tenet's been saying," he said. The next thing I knew I was hearing sections of a long statement issued by my former boss that amounted to an elaborate denial that he had received any warning of Curveball's unreliability. He also denied that I had mentioned the problems with this source on the telephone that night in February 2003.

Finally, lost my temper. "I don't give a damn what George Tenet says," I said. "he knows what the truth is."[119]

George Tenet threw his old friend Tyler Drumheller under the bus to save his own skin.

The CIA was used as a means to an end. It was used as a prop by the Bush administration to support the bogus claim that Saddam Hussein possessed weapons of mass destruction. And because he wanted to continue 'sitting at the table,' George Tenet sold his own agency, and many close friends, down the river. What Colin Powell did was worse. He sold our country down the river. Both men's ego, arrogance, and cowardice allowed them to go along with a false invasion plan of a country they had no proof was a threat, and they lacked the courage to tell their boss how they felt, or how flimsy the evidence for invasion actually was.

Curveball was the main reason George W. Bush used to invade Iraq in March 2003. The Germans had him detained, so he was easily accessible. Yet, George Tenet made no attempt to get his own interrogators to Germany to question Curveball in person prior to the invasion. The CIA made no attempt to verify Curveball's intelligence, allowing WINPAC to push it out of the way. Tyler Drumheller describes in detail how John McLaughlin, deputy CIA director, essentially blew smoke in the face of the

---

[119] Ibid, pp. 10–11.

Silverman-Robb Commission, just like George Tenet did. Cowardice and ego led both of these high ranking CIA officials to forsake their integrity, and allowed their country to get sucked into a meaningless war because that's what their boss wanted. How many lives have been lost as a result of their actions?

Time has a way of clearing the air, however. On February 16, 2010, Fox News filed a story about an Iraqi defector named Rafid Ahmed Alwan al-Janabi. Mr. al-Janabi was none other than "Curveball," the Iraqi who was our single source of intelligence on Saddam's WMP program. He was recanting his entire story, and admitted his claims that Iraq had biological weapons, a premise used to justify the 2003 U.S. invasion, were completely fabricated:

> A defector whose claims that Iraq had biological weapons were used in justifying the 2003 U.S. invasion has admitted that he lied to help get rid of Saddam Hussein, The Guardian newspaper said Tuesday.
>
> "They gave me this chance. I had the chance to fabricate something to topple the regime."[120]

Mr. al-Janabi made up his WMD story, and sold it to western intelligence services so he could play a personal role in the ouster of Saddam Hussein. No one argues that Saddam was a bad actor. But on his worst day Saddam never caused the deaths of as many people as our invasion has—all based on phony evidence from a fraud. Despite his admission, Janabi said security officials continued to take his claims that Iraq had mobile bio-weapons trucks and clandestine factories seriously. The bogus information Janabi provided was the basis Colin Powell's address to the UN on February 5, 2003.[121]

Curveball was certainly an appropriate codename.

---

[120] "Iraqi Defector Admits Lying About WMD to Topple Saddam Hussein," *Fox News*, February 16, 2010.

[121] Ibid.

The U.S. never vetted al-Janabi's claims. We invaded Iraq solely on the basis of what he said, without any verification from other sources. Invading based on the claims of one man was bad enough, but his information had already been compromised. We used it anyway.

Let me use an analogy. Bernard Madoff, the mastermind behind the biggest Ponzi scheme in U.S. history, claimed in an e-mail sent to Fox Business Network on February 22, 2011 that the banks handling his financial transactions "had to know what I was doing regarding the fraud," as if that explained everything.[122] The banks did know, and so did the Securities and Exchange Commission (SEC), but neither took appropriate action. The banks turned a blind eye to Madoff's scam because he was generating huge profits for them. The SEC did nothing because its regulators and enforcement division were cowards, and afraid the banks would get upset if they shut Madoff's operation down. Both failed their fiduciary responsibility to their clients: the banks failed their depositors, while the SEC failed the entire securities industry.

Mr. al-Janabi was like Bernie Madoff, and the Bush administration was like the banks that looked the other way so they would get what they wanted. The banks wanted continued profits, while the Bush administration wanted war. The banks have never been held accountable, and neither has the Bush administration.

> During the [UN] speech, Powell described Janabi as "an Iraqi chemical engineer" who "supervised one of these facilities."
>
> "He actually was present during biological agent production runs and was also at the site when an accident occurred in 1998," Powell told the U.N..
>
> Janabi said he was "shocked" by Powell's speech, but played down his role in the conflict.[123]

---

[122] Dunstan Prial, "Madoff to FBN: Maintain Scrutiny on Banks and Feeder Funds," *Fox Business*, February 22, 2013.

[123] "Iraqi Defector Admits...," *Fox News*, February 16, 2010.

Powell's apologists will always be around. Many say he was lied to by Bush and Cheney, that he was used for his immense popularity so they could get what they wanted. They certainly used his popularity to get what they wanted, but if Colin Powell is so brilliant how is it possible such inferior persons as Bush and Cheney could lie to him and get away with it? How could the greatest statesman alive be so easily duped? He's so much smarter than Bush, Cheney, and everyone else. It would be pretty hard for the less intelligent president to get away with lying to the most brilliant Secretary of State in our nation's history. What do Powell's apologists have to say about that? There was certainly deception at the highest levels of the Bush administration, but it was played by everyone on each other.

Lawrence Wilkerson, a retired U.S. Army Colonel, was Colin Powell's Chief of Staff at the time of his February 5, 2003 presentation to the UN Security Council. The most highly regarded official in the Bush Administration, Powell has been widely credited with turning the tide of public opinion in favor of the invasion of Iraq, which commenced weeks later. The evidence presented by Powell, said to have been culled from various intelligence agencies, turned out to be completely false. Years later, Powell described the speech as a "painful" "blot" on his career. Powell's evidence was not only wrong, however, but it was known to be wrong by many in the intelligence community by the time it was presented as fact by the well-respected Secretary of State: "Though neither Powell nor anyone else from the State Department team intentionally lied," says Wilkerson, "we did participate in a hoax."[124]

How does one "participate in a hoax," and at the same time claim not to have "intentionally lied?" For a retired U.S. Army colonel and former Powell Chief of Staff to say this, it must be credible. If not, Powell would no doubt sue Wilkerson for defamation. It would appear Col. Wilkerson's conscience was more important to him than covering up for Powell, who must

---

[124] Brad Friedman, "Powell's Chief Of Staff: Iraq Intel Was 'Outright Lies', But Powell Didn't 'Knowingly Lie' At UN," *The National Memo*, February 22, 2013 (from *Hubris: Selling the Iraq War*, NBC News documentary based on the book by David Corn and Michael Isikoff).

have been a close friend for decades. How else would Wilkerson get the job as Powell's Chief of Staff?

There is evidence Colin Powell fabricated portions of his UN testimony. The phone conversation between the two Iraqi army officers (mentioned in Chapter 5) contained wording that was not in the official State Department translation that Powell played during his UN presentation. According to *Press TV*:

> "They're inspecting the ammunition you have, yes.
>
> "Yes.
>
> "For the possibility there are forbidden ammo.
>
> "For the possibility there is by chance forbidden ammo?
>
> "Yes.
>
> "And we sent you a message yesterday to clean out all of the areas, the scrap areas, the abandoned areas. Make sure there is nothing there."
>
> *The incriminating phrases "clean all of the areas" and "make sure there is nothing there" do not appear in the official State Department translation of the exchange:* [Emphasis mine.]
>
> "Lt. Colonel: They are inspecting the ammunition you have.
>
> "Colonel: Yes.
>
> "Lt. Col: For the possibility there are forbidden ammo.
>
> "Colonel: Yes?
>
> "Lt. Colonel: For the possibility there is by chance, forbidden ammo.
>
> "Colonel: Yes.

"Lt. Colonel: And we sent you a message to inspect the scrap areas and the abandoned areas.

"Colonel: Yes."[125]

Powell re-wrote the dialogue of the two officers by inserting extra lines into the transcript that hadn't actually been said. The *Press TV* article mentions *Plan of Attack* by Bob Woodward, who had this to say about Powell's presentation:

> [Powell] had decided to add his personal interpretation of the intercepts to rehearsed script, taking them substantially further and casting them in the most negative light. Concerning the intercept about inspecting for the possibility of 'forbidden ammo,' Powell took the interpretation further: 'Clean out all of the areas. . . . Make sure there is nothing there.' None of this was in the intercept.[126]

Woodward describes the reaction of Mary McGrory, the liberal columnist for *The Washington Post*, and major Bush critic. In the lead column in the next day's op-ed page, Ms. McGrory wrote of Powell's *"J'Accuse"* speech:

> "I can only say that he persuaded me, and I was as tough as France to convince." She said that she had been hoping Powell would oppose war, but "The cumulative effect was stunning. I was reminded of the day long ago when John Dean, a White House toady, unloaded on Richard Nixon and you could see the dismay written on Republican faces that knew impeachment was inevitable." She added, "I'm not ready for war yet. But Colin Powell has convinced me that it might be the only way to stop a fiend, and that if we do go, there is reason."

---

[125] David Swanson, "Colin Powell fabricated lies to justify US-led war on Iraq," *PressTV*, February 6, 2013.

[126] Ibid.

At the White House, Dan Bartlett understood the importance of what Powell had done. He began calling it "the Powell buy-in."[127]

Imagine that, Mary McGrory was hoping Powell would oppose the war. But when he didn't oppose it with his "stunning" evidence, she was ready to lead the charge and wipe out Saddam Hussein. Reactions like hers are why Bush sent Powell to the UN that day. Bush needed "the Powell buy-in" to convince the likes of people like Mary McGrory.

Unlike Ms. McGrory, even though Powell presented it, I knew the conversation between the two Iraqi army officers was weak the day I heard it. As I have mentioned earlier in this account, I remember thinking at the time that it didn't prove anything. Look where we are all these years later. A strong case could be made that Colin Powell lied to the United Nations on February 5, 2003.

If the evidence of Saddam possessing WMD was so obvious as to be "a slam dunk," why all the hand wringing and questioning of CIA staff into the late night hours prior to his departure for New York City? Like Barack Hussein Obama's birth certificate: if it's there, just produce it. If Saddam had WMD, there would be irrefutable evidence right there at the CIA for all to see. There wasn't any.

Powell was looking for a needle in a haystack to justify an invasion that Bush wanted. He was frantic to find something to substantiate the WMD claim because the decision to invade Iraq had already been made by Bush, and if there was going to be war Powell wanted to be involved in it. Being the self-serving person that he is, Powell didn't want to miss the chance to speak in front of the UN, and the world. The problem was, he had nothing credible to tell them. Powell needed something with "meat" on it to present to the UN, something he could claim was truthful at the time he said it, regardless of whether it was proven to be false later (e.g., Curveball). All that mattered was getting the UN's permission to invade Iraq, and Colin Powell could go back to Washington with an A+ on his report card, and crowds of swooning admirers waiting for him. The details that followed his

---

[127] Bob Woodward, *Plan of Attack*, p. 188.

UN presentation would take care of themselves. But Humpty Dumpty had a great fall. The chickens all came home to roost—on Colin Powell's head.

Imagine where Powell would be today if he had the courage to stand up to Bush at that moment in time? Everyone, including me, would say Colin Powell did the right thing at the right time. Unfortunately, he failed his duty to tell the president what he thought, consequences come what may. But this was simply too big an opportunity for Colin Powell to be left out of. To Powell's supporters, nothing can possibly be his fault, it's everyone else's. To his loyal flock he's the reason why things go well, but he has no involvement when they don't.

20—The New Caliphate

Caliphate: the political-religious state comprising the Muslim community and the lands and peoples under its dominion in the centuries following the death (632CE) of the Prophet Muhammad. Ruled by a caliph (Arabic khalīfah, "successor"), who held temporal and sometimes a degree of spiritual authority, the empire of the Caliphate grew rapidly through conquest during its first two centuries to include most of Southwest Asia, North Africa, and Spain. Dynastic struggles later brought about the Caliphate's decline, and it ceased to exist with the Mongol destruction of Baghdad in 1258. (Encyclopedia Britannica)[128]

In 2008, Barack Hussein Obama was elected the 44th President of the United States, based in large part on his pledge to withdraw all American forces from Iraq and Afghanistan. Many people believed him. But many didn't believe him because they knew he would say anything to get elected. It took four years for Obama to begin withdrawing U.S. forces from Iraq, while leaving several thousand there. The United States opened its new embassy complex, hundreds of millions over budget, only to have a skeleton staff working there because of the continued threat to their security due to the never-ending insurgency. Now it's a barracks for U.S. military advisors.

The post-invasion government of Iraq has proven to be a complete disaster. Nouri al-Maliki, the former Prime Minister, was a Shi'ite. There was no way the U.S. was going to allow a Sunni to be Prime Minister because Saddam was a Sunni, and the Sunnis had run the show for decades. Little did anyone know a Shi'ite Prime Minister would not go over well with the minority Sunni population, regardless of the fact they had been in charge all those years under Saddam.

The combination of the United States invading Iraq with too few forces, Paul Bremer disbanding Iraq's security infrastructure, Coalition military forces pulling out, Obama withdrawing the

---

[128] *Encyclopaedia Britannica.*

bulk of American forces that remained, the inability of the al-Maliki government to contain the growing violence, and the growth of an insurgency that is worse and larger than al Qaeda of just a few years ago, have all laid the foundation for the final destruction of Iraq, which is now under threat of a full-scale insurgency, making 2006-2007 look like a picnic.

At the time of this writing the Islamic State controls much of north-western Iraq and Kurdistan, across the Syrian frontier. These new insurgents, the next generation of al Qaeda, want to kill as many non-believers as possible, which means as many westerners and as many Americans as possible before they're called to heaven. They want to fly their flag over the White House, yet Obama has the nerve to call them the "JV" of terrorists.

Obama took over the Iraq War (and our country) with no plan other than complete withdrawal. Obama has done nothing to stop the insurgency in Iraq. However, he got elected on the promise he would withdraw all American forces. He's only doing what he said he would do, just like Adolf Hitler only did what he said he would do in *Mein Kampf.* It's difficult to place all the blame on Obama. The people who voted for him are another matter.

If ever there was a case of wishful thinking, it was that Iraq would become a democracy as soon as America showed up in March 2003. Rumsfeld's plan to hand out tiny American flags to Iraqi children after we invaded speaks for itself. He said: "There's no question but that they would be welcomed. Go back to Afghanistan—the people were in the streets playing music, cheering, flying kites…Now, is there a risk when that dictatorial system isn't there that there could be conflicts between elements within the country, get-even type things? Yes. And we've got to be careful to see that that doesn't happen."[129] Afterward, Donald Rumsfeld had this to say about his prediction: "Never said that. Never did. You may remember it well, but you're thinking of somebody else."[130] Revisionist history, or revisionist memory?

[129] "News Hour with Jim Lehrer (transcript)," *PBS*, February 20, 2003.

[130] John B. Judis, *The Folly of Empire: What George W. Bush Could Learn from Theodore Roosevelt and Woodrow Wilson*, (New York: Scribner, 2004), p. 194.

During run-up to the invasion Dick Cheney got on the bandwagon: "We have great information. They're going to welcome us. It'll be like the American army going through the streets of Paris...The people will be so happy with their freedoms that we'll probably back ourselves out of there within a month or two."[131]

The price paid for this Parisian pipedream has been extremely high, and keeps getting higher. Who are we to tell anyone how to govern themselves? Someone tried that with us once in the late 1700's, and it didn't work out too well for them. The United States tried the same thing in Iraq, and look what the results have been. The details are different, but the issues are the same: trying to change another country into what you want it to be never works.

Hundreds of thousands of Iraqis have died because the United States invaded their country in 2003. The reasons for our invasion were phony, and have never justified what we did. Our country's leadership, political and military, is to blame. We didn't learn anything from the "quagmire" of Vietnam, which Iraq has now become.

The result of these failures has been complete and utter disaster. The Islamic State (IS) has taken the city of Mosul, the largest in Iraqi Kurdistan. It threatens Irbil, the second largest city in Kurdistan. It threatens Baghdad itself, and controls the major oil-producing areas in northern Iraq. The Islamic State is now in control of large swaths of land. At one point IS took control of Mosul Dam, which was later re-taken by Iraqi forces. It threatened to wipe out a Christian sect called the Yazidis, with accounts describing their slaughter for not converting to Islam.

David Cameron, the British Prime Minister, has called on the western democracies to prepare for a "terrorist caliphate" on the shores of the Mediterranean if the Islamic State isn't stopped. Yet, while he says airstrikes alone aren't sufficient, at the same time he refuses to commit ground forces, which makes no sense. But what does Mr. Cameron expect? In the spirit of goodwill, Britain has been allowing Muslims to enter the country by the

---

[131] Robert Draper, *Dead Certain: The Presidency of George W. Bush,* (New York: Free Press, 2007), p. 178.

thousands for decades. The most popular name given to newborn males in Britain is Mohammed.

Barack Hussein Obama has ordered airstrikes, which have been effective at the point they target, but are a pinprick compared to what is needed. The guy who promised he would not take vacations if elected president plays golf on Martha's Vineyard while Iraq explodes. As Obama opens the southern border of the United States to any alien who wants to walk in, does anyone think IS militants are not part of this wave? If Barack Hussein Obama swore to defend the Constitution of the United States, how does his violation of our national sovereignty square with that oath? It doesn't, but Congress will do nothing to stop him.

Attorney General Eric Holder wanted the Justice department to conduct a criminal investigation of the beheading by the Islamic State of American journalist James Foley. How on earth did he plan to accomplish this, or did it just fly out of his mouth like everything else he says? Did Holder think his FBI agents would be able to interview witnesses and press criminal charges? Where does Mr. Holder get the idea he can do anything he wants in a foreign country? But he's Eric Holder, and he works for Barack Hussein Obama. They can do whatever they want.[132]

Such are the responses of the Obama administration to the growing threat posed by the Islamic State. David Cameron's point is clear: if the Islamic State isn't stopped very soon, before it starts growing legs, Britain and many other countries will be in serious trouble. Islam is taking over Western Europe. It only needs to make the leap across the Atlantic and it will be knocking on our door, if it hasn't already started infiltrating our country thanks to Barack Hussein Obama.

I did not write this book because I hate my country. I love my country. However, I hate what my country's leadership has done in Iraq, and what it has done to the Iraqi people. Unfortunately, it's still going on.

My hope is that the United States stops doing things that are destructive to itself, and to other nations and people. In order to

---

[132] "Holder says criminal investigation launched into American journalist's execution," *Fox News,* August 21, 2014.

make these changes our country needs leaders with integrity and courage. We haven't had a leader that met these standards since Ronald Reagan. If this causes liberals to gag, it's their problem. Because of my Iraq experience I have come to realize the extent of our nation's political and military incompetence. Without leaders and senior government officials who possess integrity and courage, we will keep creating debacles like our invasion of Iraq.

In May of 2003, making the case that Saddam Hussein was linked to 9/11, possessed weapons of mass destruction, and posed a threat to the United States, an advisor to the Bush administration's Office of Special Plans wrote:

> I'd love to be the historian who writes the story of how this small group of eight or nine people [Bush, etc.] made the case [to invade Iraq] and won.[133]

That story hasn't been written yet.

---

[133] Seymour Hersh, "Annals of National Security: Selective Intelligence," op. cit.

Visit my website at:

www.warfare-inc.com

Bibliography

Several books provided background information on the conduct of the 2003 Iraq invasion, officially called Operation Iraqi Freedom (an oxymoron if ever there was one), and its aftermath. These have also provided a description of our intelligence capabilities, the post-invasion situation in Iraq, and warfare in general.

- *Cobra II* by Michael R. Gordon and General Bernard E. Trainor, and *Fiasco* by Thomas E. Ricks, give excellent and detailed descriptions of the planning and conduct of the war, and the initial stages afterwards.

- *On the Brink*, by Tyler Drumheller, describes the inner workings of the CIA by a senior intelligence officer and long-time colleague of George Tenet, who at one time was in charge of operations in Western Europe.

- *The Secret History of the CIA*, by Joseph J. Trento, and *The Human Factor*, by Ishmael Jones (a pseudonym) provided me with needed information about our nation's covert, and mostly futile, involvement in the political, military and domestic affairs of other countries since World War II. In just about every case the results have been disastrous. They also provided insight into the human element of our country's intelligence community. What they have to tell about this is depressing.

- *Embracing Defeat*, by John W. Dower, is the Pulitzer Prize winning history of Japan immediately after World War II, specifically the occupation from 1945 to 1952 by the United States Army under the command of General of the Army Douglas MacArthur.

- *We Meant Well*, by Peter Van Buren, provides a painfully accurate portrayal of the time, manpower, and money that has been wasted on transition from Iraqi dependence on the Coalition, to Iraq's independence. No such transition has taken place, nor is it ever likely to, regardless of what the talking heads in Washington say.

- *Washington Rules,* by Andrew J. Bacevich, provides an overview of America's military involvement just about everywhere on the globe. It poses the legitimate question: why?

- No story pertaining to the U.S.'s failure in Iraq could be written without reference to *Dereliction of Duty: Johnson, McNamara, the Joint Chiefs of Staff, and the Lies That Led to Vietnam,* by H.R. McMaster. Written by an active duty U.S. Army major at the time, it is one of the best accounts of the total lapse in leadership, judgment, ethical responsibility and ethical accountability related to the Vietnam debacle.

- One of the most important references I have used in the revision of my book is *Warrior's Rage: The Great Tank Battle of 73 Easting,* by retired U.S. Army Colonel Douglas Macgregor. Col. Macgregor was the Operations Officer of an armored cavalry squadron at the "tip of the spear" during the Iraqi Army's retreat from Kuwait. His take on the abysmal "leadership" at the highest military and political levels of our country validate my own.

- The film *Obsession,* produced by the Clarion Fund, as an excellent graphic source of reference about the true danger of radical Islamic terrorism in the world today. I highly recommend to everyone who believes in freedom and western civilization to watch this one hour DVD. It gets right to the heart of the issue. (Obsession can be watched on-line at www.obsessionthemovie.com.)

- No account of the U.S. invasion, and its aftermath, equals the documentary *No End in Sight.* Released in 2007 by Charles H. Ferguson, this DVD describes Iraq's "descent into chaos" better than any other film I have seen. It even convinced my mother who, until she watched it the night before she died in 2013, believed George W. Bush was right. The day she died my mother told me, "Michael, you were right [about the war] all along." I felt good about what she said, but terrible at the loss of such a wonderful woman.

- *Napoleon's Wars: An International History,* by Charles Esdaile, is a powerfully detailed account of the times during which Napoleon was master of Europe. The intrigue, treaties, agreements and international gamesmanship of those times are being played today by the United States. Napoleon's hubris got him into trouble in 1815, just like George W. Bush's hubris got him into trouble in 2003.

- *Infamy, Pearl Harbor and its Aftermath,* by John Toland, makes the case that President Roosevelt and General Marshal knew the Japanese were going to attack Pearl Harbor, but allowed it to happen in order to force the United States into the war. Like the assassination of JFK, we will never know the answer. There are several things, however, that lend credence to Toland's account. General Marshall could not be found for many hours after we heard of the attack, therefore no one knew what to do or how to respond. As Chief of Staff of the Army, this is simply not possible. The only way this could happen was if pre-planned. We had broken the Japanese code, and were aware of their plans, which is explained in great detail in Gordon W. Prange's *At Dawn We Slept.* Prange goes into so much detail concerning what U.S. Naval Intelligence knew before the attack, that he dis-proves his own statement in the forward of the book—that anyone who thinks FDR knew ahead of time is a conspiracy theorist, and therefore not worthy of the time of day. Prange's research adds more to the possibility that FDR knew about the attack, than it takes away.

- *The Iraq War-Part I: The U.S. Prepares for Conflict, 2001,* by Joyce Battle, is an incredible compilation of statements made by President George W. Bush, Donald Rumsfeld, Dick Cheney, Tommy Franks, Doug Feith, and others. The planning and justification for the U.S. invasion of Iraq are spoken in their own words.

- I also reference *Crush the Cell*, by my West Point classmate and former roommate, Michael A. Sheehan. Mike was the last Ambassador-at-Large for Counterterrorism the last two years of Bill Clinton's administration. His book provides insight to the inner workings of global terrorism, and how to fight it.

About the Author

Michael M. O'Brien was a political appointee in the first administration of George W. Bush, serving in the U.S. Department of State and the Office of Homeland Security in the White House. A graduate of the U.S. Military Academy at West Point, he served as an Infantry officer in the Canal Zone, Panama, the Demilitarized Zone, Korea, and Fort Sam Houston, San Antonio, Texas. He was Airborne and Ranger qualified, and left active duty service as a Captain. After leaving the Army he was a commercial helicopter pilot in New York City, and then pursued a career in commercial real estate. Michael O'Brien was the Senior Advisor to the Iraqi Ministry of Defense in Baghdad, Iraq, from July 2006 to September 2007, advising the Ministry on all matters relating to its land, facilities, bases, and construction— after the Iraqi Army had been disbanded by the Coalition Provisional Authority. He lives in Arlington, Virginia.

CPSIA information can be obtained
at www.ICGtesting.com
Printed in the USA
FFOW03n2002140715
15118FF